# TAKING ECONOMIC, SOCIAL AND CULTURAL RIGHTS SERIOUSLY IN INTERNATIONAL CRIMINAL LAW

Is the neglect of economic, social and cultural abuses in international criminal law a problem of positive international law or the result of choices made by lawyers involved in mechanisms such as criminal prosecutions or truth commissions? Evelyne Schmid explores this question via an assessment of the relationship between violations of economic, social and cultural rights and international crimes. Based on a thorough examination of the elements of international crimes, she demonstrates how a situation can simultaneously be described as a violation of economic, social and cultural rights and as an international crime. Against the background of the emerging debates on selectivity in international criminal law and the role of socio-economic and cultural abuses in transitional justice, she argues that international crimes overlapping with violations of economic, social and cultural rights deserve to be taken seriously, for much the same reasons as other international crimes.

EVELYNE SCHMID is a post-doctoral researcher and lecturer at the University of Basel, Switzerland. She was previously based at Bangor University and at the Graduate Institute of International and Development Studies (IHEID) and acted as the project coordinator for the International Criminal Court's Legal Tools Project at TRIAL in Geneva.

# CAMBRIDGE STUDIES IN INTERNATIONAL AND COMPARATIVE LAW

Established in 1946, this series produces high-quality scholarship in the fields of public and private international law and comparative law. Although these are distinct legal sub-disciplines, developments since 1946 confirm their interrelations.

Comparative law is increasingly used as a tool in the making of law at national, regional and international levels. Private international law is now often affected by international conventions, and the issues faced by classical conflicts rules are frequently dealt with by substantive harmonisation of law under international auspices. Mixed international arbitrations, especially those involving state economic activity, raise mixed questions of public and private international law, while in many fields (such as the protection of human rights and democratic standards, investment guarantees and international criminal law) international and national systems interact. National constitutional arrangements relating to 'foreign affairs', and to the implementation of international norms, are a focus of attention.

The series welcomes works of a theoretical or interdisciplinary character, and those focusing on the new approaches to international or comparative law or conflicts of law. Studies of particular institutions or problems are equally welcome, as are translations of the best work published in other languages.



*A list of books in the series can be found at the end of this volume.*

# TAKING ECONOMIC, SOCIAL AND CULTURAL RIGHTS SERIOUSLY IN INTERNATIONAL CRIMINAL LAW

EVELYNE SCHMID
*University of Basel, Switzerland*

CAMBRIDGE
UNIVERSITY PRESS

**CAMBRIDGE**
**UNIVERSITY PRESS**

University Printing House, Cambridge CB2 8BS, United Kingdom

Cambridge University Press is part of the University of Cambridge.

It furthers the University's mission by disseminating knowledge in the pursuit of education, learning and research at the highest international levels of excellence.

www.cambridge.org
Information on this title: www.cambridge.org/9781107063969



First published 2015

*Library of Congress Cataloguing in Publication data*
Schmid, Evelyne, author.
Taking economic, social and cultural rights seriously in international criminal law / Evelyne Schmid.
pages cm. – (Cambridge studies in international and comparative law ; 117)
ISBN 978-1-107-06396-9 (hardback)
1. Crimes against humanity. 2. International law and human rights. 3. Social rights – Criminal provisions. I. Title.
KZ7145.S36 2015
345′.056–dc23
2014050253

ISBN 978-1-107-06396-9 Hardback

CONTENTS

# FIGURES AND TABLE

## Figures



## Table

# ACKNOWLEDGEMENTS

This book is based on my doctoral thesis, undertaken at the Graduate Institute of International Studies and Development (IHEID), under the supervision of Andrew Clapham. I am most grateful for his encouragement, excellent feedback and cogent advice at the turn from dissertation to book. His assistance made researching and writing this book an intellectually enriching and enjoyable exercise. I also thank the other members of the jury committee – Prof. William Schabas (Middlesex University, London) and Prof. Vincent Chetail (Graduate Institute, Geneva) – for carefully reading and discussing my findings and for providing me with valuable feedback.

I gained a great deal from many conversations about my research in Geneva, Cambridge, MA, and elsewhere. Scott Leckie and Mara Bustelo found time to listen to my questions, ideas and doubts. I thank Vera Gowlland-Debbas, Eibe Riedel and Jeremy Sarkin for their encouragement. I owe much to Cristina Verones, who read the draft and provided useful comments, and to Kali Tal for efficiently proofreading the manuscript.

I would not have been able to enjoy the research and writing without help from my friends. My former colleagues at TRIAL, the United States Institute of Peace and Amnesty International, Switzerland, demonstrated inspiring commitment. Adineh Abghari, Julio Bacio-Terracino, Annyssa Bellal, Joie Chowdhury, Ioana Cismas, Thea Gelbspan, Gilles Giacca, Christophe Golay, Mamadou Hebié, Krisztina Huszti, Tahmina Karimova, Fiona Le Diraison, Daniel Mburu, Sigrid Mehring, Andreas Th. Müller, Yasmin Naqvi, Bo Viktor Nylund, Juan Carlos Ochoa Sanchez, Pablo Sandonato de Leon, Emilia Richard, Thomas Mitchell Robinson and Deborah Ruiz-Verduzco provided advice and companionship. Antoine Buyse deserves special thanks for tracking down a hard-to-find court decision.

I am grateful for the semester I spent as an exchange doctoral researcher at Harvard Law School, where I benefited from conversations with Philip Alston, Susan Farbstein, Tyler Giannini and the community of visiting researchers. Bangor University School of Law has supported my research project and I thank my former colleagues in Wales, in particular Dermot Cahill, Yvonne McDermott, Suzannah Linton and Alison Mawhinney. I am much obliged to Kathryn Davis for the generous financial assistance of a Shelby Cullom Davis and Kathryn Davis Scholarship. I, moreover, thank C.H. Beck Publishers for permission to include material in this book from an article that I previously published in the *Heidelberg Journal of International Law*, Vol. 71(3), 2011. Warm thanks are also due to Cambridge University Press and, in particular, to Elizabeth Spicer and Richard Woodham for their help in the production of this book.

I owe special thanks to my parents, who always approved of my undertakings and contributed to my studies for many years. My deepest appreciation is reserved for my husband, Andreas, who has been my constant source of support over the years.

# TABLE OF CASES AND AUTHORITIES

## I. International cases and communications

### A. *Permanent Court of International Justice and International Court of Justice*



### B. *International Criminal Court*

## C. *International Criminal Tribunal for the former Yugoslavia*

## D. *International Criminal Tribunal for Rwanda*



## E. *International Military Tribunal at Nuremberg*



## F. *Communications before United Nations treaty bodies*



## G. *Various international cases*

## II. Cases before internationalised tribunals

### A. *Bosnia War Crimes Chamber*



### B. *Special Court for Sierra Leone*



### C. *Special Panels for Serious Crimes – Timor Leste*



### D. *Extraordinary Chambers in the Courts of Cambodia*



### E. *Special Tribunal for Lebanon*

## III. Subsequent Nuremberg proceedings under Control Council Law Number 10

### A. *American Zone*



### B. *British Zone*



### C. *French Zone*



## IV. Cases before organs of regional organisations

### A. *African Commission on Human and Peoples' Rights*

## *B. Council of Europe*

### 1. European Commission of Human Rights

*Crutzescu* v. *Germany*, Application No. 8247/78, Unreported Admissibility Decision of 4 July 1979, 249, 250.

*Cyprus* v. *Turkey*, Applications Nos. 9780/74 and 6950/75 (Report of the Commission 10 July 1976), 249.

*'Greek Case'*, Applications Nos. 3321/67, 3322/67, 3323/67, 3344/67, Report Adopted on 15 April 1970, Yearbook of the European Convention on Human Rights, Vol. 12 (1972), 248.

*Tanko* v. *Finland*, Application No. 23634/94, Admissibility Decision of 19 May 1994, 250.

### 2. European Court of Human Rights

*Airey* v. *Ireland*, Application No. 6289/73, 9 October 1979, 61.

*Akdivar et al.* v. *Turkey*, Application No. 99/1995/605/693, 16 September 1996, Grand Chamber, 106.

*Aksoy* v. *Turkey*, Application No. 21987/93, 18 December 1996, 96.

*Buckley* v. *United Kingdom*, Application No. 20348/92, 25 September 1996, 106.

*Catan and Others* v. *Moldova and Russia*, Applications Nos. 43370/04, 8252/05 and 18454/06, 19 October 2012, Grand Chamber, 54.

*Chapman* v. *United Kingdom*, Application No. 27238/95, 18 January 2001, Grand Chamber, 106.

*C. R.* v. *United Kingdom*, Application No. 20190/92, 22 November 1995, 71.

*Cyprus* v. *Turkey*, Application No. 25781/94, 10 May 2001, Grand Chamber, 106.

*D.* v. *United Kingdom*, Application No. 30240/96, 2 May 1997, 250.

*D.H. and Others* v. *Czech Republic*, Application No. 57325/00, 13 November 2007, Grand Chamber, 146.

*Dybeku* v. *Albania*, Application No. 41153/06, 18 December 2007, 249.

*Ergi* v. *Turkey*, Application No. 23818/94, 28 July 1998, 284.

*Georgia* v. *Russia (No. 2)*, Application No. 38263/08, Admissibility Decision of 13 December 2011, 198, 250.

*Gladysheva* v. *Russia*, Application No. 7097/10, 6 December 2011, 105.

*Ireland* v. *United Kingdom*, Application No. 5310/71, 18 January 1978, 49, 248–9.

*Khamidov* v. *Russia*, Application No. 72118/01, 15 November 2007, 106.

*Lopez Ostra* v. *Spain*, Application No. 16798/90, 9 December 1994, 50.

*Mentes and Others* v. *Turkey*, Application No. 23186/94, 28 November 1997, Grand Chamber, 106.

*M.S.S.* v. *Belgium and Greece*, Application No. 30696/09, 21 January 2011, Grand Chamber, 250.

*Rantsev* v. *Cyprus and Russia*, Application No. 25965/04, 7 January 2010, 118.

### 3. European Committee of Social Rights



## *C. Organization of American States*

### 1. Inter-American Commission of Human Rights



### 2. Inter-American Court of Human Rights



## *D. Various regional cases*

## V. Cases before national tribunals

# TABLE OF SELECTED TREATIES AND OTHER INTERNATIONAL INSTRUMENTS

Given the number of international instruments cited in this study, I have taken the liberty to refer to short titles. Full references are given at the first mention in each chapter.

Particularly in Chapter 7, I reference a range of sources that are not pivotal to the central argument but useful to illustrate arguments or indicate additional instruments in which states have agreed to criminalise certain conduct. These instruments are mentioned in footnotes but not discussed in detail. As a result, they do not appear in this table. With a few exceptions, documents from UN supervisory organs, preparatory works, resolutions and reports from UN organs and agencies, national legislation or expert declarations are also not mentioned in this table.

## I. Instruments of the United Nations

## II. Regional treaties and instruments



## III. ICC – Assembly of States Parties



## IV. Other international instruments

# ABBREVIATIONS

| | |
|---|---|
| ACHPR | African Charter on Human and Peoples' Rights |
| ACommHPR | African Commission on Human and Peoples' Rights |
| AP I | Protocol Additional to the Geneva Conventions of 12 August 1949, and relating to the Protection of Victims of International Armed Conflicts, 8 June 1977 |
| AP II | Protocol Additional to the Geneva Conventions of 12 August 1949, and relating to the Protection of Victims of Non-International Armed Conflicts (Protocol II), 8 June 1977 |
| ATS | Alien Torts Statute (US legislation) |
| CAH | Crimes against humanity |
| CAT Committee | United Nations Committee against Torture |
| CEDAW | United Nations Convention on the Elimination of All Forms of Discrimination against Women |
| CERD | United Nations Convention on the Elimination of All Forms of Racial Discrimination |
| CESCR (or the committee) | The United Nations Committee on Economic, Social and Cultural Rights |
| CIDT | Cruel, inhuman or degrading treatment |
| CoE | Council of Europe |
| COHRE | Centre on Housing Rights and Evictions |
| CRC | United Nations Convention on the Rights of the Child |
| ECCC | Extraordinary Chambers in the Courts of Cambodia |
| ECHR | European Convention for the Protection of Human Rights and Fundamental Freedoms |
| ECommHR | European Commission of Human Rights |
| ECtHR | European Court of Human Rights |
| ECttSR | European Committee of Social Rights |
| ESCR | Economic, social and cultural rights |
| GA | General Assembly of the United Nations |

| | |
|---|---|
| GC | General Comment |
| GVA III or IV | Geneva Convention Relative to the Treatment of Prisoners of War (III) or the Protection of Civilian Persons in Time of War (IV) |
| HRC | United Nations Human Rights Council |
| HRCttee | United Nations Human Rights Committee |
| IAC | International armed conflict |
| IACommHR | Inter-American Commission on Human Rights |
| IACtHR | Inter-American Court of Human Rights |
| ICC | International Criminal Court |
| ICCPR | International Covenant on Civil and Political Rights |
| ICESCR (or covenant) | International Covenant on Economic, Social and Cultural Rights |
| ICTJ | International Center for Transitional Justice |
| ICTR | International Criminal Tribunal for Rwanda |
| ICTY | International Tribunal for the Prosecution of Persons Responsible for Serious Violations of International Humanitarian Law Committed in the Territory of the Former Yugoslavia since 1991 |
| IHL | International humanitarian law |
| ILC | International Law Commission |
| ILC Draft Code | Draft Code of Crimes against the Peace and Security of Mankind, International Laws Commission (various versions) |
| ILO | International Labour Organization |
| IMT | International Military Tribunal at Nuremberg ('major war criminals', with reports in the 'Blue Series', documentary evidence in the 'Red Series') |
| NIAC | Armed conflict not of an international character |
| NMT | Nuremberg Military Tribunals ('subsequent Nuremberg trials'), under Control Council Law No. 10 |
| OHCHR | Office of the High Commissioner for Human Rights |
| OP | Optional Protocol |
| Rome Statute or ICC Statute | Statute of the International Criminal Court |
| SC | United Nations Security Council |
| SCSL | Special Court for Sierra Leone |
| SG | Secretary-General of the United Nations |
| TWC | Reports of Trials of War Criminals Before the Nuremberg Military Tribunals Under Control Council Law No. 10 ('Green Series') |
| UDHR | Universal Declaration of Human Rights |
| UNCAC | United Nations Convention against Corruption |

| | |
|---|---|
| UNCAT | United Nations Convention against Torture |
| UNHCR | United Nations High Commissioner for Refugees |
| UNTAET | United Nations Transitional Administration in East Timor |
| UNTOC | United Nations Convention against Transnational Organized Crime |
| VCLT | Vienna Convention on the Law of Treaties |
| WHO | World Health Organization |

# 1

# Introduction

Hans Frank, a leading Nazi lawyer and the Governor-General of occupied Poland during World War II, was aware of the close relationship between economic, social and cultural wrongdoing and the commission of international crimes: 'We must annihilate the Jews, wherever we find them and wherever it is possible ... We cannot shoot or poison those 3,500,000 Jews, but we shall nevertheless be able to take measures, which will lead, somehow, to their annihilation.'[1] In September 1941, Dr Walbaum, head of public health of the Nazi administration in Poland, provided the following calculation to Frank: 'During the last week alone 1000 new spotted fever cases have been officially recorded ... If the food rations were to be diminished again, an enormous increase of the number of illnesses could be predicted.'[2] Despite his knowledge about the prevalence of disease and starvation, Frank 'approved a new plan which called for much larger contributions of foodstuffs to Germany at the expense of the non-German population'[3] in Poland: 'The new demand will be fulfilled exclusively at the expense of the foreign population. It must be done cold-bloodedly and without pity',[4] he reported in his diary.

In his diary, Hans Frank also describes the extensive paralysation of cultural life,[5] the curtailment of the influence of the Catholic

[1] *Prosecutor* v. *Frank, in Nazi Conspiracy and Aggression (Red Series): Documentary Evidence, 1946, IV TWC 1*, IMT, 892, 2233-D-PS, Diary entry of 16 December 1941.

[2] Ibid., 909, 2233-P-PS, Diary entry of 9 September 1941.

[3] *Prosecutor* v. *Frank, in Nazi Conspiracy and Aggression (Red Series): Documentary Evidence, 1946, II TWC 1*, IMT, 637–8 (emphasis omitted).

[4] Ibid.

[5] The International Military Tribunal at Nuremberg (IMT) only translated parts of Frank's diary. The original version in German contains many more passages on the socio-economic and cultural well-being of the affected population. On the right to education and participation in cultural life, Frank for instance wrote: 'We must only provide the Poles with those educational opportunities that show them the hopelessness of their ethnic [*völkisch*] destiny. Only poor movies, or movies visualising the greatness and strength of the German Empire

Church,[6] the closure of educational institutions to prevent the growth of the Polish intelligentsia[7] and how he used starvation as a method of recruiting forced labourers.[8] Frank anticipated that public attention to these abuses would not be significant: 'That we sentence 1.2 million Jews to die of hunger should be noted only marginally.'[9]

Seven decades later, contemporary human rights law qualifies such practices as violations of economic, social and cultural rights (ESCR). These rights include the right to health, water, and work or the right to take part in cultural life and to protect dignity, freedom and well-being. Hans Frank was one of the twenty-four defendants who faced the International Military Tribunal at Nuremberg. The tribunal found him guilty of war crimes and crimes against humanity and sentenced him to death, based on evidence that he introduced the deportation of Polish slave labourers and persecuted the Jews by forcing them into ghettos, subjecting them to discriminatory laws and depriving them of the food necessary to avoid starvation.[10] Frank's case is one of the precedents that suggest that conduct amounting to an international crime can sometimes simultaneously be understood as violations of ESCR.

could thus come into question.' Werner Präg and Wolfgang Jacobmeyer (eds.), *Das Diensttagebuch* (Deutsche Verlagsanstalt, 1975), 53 (translation by the author).

[6] *Prosecutor* v. *Frank, in Nazi Conspiracy and Aggression (Red Series): Documentary Evidence, 1946, III TWC 1*, IMT, 397, 437-PS, report of Hans Frank to Hitler re Situation in Poland, 19 June 1943. See further Präg and Jacobmeyer (eds.), *Das Diensttagebuch*, 55, 'The Governor-General [Frank] explained that the higher schools were already closed. As a matter of principle, seminaries ... would be closed, as they merely constitute breeding grounds of Germanophobia' (translation by the author).

[7] *Prosecutor* v. *Frank, in Nazi Conspiracy and Aggression (Red Series): Documentary Evidence, 1946, VII TWC 1*, IMT, 420, EC-344 16–17.

[8] *Prosecutor* v. *Frank, in Nazi Conspiracy and Aggression (Red Series): Documentary Evidence, 1946, IV TWC 1*, IMT, 914, 2233-Y-PS. Diary entry of 20 November 1942: 'Starting 1 February 1942 the food ration cards should not be issued to the individual Pole or Ukrainian by the Nutrition Office, but to the establishments working for the German interest. 2,000,000 people would thus be eliminated from the non-German, normal ration-consuming contingent. Now, if those ration cards are only distributed by the factories, part of those people will naturally rush into the factories.'

[9] Ibid., 900, 2233-E-PS, Diary entry on the cabinet session of 24 August 1942. The later date of the diary entry and the fact that some should be spared to continue forced labour explain why Frank refers to a lower number of Jews than in the entry of 16 December 1941 (above note 1).

[10] *United States of America, the French Republic, the United Kingdom of Great Britain and Northern Ireland, and the Union of Soviet Socialist Republics against Major War Criminals, Opinion and Judgment, in Nazi Conspiracy and Aggression (Red Series), 1 October 1946*, IMT, 125–6.

Notwithstanding Frank's trial and the development of human rights law after World War II, Frank's assessment remains accurate: other atrocities attract much more attention than deliberately starving people, which is often noted only marginally. The same tends to be true with other ESCR violations. The mechanisms of international criminal law often marginalise or ignore those crimes that overlap with ESCR abuses. Consider, for example, the Cambodian communist regime from 1975 to 1979. The extremist policies of the Khmer Rouge resulted in the worst fabricated famine in recent history.[11] The first Khmer Rouge trial at the Extraordinary Chambers in the Courts of Cambodia (ECCC) has been criticised for focusing on executions and detention in the notorious Camp S-21, to the exclusion of starvation or other abuses related to ESCR.[12] Would it have been possible for prosecutors in the ECCC to press charges for starvation, which affected many more than those executed or detained? Could charges have been brought for policies abusing cultural rights, such as the prohibition to exercise religious practices or to disperse a disenfranchised minority, the Cham, with intent to destroy them as a community?[13] Or for the destruction of entire libraries, the closing of schools and the prohibition against speaking any languages other than Khmer?[14] Could any of the instruments aiming at the suppression of certain criminal conduct in states' domestic jurisdictions, such as the United Nations (UN) Convention against Transnational Organized Crime, be invoked to address some of the ESCR abuses that continue to plague today's post-conflict Cambodia?

As another example, consider a woman living in one of the almost 140 Sudanese villages visited by the International Commission of Inquiry on Darfur. Her name could be Zeinab. While she is a fiction, the International Commission of Inquiry collected evidence on a pattern of rape followed by looting in Darfur conflict:[15] 'deliberate aggressions against women and girls, including gang rapes, occurred during the attacks on the villages ... In most of the cases, the involvement of

[11] Randle DeFalco, 'Accounting for Famine' (2011) 5 *International Journal of Transitional Justice*, 1, 142–58: 143 (in terms of the percentage of the total affected population killed).

[12] Ibid.

[13] Ben Kiernan, *The Pol Pot Regime* (Yale University Press, 1996), 262–8.

[14] Ibid., 8, 9, 39.

[15] Report of the International Commission of Inquiry on Darfur to the SG, Pursuant to SC Resolution 1564 of 18 September 2004, 25 January 2005, para. 548, see also, for instance, para. 339 for an account of a rape followed by looting.

Janjaweed [Sudanese militiamen] was reported. In many cases, the involvement of soldiers was also alleged.'[16]

After Zeinab was raped by militia members, who allegedly acted under the authority of the Sudanese state authorities, the perpetrators stole her household items and her livestock.

> Many of the villages were reportedly completely destroyed by deliberate demolition of structures and more frequently by burning down the whole village. Straw-roofs of the traditional circular houses were torched, as well as all other inflammable material, and vegetation inside and in the immediate vicinity of the village was destroyed by burning ... During the attacks Janjaweed are reported to have destroyed utensils, equipment for processing food, water containers and other household items essential for the survival of the inhabitants. Wells were reportedly poisoned by dropping the carcasses of cattle into the wells. In addition ..., the destruction seems to have been consistently combined with looting of personal valuables, cash and, above all, live-stock.[17]

If the conduct of the militia members is attributable to the state of Sudan, the perpetrators would have violated the woman's ESCR, in particular by interfering with her access to food and water. Alternatively, if state attribution cannot be established, the state of Sudan should face the allegation that it failed to protect Zeinab's ESCR by letting the militia act without hindrance.[18]

If a situation like Zeinab's is discussed in a process concerned with international crimes, the conventional reaction would usually be to classify her as a victim of sexual violence. The theft or destruction of her property is likely to be relegated to the background, considered merely to give context to the rape: past mechanisms as well as the literature have tended to conceptualise economic and social abuses as the landscape against which abuses of civil and political rights are committed.[19] Yet, Zeinab should not 'only' be considered as a victim of rape, but also of pillage and, hence, as a victim of a war crime which overlaps with ESCR violations. Her property may at first sight seem of marginal importance, but what if Zeinab desperately needs her household utensils to carry drinking water from the well? What if the theft of her livestock has deprived her of her only sources of protein and income? As the commission of inquiry emphasised, noting

[16] Ibid., paras. 334–5. [17] Ibid., para. 305.

[18] On the alleged relationship between the government of Sudan and the Janjaweed militia, see ibid., para. 99.

[19] On this tendency, see particularly Zinaida Miller, 'Effects of Invisibility' (2008) 2 *International Journal of Transitional Justice*, 266–91.

that property can be essential for the survival of victims, theft or destruction of belongings can severely affect victims' access to socio-economic rights' enjoyment.[20]

And what about Zeinab's neighbour Jamal, whose home was set on fire by soldiers to force him to leave the village? Should he 'merely' be directed to seek help from an organisation that provides reconstruction assistance? Housing rights are not usually considered relevant to determinations based on international criminal law, but perhaps he should also be acknowledged as the victim of a crime, and his testimony collected by a truth commission that examines widespread evictions as a crime against humanity. The most recently adopted African Union Convention for the Protection and Assistance of Internally Displaced Persons in Africa expressly requires that state parties 'declare as offenses punishable by law acts of arbitrary displacement that amount to genocide, war crimes or crimes against humanity'.[21] How can such acts be identified? We must know under what circumstances the human rights violation most prominently associated with arbitrary displacement – forced evictions – relate to the definitions of crimes such as genocide, war crimes and crimes against humanity.

## 1.1 The research problem and why it needs to be solved

At the core of this study are the legal aspects of the questions asked above. Can violations of ESCR – such as the ones Frank described in his diary – be addressed in processes dealing with international crimes and, if so, to what extent? International crimes denote conduct that is outlawed by international law or conduct that states deem must be prevented and repressed by international cooperation, or both. The *research question* central to the study is whether or not international criminal law is capable of accommodating claims related to conduct qualified by human rights lawyers as violations of international or regional treaties protecting ESCR. The *hypothesis* is that current definitions of international crimes (leading to criminal responsibility) can overlap with violations of ESCR (giving raise to state responsibility for internationally wrongful acts).

20 Report of the International Commission of Inquiry on Darfur to the SG, Pursuant to SC Resolution 1564 of 18 September 2004, 25 January 2005, para. 305.

21 AU Convention for the Protection and Assistance of Internally Displaced Persons in Africa, Kampala, 23 October 2009 (entered into force 6 December 2012), Art. 4(6).

The exclusion of considerations related to the rights to food, health or education poses significant legal, ethical and political questions. How should criminal tribunals deal with claims that they should convict alleged perpetrators of conduct that human rights lawyers qualify as violations of ESCR? May truth commissions with a mandate over international crimes collect testimonies on abuses of the right to non-discrimination, food, housing, education or partaking in cultural life, or do they overstep their mandates by doing so? Could instruments aiming at the suppression of criminal conduct in states' domestic jurisdictions, such as treaties against transnational organised crime, assist us in addressing ESCR abuses?

The abuses committed by the Nazis, the Khmer Rouge or the perpetrators in Darfur are illustrations of the types of claims that can be, and are being made today when societies and international actors are trying to deal with the legacies of international crimes. The examples of Nazi practices, the story of Zeinab and Jamal and the policies of the Khmer Rouge all illustrate the problems inherent in the position that certain abuses fall outside the scope of international criminal law because their underlying factual conduct primarily affects people's access to ESCR rather than civil and political rights. They raise serious and contentious questions about the scope of current international law. They also suggest that there is need for analysis and discussion: does international law accommodate claims that such abuses can amount to international crimes? If this study provokes and stimulates nuanced discussions about the unavoidable choices prosecutors, lawyers and advocates make in selecting cases, and the way lawyers determine whether or not someone is a victim of an international crime, then it will have successfully achieved its goal.

It must be stated at the outset that most violations of ESCR will not ever be relevant in a discussion of international criminal law. Nevertheless, the hypothesis represents the view that, between the complete exclusion of ESCR and the claim to consider every kind of socio-economic denial as a crime, there is an area that merits further analysis. The potential for development in this area has been recognised in recent literature, most notably by Louise Arbour and the Secretary-General of the United Nations. Arbour urged that '[t]here are still other examples [of prosecutions by domestic, hybrid and international tribunals dealing with ESCR], and the use of statutes of existing international and national courts to adjudicate economic, social, and cultural violations as international crimes should thus be further explored'.[22] The Secretary-General emphasised that '[i]nvestigating and prosecuting crimes under national or international law where the conduct involves violations of [ESCR] as well as civil and political rights' was part of the UN approach to transitional justice.[23] Today, developments at the international level suggest that overlap between ESCR violations and international crimes is considered a possibility: in 2014, the Office of the High Commissioner for Human Rights (OHCHR) published the outcome of its exploration of the potential, challenges and limitations of transitional justice processes addressing violations of ESCR – finding that 'a number of international crimes involve or might involve infringements of ESCR'.[24] A groundbreaking UN report on the human rights situation in the Democratic People's Republic of Korea released in spring 2014 moreover extensively analysed unprecedented violations of ESCR and argued that these, in many instances, constitute crimes against humanity.[25]

### *1.1.1 The current marginalisation of ESCR abuses*

Despite Hans Frank's conviction – and, as this study shows, significant other jurisprudence – the conventional position has been to assume that violations of ESCR are beyond the scope of international criminal law. The destruction of homes, cutting off water sources, excluding certain groups from education or cultural life and forcing people to work under inhumane conditions have been commonplace throughout history, particularly in situations of armed conflict. Rarely, however, have such violations been addressed through legal processes relying on international criminal law. Indeed, international criminal lawyers have generally assumed that international crimes are confined to certain violations of civil and political rights to the exclusion of their

[22] Louise Arbour, 'Economic and Social Justice for Societies in Transition' (2007) 40 *New York University Journal of International Law and Politics*, 1, 1–28: 15–16.

[23] Guidance Note of the Secretary-General on the United Nations Approach to Transitional Justice, March 2010, 10. Transitional justice denotes 'the full range of processes and mechanisms associated with a society's attempt to come to terms with a legacy of large-scale past abuses.' Ibid., 2.

[24] OHCHR, Transitional Justice and Economic, Social and Cultural Rights, HR/PUB/13/5, 2014, 24.

[25] Report of the Commission of Inquiry on Human Rights in the Democratic People's Republic of Korea, A/HRC/25/CRP.1, 7 February 2014, esp. paras. 1115–37 on violations of the right to freedom from hunger. Adopted by the HRC in Situation of Human Rights in the Democratic People's Republic of Korea, A/HRC/25/L.17, 26 March 2014.

socio-economic and cultural counterparts. Traditionally, criminal proceedings or other processes to address an abusive past have thus tended to focus on a limited number of civil and political rights abuses, such as summary executions, arbitrary detention, disappearances and, more recently, sexual violence. The constantly expanding literature on international criminal law and continuing efforts to redress the legacies of massive human rights abuses more broadly (sometimes referred to as transitional justice, post-conflict justice or 'dealing with the past') have remained detached from the human rights literature on ESCR.

The assumption that ESCR violations have no place in international criminal law has been evident in the workings of all the primary mechanisms employed to deal with the legacy of an abusive past, namely criminal proceedings, truth commissions and out-of-court reparation programmes. The mandates of such mechanisms frequently cover crimes against humanity, war crimes and other international crimes. As outlined below, and in more detail in the next chapter, most scholars, practitioners and commentators have assumed that the elements of such crimes comprised only abuses related to a narrow set of civil and political liberties. Truth commissions, particularly, demonstrate the tendency to simplistically assume that international crimes and ESCR violations do not overlap.[26] The South African Truth and Reconciliation Commission, for instance, was criticised for paying insufficient attention to violations of ESCR,[27] despite its relatively broad mandate.[28] Among the few exceptions to the pattern of excluding ESCR considerations is the Commission for Reception, Truth and Reconciliation in East Timor, which has analysed abuses of ESCR in relation to international crimes. The commission concluded that many of the examined ESCR abuses were part of a deliberate scorched earth policy that violated the laws of war seriously enough to qualify at least some of the abuses as war crimes.[29] The commission, however, set aside the practical relevance of this finding in

[26] Lisa Laplante, 'Addressing the Socioeconomic Roots of Violence' (2008) 2 *International Journal of Transitional Justice*, 3, 331–55: 335, noting how truth commissions have 'tended to interpret their mandates more narrowly, often limiting their study to crimes that constitute violations of civil and political human rights'.

[27] South African Community Law Centre et al., 'Submission to the TRC Concerning the Relevance of Economic, Social and Cultural Rights to the Commission's Mandate, 18 March 1997', www.justice.gov.za/trc/hrvtrans/submit/esc6.htm.

[28] Promotion of National Unity and Reconciliation Act 1995, Act 95–34, 26 July 1995, Section 3(1)a.

[29] Truth and Reconciliation in Timor-Leste Commission for Reception, *Chega!* (CAVR, 2005), Chapters 7.5 and 7.9.

a single sentence and recommended that 'principles of feasibility and needs-based prioritisation' should limit reparation programmes to victims of a small set of civil and political rights abuses and to certain categories of vulnerable populations such as widows, children and people with disabilities.[30] Despite the criticism this approach attracted from the UN Secretary-General,[31] and despite calls that more attention should be paid to economic, cultural and social concerns in transitional justice in general,[32] the imbalance in the treatment of ESCR has not been corrected by subsequent truth commissions.[33]

In addition to the practice of tribunals and quasi-judicial mechanisms, scholars, policy-makers and non-governmental organisations have generally tended to accept the traditional view that the consideration of abuses of ESCR have little or no place in international criminal law. Most often, the exclusion of considerations related to food, health, education, work or culture by processes applying international criminal law is not explained, but taken as given. Amnesty International, for instance, contrasts war crimes or crimes against humanity with 'mass abuses of ESCR',[34] conveying the impression that there is no overlap

[30] Ibid., Chapter 12, 40.

[31] Report of the SG on the Question of the Realization in All Countries of Economic, Social and Cultural Rights, A/HRC/4/62, 13 February 2007, para. 42.

[32] Two recent edited volumes are most notable in this respect. Gaby Oré Aguilar and Felipe Gómez Isa (eds.), *Equality and Social Justice in Societies Emerging from Conflict* (Intersentia, 2011); Dustin Sharp (ed.), *Justice and Economic Violence in Transition* (Springer, 2013).

[33] At the time of writing, the Kenyan Truth, Justice and Reconciliation Commission (TJRC) was the most recent example of a truth commission paying attention to ESCR. Although the TJRC made laudable efforts to address ESCR in some parts of the report, the report overall resembles those of earlier commissions insofar as it contains little to no specific legal analysis of ESCR violations. For further analysis of the treatment of ESCR by truth commissions, see Evelyne Schmid and Aoife Nolan, 'Economic and Social Dimensions of Transitional Justice' (2014) 8 *International Journal of Transitional Justice* 3, 362–82. Other truth commissions that have analysed (explicitly or implicitly) ESCR violations include those of Germany, Guatemala, Mauritius, Morocco, Peru and Sierra Leone. For profiles and the mandates of these commissions, see United States Institute of Peace, 'Truth Commission Digital Collection', www.usip.org/publications/truth-commission-digital-collection.

[34] Amnesty International, *The State of the World's Human Rights 2010* (Amnesty International, 2010), xvii, 'The obstacles to implementing accountability for mass atrocities in conflicts or political repression are real, but the debate at least has been won: no one denies the principle that war crimes or crimes against humanity or enforced disappearances should be punished. Yet when it comes to the mass abuses of economic, social and cultural rights, there is no comparable effort to bring law and accountability to bear.'

between the two. Others simply affirm that 'most crimes referred to in the Rome Statute [of the International Criminal Court] pertain to violations of civil and political rights'.[35] Consider moreover the OHCHR publication on reparation programmes in post-conflict countries. While the document acknowledges that reparation programmes have tended to focus on civil and political rights and marginalised ESCR, the OHCHR states in this brochure that this focus 'is not entirely unjustified' because 'arguably, it makes sense to concentrate on the most serious crimes'.[36] The problem with this statement is that it sustains views that only civil and political rights violations can constitute the most serious crimes.

In a groundbreaking lecture at the New York University School of Law in 2006, Louise Arbour asserted that efforts to address the legacy of widespread human rights abuses display a bias towards civil and political rights.[37] The former High Commissioner for Human Rights criticised the way these efforts exclude considerations of ESCR and are 'predicated on accountability for past abuses of civil and political rights as a way to achieve peace and the rule of law'.[38] Arbour believes that this bias 'reflects the hidden assumption that [ESCR] are not entitlements but aspirational expectations to be fulfilled by market-driven or political processes alone'.[39] Arbour's speech was a timely invitation for international lawyers to reconsider some of the traditional assumptions about the relevance of socio-economic and cultural rights abuses to processes established to deal with the legacy of past crimes.

To date, Sigrun Skogly, David Marcus, Mark Drumbl and Larissa van den Herik are the authors of the four most significant legal articles that explicitly examine the relationship between ESCR and international crimes.[40] Advocating that more attention be given to ESCR, Skogly notes

[35] Elodie Aba and Michael Hammer, 'Yes We Can? Options and Barriers to Broadening the Scope of the Responsibility to Protect to Include Economic, Social and Cultural Rights Abuse', in *One World Trust Briefing Paper* (One World Trust, 2009), 9. See Section 2.2 for more evidence of such assumptions.

[36] Office of the High Commissioner for Human Rights, *Rule-of-Law Tools for Post-Conflict States: Reparations Programmes* (United Nations, 2008), 19, 21 (drafted by Pablo de Greiff).

[37] Arbour, 'Economic and Social Justice for Societies in Transition', 9–10.

[38] Ibid., note 26. [39] Ibid., 4.

[40] Earlier, in 1994, Tadeusz Jasudowicz observed that the 'failure to implement [ESCR] can engage international responsibility and wilfully causing serious injury to body or health can constitute – according to its gravity and scale – genocide or some other crimes against humanity'. Tadeusz Jasudowicz, 'The Legal Character of Social Rights', in *Social Rights as Human Rights: A European Challenge*, ed. Krzysztof Drzewicki, Catarina Krause, and Allan Rosas (Åbo Akademi University, 1994), 34–9: 39.

that 'there are possible violations of economic and social human rights that are sufficiently severe to merit an inclusion into the crimes against humanity concept, such as deliberate starvation or forced evictions'.[41] At first reading, Skogly does not seem to believe that this would be possible without an expansion of existing law. She begins her analysis by asking 'whether the various definitions are open for the inclusion of crimes *other* than those listed in the various instruments'.[42] Her pioneering text, however, wavers between the opinion that international criminal law must be expanded and that a fresh interpretation of the definitions of crimes may reveal that existing definitions already overlap with ESCR violations, particularly as far as crimes against humanity are concerned: 'The question is whether the way in which crimes against humanity is understood in the instruments gives room for an inclusion of gross violations of economic and social rights.'[43]

Marcus, Drumbl and van den Herik are more assertive and argue that the scope of existing definitions of crimes already encompasses certain ESCR violations. Referring to the Ukrainian famine in the early 1930s, the Ethiopian Dergue during the late 1980s and the North Korean famine in the 1990s, Marcus observes that

> [i]nternational blindness to this criminal conduct of the most nefarious sort is odd, given that existing international law criminalizes first- and second-degree faminogenic behavior . . . [A] survey of existing international criminal law shows that faminogenic rights violations like these [i.e. abuses such as violations of the right to food], committed with the appropriate degree of intentionality, incur criminal responsibility.[44]

Drumbl, for his part, observes that there are 'crimes that are social, economic or cultural in nature', but that 'few socioeconomic crimes have been prosecuted in practice'.[45] In 2014, van den Herik asserts 'that there is ample opportunity to include socio-economic and cultural

[41] Sigrun Skogly, 'Crimes against Humanity' (2001) 5 *The International Journal of Human Rights*, 1, 58–80: 58.

[42] Ibid., 60 (emphasis added). [43] Ibid.

[44] David Marcus, 'Famine Crimes' (2003) 97 *American Journal of International Law*, 2, 245–81: 245–8, 62. Based on the US common-law understanding of mental elements, Marcus defines 'first-degree famine crimes' as 'knowingly creating, inflicting or prolonging conditions that result in or contribute to the starvation of a significant number of persons'. A second-degree famine crime would be committed by 'recklessly ignoring evidence that [the perpetrator's] policies are creating, inflicting, or prolonging the starvation of a significant number of persons'.

[45] Mark Drumbl, 'Accountability for Property and Environmental War Crimes' (ICTJ, November 2009), 6.

concerns in mainstream criminal justice modalities',[46] although, in her view, ESCR are 'less susceptible to international criminalization' than civil and political rights violations.[47]

Does international law already recognise that many types of abusive conduct that deprive people of their rights to health, food, education or other ESCR are properly considered within the ambit of international criminal law, or would the definitions of crimes first need to be expanded? The diverging analyses point to a lack of certainty about the status of international criminal law in respect of economic, social and cultural wrongs. Careful research is needed to determine if ESCR violations can, *de lege lata*, overlap with the definitions of international crimes.

### *1.1.2 Consequences of the current marginalisation of ESCR*

A refusal to consider whether and how existing international law may accommodate abuses related to ESCR in processes that deal with international crimes would have a range of consequences for the discipline of international law.

International criminal law is among the youngest, and yet most visible, branches of public international law. For better or worse, 'the institutions of international criminal justice have assumed a central place in discussions and actions around what should be done in the wake of atrocities'.[48] The perception and reputation of international law will depend, in part, upon whether its institutions and actors successfully explain its focus, orientation and limitations. If mainstream approaches continue to concentrate almost exclusively on abuses that are predominantly viewed as civil and political rights violations, there is a risk that observers will come to believe that international law is unable to address even the worst socio-economic and cultural abuses. Skogly warns that the lack of linkage between ESCR violations and international crimes indicates that 'the

[46] Larissa van den Herik, 'ESCR – International Criminal Law's Blind Spot?', in *Economic, Social, and Cultural Rights: Contemporary Issues and Challenges*, ed. Eibe Riedel, Gilles Giacca and Christophe Golay., *Economic, Social, and Cultural Rights* (Oxford University Press, 2014), 343–66: 365.

[47] Ibid., 344.

[48] Naomi Roht-Arriaza, 'Editorial Note to the Special Issue on the Role of International Criminal Justice in Transitional Justice' (2013) 7 *International Journal of Transitional Justice*, 3, 383–92: 383.

international human rights community is about to make the same mistake as it did in the 1960s and 1970s – to leave economic and social rights behind'.[49] She posits: 'If malicious state leaders know that they may be brought to trial for massacring people, they may choose to starve them to death, or inflict illness on them instead. If the concern is the kind of suffering, and the result of the actions, then a limitation to civil rights does not seem logical.'[50]

Those frustrated with the lack of attention ESCR receive in processes designed to address a legacy of international crimes sometimes accuse the discipline itself of being, at best, unsuited and irrelevant, and at worst, oppressive. They conclude that a departure from international legal norms or from 'legalism' is required to enable societies to deal with some of the crimes that defined survivors' experiences of the abusive past.[51] From a constructivist perspective, 'when people believe law matters, it will matter; when people think law does not matter, it rarely can'.[52] As long as scholars, judges, truth commissioners or advocates believe that considerations of ESCR have no place in international criminal law, international law will not be able to maximise its potential to contribute to the resolution of the complex issues that arise from ESCR violations. This study engages with the broader question: have tribunals and other mechanisms so far sparingly addressed issues related to ESCR for reasons that are inherent in international law? Should international law be blamed for the relative lack of attention paid to ESCR by the bodies that apply international criminal law? Or is the hypothesis of this study correct: Proper interpretation of legal sources allows for considerably more attention to ESCR than has so far been accorded and there must be extra-legal reasons why ESCR violations are not treated with the same emphasis as most violations of civil and political rights? To answer this

49 Skogly, 'Crimes against Humanity', 59–60. 50 Ibid., 74.

51 An example is Kieran McEvoy, 'Beyond Legalism' (2007) 34 *Journal of Law and Society*, 4, 411–40: 418, 'The criticism [to abandon the traditional social justice concerns such as poverty and health] is framed as the logical result of the legalistic bent of contemporary human rights discourse'. By 'legalism', the author means the reliance on legal norms that are – in his view – closed to considerations of concerns such as poverty or health. See also Makau Mutua, 'A Critique of Rights in Transitional Justice', in *Rethinking Transitions: Equality and Social Justice in Societies Emerging from Conflict*, ed. Gaby Oré Aguilar and Felipe Gómez Isa (Intersentia, 2011), 31–45: 35–6. Mutua is skeptic about the ability of human rights law to respond to Africa's crises, *inter alia*, because ESCR are 'impotent and vague'.

52 Jane Stromseth et al., *Can Might Make Rights?* (Cambridge University Press, 2006), 312.

question, we must know the extent to which international criminal law is open to considerations of socio-economic and cultural abuses.

We will return to the risks of a failure to engage seriously with the research question in the next chapter and will now consider why it is warranted to examine the research problem at this point in time.

### 1.1.3 *The timeliness of revisiting the traditional view*

This study is particularly pressing at this time for two reasons.

First, international human rights law concerning ESCR has significantly developed, moving beyond the point when it considered ESCR an orphan of human rights law. As we will consider in more detail in Chapter 3, the dichotomy between ESCR and civil and political rights was untenable and has been eroding in the practice of courts, human rights organs, advocacy and the scholarly literature. States have expressed their commitment to recognise ESCR on the same footing as civil and political rights,[53] and most countries have entrusted their judiciaries to adjudicate at least some claims based on ESCR.[54] At the normative level, most state obligations on ESCR have been clarified to a comparable level just as for civil and political rights. This is often effected through the state reporting procedures before the UN Committee on Economic, Social and Cultural Rights (CESCR), regional and national tribunals and expert bodies, such as the African Commission on Human and Peoples' Rights (ACommHPR) or the European Committee of Social Rights (ECttSR), domestic jurisprudence and scholarly contributions. UN special procedures (such as special rapporteurs[55]) and charter-based mechanisms, such as the UN Human Rights Council (HRC), have further elucidated the normative content of ESCR and have provided practical evidence of the importance of the international legal obligations contained in the international human rights instruments. Moreover, the negotiation and recent adoption of the Optional Protocol to the International Covenant on Economic, Social, and Cultural Rights (ICESCR) provided states with the opportunity to

[53] World Conference on Human Rights: Vienna Declaration and Programme of Action, A/Conf.157/23, 12 July 1993, para. 5.

[54] For a useful overview, see Malcolm Langford (ed.), *Social Rights Jurisprudence* (Cambridge University Press, 2008).

[55] Particularly notable are the special rapporteurs on education, housing, food and health. Christophe Golay et al., 'UN Special Procedures' (2011) 15 *International Journal of Human Rights*, 2, 299–318.

express their views about ESCR.[56] The fact that this protocol was adopted unanimously and the fact that it foresees mechanisms very similar to those of other procedural human rights instruments indicate that there is today a fairly broad consensus among states that many aspects of ESCR are not as different from civil and political rights as may traditionally have been assumed. Acknowledging that the protection of civil and political rights in isolation is insufficient has, in turn, prepared the way for an exploration of the relationships between international criminal law and ESCR, which may identify the kind of situations that could simultaneously be covered by those bodies of law.

The second reason for studying this issue now is that developments in the field of state responsibility for violations of international human rights law have been accompanied by important advances in international criminal law over the last fifteen years. As Cassese pointed out, '[i]ndividual criminal liability, as opposed to State responsibility, has enormously expanded ... The body of international criminal law has developed as a separate branch from the international law on State responsibility, although overlaps may come about ... between individual criminal liability and State responsibility.'[57] Such possible overlaps, however, have not yet been systematically studied in international law, let alone in the field of ESCR.[58] It is now a suitable time to enquire if overlap between ESCR violations and international crimes exists.

In the past, exploring the intersection between two branches of law has allowed more nuanced understandings of the definitions of crimes in other areas. For example, it has become apparent that the legal definitions of international crimes were never inherently closed to claims based on sexual violence, as had been thought earlier. They only required a more holistic interpretation in line with present-day human rights law.[59]

[56] Optional Protocol to the International Covenant on Economic, Social and Cultural Rights, GA Res. 63/117, 63 UN GAOR Supp. (No. 49), 10 December 2008 (entered into force 5 May 2013).

[57] Antonio Cassese, *International Law*, 2nd edn (Oxford University Press, 2005), 245.

[58] See also Andrea Bianchi, 'State Responsibility and Criminal Liability of Individuals', in *The Oxford Companion to International Criminal Justice*, ed. Antonio Cassese (Oxford University Press, 2009), 16–24: 16. The author emphasises that even if state responsibility and individual criminal responsibility are considered distinct in international law, '[i]t would be misleading, however, to believe that the two separate regimes of responsibility never intersect or overlap' (reference omitted).

[59] See for instance Kelly Askin, 'Prosecuting Wartime Rape and Other Gender-Related Crimes under International Law: Extraordinary Advances, Enduring Obstacles' (2003) 21 *Berkeley Journal of International Law*, 2, 288–349.

International criminal law may not prove to be as categorically opposed to claims related to ESCR as a cursory glance may suggest. It is possible that perceptions are undergoing similar change as that which occurred when international criminal lawyers started to take sexual violence against women more seriously.[60] In order to assess whether the same might be possible in the realm of ESCR, we should rigorously examine the links between the legal definitions of crimes and violations of ESCR.

## 1.2 Conceptual underpinnings and organisation of the study

The inquiry of this study is best conceived as an exploration of the ways that the contemporary international legal order encompasses diverse legal sub-orders that pursue specific and distinct, but nonetheless connected, social functions. Whether existing international criminal law accommodates claims related to ESCR is part of a growing interest in the *ius post bellum*, that is, the question how law can assist to organise the aftermath of conflict.[61] This interest demands an exploration of an ever-more complex fabric of normative frameworks, including human rights law, international criminal law and international humanitarian law (IHL). As we will see in Chapter 3, the law of state responsibility for violations of human rights law, international criminal law and IHL are each based on different premises that must be respected if the branches or sub-systems are to fulfil their specific purposes.[62] The study of the

[60] Michelle Foster, *International Refugee Law and Socio-Economic Rights* (Cambridge University Press, 2007), 15–16. Foster similarly argues that the Refugee Convention should be reinterpreted to embrace certain claims related to socio-economic rights deprivation, just as advocates for women's rights were able to overcome the reluctance of courts to embrace refugee claims related to women's human rights.

[61] For an exploration of the term, see Vincent Chetail (ed.), *Post-Conflict Peacebuilding* (Oxford University Press, 2009), 17.

[62] That international law serves a social purpose, just as any other law, not only derives from the adage *ubi societas ibi ius*, but is equally at the core of modern approaches to international law. The school of thought that can broadly be associated with the interpretative method taken in this study is the (original version of the) policy-oriented New Haven school, which viewed international law as a system of decision-making towards the attainment of values – most importantly 'the post-World War II image of international law as a creative medium devoted to building a humane world public order'. Harold Koh, 'Commentaries – Is There a "New" New Haven School of International Law?' (2007) 32 *Yale Journal of International Law*, 2, 559–73: 572. For some of the school's most influential works, see Myres McDougal et al., 'Theories about International Law: Prologue to a Configurative Jurisprudence' (1968) *Yale Faculty Scholarship Series*, 2577; Rosalyn Higgins, *Problems and Process* (Clarendon, 1994).

overlap between ESCR and the definitions of international crimes shows that they are all part of a normative order based on 'faith in fundamental human rights, in the dignity and worth of the human person'.[63] What Sørensen wrote in 1983 remains true today: the international organisational structure is characterised by an almost infinite diversity, but 'in spite of all the tendencies towards fragmentation . . . it is still accurate – to use the terms of systems analysis – to regard the general international legal order as a universal system which engulfs the great variety of existing autonomous legal orders as sub-systems'.[64]

The demonstration of overlap between human rights violations giving rise to state responsibility and the law pertaining to international crimes is an inquiry that evidences the shift from accounts of the international system that described it as a 'hierarchical pyramid structure with relatively few norms, in which states, perceived as opaque and unitary actors ("billiard balls"), interacted in a largely unconstrained manner', and towards contemporary international law today, which 'resembles a dense web of overlapping and detailed prescriptions in [diverse] subject areas'.[65] Even those who have a 'particularistic' conception of international law[66] agree that the various sub-systems or branches of international law 'do not live by themselves, each in their own area, but intersect and overlap with each other'.[67] Rather than a *bric-à-brac*,[68] international law is best considered a normative system that operates within, and for, the social context of an imperfect and

[63] Charter of the United Nations, 1 UNTS XVI, 26 June 1945 (entered into force 24 October 1945), Preamble.

[64] Max Sørensen, 'Autonomous Legal Orders' (1983) 32 *The International and Comparative Law Quarterly*, 3, 559–76: 560.

[65] Bruno Simma and Dirk Pulkowski, 'Of Planets and the Universe' (2006) 17 *European Journal of International Law*, 3, 483–529: 484.

[66] For instance, such was the view taken in *Prosecutor* v. *Tadić, Decision on the Defence Motion for Interlocutory Appeal on Jurisdiction, IT-94-1-Ar72, 2 October 1995*, ICTY, para. 11, 'In international law, every tribunal is a self-contained system (unless otherwise provided).'

[67] Andreas Fischer-Lescano and Gunther Teubner, 'Regime-Collisions' (2004) 25 *Michigan Journal of International Law*, 4, 999–1046: 1022. An illustration of this point can be found in the *Tadić* case where the Appeals Chamber made extensive use of human rights law to interpret terms of IHL, despite the fact that the same Chamber expressed a 'particularistic' view. *Prosecutor* v. *Tadić, Decision on the Defence Motion for Interlocutory Appeal on Jurisdiction, IT-94-1-Ar72, 2 October 1995*, ICTY, for instance, para. 97.

[68] Jean Combacau, 'Bric-a-brac ou système?' (1986) 31 *Annuaire de philosophie du droit*, 85–105.

diverse 'international community', composed of states, individuals and other organs of society. The present study adheres to the view that the various branches of international law not only overlap, but also share a common overarching social goal. This premise justifies that the various branches of law relevant to this study are consulted in conjunction, and this view will shape the subsequent interpretation of the different sources of international law relevant to the research question.

### *1.2.1 Organisation of the study*

We will begin with a discussion of the main argued concern that is raised against the idea of paying more attention to ESCR in international criminal law. Chapter 2 will introduce the 'legal impossibility argument' and present the evidence of widespread assumptions about a hierarchy of rights in international criminal law and outline the risks of an unquestioned adherence to these assumptions. In order to offer a systematic analysis of the relationship between the definitions of international crimes and violations of ESCR, it is then necessary to set forth the methodology and the appropriate terminology: the definitions of ESCR violations and of international crimes. Chapter 3, therefore, presents a model of the way in which the overlap between crimes and ESCR violations can be ascertained, outlines the definitions of the key concepts and explains the interaction between the various branches of law relevant to this study and the respective rules of interpretation that must be applied, including the principle of legality, which is fundamental to any analysis of criminal law.

Chapters 4, 5, 6 and 7 are the core of the study. These chapters examine the existing definitions of international crimes and their relationship with ESCR violations.

Chapter 4 deals with crimes against humanity and is the longest of the study. The development of the category of crimes against humanity was inspired by the international community's desire to punish mass abuses of human rights by states against their own citizens. The International Law Commission (ILC) in 1991 went as far as replacing the reference to 'crimes against humanity' with the description 'systematic or mass violations of human rights',[69] writing that this 'in substance covers the same

[69] ILC, Draft Code of Crimes against the Peace and Security of Mankind, A/46/10 (1991), Art. 21.

field' as crimes against humanity.[70] The relationship between international criminal law and human rights law is closest to the realm of crimes against humanity, and the most significant area of overlap with ESCR violations exists in this area. We will trace evidence of this relationship from the early Nuremberg case law to present-day examples such as a brutal governmental campaign uprooting nearly a fifth of Zimbabwe's population.

Chapter 5 examines war crimes related to ESCR violations. To conduct the analysis, this chapter will briefly revisit the relationship between human rights law in times of armed conflict, IHL and war crimes and then examine offences grouped into four types of war crimes: war crimes against persons, war crimes against property, war crimes consisting in the use of prohibited methods of warfare and war crimes consisting in the use of prohibited means of warfare. The analysis reveals that serious violations of the right to housing, food, education, work, health or other ESCR during an armed conflict often simultaneously give rise to war crimes. We will pay particular attention to the almost forgotten trial against Arthur Greiser, the Nazi *Gauleiter* of the Warthegau in western Poland, who became the very first defendant convicted according to the principles underpinning the charter of the International Military Tribunal (IMT) and whose trial report reads like a primer of how international crimes can be committed by way of violating victims' ESCR.

Genocide is the subject of Chapter 6. Since the defining legal characteristic of genocide is the intent to destroy a protected group, the evaluation will concentrate on the question of whether, and how genocidal intent 'to destroy' can be inferred from conduct affecting people's access and enjoyment of ESCR. In addition, Chapter 6 studies relationships between the *actus reus* of the various underlying acts of genocide and ESCR violations. Though this analysis, it will become apparent that Raphael Lemkin, the lawyer who coined the word 'genocide', succeeded in convincing states to include many economic, social and cultural aspects into the accepted legal definition of the crime, although he would have preferred a broader definition of the crime.

Chapter 7 extends the analysis and focuses on a range of other crimes, such as slavery-related practices, forms of corruption or acts of terrorism. Because many crimes must be discussed, the analysis is less detailed than in the previous chapters. Nonetheless, the evidence allows for the

[70] ILC, Yearbook of the International Law Commission, A/CN.4/SER.A/1994/Add.1 (Part 2), 1994, 40.

conclusion that there are interesting, yet largely untested, avenues for employing the treaties and mechanisms that address these crimes in order to curb and remedy at least certain ESCR violations. Most of the crimes examined in Chapter 7 are the subject of international suppression conventions with extensive provisions on international cooperation. Provisions on international cooperation mechanisms are often scant in instruments of human rights law. A successful demonstration of overlap between ESCR violations and criminal conduct reveals that the legal frameworks for addressing the issues overlap,[71] and thus potentially serve to enhance the protection and respect of ESCR.

As definitions of existing international crimes are interpreted, it becomes evident that critical reappraisal is required of the common assumption that considerations related to ESCR in international criminal law have no place in international criminal law. After exploring the overlap between definitions of crimes and violations of ESCR, Chapter 8 allows us to reflect on the legal corollaries of these research findings. In particular, the findings of the study have significant jurisdictional and remedial consequences which are identified in the chapter. The feasibility of addressing ESCR abuses with processes established to deal with international crimes, both at the international and national level, deserves to be contemplated.

Finally, Chapter 9 draws the presentation to its close, appraising the overlap between the definitions of international crimes and violations of ESCR and considering the questions and argued concerns that will doubtless be raised by this study. These concerns are acknowledged and confronted, with regard to the limitations of the argument. Suggestions for topics of further research and other avenues available to strengthen remedies for violations of ESCR are provided. The study concludes with a consideration of the several reasons that the salient findings of its enquiry will be useful for theorising the means by which current mechanisms of international criminal law may address certain violations of ESCR. In so doing, the study hopes to nurture much-needed reflections on the potential, limitations and the unavoidable selectivity of approaches based on international criminal law. From a broader perspective, the study has the potential to lead to a more

[71] See also Tom Obokata, *Transnational Organised Crime* (Hart, 2010), 228. 'As issues of international importance increasingly overlap with each other, so do the legal frameworks for addressing them.'

widespread acknowledgement that the selection of facts for the judicial interpretation of elements of crimes in international criminal law is no mechanical exercise as Montesquieu would have imagined the operation of the law,[72] but rather takes place in a hotly contested and constrained societal context.

[72] Montesquieu, *De l'esprit des lois* (1748), livre XI, chapitre VI. Montesquieu famously wrote that judges are '*que la bouche qui prononce les paroles de la loi; des êtres inanimés qui ne peuvent modérer ni la force ni la rigueur*' ('only the mouth that pronounces the words of the law; inanimate beings that are not able to modify either its force or its rigour').

# 2

# Rethinking hierarchies of human rights in international criminal law

The central argument of this study is that existing definitions of international crimes accommodate abusive conduct that human rights lawyers qualify as violations of economic, social and cultural rights (ESCR). Scholars, practitioners and policy-makers all have an interest in this argument, but many doubt if existing law allows for such a nexus between international criminal law and ESCR abuses. The literature reflects the hesitation whether there can be overlap between international crimes and ESCR violations within the confines of existing international criminal law. The presumption that we would have to modify the law before international criminal lawyers could engage with ESCR violations is a 'legal impossibility argument'.

Consideration of the legal impossibility argument will serve to explain why the current approach to ESCR in international criminal law should be reconsidered. The legal impossibility argument supposes that the relative lack of attention paid to ESCR in international criminal law has a *legal* explanation. It assumes that existing international criminal law is restricted to massive abuses of civil and political rights, while cultural as well as 'social and economic rights are barely covered'[1] in instruments such as the Rome Statute. This view presumes that the neglect of ESCR cannot be remedied without expanding the definitions of international offences or adding new crimes because international criminal law would prescribe a hierarchical approach to consideration of human rights, with ESCR being considered 'secondary rights'.

This chapter defines the legal impossibility argument, explores its intellectual roots and argues that the argument should be reappraised.

[1] Kirsten Ainley, 'Individual Agency and Responsibility for Atrocity', in *Confronting Evil in International Relations: Ethical Responses to Problems of Moral Agency*, ed. Renée Jeffery (Palgrave, 2008), 37–60: 55.

## 2.1 Presumed hierarchies of human rights in international criminal law

International criminal lawyers are influenced by traditional perceptions of the legal nature of ESCR when they consider the relevance and respective role of past human rights abuses. Few people nowadays disagree that ESCR are legal rights. Yet, normative advancements in the field of ESCR have not completely eradicated uncertainty as to whether ESCR can be understood as similar to other human rights. The Vienna Conference on Human Rights affirmed that all human rights should be treated in an equal manner and with the same emphasis,[2] but some still believe that ESCR have an inherently different legal nature than civil and political rights. They thus take an hierarchical approach towards past human rights violations. Leckie points out that, as a result of the perception of a dichotomy between ESCR and civil and political rights, 'responses to violations of economic, social and cultural rights – both procedural and substantive – have paled in comparison to the seriousness accorded to infringements of civil and political rights'.[3] Arbour notes, '[e]ven among those who concede that egregious violations of economic, social and cultural rights occur, a last hurdle often remains: Such rights, it is contended, do not lend themselves to judicial or quasijudicial action.'[4] According to proponents of this view, there are *legal* reasons why actors and mechanisms that apply international criminal law have rarely addressed conduct that human rights lawyers describe as violations of ESCR. A small number of authors still hold on to the view that obligations concerning ESCR are inherently vague and are mere 'aspirational goals' that states shall realise progressively, but that ESCR are not justiciable.[5] According to them, ESCR are inherently unsuitable for judicial determination in general. Those who believe that courts should not or cannot deal with ESCR in human rights cases likely conclude that ESCR considerations are even less suited to inform our thinking on international criminal law given that international criminal law depends on respect for the principle of legality and requires clearly defined prescriptions.[6]

[2] World Conference on Human Rights: Vienna Declaration and Programme of Action, A/Conf.157/23, 12 July 1993, para. 5.

[3] Scott Leckie, 'Violations of ESCR' (1998) 20 *Human Rights Quarterly*, 1, 81–124: 82.

[4] Louise Arbour, 'Economic and Social Justice for Societies in Transition' (2007) 40 *New York University Journal of International Law and Politics*, 1, 1–28: 10–11.

[5] For references, see Section 3.2.1.2. In particular, Michael Dennis and David Stewart, 'Justiciability of ESCR' (2004) 98 *American Journal of International Law*, 3, 462–515.

[6] We will address the relationship between the argument made in this study and the principle of legality in Section 3.3.1.1.

If one presumes that civil and political rights are a separate category of human rights that is normatively better developed, less complex and maybe more fundamental than ESCR, it is logical to order a hierarchy of human rights norms in which civil and political rights *en bloc* are accorded a higher value than ESCR. Of course, few explicitly make the claim that this is or should be the case. Those who argue in favour of paying more attention to ESCR in international criminal law are likely to vehemently object to the idea that there is a hierarchy of human rights, and would point to the many statements of the international community that such a hierarchy does not exist. However, as argued in the next section, the roots of the legal impossibility argument refer, in one way or another, to a presumed normative hierarchy in which civil and political rights rank higher than ESCR. It is the implicit belief in this hierarchy that leads to the widespread assumption that international criminal law simply does not deal with ESCR violations.

## 2.2 The belief that international criminal law is restricted to civil and political rights abuses

The three authors quoted in the following paragraphs believe that existing international criminal law prescribes an exclusive or at least primary focus on civil and political rights. They represent both those who favour and those who oppose attending more to ESCR in processes set up to address a violent past.

Paul Ocheje calls for more attention to ESCR in international criminal law. He complains that

> [the International Criminal Court (ICC)] represents everything desirable with modern international criminal law, except that its concept of crime follows the traditional pattern of according more importance to civil and political rights than social and economic rights. Articles 6, 7, and 8 define the three heads of crime over which the ICC has jurisdiction ... Clearly, all of these crimes relate to serious violations of civil and political rights. The serious violation of social and economic rights ... does not engage the attention of the international community in this concept of crime. This lack of regard for the complementarity of human rights casts an unseemly blight on the otherwise impressive progress of human civilization exemplified by the establishment of the ICC.

Ocheje argues that the jurisdiction of the ICC should be expanded to 'eliminate the needless dichotomy which is currently being drawn between civil/political rights on the one hand and social/economic rights on the other'.[7]

In contrast, Lars Waldorf does not think more attention should be paid to socio-economic issues in international criminal law and in related attempts to redress past abuses. Yet, he agrees with Ocheje that international criminal law is concerned with civil and political rights:

> The rise of transitional justice has been profoundly shaped by criminal justice, particularly the concomitant development of international criminal law, which mostly treats those civil and political rights linked to bodily integrity (see Rome Statute of the International Criminal Court, 1998: articles 6–8). International criminal law emphasizes individual criminal responsibility rather than structural causes. Not surprisingly then, there have been very few prosecutions under international criminal law for massive violations of [ESCR].

Ocheje and Waldorf both reference the articles in which crimes within the ICC's jurisdiction are specified – Articles 6–8 of the Rome Statute. In so doing, they take for granted that the international crimes set out in these key articles of the Rome Statute apply to civil and political rights violations and exclude ESCR. Waldorf also assumes that ESCR violations always relate to structural causes – an issue we will return to later.[8]

In her analysis of the few existing academic considerations of the relationship between international crimes and ESCR violations, Larissa van den Herik also observes that the focus of international criminal law is on civil and political rights violations. She asks if there is 'a hidden sense of hierarchy despite the lofty promises of Vienna 1993',[9] where states asserted that all human rights deserve equal treatment.[10] '[T]he articulation between international criminal law and human rights law seems rather one-sided', she notes.[11] 'International criminal law is primarily concerned with

[7] Ibid., 779. Like Ocheje, Kofele-Kale regrets that large-scale corruption does not attract international attention and outrage within international criminal law. He proposes the crime 'indigenous spoliation' be added to international criminal law to ensure that corrupt high-ranking state officials can be charged with crimes 'of universal interest'. The implication is that the crimes listed in existing instruments of international criminal law do not allow for claims based on denying people's economic and social opportunities and that the law should be expanded. Ndiva Kofele-Kale, *Economic Crimes* (Ashgate, 2006), 66–78.

[8] See Section 2.2.1.3.

[9] Larissa van den Herik, 'ESCR – International Criminal Law's Blind Spot?', in *Economic, Social, and Cultural Rights: Contemporary Issues and Challenges*, ed. Eibe Riedel, et al., *Economic, Social, and Cultural Rights* (Oxford University Press, 2014), 343–66: 344.

[10] Vienna Declaration and Programme of Action, para. 5.

[11] Van den Herik, 'ESCR – International Criminal Law's Blind Spot?': 343.

violations of civil and political rights . . . [ESCR] have, so far, less directly inspired the development of international criminal law, if at all.'[12] Van den Herik refers to 'the overall non-criminalization of violations of cultural and socio-economic rights',[13] a phrase that indicates she thinks that ESCR abuses are neglected by international criminal lawyers primarily as a matter of the law, rather than its interpretation and application.

These three authors agree not only that international criminal law treats human rights interests in a hierarchy but also that the hierarchical treatment of human rights results from positive international law. This perception is influenced by traditional understandings of the legal nature of ESCR.

### *2.2.1 The roots of the legal impossibility argument: traditional conceptualisations of ESCR*

As Larissa van den Herik notes, traditional conceptualisations of ESCR account for the neglect of ESCR issues in international criminal law: 'The bias against socio-economic and cultural rights might be explained by the traditional conceptualization of [ESCR] as having the character of programmatic aspirations rather than justiciable rights.'[14]

We will revisit the debate over the normative quality of ESCR in the next chapter in some detail, and will pay particular attention to the claim

[12] Ibid. [13] Ibid., 344.

[14] Ibid., 343 (reference omitted). While van den Herik states that human rights scholars have rebutted claims that ESCR have lesser normative content than civil and political rights, she is not entirely clear about the extent to which she shares the view that ESCR obligations cannot be approached in the same way as lawyers approach other human rights norms. She refers to the 'special character' of ESCR obligations, and implies that the 'softness' of socioeconomic rights is both only 'presumed', yet 'inherent' (ibid., 344, 349). The original quote refers to 'this generation of human rights' rather than to ESCR. The generational analogy has fallen out of favour with many human rights scholars and practitioners because such terminology may be used to distinguish within a hierarchy of rights. The classification has been criticised as 'inconsistent with the principles of universality, indivisibility and interdependence of human rights' and for assuming that human rights are exclusively the product of post-enlightenment Western liberal thought. John Mubangizi, 'Towards a New Approach to the Classification of Human Rights with Specific Reference to the African Context' (2004) 4 *African Human Rights Law Journal*, 1, 93–107: 93, 97. Foster writes that the language of 'generations' of rights 'is not a matter of mere semantics . . . rather it has important ramifications for the assessment of individual claims, because the notion that economic and social rights are inherently inferior to civil and political rights, and thus that a breach of such rights is less significant'. Michelle Foster, *International Refugee Law and Socio-Economic Rights* (Cambridge University Press, 2007), 122.

that ESCR obligations are necessarily vague and positive.[15] But first we must trace the roots of the legal impossibility argument.

Five interrelated reasons explain how outdated views on ESCR nurture the widespread belief that ESCR are not and cannot be dealt with by existing international criminal law.

#### 2.2.1.1 The tendency to conceptualise ESCR obligations as positive obligations

The assumption that ESCR obligations are necessarily positive obligations (obligations that require states to take particular action) is one of the roots of the legal impossibility argument. There is a general belief that ESCR violations arise exclusively because of a state's failure to act, rather than its active conduct. If one assumes that ESCR obligations are necessarily positive obligations, while civil and political rights obligations are negative, it is easy to conclude that ESCR issues are not as suited to approaches based on international criminal law as their civil and political counterparts are: omissions are more difficult to deal with in international criminal law than are acts of commission. Van den Herik comments on human rights conventions such as the International Covenant on Economic, Social and Cultural Rights (ICESCR): 'at first glance, they primarily spell out positive obligations, i.e. obligations of result. A violation of such obligations is mostly constituted by a failure to act. Conversely, criminal law is generally concerned with commission of acts rather than omission.'[16]

But many ESCR obligations are not positive obligations. As van den Herik points out, '[t]his prima facie incompatibility between the nature of [ESCR obligations] and the scope of international criminal law is less pronounced than it seems though. The nature of [ESCR] has been refined through the application of the threefold typology which encompasses the obligation to respect, protect and fulfil.'[17] Indeed, ESCR obligations combine negative and positive aspects. The obligation not to arbitrarily evict people from their homes and the duty not to adopt legislation that denies members of some groups access to the labour market or to health care are examples of negative dimensions of ESCR obligations.

The tendency to conceptualise ESCR obligations only in terms of positive obligations poses a significant problem as it reduces our ability

[15] See below, Section 3.2.1.2.

[16] Van den Herik, 'ESCR – International Criminal Law's Blind Spot?': 350. [17] Ibid.

to engage adequately with the negative obligations ESCR impose. From the perspective of international criminal law, overlooking these negative obligations makes the legal relevance of ESCR considerations unnecessarily difficult to see.

#### 2.2.1.2 The tendency to consider ESCR violations as unrelated to life and integrity

Assuming that ESCR obligations do not relate to the right to life or the protection of physical and mental integrity is also problematic.[18] We encounter numerous constellations in which threats to life and integrity are caused by a perpetrator's abusive interference with survivors' access to ESCR. For example, when a prison guard deliberately deprives victims under his or her control of food or water and the victims die as a result of the perpetrator's conduct, the right to life has been violated. In armed conflict, this may constitute wilful killing as a war crime. Other threats to life and integrity include denying the right to health, as when perpetrators hinder medical personnel who attempt to assist the sick and wounded. To add just one other example, denying people with a disability the basic necessities required to lead their lives in dignity can threaten both physical and mental integrity. Contrasting ESCR violations with threats to the right to life and the protection of integrity is oversimplifying them.[19] Recognising this oversimplification, in turn, allows us to consider if ESCR violations can overlap with crimes that threaten life and integrity, such as murder or torture.

#### 2.2.1.3 The tendency to equate ESCR violations with structural violence or 'root causes'

The next idea that connects the assumed legal nature of ESCR and the legal impossibility argument is based on the commonly held view that ESCR violations are 'structural', whereas civil and political rights

[18] This impression, for instance, arises in the Waldorf's text. Waldorf, 'Anticipating the Past': 174. Or in van den Herik, 'ESCR – International Criminal Law's Blind Spot?': 343. Van den Herik explains that 'the right to life and the right to physical and mental integrity are the central values shaping the register of international crimes' – as opposed to ESCR.

[19] This point is also made by Dustin Sharp, 'Economic Violence in Times of Transition' (2012) 35 *Fordham International Law Journal*, 780–814: 785. Sharp rightfully qualifies his own distinction between 'physical' versus 'economic' violence: 'Both terms are clearly oversimplifications. For example, not all violations of civil and political rights involve direct physical violence, and many violations of economic and social rights – hunger and starvation, for example – are arguably a form of physical violence.'

infringements are 'discrete' abuses. Laplante regards the addressing of ESCR violations after armed conflicts as necessarily an attempt to address 'structural violence',[20] a concept that includes entrenched poverty, tyranny, poor economic opportunities and systematic social deprivation and exclusion.[21] Carranza presents the dichotomy between civil and political rights and ESCR in transitional justice as a choice between focusing on direct violence and structural violence.[22] When more attention is paid to ESCR in approaches based on international criminal law, there is sometimes an assumption that the relationship between addressing ESCR and tackling root causes of widespread violence[23] or 'deep-rooted inequities' is almost automatic.[24] Arguing in favour of a new concept of transformative justice, Evans mentions 'addressing structural violence' in the same breath as addressing socio-economic rights abuses.[25] Buckley-Zistel writes that more attention should be paid to ESCR in processes employed to deal with human rights abuses after armed conflicts, because 'it is necessary to address the root causes of the conflict'.[26] These statements contrast civil and political rights with broad concepts of structural exclusion and inequality or the root causes of past violence. The tendency is to assume

[20] Lisa Laplante, 'Addressing the Socioeconomic Roots of Violence' (2008) 2 *International Journal of Transitional Justice*, 3, 331–55: 333.

[21] This description of structural violence goes back to Paul Farmer, *Pathologies of Power* (University of California Press, 2003), 8. Farmer's work is inspired by Johan Galtung, who conceptualised structural violence as associated with the absence of 'positive peace', namely 'poverty, corruption, radical economic, social, civil, and political inequalities, and other forms of social injustice'. Johan Galtung, 'Violence, Peace, and Peace Research' (1969) 6 *Journal of Peace Research*, 3, 167–91: 167.

[22] Ruben Carranza, 'Plunder and Pain' (2008) 2 *International Journal of Transitional Justice*, 3, 310–30: 313–15.

[23] This tendency is apparent including in one of my own early papers: Evelyne Schmid, 'ESCR in Transitional Justice' (2009) 24 *PRAXIS – The Fletcher Journal of Human Security*, 5–28: 17; Arbour, 'Economic and Social Justice for Societies in Transition': 26–7; Laplante, 'Addressing the Socioeconomic Roots of Violence'.

[24] Ismael Muvingi, 'Sitting on Powder Kegs' (2009) 3 *International Journal of Transitional Justice*, 2, 163: 177.

[25] Matthew Evans, 'Land, Socio-Economic Rights and Transformative Justice' (Paper presented at the Land Divided: Land and South African Society in 2013, Cape Town, 24–27 March 2013), www.landdivided2013.org.za/sites/default/files/Matthew%20Evans%20-%20land%20socioeconomic%20rights%20transformative%20justice.pdf, 7 or 11.

[26] Susanne Buckley-Zistel, 'Connecting Transitional Justice and Development' (Paper presented at The Contribution of Civil Society and Victim Participation in Transitional Justice Processes, Marburg, 2 December 2009), www.victim-participation.org/files/Buckley-Zistel.pdf, 8 (notes omitted). The author both tends to view ESCR violations as 'structural' and amalgamates several distinct concepts: the distribution of wealth and opportunities, socio-economic development, ESCR and international crimes.

that ESCR violations relate to entrenched, systemic issues rooted in structures, institutions and practice, while civil and political rights can be addressed independently.

Although often interlinked, human rights violations are not congruent with broader socio-economic and cultural injustices, structural violence or the root causes of violence. Confusing them may result in unsound conclusions about the potential of international law to address past ESCR abuses. As argued elsewhere,[27] many commentators who participate in the debate on the role of ESCR in addressing the legacies of past abuses do not exclusively address the narrow legal concept of ESCR. Instead, many aim to address much broader socio-economic issues, such as the root causes of a conflict or 'historically constructed inequalities'.[28] Addressing structural violence is difficult and requires more than international criminal law approaches. The assumption that all ESCR violations are related to deep-seated structural violence and maldistribution leads too easily to the conclusion that international criminal law cannot redress ESCR abuses. However, it is inaccurate to consider ESCR violations as necessarily structural and civil and political rights abuses as discrete. Such an assumption fails to acknowledge the structural components of many civil and political rights violations. Structural violations of civil and political rights can occur in the context of a conflict where a justice system is discriminatory or members of particular groups are systematically detained or harassed. Vice versa, conceiving of ESCR violations exclusively as complex structural abuses hinders our exploration of the full potential of international law to redress ESCR violations.

#### 2.2.1.4 The tendency to assume that ESCR obligations are vague

The legal impossibility argument is also based on the notion that ESCR obligations are vague and that the principle of legality does not allow international criminal lawyers to engage with ESCR-related abuses. The principle of legality prescribes specific rules for interpreting the legal definitions of international crimes to avoid miscarriages of justice (see Chapter 3). This fundamental principle requires crimes be prescribed with precision. If ESCR obligations are indeed vague, international criminal law cannot address them because the requirements of

[27] Evelyne Schmid and Aoife Nolan, 'Economic and Social Dimensions of Transitional Justice' (2014) 8 *International Journal of Transitional Justice*, 3, 362–82.

[28] Waldorf, 'Anticipating the Past': 172; Muvingi, 'Sitting on Powder Kegs': 164.

the principle of legality 'contrast sharply with the relatively vague formulation of socio-economic rights, in particular, as they have been codified in the . . . ICESCR'.[29]

If all ESCR obligations were vague, it would follow that they are difficult to address in general, and especially difficult to address in international criminal law.[30] But there are many kinds of ESCR and civil and political rights obligations and violations. Just as it is inaccurate to view ESCR obligations as necessarily positive obligations, it is also inaccurate to see them as necessarily more vague than many civil and political rights obligations. Many aspects of ESCR obligations are just as clear as aspects of civil and political rights obligations. For instance, the scope of the obligation not to ban children who belong to minority groups from attending primary education is crystal clear. On the other hand, identifying civil and political rights violations can sometimes be very complex. It can be challenging to determine if an instance of detention in a non-international armed conflict was arbitrary; the International Committee of the Red Cross (ICRC) is currently leading a major project to fill the gaps left by the very limited treaty law on this question.[31] From the point of view of the principle of legality, it cannot be assumed that engaging with ESCR-related conduct in international criminal law is necessarily more problematic than engaging with other human rights breaches.

#### 2.2.1.5 Preventing misunderstandings: no direct criminalisation of human rights violations

Another premise underlying the legal impossibility argument is the idea that ESCR violations would have to be directly criminalised before international criminal lawyers could give more attention to them. In the three arguments that prefaced this section, the authors state that ESCR violations are not criminalised, or are not explicitly mentioned in the provisions that define crimes under the jurisdiction of international criminal tribunals.[32]

[29] Van den Herik, 'ESCR – International Criminal Law's Blind Spot?': 349.

[30] This paragraph is based on Schmid and Nolan, 'Economic and Social Dimensions of Transitional Justice'.

[31] 31st International Conference of the Red Cross and Red Crescent, Geneva, Switzerland, 28 November – 1 December 2011, Resolution 1: Strengthening Legal Protection for Victims of Armed Conflicts.

[32] Van den Herik refers to 'the overall non-criminalization of violations of cultural and socio-economic rights. Ochеje writes that the crimes under the jurisdiction of the ICC follow 'the traditional pattern of according more importance to civil and political rights than social and

Yet, the absence of language related to ESCR obligations in instruments of international criminal law is unsurprising. Civil and political rights equally do not explicitly appear in any of the lists of crimes in the statutes of international criminal tribunals. Human rights law is separate from international criminal law and does not stipulate crimes. Instruments of international criminal law are crimes based, not rights based, and there is no direct correspondence between international crimes and human rights violations. Lars Waldorf, for instance, wrongly assumes that criminal courts would have to prosecute violations of ESCR *as such* before international criminal law could pay more attention to such abuses: 'International criminal law emphasizes individual criminal responsibility rather than structural causes. Not surprisingly then, there have been very few prosecutions under international criminal law for massive violations of [ESCR].'[33] Yet, no criminal court prosecutes human rights violations, whether they are civil, political, economic, social or cultural. By criminalising certain conduct, international criminal law deals indirectly rather than directly with the underlying human rights interests. The instruments of international criminal law define crimes by their specific elements. It is these elements that delineate the conduct that constitutes an international crime. Lawyers apply these elements of crime to concrete factual scenarios in order to decide on the criminality of actions. This logic applies irrespective of the type of violation, whether it is civil, economic, political, social or cultural human rights abuse. Criminal lawyers must always refer to the specific elements of crimes before they conclude whether or not human rights violations overlap with the definition of an international crime.

We should thus not expect ESCR violations (or any other human rights violations) to be directly criminalised. International criminal lawyers can pay more attention to them anyway. In fact, 'a pronounced appreciation of the socio-economic dimensions of [existing] crimes'[34] might remedy many of the problems caused by relying on criminal law approaches that neglect ESCR violations in their attempts to address a legacy of widespread human rights abuses. 'Human rights conventions postulate obligations for States, whereas international criminal law

economic rights', and Waldorf states that the Rome Statute 'mostly treats those civil and political rights linked to bodily integrity'. For the full quotes, see Section 2.2.

[33] Waldorf, 'Anticipating the Past': 173.

[34] Van den Herik, 'ESCR – International Criminal Law's Blind Spot?': 353.

targets individuals', van den Herik rightly explains.[35] This is true whether we are concerned with economic, political, social, civil or cultural abuses. Standard criminal law analysis requires that we have recourse to the elements of crimes and study the extent to which they can accommodate conduct that overlaps with abuse of human rights. It is premature to conclude that positive international criminal law obviously emphasises civil and political rights, as no one has systematically endeavoured to determine if we can interpret the elements of existing international crimes in a way that accommodates claims based on ESCR.

Now that we have uncovered the roots of the legal impossibility argument, it is time to consider the risks of refusing to engage with the assumptions that underpin that argument.

## 2.3 The shadow of the law and the risks of failing to reconsider the legal impossibility argument

Failure to challenge the assumptions underlying the legal impossibility argument is risky. If we do not question the legal impossibility argument, we risk overlooking cases and may, in turn, fail to scrutinise selectivity in international criminal law.

### *2.3.1 Failing victims*

If the legal impossibility argument is not valid, and we do not challenge its assumptions, we may fail to recognise cases and may fail to acknowledge the suffering of those against whom international crimes have been committed. In the previous chapter, the fictive examples of Zeinab and Jamal revealed the tendency to relegate abuses pertaining to ESCR to the background, even though it might have been possible to consider alternative (or additional) selections of facts for criminal law purposes. Adhering to the legal impossibility argument puts us at risk of dismissing the stories of survivors without even giving them a preliminary examination.

In addition, research on gender suggests that the unquestioned marginalisation of ESCR concerns in international criminal law may have negative consequences on the prospect that it will fulfil its promise to uphold the equality and dignity of the human person. Developments in the field of ESCR have brought increasing awareness that pre-existing

35 Ibid., 351.

inequalities in access to ESCR make women and girls disproportionately vulnerable to ESCR violations.[36] The assumption that ESCR considerations have no place in international criminal law, therefore, also risks the failure to incorporate a gender perspective into attempts to address abuses in armed conflict[37] and other situations of widespread human rights violations.[38]

At a practical level, if lawyers, non-governmental organisations (NGOs) or donors simply accept the legal impossibility argument, they will dismiss out of hand strategies that could be useful in addressing ESCR violations through international criminal law. Facts 'are more than merely raw observations made by scientists';[39] presumptions about the nature of a 'typical' international crime shape the strategies lawyers and other advocates choose from the earliest stage of their involvement with a situation. Fact-finding – for criminal investigations, truth commissions, or other mechanisms – is fraught with challenges. Max Weber pointed out, long ago, that facts do not speak for themselves.[40] Conscious or unconscious assumptions in the fact-finding stage and at crime-scene investigations often shape decisions about the relevance of the material collected. Gready criticises the 'emphasis on facts ("speaking for themselves") over interpretation' in

[36] Commission on the Status of Women, African Platform for Action Adopted by the Fifth Regional Conference on Women (Dakar), E/CN.6/1995/5/Add.2, 29 December 1994, paras 9–10; Hilary Charlesworth, 'Feminist Methods in International Law' (1999) 93 *American Journal of International Law*, 2, 379–94: 388. Charlesworth writes: 'A different type of silence that might be identified in the legal protection of the human rights of women in armed conflict is the almost exclusive focus on sexual violence . . . This emphasis obscures many other human rights issues in times of armed conflict, particularly the protection of economic, social and cultural rights of women. Conflict exacerbates the globally unequal position of women and men in many ways.'

[37] Women, Peace and Security, S/RES/1325, 13 October 2000.

[38] Guidance Note of the Secretary-General on the United Nations Approach to Transitional Justice, March 2010, para. 4. See also Report of the SG on the Rule of Law and Transitional Justice in Conflict and Post-Conflict Societies, S/2011/634, 12 October 2011, para. 45. The Secretary-General advocates that underlying economic and social issues driving gender inequality as well as the socio-economic consequences of human rights violations must be taken into account when setting up processes to deal with the legacies of past abuses.

[39] Sheila Jasanoff, 'What Judges Should Know About the Sociology of Science' (1992) 32 *Jurimetrics*, 3, 345–59: 77. Recommending Bruno Latour and Steve Woolgar, *The Construction of Scientific Facts* (Princeton University Press, 1986).

[40] Max Weber, *From Max Weber: Essays in Sociology*, trans. Hans Heinrich Gerth and Charles Wright Mills (Routledge, 1991), 146. Weber points out that relevant facts are largely determined by the spectacles through which we view the world.

truth commissions and reports by human rights NGOs[41] and urges us not to take the selection and interpretation of what is found for granted. Andreu-Guzman shares this unease in his analysis of forced displacement and related abuses of housing rights:

> Too frequently, I would argue, examining magistrates, public prosecutors, and judicial investigators focus their attention on these connected crimes [such as massacres, extrajudicial executions and enforced disappearances] and do not develop methodologies to investigate the crime of forced displacement in particular. In such situations, displacement is seen by investigating authorities and judges as a 'natural' consequence of those other crimes or as an inherent effect of the armed conflict. Investigating authorities and judges therefore do not investigate the crime of forced displacement itself or its rationale and purpose (for example, whether it was part of a military strategy, a strategy to dispossess people of land, or a political strategy to control an electorate). The criminal responsibility of actors involved in these crimes is ignored, opening an avenue for impunity.[42]

Conversely, if lawyers are open to the possibility that the legal impossibility argument does not hold, they may collect factual information more broadly and include information that pertains to people's enjoyment of ESCR. This openness makes room for cautious analysis of collected material to determine its relevance and avoids the quick assumption that ESCR-related problems lie outside the concern of international criminal lawyers.

In 2013, the Prosecutor of the ICC adopted a new investigative strategy. The office announced that it was moving away from 'focused investigations' towards 'a new model of in-depth, open-ended investigations' with an expansion and diversification of its collection of evidence.[43] This approach may open space for victims who hope to convince the ICC that ESCR violations overlapped with a crime under the jurisdiction of the ICC when their socio-economic or cultural well-being was harmed.

### 2.3.2 *Selectivity in international criminal law*

If the legal impossibility argument is not challenged, we cannot determine whether the relative neglect of ESCR in international criminal law results from selective choices made by lawyers or from a problem of positive law.

[41] Paul Gready, 'The Methodological Challenges of Truth Commissions', in *Methods of Human Rights Research*, ed. Fons Coomans, Fred Grünfeld and Menno T. Kamminga (Intersentia, 2009), 159–85: 171.

[42] Federico Andreu-Guzman, 'Forced Displacement', in *Transitional Justice and Displacement*, ed. Roger Duthie (Social Science Research Council, 2012), 233–53: 248.

[43] ICC Office of the Prosecutor, 'Strategic Plan June 2012–2015' (ICC, 2013), 6, 34.

In recent literature on international criminal law, the selective prosecutions of international criminal tribunals are increasingly described as a threat to the legitimacy of international criminal institutions like the ICC.[44] While the former prosecutor of the ICC maintained that he did not exercise any discretion in selecting facts or cases,[45] many have pointed out that international prosecutors select facts, cases and defendants from a much broader universe of abuses.[46] Sloane and Brownlie point out that discretionary decisions inevitably determine what will attract the attention of international criminal lawyers.[47] Sharp notes that truth commissions also cannot avoid selectivity.[48] Selectivity is a factor in international criminal law in general, and it is possible that the relative neglect of ESCR results from such selectivity, as well as the focus on some civil and political rights to the exclusion of others.

As long as we do not confront the problem of hierarchical categorisation based on the normative value of different types of human rights, we will not confront international criminal lawyers with the thorny question of selectivity in the case of ESCR. If the legal impossibility argument is correct, international criminal lawyers can justify the neglect of ESCR abuses by referring to international law. But if the legal impossibility argument does not hold, neglect of ESCR abuses is the result of choices – conscious or unconscious – made by lawyers, prosecutors, truth commissioners, advocates and others.

In case ESCR-related issues are neglected by international criminal lawyers for extra-legal reasons, we must ask if selective focus on some types of abuses is justified. We will return to the benefits of such a debate

[44] In particular, Margaret DeGuzman, 'Choosing to Prosecute' (2012) 33 *Michigan Journal of International Law*, 2, 265–320: 271.

[45] ICC Observers, 'Interview with William Schabas', http://iccobservers.wordpress.com/2009/03/26/icc-observers-exclusive-interview-william-schabas-professor-of-human-rights-law-and-director-of-the-irish-centre-for-human-rights-at-the-national-university-of-ireland-galway. Schabas cites the former Prosecutor to have said: '"I investigate the facts, I'm just an apolitical prosecutor who investigates the facts and goes where they lead me", as if he were Colombo or Sherlock Holmes. But that's not what he's doing.'

[46] DeGuzman, 'Choosing to Prosecute': 266–7 (with further references).

[47] Robert Sloane, 'The Expressive Capacity of International Punishment', 2007) 43 *Stanford Journal of International Law*, 1, 39–94: 50; Ian Brownlie, *Principles of Public International Law* (Oxford University Press, 2008), 604. Brownlie states that '[p]olitical considerations, power, and patronage will continue to determine who is to be tried for international crimes and who [is] not.' Discussed in DeGuzman, 'Choosing to Prosecute': 267.

[48] Dustin Sharp, 'Conclusion: From Periphery to Foreground', in *Justice and Economic Violence in Transition*, ed. Dustin Sharp (Springer, 2013), 289–97: 293.

on selectivity in international criminal law towards the end of this book.[49]

### 2.3.3 *The shadow of the law: maximising the expressive function of international criminal law*

If the legal impossibility argument is not scrutinised, we accept without question that the condemnation associated with a finding that something amounts to an international crime is not available for ESCR violations. But if the legal impossibility argument is mistaken, the refusal to reconsider the relationship between ESCR violations and international crimes belittles ESCR violations. Miller convincingly points out that addressing the legacies of armed conflict and violence is ultimately a definitional project that explains 'who has been silenced by delineating who may now speak, describing past violence by deciding what and who will be punished'.[50] If ESCR violations are presumed as not overlapping with existing definitions of international crimes, then ESCR violations are unlikely to gain attention, perpetuating the 'invisibility and silence' that often surrounds them.[51] Crimes result from adverse human agency. If it is legally possible to conclude that violations of ESCR can overlap with international crimes, we can claim that the sufferings of victims result from adverse human agency rather than 'simply' from misguided policies, bad weather or other unfortunate circumstances. Roht-Arriaza describes this as 'moving beyond seeing [ESCR] as simply background conditions'.[52]

Inspired by the philosophical work of Joel Feinberg,[53] expressive theories of international criminal law assert that condemnations associated with a finding that something amounts to an international crime reflect collective beliefs, values and attitudes. They underline the intolerable nature of the criminalised conduct and demonstrate that it is

[49] See Section 9.6.

[50] Zinaida Miller, 'Effects of Invisibility' (2008) 2 *International Journal of Transitional Justice*, 266–91: 267.

[51] Ibid.

[52] Naomi Roht-Arriaza, 'Reparations and Economic and Social Rights', in *Justice and Economic Violence in Transition*, ed. Dustin Sharp (Springer, 2013), 109–38: 110. See also, Amanda Cahill-Ripley, 'Foregrounding Economic and Social Rights in Transitional Justice' (2014) 32 *Netherlands Quarterly of Human Rights*, 2, 183–213.

[53] Joel Feinberg, 'The Expressive Function of Punishment' (1965) 49 *The Monist*, 3, 397–423.

worthy of special international attention.[54] The expressive function of international criminal law has recently been called the 'shadow of the law': This notion captures the idea that the work of a court like the ICC extends beyond the cases it adjudicates. The attention such courts focus on certain conduct taxed as criminal and worthy of international attention may lead to behavioural changes in many situations that are beyond the court's purview.[55] DeGuzman argues that expressionist theories are the best justification of international criminal law but that they raise questions about which global norms international criminal tribunals should seek to express, and their priority.[56]

If the legal impossibility argument is unsound, the expressive capacity of international criminal law can be used for socio-economic and cultural harm. Van den Herik argues that '[i]t is within the confines of [the concept of the "shadow of the law"], which acknowledge [*sic*] the great symbolic or educational function of the ICC, that attention to socio-economic abuses may be encouraged, but only to the extent that this does not trespass the boundaries set for a criminal court'.[57] Drumbl explains that '[c]riminal prosecutions for socioeconomic ... crimes can serve expressive goals' because they 'can expose wrongdoing and stigmatize it as criminal', 'help prospectively build a culture supportive of socioeconomic ... rights' and 'offer a more fulsome picture of justice for victim communities and narrate a story that is much more representative of the multi-causal origins of mass atrocity and its gradual, and often incremental, implementation'.[58] Yet, we will only know if this potential expressive capacity of international criminal law is available for ESCR violations once we know if ESCR violations can already be taken into account by international criminal lawyers.

## 2.4 Conclusion

In this chapter, we considered the view that existing international criminal law is incapable of addressing claims related to ESCR violations,

[54] DeGuzman, 'Choosing to Prosecute': 312–13, with further references.

[55] Moreno-Ocampo to the Council on Foreign Relations, 4 February 2010, 9–10; Nicole Samson, 'Keynote Address' (2012) 2 *Issues in International Criminal Justice*, 1, 39–45: 41–2.

[56] DeGuzman, 'Choosing to Prosecute': 270.

[57] Van den Herik, 'ESCR – International Criminal Law's Blind Spot?': 366.

[58] Mark Drumbl, 'Accountability for Property and Environmental War Crimes' (ICTJ, November 2009), 22.

which we called the legal impossibility argument. The legal impossibility argument depends on underlying assumptions about ESCR – in particular, assumptions that ESCR violations are structural and describe violations of positive, aspirational and vague obligations. Once we question the soundness of these assumptions, the possibility is raised that contemporary international criminal lawyers have more leeway than is commonly thought for addressing factual situations that give rise to ESCR violations. We saw that refusing to reconsider the relationship between ESCR violations and international crimes could obstruct international criminal law in its evolution towards accounting for socio-economic and cultural harms.

In essence, this book will provide the evidence that the legal impossibility argument is untenable from a legal point of view and that some of the problems related to the undervaluation of ESCR in approaches that rely on international criminal law can be rectified by reference to relevant human rights law. Today, many normative aspects of ESCR are abundantly clear and identifying the state's corresponding obligations is not a significant legal challenge. Moreover, the perceived nature of the rights at issue cannot be the decisive factor in assessing whether a crime has been committed. The only relevant legal enquiry is whether the elements of the alleged conduct constitute a crime. This book is the first systematic enquiry into the relevance of ESCR violations to the elements of international crimes, and it provides ample evidence that the elements of many crimes are open to consideration as violations of ESCR. The analysis does not suggest that ESCR-related issues should unconditionally be a focus in all situations; rather, readers are invited to consider the extent of international criminal law and reflect on the principles and assumptions we employ when we decide which facts deserve how much attention from international criminal lawyers.

The next chapter addresses the traditional conceptualisations of ESCR; refutes the claims that ESCR are exclusively aspirational, vague and limited to positive obligations; and presents the methodology. The study will then set out to consider a wide range of international crimes and their relationship to ESCR violations. Throughout the analysis, we will encounter examples in which the legal history of international criminal law has been shaped by those with an interest in protecting the social, economic and cultural well-being of affected populations. No argument is made that criminal law approaches are always the best, or even always a suitable, strategy for addressing human rights abuses. But when we examine the evidence against the legal impossibility argument, we will see towards the end of the book that the limitations of international criminal law are not specific to ESCR violations. In particular, we must proceed with great care and respect for the principle of legality whenever international crimes are interpreted in light of international human rights interests – whether they relate to economic, social, political, civil, social or cultural rights.

# 3

# Relating international crimes to ESCR violations

Before presenting the research and analysis undertaken to answer the question formulated in the introductory chapter, it is warranted to clarify the methodology, to define key concepts and to explain why it is legitimate to perform an analysis that enquires into the overlap between international criminal law, human rights law and international human rights law.

## 3.1 Methodology

How can we consistently conceptualise overlap between ESCR violations and the definitions of international crimes? The principal subjects of this study are (i) violations of ESCR under international and regional treaties and (ii) the existing definitions of international crimes. Note that the focus is on treaty law related to ESCR, rather than on customary international law obligations.

The model shown in Figure 3.1 illustrates the relationship that must be analysed if an overlap between violations of ESCR and international offences is to be demonstrated. The model illustrates that the area of the first building block is significantly larger than that of the second. This represents the fact that, by far, not every ESCR violation gives rise to criminal responsibility. Human rights law violations cannot simply be transposed into international criminal law.

The two building blocks of the model overlap if the same factual situation can at the same time be described as a violation of ESCR and as an international crime. Imagine the following scenario: a criminal lawyer and a human rights lawyer analyse the same facts. If the criminal lawyer correctly finds an international crime and the human rights lawyer correctly identifies a violation of ESCR under an existing human rights treaty, we can conclude that the same factual background gives rise to both a crime and a violation of ESCR. While the criminal lawyer will be concerned with individual criminal responsibility and the

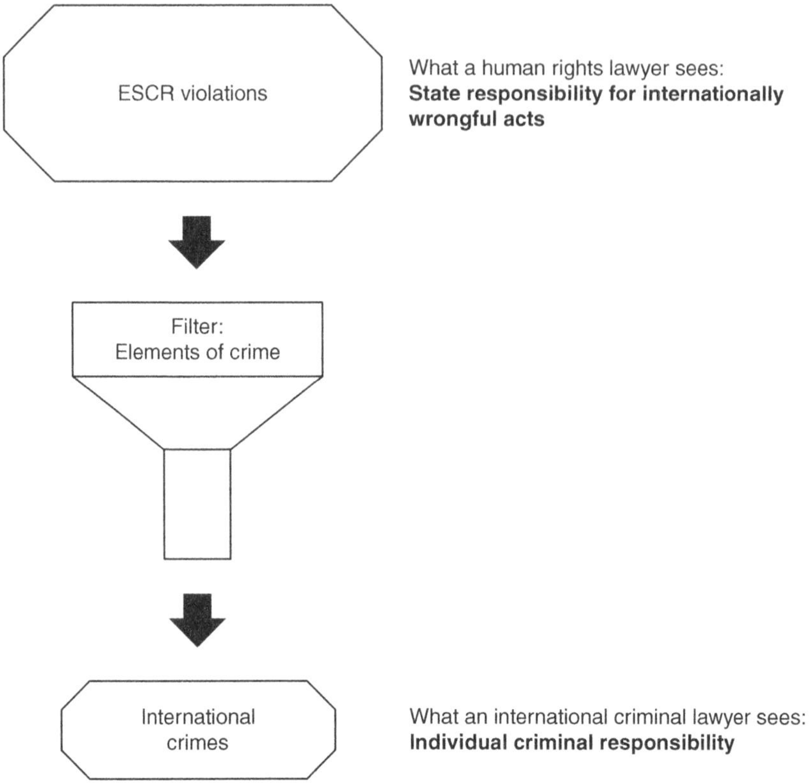


**Figure 3.1** Analysing if an ESCR violation overlaps with an international crime

question of whether the conduct meets the elements of a crime, the human rights lawyer will undertake to examine whether the state – through conduct attributable to it – has breached an international obligation of the state dealing with ESCR. It is not always clear if a violation of ESCR has occurred (or is occurring). Is the interference with existing access to food, health or education imputable to the state? Did the state fail to protect a right by doing nothing against non-state abuse even if the state had the required capacity? Did the state take adequate measures to fulfil ESCR with the level of resources available? Section 3.2.1 reveals that some controversies remain when it comes to ascertaining violations of ESCR. Nonetheless, the UN Committee on Economic, Social and Cultural Rights (CESCR) and other bodies have gone a long way to elucidating the content of state obligations in respect of ESCR. There is a considerable area of human rights law relating to ESCR that is sufficiently accepted to merit a detailed analysis of how it relates to international criminal law.

Before one can determine that the same factual situation can at the same time be described as a violation of ESCR and an international crime, the elements of the crimes are the filtering prism to identify the existence of a crime. Elements of crimes are components of a material or mental nature. Taken together, the elements provide the necessary and sufficient conditions to establish guilt. Material elements of crimes can be of three types: conduct (acts or omissions), consequences (if required) and circumstances (such as the existence of an armed conflict for war crimes). These elements derive from the criminal provisions of the relevant instruments and sometimes from customary international law. To minimise ambiguity in the interpretation of the crimes of the Rome Statute, states have also adopted a sophisticated list of non-binding elements of crimes for the purposes of the ICC Statute,[1] in order to 'assist the Court in the interpretation and application' of the definitions of crimes.[2] The ICC Elements of Crimes provide useful, but not exclusive, legal guidance in relation to those crimes included in the Rome Statute. Where it is apparent that the ICC Elements of Crimes are more restrictive than the elements of the same crime under other legal sources, this will be made explicit.[3]

An uncontroversial example illustrates how the methodological model is applied to specific crimes. In order to determine whether there is overlap between the crime against humanity of enforced sterilisation and a violation of the right to health, for instance, it is necessary to assemble the elements of the crime against humanity of enforced sterilisation and to scrutinise them in order to assess the extent to which the ESCR violations would be canvassed by the definition of the crime of enforced sterilisation (Figure 3.2). The assertion that a practice constitutes a violation of ESCR cannot be taken for granted; therefore, at least one legal basis for concluding that a certain act or omission constitutes a violation of ESCR must be provided. The study concentrates on the rights recognised in the ICESCR, but will often make reference to relevant norms contained in other (international and regional) treaties concerned with ESCR, as well as findings by supervisory bodies.

Hence, the demonstration that enforced sterilisation can simultaneously be understood as a crime against humanity, as well as a

[1] ICC Elements of Crimes, ICC-ASP/1/3, 9 September 2002.

[2] Rome Statute of the International Criminal Court, 2187 UNTS 90, 17 July 1998 (entered into force 1 July 2002), Art. 9.

[3] This is, for instance, the case with the war crime of pillage. See Section 5.2.2.1.

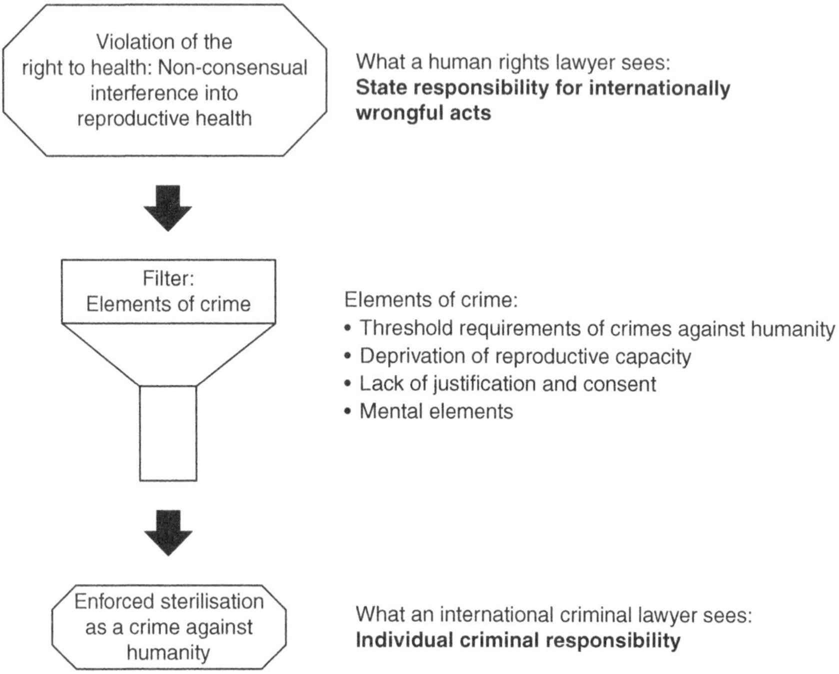


**Figure 3.2** Application of the model from Figure 3.1 to show overlap between violations of the right to health and enforced sterilisation as a crime against humanity

violation of ESCR requires evidence that enforced sterilisations attributable to the state amount to a violation of ESCR – in this case particularly the right to health. If actors acting on behalf of a state forcibly deprive victims of their reproductive capacity, the state is responsible for a violation of the right to health. To conclude that the violation of the right to health (through enforced sterilisation) can be a crime against humanity, the conduct must satisfy all elements of the particular crime against humanity, namely the conduct must be part of a widespread or systematic attack directed against any civilian population (threshold requirements), must have deprived the victim(s) of reproductive capacity and must have been carried out without any justification or consent, and the perpetrator must satisfy the mental elements of the offence.

The ease with which such overlap can be demonstrated varies depending on whether or not the perpetrator of the crime is a state actor. Where state officials order enforced sterilisations, overlap between the crime and violations of the right to health is relatively straightforward to demonstrate. In such cases, the conduct of the criminal perpetrator is attributable to the state. The human rights lawyer will be able to identify a violation of a treaty protecting ESCR. The criminal lawyer will assess the alleged perpetrator's conduct and his or her *mens rea* to verify whether the scenario meets the elements of the examined international crime. If it does, overlap between the international crime and the ESCR violation exists.

We will also consider examples in which overlap between a crime and ESCR violations is less obvious. Particularly in cases of a state's failure to *protect* ESCR, the establishment of overlap between ESCR violations and a crime is complicated by the fact that the perpetrator of the crime is not the same entity as the actor responsible for violating ESCR. Consider, for instance, a non-state actor which dumps hazardous waste that harms human health. In this scenario, a criminal lawyer and a human rights lawyer would examine the conduct of different actors. Depending on the facts of the case, a human rights lawyer might identify an ESCR violation based on the state's failure to sufficiently protect the right to health, for instance, because the state failed to enforce hazardous waste disposal regulations. For the criminal lawyer, the perpetrator of the crime is the non-state actor whose conduct must be criminalised by the state at the national level.[4] Though the relationship is less obvious, the scenario still displays overlap between the ESCR violation and a crime: both lawyers examine the same factual background and conclude that there is both a violation of ESCR and an international crime.

Both key concepts, ESCR violations and international crimes, are sometimes understood differently by different people and the use of these terms must be defined carefully before we can examine examples that illustrate how overlap between ESCR violations and international crimes occurs.

## 3.2 Key concepts

### *3.2.1 Violations of economic, social and cultural rights*

The research problem of this study raises the question how we can ascertain with certainty whether ESCR are violated. It is important to proceed with care before labelling something as a violation of ESCR, since, as Leckie cautions: 'Characterising all displeasing situations as

[4] For such scenarios, see Section 7.10.

violations of human rights is to erode the seriousness of the term.'[5] Human rights violations only exist where an act or omission of a state is not in conformity with a human rights obligation. In the absence of circumstances precluding wrongfulness,[6] non-compliance with an international obligation gives rise to the responsibility of the state for an internationally wrongful act if that act can be attributed to the state.[7] These rules stem from the ILC's articles on state responsibility, which are widely regarded as reflecting customary international law and that have been applied as such by the ICJ and by other international mechanisms.[8]

Human rights treaties are concluded by states. To identify a violation of a treaty protecting ESCR, it is necessary to impute a conduct to a state.[9] The rules of attribution are equally codified in the ILC articles on state responsibility.[10] Many examples analysed in this study concern behaviour that can be attributed to states under Art. 4 of the ILC's articles on state responsibility (conduct of organs of a state), including failures to protect ESCR.[11] More rarely, attribution can be established by reference to Art. 8 (conduct instructed, directed or controlled by a state). According to the ICJ, attribution under Art. 8 requires that the state had 'effective control' over the relevant conduct.[12] Where conduct cannot be attributed to a state, this does not inhibit the finding of a crime, but the same conduct cannot legally be described as a violation of ESCR as this concept is traditionally understood in international law. The conduct therefore falls outside the purposive scope of this study.[13]

[5] Scott Leckie, 'Violations of ESCR' (1998) 20 *Human Rights Quarterly*, 1, 81–124: 96.

[6] See Section 3.2.1.3.

[7] ILC Articles on State Responsibility, Annex to GA Res. 56/83, 12 December 2001, Art. 12.

[8] See *Application of the Convention on the Prevention and Punishment of the Crime of Genocide (Bosnia and Herzegovina* v. *Serbia and Montenegro), 26 February 2007*, ICJ, for instance, at para. 398; *Gabcïkovo-Nagymaros Project (Hungary* v. *Slovakia), 25 September 1997*, ICJ, para. 83. See also *Noble Ventures, Inc.* v. *Romania, Award, ICSID Case No. Arb/01/11, 12 October 2005*, International Centre for Settlement of Investment Disputes, para. 69.

[9] ILC Articles on State Responsibility, Art. 2.

[10] Ibid., Arts. 4–11.

[11] Where the state fails to protect ESCR, the conduct attributable to the state is, of course, the failure to regulate the behaviour of the abusive non-state actor, not the conduct of the individual responsible for the crime.

[12] *Military and Paramilitary Activities in and against Nicaragua (Nicaragua* v. *USA), (Merits), 27 June 1986*, ICJ, para. 115. See in particular also *Application of the Convention on the Prevention and Punishment of the Crime of Genocide (Bosnia and Herzegovina* v. *Serbia and Montenegro), 26 February 2007*, ICJ, paras. 403–7, affirming the 'effective control' test for the purpose of state responsibility.

[13] For an analysis of how international legal obligations could pertain to non-state actors, see Andrew Clapham, *Human Rights Obligations of Non-State Actors* (Oxford University Press, 2006) See also Section 8.4.

Hence, before concluding that a factual situation amounts to a violation of ESCR, we must assess whether the concerned state fails to comply with a legal obligation of international law pertaining to ESCR.[14] Standard legal reasoning demands that we must first identify the obligations of states before we can assess whether or not the conduct of the state is consistent with these obligations. Whether there is or has been a breach of an obligation 'depends on the precise terms of the obligation, its interpretation and application, taking into account its object and purpose and the facts of the case'.[15]

Since the adoption of various national constitutions and the Universal Declaration of Human Rights (UDHR), ESCR or aspects thereof have been included in a range of international and regional treaties, international customary law and national law. As one of the two core treaties of the International Bill of Rights, the widely ratified ICESCR includes rights to self-determination, education, work and the highest attainable standard of health, the right of everyone to take part in cultural life, the right to benefit from scientific, literary or artistic production and the right to an adequate standard of living.[16] The latter right encompasses the right to be free from hunger, the right to food and the right to clothing, housing and water.[17]

[14] Historically, there have been proposals that a state party could be in non-compliance with covenant obligations, without violating a right contained in the treaty: Final Utrecht Draft Optional Protocol Adopted by the Utrecht Expert Meeting on 28 January 1995 in Fons Coomans and Fried van Hoof (eds.), *The Right to Complain* (SIM, 1995), Chapter 24. At odds with general international law, this approach has, however, rightly been abandoned. There have also been proposals that violations of ESCR could be directly enumerated without first establishing that a state had a corresponding legal obligation. Audrey Chapman, 'Violations Approach' (1996) 18 *Human Rights Quarterly*, 1, 23–66. This view has rightly been criticised for reversing standard legal reasoning by concluding on the existence of violations without first clarifying the legal obligations incumbent on the state for the specific right under examination. This critique is at the core of the seminal study of Magdalena Sepúlveda, *The Nature of the Obligations under the ICESCR* (Intersentia, 2003), 20.

[15] ILC Articles on State Responsibility, Commentary to Art. 12.

[16] As of December 2014, the ICESCR was ratified by 162 states.

[17] International Covenant on Economic, Social and Cultural Rights, GA Res. 2200a (XXI), 16 December 1966 (entered into force 3 January 1976), Art. 11. The right to food has been interpreted to encompass the right to safe drinking water. Committee on Economic, Social and Cultural Rights, *General Comment 15 on the Right to Water*, 20 January 2003, E/C.12/2002/11; Human Rights and Access to Safe Drinking Water and Sanitation, A/HRC/RES/15/9, 6 October 2010, para. 3. This interpretation was confirmed by states in the GA Third Committee in 2013: General Assembly Third Committee, Third Committee Approves Text on Human Right to Safe Drinking Water and Sanitation, Press release, 21 November 2013.

Part II of the ICESCR contains the general obligations of the realisation of the rights recognised in the instrument, recognises the principle of non-discrimination and specifies the narrow circumstances in which these rights may be limited.[18] Article 2(1) of the ICESCR contains the general framework of legal obligations incumbent upon states. It stipulates that each state party undertakes 'to take steps, individually and through international assistance and co-operation, especially economic and technical, to the maximum of its available resources, with a view to achieving progressively the full realization of the rights recognized in the present Covenant by all appropriate means, including particularly the adoption of legislative measures'.[19] With the exception of the right to self-determination and non-discrimination, Part III (Arts. 6–15) contains the rights themselves.

The material analysed to assist the determination of violations of ESCR primarily stems from the CESCR, the experts mandated to monitor the implementation of the ICESCR.[20] For most of the rights contained in the ICESCR, the committee has indicated a number of criteria to assess whether a state is complying with the legal obligations under the treaty. These indications can be found in the concluding observations of the committee,[21] General comments and other statements made by the committee. General comments contain the most coherent and detailed information on the position of the committee in relation to a considerable number of issues. Resolution 1987/5 of the United Nations Economic and Social Council (ECOSOC) invited the committee to prepare such documents 'with a view to assisting the States Parties to fulfil their reporting obligations'.[22] While such documents are non-binding, the committee is well placed for establishing the common agreement of states as to the interpretation of the treaty.[23] Before the ICJ, concluding observations and general comments of the CESCR would be considered

[18] See Section 3.2.1.3. [19] ICESCR, Art. 2(1).

[20] Ibid. The CESCR was established in Resolution, ECOSOC Res. E/1987/5, Supp 1, 10–11, 26 May 1987.

[21] Concluding Observations are the documents adopted by the CESCR after a state has presented and discussed its periodic report.

[22] Resolution, ECOSOC Res. E/1987/5, Supp 1, 10–11, 26 May 1987.

[23] Theodor Meron, *Human Rights Law-Making in the United Nations* (Clarendon, 1986), 10. Writing on the CERD Committee: 'Such an interpretation [of the CERD Committee] *per se* is not binding on States Parties, but . . . shapes the practice of States in applying the convention and may establish and reflect the agreement of the parties regarding its interpretation.'

as subsidiary means for the determination of rules of law.[24] The material issued by the committee carries considerable legal weight particularly because human rights treaties as well as treaties of international humanitarian law (IHL) are not simply reciprocal obligations in interstate relations,[25] but entail a system of 'collective enforcement'.[26] As the primary organ responsible for the implementation of the covenant, states entrusted the committee with interpretative functions.

In addition to the material of the CESCR and the decisions of various tribunals, several instruments of 'soft law' and the teachings of publicists assist the interpretation of treaties related to ESCR. In 1997, experts elaborated the Maastricht Guidelines on Violations of ESCR.[27] These guidelines are not legally binding, but they may usefully supplement our considerations in determining whether an obligation related to ESCR has been breached.[28] Similar guidelines exist at the African regional level.[29]

#### 3.2.1.1 International legal obligations related to the realisation of ESCR

ESCR entail an obligation of the state to respect, protect and fulfil the rights recognised in the applicable treaties. This useful tripartite typology of interdependent duties was first developed by Henry Shue,[30] and has entered general comments and concluding observations of the

[24] Statute of the International Court of Justice, 3 Bevans 1179, 26 June 1945 (entered into force 24 October 1945), Art. 38(1)d.

[25] Paul Sieghart, *The Lawful Rights of Mankind* (Oxford University Press, 1985), 92.

[26] *Ireland* v. *United Kingdom, Application No. 5310/71, 18 January 1978*, ECtHR, para. 239.

[27] Maastricht Guidelines on Violations of Economic, Social and Cultural Rights, Commission of Jurists, the Faculty of Law of the University of Limburg and the Urban Morgan Institute for Human Rights University of Cincinnati, 1997; Victor Dankwa et al., 'Commentary to the Maastricht Guidelines' (1998) 20 *Human Rights Quarterly*, 3, 705–30. The Maastricht Guidelines complement the Limburg Principles on the Implementation of the International Covenant on Economic, Social and Cultural Rights, Note Verbale from the Permanent Mission of the Netherlands to the United Nations Office at Geneva, E/CN.4/1987/17, 8 January 1987.

[28] Statute of the International Court of Justice, 3 Bevans 1179, 26 June 1945 (entered into force 24 October 1945), Art. 38.

[29] Principles and Guidelines on the Implementation of Economic, Social and Cultural Rights in the African Charter on Human and Peoples' Rights, adopted in Nairobi at the 48th Session of the African Commission on Human and Peoples' Rights (ACommHPR), November 2010.

[30] Henry Shue, 'Rights in the Light of Duties', in *Human Rights and US Foreign Policy*, ed. Peter Brown and Douglas MacLean (Lexington Books, 1979), 65–81. Further elaborated and refined in Henry Shue, 'The Interdependence of Duties', in *The Right to Food*, ed. Philip Alston and Katarina Tomasevski (Nijhoff, 1984), 83–95.

CESCR,[31] the committee monitoring the implementation of the Convention on the Elimination of All Forms of Racial Discrimination (CERD),[32] and the committee monitoring the implementation of the Convention on the Elimination of All Forms of Discrimination against Women (CEDAW).[33]

The obligation to *respect* means that the state has a duty to refrain from interfering with existing access to the enjoyment of rights. The obligation to respect the right to social security, for instance, implies that states must not arbitrarily or unreasonably interfere with private institutions or initiatives that have been established to provide social security.[34]

States must *protect* human rights by ensuring that other actors do not interfere with rights, for instance by regulating the behaviour of non-state actors, such as by adopting and enforcing legislation to protect workers from unfavourable working conditions.[35] The duty to protect was well explained in a decision by the ACommHPR, where the commission found that the Nigerian state failed to adequately monitor oil activities and thus failed to protect people from abuses by private actors.[36] Similarly, the European Court of Human Rights (ECtHR) and the committee supervising the implementation of the UN Convention against Torture (CAT Committee) found governments responsible for human rights violations related to ESCR because they failed to protect people from abuse by non-state actors.[37]

The obligation to *fulfil* entails that the state must take steps to progressively realise human rights by facilitating and providing access to entitlements, especially to those unable to satisfy their own needs, to the

[31] Committee on Economic, Social and Cultural Rights, *General Comment 12 on the Right to Adequate Food*, 12 May 1999, E/C.12/1999/5, para. 15; Committee on Economic, Social and Cultural Rights, *General Comment 14 on the Right to the Highest Attainable Standard of Health*, 11 August 2000, E/CN.12/2000/4, para. 33.

[32] Concluding Observations, Lithuania, CERD/C/60/CO/8, 21 March 2002, para. 5.

[33] CEDAW Committee, *General Recommendation No. 26 on Women Migrant Workers*, 5 December 2008, CEDAW/C/2009/WP.1/R, para. 2.

[34] Committee on Economic, Social and Cultural Rights, *General Comment 19 on the Right to Social Security*, 4 February 2008, E/C.12/GC/19, para. 44.

[35] For an analysis of (regional) case law on the obligation to protect, see Aoife Nolan, 'Addressing Economic and Social Rights Violations by Non-State Actors' (2009) 9 *Human Rights Law Review*, 2, 225–55.

[36] *Social and Economic Rights Action Center (SERAC) and Center for Economic and Social Rights* v. *Nigeria, Communication 155/1996, 27 October 2001*, ACommHPR, paras. 57–8; see also paras. 44–7 for a useful outline of the obligations typology.

[37] Notable cases include *Dzemajl et al.* v. *Yugoslavia, CAT/C/29/D/161/2000, 2 December 2002*, CAT Committee; *Lopez Ostra* v. *Spain, Application No. 16798/90, 9 December 1994*, ECtHR.

maximum of available resources and by all appropriate means. The CESCR emphasised the importance of distinguishing 'the inability from the unwillingness of a State party to comply with its obligations'.[38] Fulfilment aspects of human rights obligations mean that states must work towards creating the conditions that allow the realisation of human rights and to provide the material benefits required for the substance of a right (for instance, by providing free primary education or assistance to vulnerable groups or making public streets available for the exercise of freedom of expression, etc.).[39] A peculiarity of many ESCR is that they refer to 'adequate' food, housing or other rights. In various general comments, the CESCR elaborated a set of criteria for evaluating 'adequacy': entitlements must be available (in sufficient quantity and quality), accessible (physically and economically) and acceptable (culturally and gender sensitive).[40]

As Kälin and Künzli posit, it is fair to say that ESCR slightly differ from other human rights norms 'inasmuch as they place greater weight on the fulfillment components',[41] but they do not differ in terms of their fundamental nature. The relatively greater weight placed on the dimension to fulfil does not imply that the obligations to respect and protect ESCR are insignificant. As Kälin and Künzli appropriately suggest,

> [a]rguably, the most common and serious violations of ESCR consist of denial by the state of access to available goods and services protected by these rights or the refusal to provide protection against such infringements by third parties. Very often, such violations target specific groups of people (women, members of particular minorities, persons with disabilities, etc.) and are based on discriminatory intent.[42]

Indeed, many of the examples of ESCR violations analysed in this study concern violations based on a failure to respect and protect ESCR, either by the state's unlawful interference with people's health or access to

[38] The state has to show that it has used all available resources. Committee on Economic, Social and Cultural Rights, *General Comment 14 on the Right to the Highest Attainable Standard of Health*, para. 47.

[39] The examples are taken from Walter Kälin and Jörg Künzli, *International Human Rights* (Oxford University Press, 2009), 112–13.

[40] See particularly Committee on Economic, Social and Cultural Rights, *General Comment 4 on the Right to Adequate Housing*, 13 December 1991, E/1992/23; Committee on Economic, Social and Cultural Rights, *General Comment 12 on the Right to Adequate Food.*

[41] Kälin and Künzli, *International Human Rights*, 114. Based on Philip Alston and Gerard Quinn, 'States Parties' Obligations under the ICESCR' (1987) 9 *Human Rights Quarterly*, 156–299: 184.

[42] Kälin and Künzli, *International Human Rights*, 114.

housing, food, water or education or by the state's lack of measures to protect people from abuses by private actors.

A universally applicable list of violations for each right recognised in the ICESCR would be elusive, but a few principles serve as indicators when a violation is likely to have occurred:

- Violations of rights under the ICESCR can arise through *acts of commission* and *omission*.[43] As mentioned in the previous chapter, ESCR entail a combination of positive and negative obligations. Typical acts of commission contrary to the enjoyment of ESCR are, for instance, the intentional withdrawal of a currently enjoyed right or the erection of barriers designed to preclude the enjoyment of rights not currently enjoyed, the unjustified prevention of access to humanitarian aid, the repeal of protective legislation or the imposition of policies detrimental to the enjoyment of ESCR. Acts of omission amounting to a violation of ESCR could be the conscious failure to intervene in social or other situations manifestly inconsistent with legal obligations, or 'the failure to regulate activities of [non-state actors] so as to prevent them from violating the [rights of others], or the failure of a State to take into account its international legal obligations regarding [ESCR] when entering into agreements with other States or with international organizations'.[44]
- There is a presumption of *non-retrogression*, that is the state must not deliberately decrease people's access to a right without good cause.[45]
- The obligation of *non-discrimination* is immediate, and the failure to ensure the equal right to the enjoyment of ESCR, in law and in practice, therefore *prima facie* constitutes a violation of ESCR.[46]
- The failure to take special measures on behalf of children below the age of eighteen is often a violation of ESCR.[47]

[43] ILC Articles on State Responsibility, Art. 2; Committee on Economic, Social and Cultural Rights, *General Comment 14 on the Right to the Highest Attainable Standard of Health*, 49.

[44] Committee on Economic, Social and Cultural Rights, *General Comment 12 on the Right to Adequate Food*, para. 19.

[45] Committee on Economic, Social and Cultural Rights, *General Comment 15 on the Right to Water*, para. 19; Committee on Economic, Social and Cultural Rights, *General Comment 14 on the Right to the Highest Attainable Standard of Health*, para. 47.

[46] Committee on Economic, Social and Cultural Rights, *General Comment 20 on Non-Discrimination in Economic, Social and Cultural Rights*, 10 June 2009, E/C.12/GC/20, para. 14.

[47] ICESCR, Art. 10; Convention on the Rights of the Child, GA Res. 44/25 (1989), 20 November 1989 (entered into force 2 September 1990), Art. 27 and others.

- The obligation to *take steps* towards the full realisation of the rights recognised in the ICESCR is immediate.[48] If a state fails to take any steps whatsoever, it is likely that the state fails to comply with the ICESCR.[49] This obligation to take steps is particularly relevant in times of crisis. As van Hoof pointed out in relation to the right to be free from hunger, 'a State violates [the obligation to fulfil the right to food] when, in the face of food shortage, it does nothing'.[50] If the state fails to ensure the satisfaction of the minimum essential levels of each of the rights, a violation may be occurring.[51]

Cultural rights are particularly neglected in the legal literature,[52] and violations thereof rarely discussed. Cultural rights include the right to participate in cultural life, the right to education, the right to enjoy the benefits of scientific, literary or artistic production, the freedom for scientific research and the right of ethnic, religious or linguistic minorities to their own culture.[53]

48 This follows from the ordinary wording of the ICESCR and the object and purpose of the treaty. In September 2012, the HRC emphasised the obligation to take steps in relation to poverty eradication: 'States have an immediate obligation to take steps towards the full realization of [ESCR] ... At all times, States need to demonstrate the specific measures taken to tackle poverty and prove that they have done so to the maximum of their available resources, including through international assistance and cooperation.' See Final Draft of the Guiding Principles on Extreme Poverty and Human Rights, Submitted by the Special Rapporteur on Extreme Poverty and Human Rights (Magdalena Sepúlveda Carmona), A/HRC/21/39, 18 July 2012, para. 48.

49 Committee on Economic, Social and Cultural Rights, *General Comment 14 on the Right to the Highest Attainable Standard of Health*, para. 52.

50 Godfried van Hoof, 'The Legal Nature of ESCR', in *Right to Food*, ed. Philip Alston and Katarina Tomasevski (Nijhoff, 1984), 97–110: 97.

51 The CESCR has argued that these minimum core obligations are 'non-derogable'. At the regional level, the European Committee of Social Rights (ECttSR) has developed a similar approach, referring to a 'decency threshold' to interpret the European Social Charter. Council of Europe, *Digest of the Case Law of the European Committee of Social Rights* (Council of Europe, 2008), 217.

52 Janusz Symonides, 'Cultural Rights' (1998) 50 *International Social Science Journal*, 4, 559–72.

53 See Universal Declaration of Human Rights, GA Res. 217a (III), A/810 at 71, 10 December 1948, Art. 27; ICESCR, Arts. 13, 5; International Covenant on Civil and Political Rights, GA Res. 2200a (XXI), 999 UNTS 171, 16 December 1966 (entered into force 23 March 1976), Art. 27; International Convention on the Elimination of All Forms of Racial Discrimination, GA Res. 2106 (XX), 660 UNTS 195, 7 March 1966 (entered into force 4 January 1969), Art. 2; Convention on the Elimination of All Forms of Discrimination against Women, GA Res. 34/180 (1979), Arts. 3, 13, 4; CRC, Arts. 17, 20, 3, 9, 31; International Convention on the Protection of the Rights of All Migrant Workers and Members of Their Families, GA Res. 45/158, 18 December 1990 (entered into force 1 July 2003), Arts. 17, 26, 31, 40, 3, 5. See also Committee on Economic, Social and Cultural

Examples of violations of cultural rights arise, as Elsa Stamatopoulou enumerates in the most comprehensive study on the subject, in cases of prohibitions of speaking languages, lack of state sanctions for acts of harassment by non-state actors, the exclusion of minority or indigenous representation in schools or other public institutions, the unjustified inaccessibility of sacred sites or prejudicial language about minority cultures in public documents or school curricula.[54] The ECtHR recently identified violations of the right to education based on the closure of schools, the alleged harassment and intimidation of children on their way to school and legislation criminalising the use of an alphabet.[55]

Despite these indications from cases and the literature, not everyone agrees that ESCR violations can be identified as suggested above.

#### 3.2.1.2 Objections against ESCR

The Vienna World Conference on Human Rights in 1993 famously acknowledged that '[a]ll human rights are universal, indivisible and interdependent and interrelated' and should be treated 'on the same footing, and with the same emphasis'.[56] Today, there is a basic agreement that as treaty norms, provisions relating to ESCR or to aspects thereof can

Rights, *General Comment 13 on the Right to Education*, 8 December 1999, E/C.12/1999/10; Committee on Economic, Social and Cultural Rights, *General Comment 17 on the Right of Everyone to Benefit from the Protection of the Moral and Material Interests Resulting from Any Scientific, Literary or Artistic Production of Which He or She Is the Author*, 12 January 2006, E/C.12/GC/17; and Committee on Economic, Social and Cultural Rights, *General Comment 21 on the Right of Everyone to Take Part in Cultural Life*, 20 November 2009, E/C.12/GC/21. At the regional level, the Charter of Fundamental Rights of the European Union includes a specific right of elderly people to participate in cultural life. Charter of Fundamental Rights of the European Union (200/C364/01), Art. 25.

54 Elsa Stamatopoulou, *Cultural Rights in International Law* (Nijhoff, 2007), 162; Committee on Economic, Social and Cultural Rights, *General Comment 21 on the Right of Everyone to Take Part in Cultural Life*, paras. 60–5. Moreover, ICCPR, Art. 27, entails a 'negative obligation of states to abstain from conduct aimed at the destruction, damage, alteration or desecration of cultural objects or spaces that are of significant importance for the practice and enactment of a people's culture, be it a library, a temple, a civic monument or a sacred site for indigenous peoples'. Francesco Francioni and Martin Scheinin (eds.), *Cultural Human Rights* (Nijhoff, 2008), 9.

55 *Catan and Others* v. *Moldova and Russia, Applications Nos. 43370/04, 8252/05 and 18454/06, 19 October 2012*, ECtHR Grand Chamber, paras. 141–4, 149–50.

56 World Conference on Human Rights: Vienna Declaration and Programme of Action, A/Conf.157/23, 12 July 1993, para. 5.

and should be approached much in the same way as any other norm contained in an international human rights treaty.[57]

As we saw in Chapter 2, however, there is still a tendency to view ESCR as inherently different from civil and political rights. Two common objections are raised against interpreting ESCR in the same way as other human rights norms: first, some claim that ESCR violations cannot be identified with certainty because the wording of provisions related to ESCR would be vague and indeterminate.[58] Second, some argue that courts would infringe on the powers of other branches of government if they would adjudicate ESCR because they believe that all ESCR require progressive positive action while civil and political rights could be realised by abstentions of the state.[59]

These objections characterise the justiciability debate surrounding ESCR, a debate that is relevant to this study insofar as proponents of non-justiciability for ESCR tend to believe that ESCR violations cannot be identified by standard legal reasoning.[60] The term 'justiciability' refers to the suitability of a question for invocation in a judicial or quasi-judicial mechanism.[61] In response to the first objection, we already considered in Chapter 2 that a closer look reveals that ESCR provisions are not inherently vaguer than civil and political rights: consider the controversies around the specific elements of the right to a fair trial (a classic civil and political right) in times of terrorism compared to the international consensus that bulldozing homes and arbitrarily evicting people from their homes (a classic socio-economic rights abuse) amounts to a clear violation of human rights.[62] The

[57] Ibid. See also OHCHR, Report on Implementation of Economic, Social and Cultural Rights, E/2009/90, 8 June 2009, para. 55. 'As do any other human rights, economic, social and cultural rights create legal obligations for States and non-compliance with those obligations amounts to violation of the rights.'

[58] Michael Dennis and David Stewart, 'Justiciability of ESCR' (2004) 98 *American Journal of International Law*, 3, 462–515: 476.

[59] This belief is summarised in Philip Alston, 'US Ratification of the ICESCR' (1990) 84 *American Journal of International Law*, 2, 365–93: 372–3, recounting the justifications advanced by the Secretary of State, Elliott Abrams, for the deletion of ESCR from the State Department's annual *Country Reports on Human Rights Practice* in the early 1980s.

[60] For the view that ESCR are inherently non-justiciable, see Egbert Vierdag, 'The Legal Nature of the Rights Granted by the ICESCR' (1978) IX *Netherlands Yearbook of International Law*, 69–105: 68; Marc Bossuyt, 'La distinction juridique entre les droits civil et politiques et les droits économiques, sociaux et culturels', 1981) 7 *Revue des droits de l'homme*, 783–820. For a response: van Hoof, 'The Legal Nature of ESCR'; Matthew Craven, 'The Domestic Application of the ICESCR' (1993) 403 *Netherlands International Law Review*, 367–404; Asbjørn Eide et al. (eds.), *ESCR Textbook* (Nijhoff, 1995).

[61] Vierdag, 'The Legal Nature of the Rights Granted by the ICESCR', 69, 73.

[62] See also Section 2.2.1.4.

committee,[63] a considerable number of domestic and regional decisions[64] and many academic commentators[65] have long argued, and in some instances demonstrated in practice, that many aspects of ESCR are of sufficient normative determinacy for judicial or quasi-judicial implementation.

The second objection concerns separation-of-power arguments and is based on two related assumptions. First, it is assumed that the realisation of civil and political rights merely requires the state to abstain from certain acts such as torture or interfering with the freedom of assembly. Second, proponents of this view believe that no ESCR can be realised immediately, while all civil and political rights can. These two 'characteristics' would make ESCR unsuitable for judicial determinations. Both assumptions are misconceptions. Proponents of the second objection correctly note that the wording of the International Covenant on Civil and Political Rights (ICCPR) is different than the wording of the ICESCR. The ICESCR indicates that the full realisation of ESCR is achieved progressively,[66] but different wording does not imply that ESCR violations cannot be ascertained. The implementation of all human rights requires both negative as well as positive action, and courts regularly adjudicate cases with budgetary implications in the realm of civil and political rights, implying that the realisation of civil and political rights is often far from resource free. While it is true that ESCR require 'relatively greater state action for their realization than do civil and

[63] For instance, in Committee on Economic, Social and Cultural Rights, *General Comment 9 on the Domestic Application of the Covenant*, 3 December 1998, E/C.12/1998/24, para. 10.

[64] The unanimous adoption of the OP-ICESCR provides further indication that states accept the judicial and quasi-judicial enforcement of ESCR. A full list of relevant domestic case law from diverse jurisdictions would go far beyond the constraints of this book. For a *tour d'horizon*, see Malcolm Langford (ed.), *Social Rights Jurisprudence* (Cambridge University Press, 2008).

[65] Scott Leckie, 'The UN Committee on ESCR and the Right to Adequate Housing' (1989) 11 *Human Rights Quarterly*, 522–60; Philip Alston, 'A Right to Petition under the ICESCR', in *Collected Courses of the Academy of European Law. The Protection of Human Rights in Europe* (European University Institute, 1993), 115–53; Craven, 'The Domestic Application of the ICESCR'; Virginia Leary, 'Justiciability' (1995) *Review – International Commission of Jurists*, 55, 105–22; Coomans and Hoof (eds.), *The Right to Complain*; Kitty Arambulo, *Supervision of the ICESCR* (Intersentia, 1999); Sepúlveda, *The Nature of the Obligations under the ICESCR*; Christophe Golay, *Droit à l'alimentation* (Bruylant, 2011).

[66] The ICCPR stipulates that 'every human being has the right' or 'everyone shall have the right', while in the ICESCR, states 'recognise the rights' contained in the Covenant and 'undertake to take steps ... with a view to achieving progressively the full realization of the rights'. ICCPR, for instance, Art. 6; ICESCR, Art. 2(1).

political rights',[67] Alston and Quinn aptly summarise that the 'difference separates the two sets of rights more in terms of degree than in kind'.[68]

As mentioned, the relatively greater weight placed on the dimension to fulfil does not imply that the immediate obligations to respect ESCR, such as to abstain from unlawful interference with existing access to rights, could not or should not be adjudicated in courts, or that we could not identify ESCR violations for the purpose of this study. The right not to be forcibly evicted (as part of the right to housing), for instance, is as immediately realisable as many civil and political rights. The obligation of non-discrimination and the obligation to take steps are of equally immediate character. Other aspects of ESCR call for long-term investment; yet, the same is true for many aspects of civil and political rights, such as the right to equality before the law, which requires considerable investment into a functioning court system. In addition, even progressively realisable aspects of ESCR can be justiciable.[69] The best-known national case in which a tribunal found a violation of a progressive obligation in the realm of socio-economic rights is the *Grootboom* decision of the South African Constitutional Court. The court held that the absence of any coordinated housing programme providing for those in most desperate need implied that the state had failed to take reasonable measures to progressively realise the right to housing.[70]

In addition to the two objections of the alleged indeterminacy of ESCR obligations and their progressive nature, a third type of query is sometimes raised: the claim that human rights law related to ESCR does not apply in times of conflicts.

#### 3.2.1.3 Violations of ESCR in situations of armed conflict and other exceptional circumstances

History shows that the burning of homes or villages, forced displacement and the destruction of food crops are common in armed conflict alongside other gross abuses of human rights. It is thus particularly relevant for the purpose of this book to consider whether such abuses can properly be

[67] Alston and Quinn, 'States Parties' Obligations under the ICESCR', 183–4.

[68] Ibid., 184.

[69] National courts, particularly in South Africa, have adjudicated progressive obligations related to economic and social rights. See Sandra Liebenberg, 'South Africa', in *Social Rights Jurisprudence: Emerging Trends in International and Comparative Law*, ed. Malcolm Langford (Cambridge University Press, 2009), 75–101.

[70] *Government of the Republic of South Africa* v. *Grootboom 2001 (1) SA 46 (CC)*, South Africa. For another landmark case, see *Minister of Health* v. *Treatment Action Campaign 2002 (5) SA 703 (CC)*, South Africa.

considered ESCR violations. We must know if the identification of ESCR violations is affected in times of armed conflict or other exceptional circumstances. Legal protection in the realm of economic, social and cultural matters does not cease in times of armed conflict and other exceptional situations. Consequently, ESCR violations can occur in such situations.

Treaties in international human rights law, such as the ICESCR, remain applicable in armed conflict.[71] The only partial way how provisions of human rights treaties can cease to apply in armed conflicts is through so-called derogations. In situations of public emergency, such as armed conflicts, certain terrorist attacks or natural disasters, some human rights treaties allow states to temporarily lower the human rights protection, provided that strict limits are respected.[72] The ICJ confirmed in the *Nuclear Weapons Opinion*,[73] as well as in the *Wall Opinion*[74] that as long as a state has not notified a valid derogation from a provision, the norm applies irrespective of the existence of a public emergency. The ICJ affirmed the simultaneous application of IHL and human rights law in *Democratic Republic of the Congo (DRC)* v. *Uganda* and concluded that IHL and human rights obligations were binding on the Ugandan troops occupying the DRC.[75] Hence, the legal considerations presented above can be used to identify ESCR violations even if the situation takes place during an armed conflict.

The ICESCR contains no derogation provision,[76] and the same is true for a number of other international treaties protecting ESCR, namely CEDAW, the United Nations Convention on the Rights of the Child (CRC), CERD and the Convention on the Protection of the Rights of All Migrant Workers and Members of Their Families. In the context of the similarly worded African Charter on Human and Peoples' Rights (ACHPR), the absence of a derogation provision was interpreted to

[71] On this point, see Section 5.1.

[72] See for instance, ICCPR, Art. 4; European Convention for the Protection of Human Rights and Fundamental Freedoms, as amended by Protocol Nos. 11 and 14, Rome, 4 November 1950 (entered into force with Protocol 14: 1 June 2010), Art. 15.

[73] *Legality of the Threat or Use of Nuclear Weapons, Advisory Opinion of 8 July 1996*, ICJ, para. 25.

[74] *Legal Consequences of the Construction of a Wall in the Occupied Palestinian Territory, Advisory Opinion of 4 July 2004*, ICJ, para. 106.

[75] *Case Concerning Armed Activities on the Territory of the Congo (DRC* v. *Uganda), 19 December 2005*, ICJ, para. 220.

[76] See also Amrei Müller, 'Limitations to and Derogations from ESCR' (2009) 9 *Human Rights Law Review*, 4, 557–601.

imply the impossibility of derogation.[77] As Alston and Quinn explain, it can only be speculated why the drafters of the ICESCR did not even discuss a derogation clause during the preparatory work.[78] The context and the object and purpose of the covenant support the view that it was considered unnecessary to include a derogations clause in the ICESCR. The existence of an emergency would in any event not provide the state with an excuse to arbitrarily or unlawfully interfere with existing access to ESCR (duty to respect), nor would an emergency, for instance, require the state to repeal legislation protecting from third-party abuse (duty to protect). Rather, the level of available financial and other resources will in most cases be reduced in situations of emergency, and a lowered level of available resources and capacities is inherently part of the assessment of the state's duty to protect and fulfil the rights recognised in the ICESCR. It is also interesting to note that no state has ever notified a derogation under the European Social Charter, which allows for derogations in times of public emergencies threatening the life of the nation.[79] Less than a handful of derogations have been notified under the ECHR, most recently by Armenia in 2008 and Georgia in 2007. Both of these states are also parties to the European Social Charter but apparently did not consider it necessary to derogate from that instrument.[80] This state practice illustrates that the wording of treaties on ESCR is flexible enough to take into account a more limited availability of resources in times of an emergency, including an armed conflict.

Restrictions or limitations are a separate concept from derogations and are allowed under most human rights treaties.[81] Limitations allow the state under exceptional circumstances to lower the protection of a right 'solely for the purpose of promoting the general welfare in a democratic society'.[82] The ICESCR contains a general limitations clause applicable to

[77] *Media Rights Agenda* v. *Nigeria, Communication 224/98, 6 November 2000*, ACommHPR. But see Alston and Quinn, 'States Parties' Obligations under the ICESCR', 219, arguing that the ICESCR should not be interpreted as foreclosing a possibility of derogation.

[78] Alston and Quinn, 'States Parties' Obligations under the ICESCR', 217.

[79] European Social Charter of the Council of Europe, as revised on 3 May 1996 (entered into force 1 July 1999), Art. F. Derogations must be limited to what is 'strictly required by the exigencies of the situation' and must not be 'inconsistent with [the state's] other obligations under international law'.

[80] Council of Europe, '[Derogation Notifications in the Council of Europe Human Rights System]', www.conventions.coe.int/?pg=/Treaty/Notifications/Notifications_Keyword_en.asp.

[81] The ACHPR is the only human rights treaty not expressly containing a limitations clause.

[82] ICESCR, Art. 4.

all of the rights in Part III of the covenant.[83] Limitations are, however, only permissible if they are taken in pursuit of a pressing goal and if they are proportionate to achieve that goal, that is, if no other less restrictive measure is available, and only if determined by law.[84] The ECttSR emphasised that human rights treaties require a purposive interpretation 'so as to give life and meaning to fundamental social rights', hence limitations must be read narrowly.[85] As Alston and Quinn point out, Art. 4 of the ICESCR restricts both the purposes for which limitations can be imposed as well as the way in which such restrictions can be imposed.[86] Since Art. 2(1) already takes into account limitations on the grounds of resource scarcity, the concept of limitations is of little relevance to identify ESCR violations relevant to the present study. It could well be, as Alston and Quinn believe, that Art. 4 is solely intended to deal with situations in which an unlimited interpretation of a right would lead to absurd results, such as by denying 'a state the necessary authority to enact detailed regulatory provisions'.[87] The authors continue that it is difficult to see 'how rights such as those dealing with food, health-care, housing, and clothing are readily susceptible to limitations on the aforementioned grounds'.[88]

A related question is whether general international law allows states to breach obligations related to ESCR without such a breach giving rise to state responsibility, that is when that conduct would not constitute a violation of ESCR. Circumstances precluding wrongfulness under general international law include *force majeure* and necessity.[89] To successfully invoke *force majeure*, a state would have to show that it is 'materially

[83] Ibid. Art. 8 (trade union rights), specifically emphasises the limits placed upon states when limiting rights. For a detailed discussion of the concept of limitations under the ICESCR and a critique of the CESCR's lack of attention to the issue, see Müller, 'Limitations to and Derogations from ESCR', 559ff.

[84] ICESCR, Art. 4.

[85] *FIDH* v. *France, Complaint No. 14/2003, 8 October 2004*, ECttSR, para. 29.

[86] Alston and Quinn, 'States Parties' Obligations under the ICESCR', 193.

[87] Ibid., 194–7. [88] Ibid., 197.

[89] ILC Articles on State Responsibility, Arts. 20–5. The other circumstances precluding wrongfulness are consent, self-defence, countermeasures (all of them inapplicable in respect of human rights treaties) and distress. Distress precludes wrongfulness of an act of a state if the author of the act has no other way of saving his or her life or the lives of others in his or her care. It is technically possible to imagine that acts not in conformity with an obligation under the law of ESCR could be due to an attempt of the author to save lives (e.g., where a prison guard reduces food rations of inmates to feed his or her children). As Art. 24(2) of the ILC's articles on state responsibility emphasises, distress is, however, no excuse if 'the act in question is likely to create a comparable or greater peril'.

impossible to perform the obligation',[90] implying that this is a defence that is rarely available to a state.[91] Necessity may not be invoked if the act seriously impairs an essential interest of the international community as a whole,[92] and thus is no defence for serious human rights violations.[93]

In sum, the protection of ESCR continues in all situations. While less is demanded of a conflict-affected state in respect of its duty to protect and fulfil ESCR, the determination that the straightforward examples studied in this book constitute violations of ESCR remains unaffected.

In line with these developments in the understanding of ESCR violations, today, even those arguing that ESCR are inherently non-justiciable have become open to considering remedial frameworks,[94] and would agree that ESCR violations can be identified in many situations of human rights abuse even if other aspects of ESCR remain controversial.

It should also be stressed that a state can violate ESCR even if it has not ratified the ICESCR or other instruments specifically dealing with ESCR. All international human rights instruments protect at least some aspects of ESCR, including the ICCPR.[95] The right to life guaranteed in ICCPR, Art. 6, for instance, not only is a civil and political right but also protects ESCR given that basic socio-economic entitlements play a major role in safeguarding human existence.[96] The CERD, the ICCPR, CEDAW,

[90] Ibid., Art. 23(1).

[91] For a discussion of *force majeure*, see Sepúlveda, *The Nature of the Obligations under the ICESCR*, 300.

[92] ILC Articles on State Responsibility, Art. 24(1)b.

[93] Necessity and *force majeure* play a small role in the area of human rights and IHL since both bodies contain more specific rules that govern necessity or states of emergencies. By already factoring in necessity and exceptional circumstances, human rights and IHL treaties largely preclude invocation of the general defence of necessity under the law of state responsibility. See also Cedric Ryngaert, 'State Responsibility, Necessity and Human Rights' (2011) 41 *Netherlands Yearbook of International Law*, 79–98.

[94] Even the authors of the most fervent articles against remedial procedures for violations of ESCR no longer 'reject out of hand the notion that some economic and social rights may be domestically justiciable', which presumes that ESCR violations can properly be identified. Dennis and Stewart, 'Justiciability of ESCR', 476.

[95] The idea that ESCR aspects are protected under treaties otherwise considered to be mainly concerned with civil and political rights is sometimes called 'permeability' or 'the integrated approach.' *Airey* v. *Ireland, Application No. 6289/73, 9 October 1979*, ECtHR. The ECtHR recognised that many civil and political rights have social and economic implications involving positive obligations.

[96] On the relationship between the right to life and subsistence rights, see Kälin and Künzli, *International Human Rights*, 303. For a domestic landmark decision, see also *Olga Tellis and Others* v. *Bombay Municipal Corporation and Others, 1985 SCC (3) 545, Judgment of 10 July 1985, Supreme Court, India*, deriving a right to livelihood and housing from the right to life.

UNCAT, CRC, the Convention on the Protection of the Rights of Migrant Workers, the Convention on the Rights of Persons with Disabilities, as well as numerous International Labour Organization (ILO) treaties and the Convention against Discrimination in Education of the UN Educational, Social and Cultural Organization (UNESCO) all either explicitly protect at least aspects of ESCR or have been interpreted to do so.[97] The more recent conventions such as the CRC, the Convention on the Rights of Persons with Disabilities or the ILO Convention Concerning Decent Work for Domestic Workers explicitly contain language referring to ESCR.[98]

With this background, the first key concept of the study has been established. The next step requires clarifying the meaning and scope of 'international crimes'.

### 3.2.2 *International crimes*

#### 3.2.2.1 The definition and sources of international crimes

Understandings of the term 'international crimes' vary: International criminal law means many different things to many different people.[99]

At its most basic level, international crimes are distinctive from purely national crimes insofar as the origin of the norm is found in international law and/or it is not entirely left to states to decide whether or not the conduct should be criminalised domestically.[100] Some well-known international crimes are criminalised directly at the international level, such as genocide, crimes against humanity or war crimes. Other international crimes are governed by international conventions that are concluded because states recognised that effective strife against conduct such as slavery-related practices, certain forms of corruption, movement of toxic waste or the suppression of terrorist acts requires international cooperation. In both cases, the desired result of international law is that states

97 For an overview of how procedures of the international human rights system and the ILO protect ESCR, see Langford (ed.), *Social Rights Jurisprudence*, Parts IV and V.

98 The ILO Convention Concerning Decent Work for Domestic Workers currently constitutes the youngest member of the family of treaties protecting ESCR. ILO Convention No. 189 Concerning Decent Work for Domestic Workers, 16 June 2011 (entered into force 5 September 2013), Arts. 2–15.

99 Robert Cryer, et al., *An Introduction to International Criminal Law and Procedure* (Cambridge University Press, 2007), 1–2.

100 In cases of crimes that do not exist under customary international law, a state can, of course, decide not to ratify a convention, in which case it does not have to criminalise the conduct criminalised in the convention domestically.

adopt domestic legislation and implement the offences in national law and/or create an international tribunal, enabling the effective repression of criminal conduct.[101]

Two features characterise all international crimes:

*First, to constitute an international crime, international law must either directly establish criminal liability at the international level or require states to criminalise conduct in domestic criminal law.*

The three most well-known international crimes – genocide, crimes against humanity and war crimes – are examples of crimes that are criminalised at the international level itself. In other words, criminal liability originates at the level of general international law.[102] Such crimes are often the subject of treaties, but they have acquired the additional dimension of direct criminalisation in customary law. Some authors limit their use of the term 'international criminal law' to the body of law dealing with these crimes only.[103]

Other international crimes deal with conduct that is not directly criminalised by general international law, but conduct that states must, by virtue of international law, criminalise in their domestic legal systems. Some authors refer to these crimes as 'transnational'.[104] The perpetrator does not incur penal responsibility directly under international law, but indirectly under national criminal laws which the state must adopt by virtue of state obligations under international law to criminalise the conduct. Such obligations are contained in international treaties and sometimes in customary international law to the extent that the treaty provisions reflect custom. Because the criminal conduct actually or potentially affects the interests of more than one state, states consider that they have a mutual interest in suppressing these crimes.

*Second, for all international crimes, international law foresees mechanisms for international cooperation and enforcement in the repression of certain conduct.*

[101] Compare, for instance, the surge of national implementation of international crimes in domestic law following the adoption of the Rome Statute with the adoption of national criminal legislation following the adoption of conventions on other international crimes. In both cases, the result is the enabling of accountability for conduct described as harmful by international law.

[102] Yoram Dinstein, 'International Criminal Law' (1985) 20 *Israel Law Review*, 206–42: 221.

[103] For instance, Robert Cryer, *Prosecuting International Crimes: Selectivity and the International Criminal Law Regime* (Cambridge University Press, 2005), chapter 1.

[104] Neil Boister, 'Transnational Criminal Law?' (2003) 14 *European Journal of International Law*, 5, 953–76.

Conduct criminalised as an international crime cannot be adequately dealt with in the jurisdictional sphere of ordinary crimes alone. In 1948, a US military tribunal in the *Hostage Case* defined an international crime as an act 'universally recognized as criminal, which is considered a grave matter of international concern and for some valid reason cannot be left within the exclusive jurisdiction of the state that would have control over it under ordinary circumstances'.[105] This 'valid reason' to extend the jurisdiction for international crimes is that the international community has accepted that the effective repression of certain conduct requires mechanisms for international enforcement and cooperation, because of two key considerations. The first one pertains to international crimes such as the ones prosecuted after World War II and concerns the fact that states are often implicated or complicit in the commission of international crimes, as was the case with atrocities perpetuated by the Nazis. In the absence of international mechanisms, impunity would easily prevail. The second reason pertains to the absence of a vertical system of enforcement in international law. International law accords national systems a crucial role in the enforcement of international criminal law. States deemed it necessary that for the prevention, suppression and punishment of international criminal conduct, special jurisdictional and cooperative mechanisms be created, including mechanisms that transcend the forum of ordinary jurisdiction.

Against this background, we can draw a list of criteria that will guide the determination whether an instrument is relevant for this study, that is, whether it actually contains a definition of an international crime. Cherif Bassiouni conducted an influential attempt to delineate the scope of international criminal law.[106] To decide whether or not an international instrument forms part of international criminal law, Bassiouni established a list of ten characteristics, the presence of any of which qualifies an instrument as belonging to the field of international criminal law.[107] One major difficulty with the list of criteria compiled by Bassiouni is that it risks casting the net too wide by including provisions that only implicitly recognise the penal nature of certain conduct (such as by establishing a duty to *prevent*) or instruments that merely refer to a *permission* to punish or to cooperate with other states. Numerous human rights treaties contain a duty to prevent abuses, but it would

[105] *United States of America* v. *List et al. (Hostage Case), XI TWC 1230*, NMT, 1241.
[106] Cherif Bassiouni, *International Criminal Law*, 3 vols., vol. 1 (Transnational, 1986).
[107] Ibid., 4.

seem far-fetched to argue that the instrument would therefore contain a definition of an international crime. Similarly, the application of Bassiouni's criteria would include all treaties that simply include a right to extradite. This would be too low a threshold. Nevertheless, with some modifications, Bassiouni's list is useful to delineate what should be considered an international crime. Two main modifications are necessary:

First, if an instrument merely establishes a 'duty to prevent' or a 'duty to take appropriate measures' domestically, it does not contain a definition of an international crime and is, therefore, not relevant for this study. This reduction, for instance, excludes treaties such as the Roerich Pact, which merely establishes a duty of states to adopt internal legislation to protect artistic and scientific objects and institutions, but such legislation need not necessarily be of a penal nature.[108] Second, excluded are instruments that only provide for a right (rather than a duty) to prosecute, punish, extradite or cooperate. Based on Bassiouni's scholarship, an instrument pertains to international criminal law if any of the following criteria is met: the treaty either (1) explicitly recognises proscribed conduct as constituting an international crime or a crime under international law or a crime, (2) criminalises the proscribed conduct, (3) establishes a duty to prosecute, (4) establishes a duty to punish, (5) establishes a duty to extradite, (6) establishes a duty to cooperate in prosecution and/or punishment, (7) establishes a criminal jurisdictional basis, (8) refers to the establishment of an international criminal tribunal or (9) eliminates the defence of superior orders. An instrument contains a definition of an international crime if it includes a provision that meets any of these nine alternative criteria.

Note that the study does not limit itself to those crimes over which the ICC has jurisdiction. It would be unwarranted to limit the analysis to ICC crimes, especially since other bodies, such as national criminal tribunals, truth commissions or hybrid courts, are mandated (and sometimes obliged) to deal with crimes that are not included in the Rome Statute. Yet because of the complementarity mechanism of the ICC, many states follow the Rome Statute definitions when they implement international crimes into domestic legislation. The Rome Statute is thus a useful starting point to understand the elements of international crimes but it is crucial to

[108] Treaty between the USA and the Other American Republics on the Protection of Artistic and Scientific Institutions and Historic Monuments (Roerich Pact), 15 April 1935, 167 LNTS 289 (entered into force 26 August 1935), Art. II.

stress that the ICC Statute does not exhaust international criminal prohibitions.[109] Other international crimes also deserve to be included in this study. The remaining question we need to briefly consider is whether individuals are the only possible authors of international crimes.

Some authors question whether international criminal law should really be viewed as exclusively concerned with *individual* criminal liability. The question arises whether collective non-state actors, such as corporations or armed groups (as such, and not their individual members), can be the authors of international crimes even though most international tribunals limit jurisdiction to natural persons.[110] Clapham posits that 'the exclusion of non-natural persons [from the jurisdiction of international criminal tribunals] can be seen as the consequence of a "rule of procedure" rather than the inevitable result of application of international criminal law'.[111] The present study concentrates on individual criminal liability and thus the traditional understanding of international criminal law. Yet, it should be noted that this focus does not rule out the possibility that the statutes of existing tribunals could be modified in order to allow them to exercise jurisdiction over non-natural persons, nor should it be forgotten that domestic tribunals may in some circumstances already be competent to prosecute persons other than individuals for international crimes.[112] Where a domestic tribunal can prosecute actors other than individuals, this study can be used to ascertain how the elements of a crime relate to ESCR abuses independent of whether the defendant is a natural person or not.

To summarise, international criminal law is the body of law dealing with crimes for which international law directly establishes criminal liability at the international level or, alternatively, crimes for which states have accepted international legal obligations to criminalise conduct in domestic criminal law. In either case, the enforcement of the prohibition of criminalised conduct is not left exclusively to the state, but states share a collective responsibility to enforce such rules by way of international tribunals or the exercise of national jurisdiction or judicial cooperation,

[109] That states choose to entrust the ICC with jurisdiction over a limited number of crimes (and sometimes choose a slightly different definition of a particular crime as compared to how the crime is arguably defined in general international law) does not prejudice other rules of law. See Rome Statute, Arts. 10 and 22(3).

[110] Andrew Clapham, 'Extending International Criminal Law' (2008) 6 *Journal of International Criminal Justice*, 5, 899–926: 902.

[111] Ibid.

[112] For a brief review of the relevance of domestic legal systems and for further references, see Clapham, 'Extending International Criminal Law', 913–19. See also Section 8.4.

and such obligations are contained in instruments with at least one of the above-mentioned criteria.

## 3.3 The relationship between international criminal law, human rights law and international humanitarian law

International criminal law often interacts with international human rights law and IHL. Although these branches mutually influence each other and are all part of public international law, their main functions and subjects are different. An inquiry based on the premise that the various branches of international law can be consulted and interpreted in conjunction requires us to briefly note the specificities of the different branches and their main function in the normative system.

Let us first consider human rights law and IHL. Human rights law and IHL both serve a protective purpose, but have different functional emphases and have evolved independently despite similar intellectual origins.[113] Human rights law essentially tasks states to protect individuals from interference and abuse by the state and by third parties and promotes 'better standards of life in larger freedom'.[114] International human rights law, including the law on ESCR, establishes a catalogue of rights that states must respect, protect and fulfil. Failure to uphold the international legal obligations arising from human rights law gives rise to state responsibility. As mentioned, human rights law applies at all times, that is, during peace and in times of conflict.

IHL, in contrast, 'intends to solve humanitarian problems directly arising from . . . armed conflicts'[115] and therefore limits the permissible methods and means of warfare and establishes rules of protection and care for individuals and objects. The purpose of IHL is to mitigate the human suffering in armed conflict. But this protective purpose coexists with the competing interest of military necessity that must be taken into account if IHL is to operate as a relevant guide to those engaged in hostilities.[116] As with human rights law, the law of state responsibility

[113] See for instance Hans-Peter Gasser, 'International Criminal Law, Human Rights Law and Humanitarian Law', in *The Legal Regime of the International Criminal Court: Essays in Honour of Professor Igor Blishchenko*, ed. José Doria et al. (Nijhoff, 2009), 1111–19.

[114] UDHR, Preamble.

[115] Yves Sandoz et al., *Commentary on the Additional Protocols* (Nijhoff, 1987), xxvii.

[116] This balance is a foundational idea of modern IHL. Declaration Renouncing the Use, in Time of War, of Explosive Projectiles under 400 Grammes Weight, Saint Petersburg, 11 December 1868, para. 1.

comes into play when states fail to comply with IHL. States violating IHL are internationally responsible for wrongful conduct, but states are not the only actors that can violate IHL. Individuals, armed groups and other non-state actors are bound by at least some rules of IHL.[117] IHL protects socio-economic and cultural well-being by prohibiting, for instance, the destruction of objects indispensable to the survival of the civilian population, such as foodstuffs or drinking water installations.[118]

The idea that the different branches of international law operate within the normative system of international law as a whole is expressed in the first two additional protocols to the Geneva Conventions, which both contain a reference to other applicable rules of international law relating to the protection of human rights during conflicts.[119] Yet, despite similar protective objectives, the consideration given to military necessity means that IHL remains distinct from human rights law.

Turning to international criminal law, we can observe that international criminal law primarily serves to decide on the guilt or innocence of individuals accused of criminal conduct and to establish mechanisms of cooperation in the repression of certain conduct. In so doing, international criminal law aims to serve an indirect protective purpose by deterring future crimes and by affirming the importance of the normative values protected.

Despite the different functions and subjects of these sub-systems of international law, the definitions of crimes bear on other branches of law, such as IHL and international human rights law. Just like the International Bill of Rights is part of an attempt by the international community to prevent the recurrence of the 'scourge of war',[120] the

[117] The applicability of IHL to non-state actors is least controversial with regard to Common Article 3 of the Geneva Conventions. It is generally accepted that at least this provision applies to non-state actors. For further analysis, see Annyssa Bellal et al., 'International Law and Armed Non-State Actors in Afghanistan' (2011) 93 *International Review of the Red Cross*, 881, 47–79.

[118] Protocol Additional to the Geneva Conventions of 12 August 1949, and Relating to the Protection of Victims of International Armed Conflicts, 1125 UNTS 3, 8 June 1977 (entered into force 7 December 1978), Art. 54. It has been convincingly argued that this prohibition is part of customary international law. Jean-Marie Henckaerts and Louise Doswald-Beck (eds.), *Customary IHL*, 2 vols., vol. 1 (Cambridge University Press, 2005), Rule 54.

[119] AP I, Art. 72; Protocol Additional to the Geneva Conventions of 12 August 1949, and Relating to the Protection of Victims of Non-International Armed Conflicts, 1125 UNTS 609, 8 June 1977 (entered into force 7 December 1978), Preamble.

[120] Charter of the United Nations, 1 UNTS XVI, 26 June 1945 (entered into force 24 October 1945), Preamble.

prosecutions in Nuremberg, in the Far East and in national jurisdictions were a reaction to the denial of human dignity during World War II. The social values pursued by the different branches thus share common origins.

Moreover, a correct interpretation of international criminal law frequently depends upon precise understanding of the legal terms employed in international human rights law or in IHL. For instance, IHL must be referred to in order to decide whether a certain property was protected, and thus whether it can trigger the possible finding of war crimes. On the other hand, human rights law assists in the interpretation of many elements of crimes; for instance, it helps determine whether a conflict-related displacement should qualify as a forcible transfer.[121] By requiring 'that the application and interpretation of criminal law must be consistent with internationally recognised human rights',[122] the provision on applicable law in the ICC expressly supports the view that the branches relevant to this study do not live by themselves as separate pieces in a '*bric-à-brac*'.[123] That said, the various branches remain distinct. It would be erroneous to assume that the norms of international criminal law 'are coextensive with their human rights or humanitarian counterparts, and uncritically transplant concepts and jurisprudence from other domains to flesh out their content. Such assumptions overlook the fact that these bodies of law have different purposes and consequences and thus entail different philosophical commitments.'[124]

Remaining distinct, but mutually influencing each other, the various branches relevant to this study interact in complex ways. The main implication is the following: the distinctiveness of the various branches does not prevent us from analysing them together, but their specificity must be kept in mind. This thought was best summarised by the ICTY Trial Chamber in *Kunarac*. The chamber confirmed that those who interpret the definitions of crimes must be 'mindful of the specificity' of IHL and human rights law.[125] At the same time, the trial chamber

[121] *Prosecutor* v. *Stakić, IT-97-24-T, 31 July 2003*, ICTY, para. 677. The Trial Chamber referred to the concepts employed in human rights law, namely 'the right and expectation of individuals to be able to remain in their homes and communities without interference.'

[122] Rome Statute, Art. 21(3).

[123] Jean Combacau, 'Bric-a-brac ou système?' (1986) 31 *Annuaire de philosophie du droit*, 85–105.

[124] Darryl Robinson, 'Identity Crisis' (2008) 21 *Leiden Journal of International Law*, 4, 925–63: 946.

[125] *Prosecutor* v. *Kunarac, Kovac and Vukovic, IT-96-23-T, 22 February 2001*, ICTY, para. 470.

emphasised the increasing relevance of studying the interplay between human rights law, IHL and international criminal law, considering that the recourse to 'instruments and practices developed in the field of human rights law' was 'needed to determine the content of customary international law'.[126] This approach was further elaborated upon by the ICTY Trial Chamber in *Krnojelac*:

> In attempting to define an offence or to determine whether any of the elements of that definition has been met, the Trial Chamber is mindful of the specificity of [IHL] ... In particular ..., the Trial Chamber must take into account the structural differences which exist between [human rights law] and [IHL], in particular the distinct role and function attributed to states and individuals in each regime. However, this does not preclude recourse to human rights law in respect of those aspects which are common to both regimes.[127]

In considering the correct interpretation of the international legal norms discussed in this study, the general rules of interpretation, codified in the Vienna Convention on the Law of Treaties (VCLT), warrant that treaty norms shall be interpreted 'in accordance with the ordinary meaning to be given to the terms of the treaty in their context and in the light of [the treaty's] object and purpose'.[128] Subsequent developments in the international legal system also affect the interpretation of international treaties.[129] Supplementary means of treaty interpretation such as preparatory works will be referred to if necessary and justified.[130] The ICESCR as well as the treaties containing the definitions of international crimes are subject to these rules of interpretation.[131]

[126] Ibid., paras. 467–82.

[127] *Prosecutor* v. *Krnojelac, IT-97-25-T, 15 March 2002*, ICTY, para. 181 (notes omitted).

[128] Vienna Convention on the Law of Treaties, 1155 UNTS 331, 23 May 1969 (entered into force 27 January 1980), Art. 31. For the Rome Statute, see also Rome Statute, Art. 22(2).

[129] *Legal Consequences for States of the Continued Presence of South Africa in Namibia (South West Africa) Notwithstanding Security Council Resolution 276 (1970), Advisory Opinion of 21 June 1971*, ICJ, para. 53. The ICJ emphasises that 'an international instrument has to be interpreted and applied within the framework of the entire legal system prevailing at the time of the interpretation'.

[130] VCLT, Art. 32.

[131] See also *Situation in the Democratic Republic of the Congo, Judgment on the Prosecutor's Application for Extraordinary Review of Decision Denying Leave to Appeal, 13 July 2006, Appeals Chamber, ICC-01/04*, ICC, para. 33: 'The interpretation of treaties, and the Rome Statute is no exception, is governed by the [VCLT].'

#### 3.3.1.1 *The principle of legality and its corollaries*

Having highlighted the characteristics of international crimes, their relationship with other branches of international law and the general rules of treaty interpretation, we must turn to a fundamental principle of criminal law that guides the interpretation of the definitions of international crimes. Because of the specific social function of criminal law within the broader international legal system, the principle of legality and its corollaries restrict the permissible tools of interpretation that may be applied when dealing with the substantive definitions of international crimes and their relationship with ESCR violations.

Criminal sanctions interfere with important legal interests, such as the liberty or property of the individual who is convicted of a crime. Only strictly confined categories of conduct are criminalised. The principle of legality complements and narrows the general rules of interpretation codified in the VCLT. Awareness of the interpretative implications of the principle of legality is crucial in the context of a study that interprets international criminal law from the perspective of ESCR that continue to be viewed with undue suspicion. It must therefore be shown that the principle of legality does not bar the arguments made in this book.

The principle of legality signifies that a person may only be convicted and punished on the basis of clear and ascertainable law that was in force at the time of the conduct. The principle of legality is a non-derogable norm of human rights law.[132] It enshrines the idea that the legal consequences of human behaviour must be predictable, so that the individual is in a position to know or at least to readily establish that his or her conduct entails penal consequences.[133] The absence of previous successful prosecutions in respect of similar conduct is, however, not an infringement of the principle of legality to the extent that the essence of the original crime is maintained and the conduct falls within the reasonable implications of the elements of a crime which existed at the time of the conduct.[134] This means that the scarcity of prosecutions for abuses in the

[132] See for instance ICCPR, Arts. 4, 15.

[133] The ECtHR has an elaborate jurisprudence on the principle of legality, and criminal tribunals routinely cite this jurisprudence. The case law stresses the accessibility and foreseeability of law. For example *Sunday Times* v. *United Kingdom, Application No. 6538/74, 26 April 1979 (Plenary)*, ECtHR, para. 49. One 'must be able – if need be with appropriate advice – to foresee . . . the consequences which a given action may entail'.

[134] *C. R* v *United Kingdom, Application No. 20190/92, 22 November 1995*, ECtHR, paras. 13, 34. In this case, the accused unsuccessfully argued that the prosecution against him for spousal rape infringed the principle of legality. The ECtHR found no violation of the

realm of ESCR does not inhibit a nuanced interpretation of the existing definitions of crimes from the perspective of conduct that can be qualified as a violation of ESCR.

No person can be criminally responsible for conduct that was not criminalised at the time of commission. Non-retroactivity must be distinguished from retrospective criminal prosecution, which refers to the codification of already existing legal rules. In the *Einsatzgruppen* trial, the tribunal held that Control Council Law No. 10 constituted such a retrospective, but not retroactive, criminal legislation,[135] and the same conclusion was reached by the Canadian Supreme Court in *R.* v. *Finta* for war crimes committed during World War II for which extraterritorial jurisdiction was established only after the facts.[136] The distinction between retroactivity and retrospectiveness is particularly relevant for this study in the realm of crimes against humanity. National tribunals of states with newly adopted legislation on crimes against humanity may adjudicate conduct related to ESCR without infringing the principle of legality as long as the conduct was previously criminalised as a crime against humanity in customary international law.

The principle of legality entails two corollaries. The first corollary of the principle of legality is that provisions of criminal law must be strictly construed. If a provision is ambiguous, and if a reading fails to resolve an ambiguity, the matter has to be resolved in favour of the accused, independent of whether or not the underlying conduct relates to a violation of ESCR. The requirement of strict construction is satisfied if the individual can know from the wording, and, if need be, with the assistance of the courts' interpretation of it, what acts and omissions will make him or her liable,[137] but it is not necessary that the individual is aware that the conduct belongs to the category of international offences. For the purposes of this study, this corollary of the principle of legality means that we may not interpret the definitions of crimes in a way that leads to unpredictably broad constructions giving the individual no chance to know that the conduct will make him or her liable.

principle of legality since the resultant development of the law is consistent with the essence of the offence and could reasonably be foreseen. For a discussion, see also Mohamed Shahabuddeen, 'Principle of Legality' (2004) 2 *Journal of International Criminal Justice*, 4, 1007–17: 1011.

135 *United States of America* v. *Ohlendorf et al. (Einsatzgruppen Trial), IV TWC 411*, NMT, 459.

136 *R.* v. *Finta (No. 3), 104 ILR 285, 24 March 1994, Supreme Court, Canada*, 306–8.

137 *Veeber* v. *Estonia (No. 2), Application No. 45771/99, 21 January 2003*, ECtHR, para. 31.

The second corollary of the principle of legality is the prohibition of analogy. This prohibition bars the use of analogy as a basis for imposing criminal responsibility for what would amount to substantially new crimes. In 1935, the Permanent Court of International Justice emphasised that judges infringe the principle of legality if they confirm charges on previously unknown crimes on the basis of their similarity to known ones.[138] The restriction of analogy does, however, not prevent a court from determining an issue through a process of interpretation as to the elements of a particular crime.[139] What would be impermissible is the addition of new crimes, but the restriction does not affect the argument that a number of crimes can be *interpreted* to encompass violations of ESCR.[140]

## 3.4 Conclusion

The outline of the key concepts employed in this study reveals that violations of ESCR as well as international crimes must be carefully determined. If a state fails to comply with an international obligation pertaining to ESCR and cannot invoke a circumstance precluding wrongfulness, then that state is responsible for a violation of ESCR. International criminal law either directly establishes criminal liability at the international level or requires states to criminalise conduct in domestic criminal law. In either case, international law foresees mechanisms for states to cooperate in the repression of the conduct defined as criminal. A list of nine criteria serves to identify if a provision defines an international crime and can therefore be included within the scope of this study.

If looking at the same factual background, a criminal lawyer correctly finds an international crime, and a human rights lawyer correctly identifies an ESCR violation under an existing human rights treaty, we can conclude that the same factual circumstances give rise to both a crime *and* a violation of ESCR. The analysis undertaken in the following chapters sets forth evidence that the area of overlap between the definitions of international crimes and violations of ESCR is currently underestimated.

138 *Consistency of Certain Danzig Legislative Decrees with the Constitution of the Free City, Advisory Opinion No. 27 of 4 December 1935*, Permanent Court of International Justice, 51. The Nazi decree in the Free City of Danzig made criminal punishment subject to 'sound popular feeling' and thus allowed for the impermissible creation of law by analogy.

139 Otto Triffterer (ed.), *Commentary on the Rome Statute* (Beck, 2008), 725 (Broomhall).

140 For instance, the crime against humanity of apartheid requires that the inhumane acts are of a similar character to other crimes against humanity. A careful use of analogy is required to interpret this element. A similar argument has been made in respect of the Rome Statute's Art. 7(1)k. See also ibid., 233 (Machteld Boot).

# 4

## Crimes against humanity revisited

### *From Nuremberg to Zimbabwe*

*Murambatsvina* is a word in Shona, a Bantu language spoken in Zimbabwe and southern Zambia. It was the name given to an operation conducted by the Zimbabwean authorities in 2005.[1] Some have called it 'Operation Restore Order'[2] while others translate the name to mean 'Operation Drive Out the Trash'.[3] In any event, for some 700,000 Zimbabweans, Operation Murambatsvina was devastating. As the UN reported, '92,460 housing structures had been destroyed, affecting 133,534 households at more than 52 sites' in blatant disrespect for people's right to housing, health and many other human rights.[4] 'Bulldozers played a major role in flattening structures, but frightened residents were also forced to pull down their own property', adds the International Crisis Group.[5] Given the scale and brutality of the evictions, did Operation Murambatsvina amount to a crime against humanity? Questions about crimes against humanity also arise in relation to reports alleging that the Rohingya population in Burma/Myanmar is subjected to forced labour and exploitative conditions of work. Should international criminal lawyers consider that the situation of the Rohingya population in Burma/Myanmar amounts to persecution or another crime against humanity because victims are allegedly subjected to forced labour and unjust conditions of work, based on documentation the former ICC Prosecutor Moreno-Ocampo received in 2009 from the ILO?[6] Are UN experts correct in their assessment that abuses perpetrated

[1] International Crisis Group, *Zimbabwe's Operation Murambatsvina: The Tipping Point?* (ICG, 2005), note 1.

[2] Report of the Fact-Finding Mission to Zimbabwe to Assess the Scope and Impact of Operation Murambatsvina, UN Special Envoy on Human Settlements Issues in Zimbabwe (Anna Tibaijuka), 17 July 2005, 7.

[3] Katherine Hughes, 'Operations "Drive Out the Trash"' (2007) 76 *Fordham Law Review*, 1, 323–86.

[4] Report of the UN Fact-Finding Mission to Zimbabwe, 17 July 2005, 12, 32.

[5] International Crisis Group, *Zimbabwe's Operation Murambatsvina: The Tipping Point?*, 1.

[6] See note 182.

in North Korea warrant international prosecution because the widespread starvation and forced labour reach the level of crimes against humanity?[7] Can we consider that the early case law of the post-World War II prosecutions in Nuremberg, such as the cases against Nazi doctors or industrialists, provides precedents for holding perpetrators criminally accountable for crimes against humanity related to abusive conduct in the realm of health, work or education?

To answer these questions, this chapter examines the circumstances under which ESCR violations can constitute crimes against humanity. Today, crimes against humanity are a major category of crimes. They focus on massive violations of human rights norms, and their potential overlap with violations of ESCR is particularly significant. Crimes against humanity were first prosecuted after World War II in order to capture abuses committed by authorities against their own nationals.[8]

The contours of crimes against humanity are vague in many respects,[9] and the detailed provisions adopted for the purposes of the ICC differ from other authoritative definitions that are at times broader than those contained in the Rome Statute.[10] First outlined are the threshold elements of crimes against humanity. These thresholds of crimes against humanity, the so-called *chapeau* requirements, are common to all crimes against humanity. Second, a methodological note will be made about the need to separate the analysis of threshold elements from the analysis of the underlying acts of crimes against humanity. Third, the punishable acts will be presented, commencing with those that most readily capture ESCR violations within their definition. Examples illustrate the manifold ways in which ESCR violations can overlap with specific crimes against humanity.

[7] Report of the Commission of Inquiry on Human Rights in the Democratic People's Republic of Korea, A/HRC/25/CRP.1, 7 February 2014.

[8] Only two defendants, Streicher and von Schirach, were prosecuted and convicted solely for crimes against humanity, but not for war crimes or crimes against peace. See *United States of America, the French Republic, the United Kingdom of Great Britain and Northern Ireland, and the Union of Soviet Socialist Republics against Major War Criminals, Opinion and Judgment, in Nazi Conspiracy and Aggression (Red Series), 1 October 1946*, IMT, 129–31 (Streicher) and 144–6 (von Schirach).

[9] A number of issues lack clarity, such as whether there is a requirement for a state plan or policy. See Section 4.1.2.

[10] Where the Rome Statute definition is clearly different from the definition of the same crime or element in customary international law, mention will be made. In particular, this is the case for the definition of the attack requirement under the ICC Statute.

## 4.1 Threshold requirements

Only conduct that is 'committed as part of a widespread or systematic attack directed against any civilian population, with the perpetrator's knowledge of the attack',[11] can be a crime against humanity. All of the following groups of threshold elements can be met by ESCR violations:

### *4.1.1 There must be an attack and the conduct must have a nexus to that attack*

An attack against any civilian population means a pattern of activity, 'in the context of which the conduct of the accused must have taken place to be regarded as a crime against humanity'.[12] The case law and the literature have paid little attention to the definition of attack for the purpose of crimes against humanity, leaving an important lacuna in the interpretation of the elements of these crimes. Existing literature on crimes against humanity in general as well as in relation to conduct affecting people's enjoyment of ESCR tends to focus on the requirement that the attack be widespread or systematic but glosses over the meaning of the term 'attack' itself.[13] Sluiter justifiably complains that 'the *intrinsic* definition of attack remains unclear, especially the question of intensity, namely whether nonviolent measures can constitute an attack and if so, on what basis'.[14] Yet, understanding the term 'attack' is crucial if the conditions under which legislative or other policies to deprive people of their ESCR can constitute an attack are to be ascertained.

Under general international law, the acts or omissions which form part of the attack need not amount to any crime,[15] nor to a military attack,[16]

[11] Rome Statute of the International Criminal Court, 2187 UNTS 90, 17 July 1998 (entered into force 1 July 2002), Art. 7(1).

[12] Guénaël Mettraux, *International Crimes* (Oxford University Press, 2005), 161. See also *Prosecutor* v. *Kayishema and Ruzindana, ICTR-95-1-T, 21 May 1999*, ICTR, para. 122, considering that the attack is 'the event in which the enumerated crimes must form part'.

[13] See, for instance, David Butler, 'Enforced Starvation' (2007) 3 *Human Rights Law Commentary*, 16–17; David Marcus, 'Famine Crimes' (2003) 97 *American Journal of International Law*, 2, 245–81: 271.

[14] Göran Sluiter, '"Chapeau Elements"', in *Forging a Convention for Crimes against Humanity*, ed. Leila Sadat (Cambridge University Press, 2011), 102–41: 125 (emphasis in original).

[15] *Prosecutor* v. *Kunarac, Kovac and Vukovic, IT-96-23-T, 22 February 2001*, ICTY, 415.

[16] *Prosecutor* v. *Kunarac, Kovac and Vukovic, IT-96-23-A, 12 June 2002*, ICTY, para. 86; ICC Elements of Crimes, ICC-ASP/1/3, 9 September 2002, Art. 7, Introduction, para. 3; *Prosecutor* v. *Bemba, Decision on the Charges of the Prosecutor, 15 June 2009, Pre-Trial Chamber II, ICC-01/05-01/08-424*, ICC, para. 75; *Prosecutor* v. *Akayesu, ICTR-96-4-T, 2 September 1998*, ICTR, para. 581.

but the notion of 'attack' should be interpreted as necessarily involving violent conduct. This means that ESCR violations on their own only constitute an attack if they involve violent conduct. This interpretation is warranted even if the ICTR Trial Chamber in *Akayesu* argued that an attack could be non-violent, such as the imposition of a system of apartheid.[17] The notion of an attack would lose its function to limit the scope of crimes against humanity if it was interpreted to encompass non-violent measures alone.[18] However, much depends on the way violence is conceptualised. If one emancipates the concept of violence from a narrow notion of *armed* violence,[19] 'violent conduct' includes abusive policies that do not directly kill or maim immediately, and many ESCR violations involve such violent conduct. In this vein, it is difficult to imagine that a system of apartheid could be imposed in an entirely non-violent manner.[20] Violence must be understood broadly, going beyond direct violence inflicted through firearms, machetes or raw physical force. The conceptualisation of violence must take into account research showing that violence is not simply a measurement of the number of people shot or injured.[21] Violence is best understood similar to what James Gilligan proposed: as long as we can identify that adverse human agency played the key role in the creation of the outcome, violence for the purpose of the attack requirement encompasses 'the increased rates of death and disability suffered by those who occupy the bottom rungs of society, as contrasted with the relatively lower death rates experienced by those who are above them'.[22] That said, it is not necessary to adopt Johan Galtung's very broad definition of violence ('the cause of the difference between the potential and the actual'[23]). This study still employs a definition of violence that Galtung would criticise as narrow, namely the 'incapacitation, or deprivation of health, alone (with killing as the extreme form), at the hands of an *actor*'.[24]

[17] *Prosecutor* v. *Akayesu, ICTR-96-4-T, 2 September 1998*, ICTR, para. 581.

[18] This is particularly true in the case of persecution, where 'ordinary' cases of discrimination must be distinguished from cases that amount to crimes against humanity. For a strong view on this point, see David Luban, 'Crimes against Humanity' (2004) 29 *Yale Journal of International Law*, 1, 85–167: 103, note 68.

[19] Sluiter's conceptualisation of violence seems narrow and too reliant on *armed* violence. Sluiter, '"Chapeau Elements"', 125, deriving that punishable acts would not need to be accompanied by acts of violence from the crime's applicability in times of peace.

[20] This is also the view of Mettraux, *International Crimes*, 156, note 3.

[21] Johan Galtung, 'Violence, Peace, and Peace Research' (1969) 6 *Journal of Peace Research*, 3, 167–91: 168–72.

[22] James Gilligan, *Violence* (Vintage Books, 1997), 89.

[23] Galtung, 'Violence, Peace, and Peace Research', 168.

[24] Ibid., 168 (emphasis in original).

Sluiter agrees that the ordinary meaning of the term 'attack' involves acts of violence[25] and that a definition based on acts of violence 'finds a very solid basis in international law'.[26] At the same time, he worries that this interpretation 'may not correspond with a broader protective function underlying crimes against humanity'.[27] This concern is alleviated if one adopts the view suggested in this study that violence must be defined as broader than armed violence.

Most tribunals have not devoted much attention to the attack requirement, most probably because the existence of an attack was undisputed after the Holocaust or after the atrocities in Rwanda and the former Yugoslavia. Mettraux usefully summarises the six factors taken into account by the Trial Chamber of the International Tribunal for the Prosecution of Persons Responsible for Serious Violations of International Humanitarian Law Committed in the Territory of the Former Yugoslavia since 1991 (ICTY) in finding that there was an attack against the civilian population:

> (i) whether there has been an authoritarian takeover of the region; (ii) whether a new authoritarian power structure has been established; (iii) whether discriminatory measures such as restrictions on bank accounts held by one group of citizens, or laissez-passer requirements have been imposed; (iv) whether summary arrests, detention, torture, and other crimes have been committed; (v) whether massive transfers of civilians to camps have taken place; (vi) whether the enemy population has been removed from the area.[28]

For the purposes of the threshold of crimes against humanity, an attack can thus constitute a range of social phenomena wider than acts of direct armed violence. While administrative and legislative measures imposed against a population that deprive it of access to ESCR do not in themselves constitute an attack, they can do so if the imposition of such measures is itself violent or is accompanied by acts of violence. The International Criminal Tribunal for Rwanda (ICTR) has repeatedly considered that there is an overarching attack in extermination cases and emphasised that extermination could be committed by way of depriving people of food and other socio-economic assets, but it has failed to

[25] Sluiter, '"Chapeau Elements"', 123. [26] Ibid., 125. [27] Ibid., 123.

[28] Guénaël Mettraux, 'Crimes against Humanity' (2002) 43 *Harvard International Law Journal*, 237–316: 249. Referring to *Prosecutor* v. *Nicolić, Review of Indictment Pursuant to Rule 61 on the Rules of Procedure and Evidence, IT-94-2-R61, 20 October 1995*, ICTY, para. 27.

explicitly define the broader attack.[29] In any event, serious ESCR abuses amounting to the creation of conditions of life that lead to mass deaths and harm are inevitably violent, either because they are accompanied by acts of direct physical violence or based on the definition above, which allows us to take into account forms of violence that do not involve arms and that do not immediately lead to death or harm but do so over time. In such scenarios, to constitute an attack, prosecutors must show that the conditions of life that lead to extermination were manufactured in a violent manner, for instance by comparing conditions with a neighbouring country or region with a similar agricultural system or by showing evidence of violent impediments to people's access to humanitarian assistance. Other examples of how the attack requirement can be met by conduct relating to ESCR violations are contained in the recent UN report of the Commission of Inquiry on Human Rights in the Democratic People's Republic of Korea. This commission found that the North Korean regime perpetrates an attack against the population by 'knowingly aggravating starvation in order to preserve the political system' and by abducting and displacing persons in order to gain labour and skills.[30] Given the level of violence described throughout the report,[31] it is convincing to argue that the criteria for an attack for the purposes of crimes against humanity have indeed been met.

The understanding of the term 'attack' is slightly more restrictive for the purposes of the Rome Statute than for customary law. To conclude that there is an attack, the ICC Statute requires that there is 'a course of conduct involving the multiple commission of acts referred to in paragraph 1 [of Art. 7] against any civilian population'.[32] The above reasoning thus only applies to the Rome Statute definitions as long as the violent conduct involves abuses that can be described as the *actus reus* of one or several of the underlying acts mentioned in Art. 7(1) of the Rome Statute. For the purposes of the threshold of crimes against humanity in the Rome

[29] *Prosecutor* v. *Kayishema and Ruzindana, ICTR-95-1-T, 21 May 1999*, ICTR, para. 144; *Prosecutor* v. *Bisengimana, ICTR-00-60-T, 13 April 2006*, ICTR, para. 72; *Prosecutor* v. *Bagilishema, ICTR-95-1a-T, 7 June 2001*, ICTR, para. 90.

[30] North Korea Inquiry, A/HRC/25/CRP.1, 7 February 2014, para. 1025; see also para. 1133.

[31] Ibid., para. 1133: 'Decisions and policies [aggravating starvation and related deaths] were enforced through executions and other violent measures.'

[32] Rome Statute, Art. 7(2)a. On the requirement of multiplicity, see Josh Scheinert, 'Refusal to Save Lives' (2013) 13 *International Criminal Law Review*, 3, 627–63: 646–7. Scheinert interprets this element to refer to the fact 'that a multiplicity of victims denotes a crime's commission multiple times and that the term attack can refer to either a singular attack or plurality of attacks'.

Statue, the ordinary wording of the provision further implies that active conduct is required.[33]

### *4.1.2 The attack must be directed against any civilian population*

A civilian population is a group (as opposed to individuals in isolation) that is not taking part in hostilities or in the use of force.[34] The ICTR and the ICC have both concluded that civilian populations 'include all persons except those who have the duty to maintain public order and have the legitimate means to exercise force',[35] regardless of any other criteria such as nationality or ethnicity. The interpretation of this criterion does not appear to pose additional difficulties for conduct related to ESCR violations.

More challenging from the perspective of ESCR violations is the requirement that the overall attack must be 'directed' against the civilian population. If we want to argue that ESCR violations constitute an attack, this requirement excludes ESCR violations that incidentally victimise the civilian population: the civilian population must be the primary object of the attack.[36] The requirement of a state or organisational policy also implies that a collection of recklessly committed ESCR violations leading to incidental harm of the civilian population can not constitute an attack. The idea that a 'directed' attack through ESCR violations can be arrived at recklessly makes little sense. Although individual prohibited acts may be committed recklessly, it is insufficient if the overall attack is committed recklessly. Some authorities have submitted that since 'widespread' or 'systematic' are disjunctive terms, then 'systematicity' could be demonstrated by the presence of a policy. Alternatively, the acts under consideration have to be widespread,

[33] Before the ICC, an attack should, therefore, not be based solely on omissions. The *policy* furthered by the attack can, however, in exceptional circumstances be implemented solely by a failure to act. See ICC Elements of Crimes, footnote 6. For a discussion of the significance of the use of the term 'acts' (rather than conduct, i.e., acts and omissions) in the Rome Statute definitions of the various guilty acts, see Section 5.2.1.1.

[34] *United States of America* v. *Altstoetter et al. (Justice Trial), III TWC 954*, NMT, paras. 278, 284; *Prosecutor* v. *Bemba, Decision on the Charges of the Prosecutor, 15 June 2009, Pre-Trial Chamber II, ICC-01/05-01/08-424*, ICC, para. 77.

[35] *Prosecutor* v. *Bemba, Decision on the Charges of the Prosecutor, 15 June 2009, Pre-Trial Chamber II, ICC-01/05-01/08-424*, ICC, para. 78; *Prosecutor* v. *Kayishema and Ruzindana, ICTR-95-1-T, 21 May 1999*, ICTR, paras. 127–9.

[36] *Prosecutor* v. *Kunarac, Kovac and Vukovic, IT-96-23-A, 12 June 2002*, ICTY, para. 91.

regardless of whether a policy has been formulated or not.[37] According to Marcus, recklessly committed conduct leading to famine *without* a 'directed' overall attack would therefore fit within the parameters of crimes against humanity if they are 'widespread'.[38] This interpretation is based on a controversial paragraph in the *Tadić* decision of the ICTY.[39] Early decisions of the ICC plainly indicate that it is unlikely that the court will follow the reasoning in the *Tadić* decision,[40] which does not seem to correspond to customary international law.[41]

There is controversy whether the verb 'directed' also implies that crimes against humanity can only arise if an attack is inflicted pursuant to or in furtherance of a policy. Canvassing the debate on the policy requirement is important in order to consider how ESCR violations relate to the threshold elements of crimes against humanity. If an attack is required to be directed in furtherance of a policy, then prosecutors must prove that there was such a policy. Such a requirement limits the scope of crimes against humanity, but does not make a finding of overlap between ESCR violations and crimes against humanity impossible. The requirement of a policy is debated both at the level of the Rome Statute and under customary international law. Three specific questions arise: (i) is there a policy requirement in the first place; (ii) if so, does the entity behind the policy need to be a state; and, if not, (iii) what types of organisations besides states could be behind such a policy?

As Cassese points out, in light of conflicting authorities, proponents and opponents of a policy requirement alike support their positions in

37 *Prosecutor* v. *Tadić, IT-94-1-T, 7 May 1997*, ICTY, para. 653: crimes against humanity occur 'if the acts occur on a widespread or systematic basis that demonstrates a policy to commit those acts'.

38 Marcus, 'Famine Crimes', 273.

39 See note 37. Cherif Bassiouni, *Legislative History*, International and Comparative Criminal Law Series (Transnational, 2005), 150. It has also been rejected that the policy requirement could be interpreted as being the same as the element of systematicity. This interpretation would run counter to the presumption that no statutory provision is superfluous. Margaret DeGuzman, 'The Road from Rome' (2000) 22 *Human Rights Quarterly*, 2, 335–403: 372.

40 *Prosecutor* v. *Katanga and Chui, Decision on the Confirmation of Charges, 30 September 2008, Pre-Trial Chamber I, ICC-01/04-01/07*, ICC, para. 396; *Decision Pursuant to Article 15 of the Rome Statute on the Authorization of an Investigation into the Situation in the Republic of Kenya, 31 March 2010, Pre-Trial Chamber II, ICC-01/09*, ICC, 84, 6; *Decision on the Prosecutor's Application Pursuant to Article 58 as to Gaddafi, Gaddafi and Alsenussi, 27 June 2011, Pre-Trial Chamber I, ICC-01/11*, ICC, para. 35.

41 It is doubtful that the position in *Tadić* would correspond to customary international law since it would effectively make the attack requirement of the definition redundant.

line with their views on the nature and purposes of international criminal law, and the legal texts do not unambigously clarify the matter. In light of the existing uncertainties, the most plausible view is to suppose that a policy is required to qualify conduct as a crime against humanity, but that the author of such a policy can be a non-state actor.

As far as the first question is concerned, we must know whether there is a policy requirement at all. This is straightforward under the Rome Statute. The ordinary meaning of the relevant provision in the Rome Statute confirms a policy requirement for crimes against humanity under the jurisdiction of the ICC.[42] This means that the attack must be qualified. To show overlap between ESCR violations and the attack, the ESCR violations must be inflicted in furtherance of a policy, for example, a policy to reach certain macroeconomic goals or to maintain a certain regime. We will return to the nature of the policy itself below.

Under customary international law, what the prosecutor must prove is that the conduct of the accused had a nexus to an overall attack that was 'directed'. There is support for the view that a 'directed overall attack' also implies a policy requirement connecting an aggregate of abuses committed by individuals with a civilian population being the primary object of the attack. Some contend otherwise. Guénaël Mettraux argues that 'there is no requirement in customary international law that a crime against humanity be committed pursuant to or in furtherance of a plan or policy'.[43] Before the ICTY and the Special Court for Sierra Leone (SCSL), the existence of a policy has been rejected as a legal element of crimes against humanity.[44] In the most prominent case on the policy issue before the ICTY, the ICTY Appeals Chamber, however, failed to justify how isolated and unconnected acts of individuals would be excluded from the province of crimes against humanity if no policy element was required.[45] For the time being,

[42] Rome Statute, Art. 7(2)a: 'a course of conduct . . . pursuant to or in furtherance of a State or organizational policy to commit such attack'.

[43] See Mettraux, 'Crimes against Humanity', 281.

[44] For instance, *Prosecutor* v. *Kunarac, Kovac and Vukovic, IT-96-23-A, 12 June 2002*, ICTY, para. 98, note 114. See also *Prosecutor* v. *Kunarac, Kovac and Vukovic, IT-96-23-T, 22 February 2001*, ICTY, para. 144, note 1109; *Prosecutor* v. *Sesay, Kallon and Gbao, SCSL-04-15-T, 2 March 2009*, SCSL, para. 79; *Prosecutor* v. *Taylor, SCSL-03-1-T, 26 April 2012*, SCSL, para. 511, note 1200.

[45] *Prosecutor* v. *Kunarac, Kovac and Vukovic, IT-96-23-A, 12 June 2002*, ICTY, para. 98. If crimes against humanity did not have a policy requirement, the widespread crimes in post-apartheid South Africa would, for instance, qualify as crimes against humanity, since they are widespread and the victims are civilians. But as Darryl Robinson points out, '[e]ven opponents of the policy element would answer that such a scenario is not a [crime against humanity]'. Only the inclusion of some sort of a policy requirement in the definition of the

it is difficult to identify state practice and *opinio juris* for or against the finding of a policy requirement under customary international law.[46] It seems prudent to assume that a policy is also required under customary international law. The implication relevant to the argument made in this study is that lawyers must be ready to adduce evidence of such a policy.

What is meant by a policy? The policy does not need to be formalised, but can be deduced from the manner and circumstances in which the acts occur.[47] In exceptional circumstances, a policy can be implemented by a deliberate failure to take action.[48] This is important, as many ESCR violations are committed by depriving individuals of essential entitlements. While it is not enough to infer a policy solely from the absence of action,[49] policies in practice rarely consist of pure conduct or pure abstention. In the realm of ESCR violations, policies often involve a combination of acts and abstentions, such as failure to provide access to food (failure to act), combined with threats against those who try to deliver it (active conduct).

To qualify an atrocity as a crime against humanity under the Rome Statute, the underlying policy reflected by the victimising conduct must also be considered. As the UN Commission of Inquiry on Human Rights in the Democratic People's Republic of Korea noted, it is not necessary that the policy pursues the objective to harm the population. For instance, a state could have a general policy to harass certain groups or a policy to do whatever it takes to achieve a certain outcome (attract foreign investment, construct major infrastructure, etc.) without necessarily having a policy to infringe ESCR. As long as perpetrators are aware of the causal relationship between the policy and the harm done,[50] it is

attack will ensure that such unconnected crimes fall outside the province of crimes against humanity. Darryl Robinson, 'Essence of Crimes against Humanity Raised by Challenges at ICC', www.ejiltalk.org/essence-of-crimes-against-humanity-raised-by-challenges-at-icc/. Schabas further contends that the authorities cited in footnote 114 in the *Kunarac* appeal do not stand up to scrutiny. William Schabas, *Unimaginable Atrocities* (Oxford University Press, 2012), 133–40.

[46] See Otto Triffterer (ed.), *Commentary on the Rome Statute* (Beck, 2008), 235 (Dixon) and note 374, for the argument that no international instrument except the Rome Statute includes a state or organisational policy requirement. Dixon also contends that national jurisprudence offers little support for a policy requirement.

[47] *Prosecutor* v. *Tadić, IT-94-1-T, 7 May 1997*, ICTY, para. 653.

[48] ICC Elements of Crimes, footnote 6. [49] Ibid.

[50] North Korea Inquiry, A/HRC/25/CRP.1, 7 February 2014, para. 1135. The commission pointed out that my doctoral thesis contained a sentence that would have introduced an element of criminal intent into the requirement of a policy. My sentence that 'there must be an overall attack that targets civilians' in the section on the policy requirement was open to this interpretation and, therefore, omitted in this book. Importantly, it is not necessary that the policy, for example, aims at depriving victims of their right to food.

not required that the policy aims at violating ESCR. In North Korea, the criteria for an attack directed against a civilian population are, therefore, met because the attack (the aggravation of starvation)[51] is pursuant to or in furtherance of a policy (e.g., to preserve the political system) even though this policy may not aim at starving people.

The second question that arises is whether the policy must be that of a state. As mentioned above, the very existence of a policy requirement is in dispute, as is the question of whether such a policy must be a state policy or whether policies of non-state organisations also qualify. In the latter case, the standard of what constitutes an organisation is debatable. William Schabas, a proponent of a *state* policy requirement, centres his argument on the claim that the main purpose of international criminalisation is to establish accountability over abuses that would otherwise escape prosecution in states that usually exercise jurisdiction, because the state – through its policies – is itself complicit in the abuses.[52] This relationship between the state and the perpetrator would render an abuse a crime against humanity,[53] and, according to Schabas, a state policy is therefore implicit in any definition of crimes against humanity.[54] If one takes this view, ESCR violations will only overlap with the policy requirement of crimes against humanity if it can be shown that the attack was committed in the promotion of a policy of a state, for example, if the state has a policy that impacts on people's enjoyment of ESCR.

There is, however, also support for the view that crimes against humanity may be committed even in the absence of a state policy but pursuant to or in furtherance of a policy originating with another type of organisation. A policy of an organisation acting independently of the state may suffice. If this view is adopted, it is enough if a non-state actor has a policy that affects people's socio-economic and cultural well-being and the state fails to protect from such harm. It is not required that the state's failure to protect amounts to a policy. The ordinary wording of the term 'state or organisational policy' in the Rome Statute indicates that organisations other than states can be at the origin of a policy. An interpretation based on the object and purpose of the policy requirement seems to lead to the same result: the object and purpose of the policy requirement is to ensure that random and unconnected acts are excluded

Rather, it suffices that the attack is pursuant to or in furtherance of *a* policy (such as to maintain the regime or to introduce self-sufficiency, as the Khmer Rouge intended). I agree with the commission that the policy must not aim at pursuing the attack.

51 Ibid., para. 1025. 52 Schabas, *Unimaginable Atrocities*, 149–50 and 436.

53 Ibid., 44. 54 Ibid., 149.

from the definition of crimes against humanity and that the jurisdiction for international crimes is limited to those crimes for which the territorial state is likely to fail to establish accountability. This object and purpose requires that a policy element is part of the definition of crimes against humanity, but it does not imply that a *state* policy is required. Armed groups or organised criminal networks can escape prosecutions even where the territorial state is not complicit in their abuses. The state may be unable or unwilling to contain these organisations for reasons other than state complicity, particularly if the non-state organisation holds significant power and influence. Given that the ordinary meaning of the terms in the Rome Statute unambiguously refers to states *or* organisations, it is unwarranted to consult the preparatory works of the Rome Statute or the ILC Draft Codes,[55] which would, in any event, not confirm the limitation to a state policy.[56]

Case law and parts of the literature[57] also point out that the nature of the entity behind the policy can be an 'organisation' unconnected to a

55 Vienna Convention on the Law of Treaties, 1155 UNTS 331, 23 May 1969 (entered into force 27 January 1980), Art. 31. The rules of treaty interpretation only allow for recourse to the preparatory work in order to *confirm* an interpretation that can be based on the ordinary wording of the terms, the context and object and purpose of a treaty.

56 The inclusion of the 'state or organisational policy' requirement in the Rome Statute was a compromise that found its way into the draft statute in the first week of July 1998 only, with no indications that the drafters intended to require a *state* policy. UN Diplomatic Conference of Plenipotentiaries on the Establishment of an International Criminal Court, Committee of the Whole, Art. 5, Crimes against Humanity, Recommendations of the Coordinator, A/CONF.183/C.1/L.44, 7 July 1998, 3. The ILC Draft Code of 1954 included a state policy element, while the later version of 1996 did not. Compare: ILC, Draft Code of Crimes against the Peace and Security of Mankind 1954, *Yearbook of the International Law Commission*, vol. II, 1954, Art. 2(11); and ILC, Draft Code of Crimes against the Peace and Security of Mankind 1996, *Yearbook of the International Law Commission*, vol. II, Part Two, 1996, 47, Commentary to Art. 18. As the ICC Pre-Trial Chamber II concluded, 'had the drafters of the [Rome Statute] intended to exclude non-State actors from the term "organization", they would not have included this term in article 7(2)a of the Statute'. *Decision Pursuant to Article 15 of the Rome Statute on the Authorization of an Investigation into the Situation in the Republic of Kenya, 31 March 2010, Pre-Trial Chamber II, ICC-01/09*, ICC, para. 92.

57 Bassiouni is often cited as one of the publicists arguing in favour of a *state* policy requirement. But this is not entirely accurate. In 1999, Cherif Bassiouni, *Crimes against Humanity* (Kluwer, 1999), 246, asserted that the jurisdictional element of crimes against humanity is a state action or policy for state actors *or* an organisational policy for non-state actors. At p. 275: '[Art. 7] extended the application of the proscribing norm from state actors to non-state actors.' The same author only later, in 2005, held otherwise: Bassiouni, *Legislative History*, 151–2, arguing that '[t]he text [of Art. 7(2)] clearly refers to state policy, and the words "organisational policy" do not refer to the policy of an organisation, but the policy of a state'. Bassiouni's position in 1999 does not support the view that only organisations of a

state.[58] The notion of 'organisational policy' appears broad enough to encompass entities other than state actors. This means that the policy that negatively affects the enjoyment of ESCR can originate either from a state or from a non-state actor.

The third question remains: by what standard do we determine the existence of an organisational policy of a non-state actor? One argument is that the entity at the origin of the policy needs to possess features that are characteristic of an 'organisation', that is some institutional attributes allowing it to direct, instigate or encourage crimes.[59] This is the most plausible understanding of the term. Others contend that the capacity to commit abuses is the decisive criterion. Pre-Trial Chamber II of the ICC interpreted the term 'organisational policy' when it authorised an investigation into the *Situation in the Republic of Kenya* and more recently in the judgment against Katanga. In the *Kenya* decision, the majority concluded that the test was whether or not the group was capable of performing 'acts which infringe on basic human values'.[60] Later in the same decision, the chamber indicated considerations that it 'may take into account' when deciding whether a group qualifies as an 'organisation'. Factors such as hierarchy, capacity, control over territory or an articulation of an intention to attack civilians would be relevant.[61] In the *Katanga* judgment, Trial Chamber II in spring 2014 explained that the organisation must have sufficient means to facilitate or encourage the attack.[62] While the two chambers are correct to consider a policy by a non-state

state qualify (only his later book does). Thus, contrary to the ICC's reference in the *Kenya* decision, Bassiouni's 1999 work is no example of commentators arguing that only state-like organisations qualify. See *Decision Pursuant to Article 15 of the Rome Statute on the Authorization of an Investigation into the Situation in the Republic of Kenya, 31 March 2010, Pre-Trial Chamber II, ICC-01/09*, ICC, note 83.

58 *Decision Pursuant to Article 15 of the Rome Statute on the Authorization of an Investigation into the Situation in the Republic of Kenya, 31 March 2010, Pre-Trial Chamber II, ICC-01/09*, ICC, para. 90; *Prosecutor* v. *Tadić, IT-94-1-T, 7 May 1997*, ICTY, para. 654.

59 Bassiouni, *Crimes against Humanity*, 275.

60 *Decision Pursuant to Article 15 of the Rome Statute on the Authorization of an Investigation into the Situation in the Republic of Kenya, 31 March 2010, Pre-Trial Chamber II, ICC-01/09*, ICC, para. 90.

61 Ibid., para. 93.

62 *Prosecutor* v. *Katanga, Jugement rendu en application de l'article 74 du Statut, 7 March 2014, Trial Chamber II, N° ICC-01/04–01/07*, ICC, para. 1119. The paragraph is somewhat imprecise. The chamber first refers to the capacity to committ the attack ('*assurer la coordination nécessaire à la réalisation d'une attaque*'). In the next sentence, the mere facilitation or encouragement ('*des moyens suffisants pour favoriser ou encourager l'attaque*') suffices.

actor, they probably cast the net too wide by emphasising the capacity to commit abuses and by merely stating that institutional attributes 'may be taken into account'.[63] If one would take the view of the pre-trial chamber in the *Kenya* decision, any collectivity which can infringe basic human values could be the author of an organisational policy. A group of medical doctors in a hospital, for instance, who carelessly fail to provide adequate medical treatment during a surgery has the capability to infringe basic human values but it would seem far-fetched to consider the group of surgeons as an organisation. The trial chamber in *Katanga*, in contrast, circularly amalgamates the commission of the attack with the requirement that this attack is directed in furtherance of an organisational policy. According to the chamber's reasoning, whenever there is a finding that an attack has occurred, judges will always have to conclude that the organisational requirement is met because an attack cannot be committed without the capability of committing it.

This study proposes that the term 'organisation' should be interpreted as requiring at least some institutional attributes, such as the ones mentioned in Paragraph 93 by the Pre-Trial Chamber II.[64] Judge Kaul, who dissented from the majority's interpretation of the organisational policy requirement in the *Kenya* decision, criticised the majority's claim that one must merely analyse 'whether a group has a capability to perform acts which infringe basic human values'.[65] In his view, this statement by the pre-trial chamber is too elastic and 'may expand the concept of crimes against humanity to any infringement of human rights'.[66] Kaul does not dispute the relevance of the above-mentioned considerations relating to the nature of the group, but he concludes that such considerations must necessarily form part of the identification of an 'organisational policy', rather than be considered voluntary considerations which 'may be taken into account' by a chamber.[67] At the same time, Judge Kaul's requirement that an 'organisational policy' requires functional equivalence with a state policy might be unduly restrictive, and there is support for the view that organisations possessing some institutional attributes will suffice.[68] If this

[63] *Decision Pursuant to Article 15 of the Rome Statute on the Authorization of an Investigation into the Situation in the Republic of Kenya, 31 March 2010, Pre-Trial Chamber II, ICC-01/09*, ICC, para. 93.

[64] The list provided by the Pre-Trial Chamber II should, however, not be considered exhaustive. Ibid.

[65] Ibid., Dissenting Opinion of Judge Kaul, para. 53. [66] Ibid. [67] Ibid., para. 51.

[68] Ibid., arguing that organisations 'should partake of some characteristics of a State'. Such a requirement of 'quasi-state abilities' is not contained in the text of the statute.

interpretation is accepted, the threshold elements for crimes against humanity can be met if an attack is inflicted in furtherance of a policy of a non-state organisation as long as this organisation has a certain hierarchy, control over territory or other institutional characteristics. This view has potentially significant implications in relation to ESCR abuses. If accepted, a non-state actor such as an organised armed group which hinders access to humanitarian food relief, for instance, could be the author of a policy relevant for the *chapeau* of crimes against humanity. Where, in line with the focus of this study on ESCR violations attributable to a state, a state fails to protect people from abuses from that non-state actor or the state exercises effective control over the non-state actor,[69] a violation of ESCR could be identified, and the overlap between a violation of ESCR and the policy requirement is straightforward. However, if one would take the view that only state-like organisations qualify (or if there must be a state policy *tout court*), the policy requirement could only be met by ESCR violations if the state or a state-like organisation (such as a non-recognised government) is the actor behind the policy.

Dixon concludes that the policy element, in essence, requires that the acts of individuals, which are isolated, uncoordinated and haphazard, be excluded.[70] This is a proposition with which most commentators will agree. The rejection of a *state* policy does not imply that all 'individual crimes committed in isolation'[71] would be covered: merely that non-state actors committing abuses pursuant or in furtherance of 'an organisational policy' could qualify as the entity behind a policy necessary for the attack requirement of crimes against humanity.[72] An armed non-state organisation which enforces a policy that has the effect to deprive civilians of access to employment or education, for instance, could well be the author of a policy pursuant to which an attack is carried out. In such a scenario, the potential ESCR violation is the state's failure to protect the right to work or education. It is not necessary that such a failure is part of

[69] See Section 3.1 on the attribution of conduct to a state.

[70] Triffterer (ed.), *Commentary on the Rome Statute*, 236 (Dixon). In Dixon's view, such a requirement only exists for the Rome Statute, but not under customary international law. See Note 46.

[71] Schabas, *Unimaginable Atrocities*, 150–1.

[72] It is interesting that Schabas himself qualifies his view that only those acting on behalf of the state would require international criminalisation. See, for instance, ibid., 150. He writes that we 'do not, *by and large* have the same problem [of impunity] with respect to "non-state actors"' (emphasis added).

a policy it suffices if the non-state actor has a policy that is furthered by the attack.

To conclude, the interpretation of the requirement that an attack must be 'directed' for the purposes of crimes against humanity remains unresolved and fraught with doctrinal controversies. The strictest interpretation is that a policy requirement exists and that the author of such a policy must be state. Even then, overlap between ESCR violations and the attack requirement of crimes against humanity is undoubtedly possible, such as when governments exercise violence against any civilian population and such conduct is inflicted pursuant to or in furtherance of a policy that has the effect of harming the enjoyment of socio-economic or cultural rights. Apartheid policies in the field of employment, housing, education or health are archetypal examples, but essentially any policy originating from the state will be relevant as long as the overall attack is inflicted 'in furtherance' of this policy. Importantly, the policy does not need to be inferred from the attack itself and might not relate to socio-economic or cultural infringements. While it is possible that the attack as such, as well as the policy and the underlying acts all overlap with ESCR violations, such a constellation is not necessary to identify overlap between crimes against humanity and ESCR violations.[73] As will be further explained below,[74] overlap between the definition of a crime against humanity and ESCR violations can also be shown to exist if the attack requirement is met in any other way independent of socio-economic or cultural abuses, but one of the underlying offences is committed by way of violating ESCR. In the next step, we consider the requirement that the attack be widespread or systematic.

### *4.1.3 The attack must be widespread or systematic*

The attack (but not the individual conduct of the accused) generally has to involve multiple acts.[75] Episodic and/or unconnected conduct does not suffice to constitute an attack.[76] The term 'widespread' refers to a

[73] As van den Herik seems to imply. Larissa van den Herik, 'ESCR – International Criminal Law's Blind Spot?', in *Economic, Social, and Cultural Rights: Contemporary Issues and Challenges*, ed. Eibe Riedel, et al., *Economic, Social, and Cultural Rights* (Oxford University Press, 2014), 343–66: 351.

[74] See Section 4.2. [75] ICC Elements of Crimes, Art. 7, Introduction, para. 3.

[76] *Prosecutor* v. *Tadić, IT 94 1 T, 7 May 1997*, ICTY, para. 644; Triffterer (ed.), *Commentary on the Rome Statute*, 234 (Dixon).

massive, frequent or large-scale action, while the term 'systematic' refers to an act or omission which is thoroughly organised, follows a pattern or a common policy and/or involves the use of state resources.[77] Importantly, the two terms 'widespread' and 'systematic' are disjunctive.[78] The requirement that the attack be widespread or systematic does not pose specific difficulties for the argument that ESCR violations can overlap with the threshold elements of crimes against humanity.

### 4.1.4 *The perpetrator must have had knowledge of the attack*

Under customary international law,[79] as well as under the Rome Statute, perpetrators must have knowledge of the attack and know that their act is part of that attack.[80]

The mental element of the *chapeau* therefore requires that the accused know that his or her conduct fits within the context of other widespread or systematic acts. These determinations have to be made in the same way whether the alleged conduct concerns civil and political rights, ESCR, or both.

### 4.1.5 *Absence of other requirements*

Crimes against humanity do not require the existence of further threshold elements. Particularly, they do not require a nexus to an armed conflict, nor discriminatory grounds or specific motives. The following three factors expand the scope of possible overlap between crimes against humanity and ESCR violations and other human rights violations.

First, crimes against humanity no longer need to be linked to crimes against peace or war crimes. Originally, the exercise of jurisdiction over

[77] The terms 'widespread' and 'systematic' have been interpreted by the ICTR in *Akayesu* and this interpretation is settled. *Prosecutor* v. *Akayesu, ICTR-96-4-T, 2 September 1998*, ICTR, para. 580. This was confirmed in *Prosecutor* v. *Bemba, Decision on the Charges of the Prosecutor, 15 June 2009, Pre-Trial Chamber II, ICC-01/05-01/08-424*, ICC, para. 83; *Prosecutor* v. *Katanga and Chui, Decision on the Confirmation of Charges, 30 September 2008, Pre-Trial Chamber I, ICC-01/04-01/07*, ICC, para. 394.

[78] See also ILC, Draft Code of Crimes against the Peace and Security of Mankind 1996, *Yearbook of the International Law Commission*, vol. II, Part Two, 1996, Art. 18 and commentary to Art. 18.

[79] This point is uncontroversial. For references, see William Schabas, *Commentary on the Rome Statute* (Oxford University Press, 2010), 155, note 29.

[80] Rome Statute, Art. 7(1). See also *Prosecutor* v. *Kayishema and Ruzindana, ICTR-95-1-T, 21 May 1999*, ICTR, paras. 133–4. Cited by the ICTY in *Prosecutor* v. *Kupreškić, IT-95-16-T, 14 January 2000*, ICTY, para. 557.

crimes against humanity needed to be linked to an armed conflict.[81] The Nuremberg and Tokyo charters required the existence of an international armed conflict, while the ICTY Statute expanded crimes against humanity to non-international armed conflicts.[82] Under the Rome Statute, crimes against humanity do not need to have any nexus to an armed conflict. State practice and *opinio juris* point out that this same rule applies today under customary international law.[83] As Ambos and Wirth aptly observe, it is now widely recognised that crimes against humanity are no longer primarily linked to the laws of war, but rather to international human rights law.[84] This is highly significant as ESCR abuses such as those committed in North Korea could not be captured under the law of crimes against humanity if a nexus to armed conflict would be required.

Second, the threshold of crimes against humanity does not require that the attack be committed on discriminatory grounds,[85] that is, the overall attack is targeted against a particular group. As the ICTY Appeals Chamber explained, such a requirement was rejected in the drafting of

[81] The definition of crimes against humanity may never have required a nexus to an armed conflict, but only the exercise of jurisdiction may have done so. Bernard Röling and Antonio Cassese, *The Tokyo Trial and Beyond* (Polity Press, 1993), 56; Arthur Watts and Robert Jennings, *Oppenheim's International Law*, vol. 1, 9th edn (Longman, 1992), 996. The United States contended that even at Nuremberg, nexus to armed conflict was not an element of crimes against humanity. David Scheffer, 'The United States and the International Criminal Court' (1999) 93 *American Journal of International Law*, 1, 12–22: 14.

[82] Statute of the International Tribunal for the Prosecution of Persons Responsible for Serious Violations of International Humanitarian Law Committed in the Territory of the Former Yugoslavia since 1991, Annex to Security Council S/Res/827, 25 May 1993, Art. 5. The ICTR provision on crimes against humanity does not mention any nexus to armed conflict, but since the tribunal's jurisdiction was limited to serious violations of IHL, a link to armed conflict was still required. Statute of the International Tribunal for Rwanda, Annex to S/Res/955, 8 November 1994, Art. 1.

[83] *Prosecutor* v. *Tadić, Decision on the Defence Motion for Interlocutory Appeal on Jurisdiction, IT-94-1-Ar72, 2 October 1995*, ICTY, paras. 140–1: 'It is by now a settled rule of customary international law that crimes against humanity do not require a connection to international armed conflict.' See also *Prosecutor* v. *Tadić, IT-94-1-A, 15 July 1999*, ICTY, para. 251; *Prosecutor* v. *Vasiljevic, IT-98-32-T, 29 November 2002*, ICTY, para. 30; Schabas, *Commentary on the Rome Statute*, 142–7, for the drafting history on the nexus issue in the Rome Statute; Yoram Dinstein, 'Crimes against Humanity after Tadic' (2000) 13 *Leiden Journal of International Law*, 2, 373–93; *Regina* v. *Bartle (Ex Parte Pinochet No. 3); Regina* v. *Evans, 6 BHRC 24, 24 March 1999, House of Lords*, United Kingdom, 19, Lord Wilkinson concluding that the link to war 'fell away' over time.

[84] Kai Ambos and Steffen Wirth, 'Crimes against Humanity' (2002) 13 *Criminal Law Forum*, 1, 1–90: 24.

[85] *Prosecutor* v. *Tadić, IT-94-1-A, 15 July 1999*, ICTY, para. 305.

the ILC Draft Code as well as in the negotiations of the Rome Statute.[86] Only the crime of persecution requires that the underlying acts (but not the overall attack) be committed on discriminatory grounds.

Third, the perpetrator's personal motives are irrelevant for the finding of crimes against humanity. An accused claiming that his or her policies harming victims' access to the right to food, for instance, should be justified because the policies would result in better macroeconomic outcomes would clearly fail before a court.[87]

## 4.2 A methodological note: separating threshold elements from the elements of underlying offences

It is important to separate threshold elements from the elements of the specific underlying offences. Given the complexities of the threshold requirements of crimes against humanity and the legal impossibility argument considered in Chapter 2, it is warranted to emphasise this point. It does not matter whether or not the threshold elements are met by the very same conduct as the one giving rise to the particular crime against humanity. It is entirely possible to find that the threshold elements of crimes against humanity are met because of conduct *other* than the conduct that meets the elements of the underlying offence. The ICC emphasised this fundamental point in the *Katanga* judgment by stating the need to consider the attack, the qualification of the attack and the underlying acts in separate steps.[88] Crucially, this means that there can be overlap between crimes against humanity and ESCR because the attack against a civilian population was committed by way of ESCR violations (i.e., if we find overlap between ESCR violations and the threshold elements), *or* because the attack was committed in furtherance of a policy that resulted in harm to ESCR *or* because one of the underlying offences of crimes against humanity was inflicted by depriving victims of their enjoyment of ESCR. The threshold elements as well as the conduct of the underlying act can be based on different conduct.

[86] Ibid., para. 291. It is widely accepted that Art. 3 of the ICTR Statute, requiring that the attack itself is discriminatory, does not reflect customary international law.

[87] For a discussion of 'good motives' as an unavailable defence, see DeGuzman, 'The Road from Rome', 390. Refer to *United States of America* v. *Brandt et al.* (Medical Trial), *II TWC 171*, NMT, 263, and *United States of America* v. *Altstoetter et al.* (Justice Trial), *III TWC 954*, NMT, 1086–7.

[88] *Prosecutor* v. *Katanga, Jugement rendu en application de l'article 74 du Statut, 7 March 2014, Trial Chamber II, N° ICC-01/04-01/07*, ICC, paras. 1096–9.

A concrete example illustrates the point. We can return to the crime of enforced sterilisation, previously mentioned in the methodological chapter,[89] where we saw how the underlying conduct of the crime against humanity of enforced sterilisation can overlap with violations of the right to health. It is not necessary that we simultaneously find that the threshold elements also overlap with ESCR violations. Instead, criminal lawyers can consider the full range of abuses when determining whether certain conduct was committed in the context of a widespread or systematic attack. In the Nuremberg jurisprudence, for instance, the Holocaust as such was considered the relevant context of the crimes whereas tribunals analysed a range of specific abuses in order to decide whether the elements of crimes of various underlying offences were met. In one case after World War II, the tribunal considered the 'despotic rule of violence of the Nazis' or the 'National Socialists' regime of violence and arbitrariness' as the overarching attack, while the destruction of one cultural object (a synagogue) constituted conduct sufficiently linked to that attack for a crime against humanity charge.[90] The destruction of cultural property can be a crime against humanity overlapping with a violation of cultural rights irrespective of whether the threshold elements were also met by conduct that relates to ESCR violations. Vice versa, crimes against humanity can overlap with ESCR violations because their threshold requirements are met by ESCR violations. The most straightforward way how ESCR violations can overlap with crimes against humanity is when ESCR violations overlap with one of the various prohibited offences underlying crimes against humanity. As we just saw, the threshold elements of crimes against humanity can also overlap with ESCR violations, but there will be more instances in which ESCR violations overlap with one of the specific prohibited offences forming part of crimes against humanity. The main part of this chapter therefore analyses the link between selected underlying offences and ESCR violations, starting with the crimes against humanity for which the largest amount of information relevant to the research question could be identified.

[89] See Section 3.1.

[90] *Strafsache 78/48, 9 November 1948, Entscheidungen des obersten Gerichtshofes für die britische Zone in Köln,* Courts in the British Zone of Control in Germany under Control Council Law 10, 19. Cited and discussed in Mettraux, 'Crimes against Humanity', 252, note 66.

## 4.3 Deportation or forcible transfer of population

'Deportation or forcible transfer of population' means the forced displacement by expulsion or other coercive acts from the area in which [the victims] are lawfully present, without grounds permitted under international law.[91] In human rights law, forcibly removing individuals from their homes or lands is most often synonymous with forced evictions, which *prima facie* constitute a violation of the right to housing and thus an ESCR violation. In a first step, the term 'forced eviction' is clarified, after which the elements of the crime against humanity of deportation or forcible transfer will be considered in order to ascertain when the conduct prohibited by this crime overlaps with violations of the right to housing.

It is important to note that aside from forced evictions, a number of other human rights violations could also demonstrate that this crime encompasses violations of ESCR. The rights to work or education are, for instance, also particularly relevant because 'expulsion or other coercive acts' 'include the full range of coercive pressures on people to flee their homes, including . . . depriving members of a group of employment, [or] denying them access to schools'.[92] Where the right to water is infringed, or where property is destroyed or stolen, electicity cut off or health care denied with intent to pressurise people to leave, the elements of forcible transfer deserve to be analysed. But, as Duthie points out, certain human rights abuses such as the destruction of homes and property 'are more likely to lead to displacement than others'.[93] The following part therefore focuses particularly on the intersection between housing rights violations and this crime against humanity, without implying that other ESCR abuses could not be relevant.[94]

First, it has to be observed that UN bodies and others employ a range of terminology to describe displacement-related phenomena. As Stavropoulou aptly pointed out in 1998, '"forced evictions," "population transfers," "mass exoduses," and "internal displacement" are all used as if they mean different things, and constitute different subject matters of

[91] Rome Statute, Art. 7(2)d.

[92] Triffterer (ed.), *Commentary on the Rome Statute*, 250 (Hall).

[93] Roger Duthie, 'Displacement' (2011) 5 *International Journal of Transitional Justice*, 241–61: 244.

[94] It is recommended to read this section in conjunction with the section on deportation and forcible transfer as a war crime where additional examples of overlap between this crime and ESCR-related abuses are provided. See Section 5.2.1.2.

study, although they all refer to the same phenomenon (namely, removal from one's home and/or land against one's will)'.[95]

The CESCR has held that forced evictions are '*prima facie* incompatible with the requirements of the Covenant'.[96] The CESCR defined forced evictions 'as the permanent or temporary removal against their will of individuals, families and/or communities from the homes and/or land which they occupy, without the provision of, and access to, appropriate forms of legal or other protection'.[97] Tolerance or support of evictions equally amounts to a violation of the covenant, as well as punitive evictions.[98] Other UN bodies have also condemned the practice of forced evictions as being contrary to international law.[99] The former Human Rights Commission has unanimously qualified forced evictions as 'a gross violation of a broad range of human rights'.[100] The Human Rights Committee (HRCttee) condemned forced evictions in Kenya,[101] Israel[102] and Bulgaria. In the concluding observations on Bulgaria, the HRCttee affirmed that forced evictions 'constitute potential gross violations of a wide range of internationally recognized human rights', including Arts. 17 and 26 of the ICCPR (the right not to be subjected to arbitrary or unlawful interference with privacy, family, home or correspondence and the prohibition of discrimination).[103] Regional human rights instruments have all been interpreted to prohibit forced evictions. The African Commission on Human and Peoples' Rights (ACommHPR) affirmed that the protection against forced evictions is part of the right to

[95] Maria Stavropoulou, 'Displacement and Human Rights' (1998) 20 *Human Rights Quarterly*, 3, 515–54: 517.

[96] Committee on Economic, Social and Cultural Rights, *General Comment 4 on the Right to Adequate Housing*, 13 December 1991, E/1992/23, para. 18, and Committee on Economic, Social and Cultural Rights, *General Comment 7 on the Right to Adequate Housing: Forced Evictions*, 13 December 1997, E/1997/4, para. 1.

[97] Committee on Economic, Social and Cultural Rights, *General Comment 7 on the Right to Adequate Housing: Forced Evictions*, para. 3.

[98] Ibid., para. 12.

[99] Scott Leckie, *When Push Comes to Shove* (Habitat International Coalition, 1995), 61–4, containing an overview of early statements of UN bodies on the issue of forced evictions.

[100] Forced Evictions, Resolution 1993/77, Commission on Human Rights, 10 March 1993, para. 1. See also the later resolution Prohibition of Forced Evictions, Resolution 2004/28, Commission on Human Rights, E/CN.4/2004/127, 17 April 2004, para. 1.

[101] Concluding Observations, Kenya, HRCttee, CCPR/CO/83/KEN, 29 April 2005, para. 22.

[102] Concluding Observations, Israel, HRCttee, CCPR/C/ISR/CO/3, 3 September 2010, para. 24.

[103] Concluding Observations, Bulgaria, HRCttee, CCPR/C/BGR/CO/3, 19 August 2011, para. 24.

adequate housing derived from the express rights to property, health and family and that '[t]he State's obligation to respect housing rights requires it, and thereby all of its organs and agents, to abstain from carrying out, sponsoring or tolerating any practice, policy or legal measure violating the integrity of the individual or infringing upon his or her freedom to use those material or other resources available to them in a way they find most appropriate to satisfy individual, family, household or community housing needs'.[104] The European Court of Human Rights (ECtHR) and the European Committee of Social Rights (ECttSR) have also condemned the practice.[105] The new Convention for the Protection and Assistance of Internally Displaced Persons in Africa is the first regional instrument to specifically require states to prevent political, social, cultural and economic exclusion and marginalisation likely to cause displacement of populations, complementing states' other human rights obligations.[106] In addition, as courts and reports have recognised, forced evictions cannot only constitute housing rights violations, but often have an immediate impact on the right to education, 'as children and young people are forced to move away from their schools, while increased poverty among those affected, as a result of destruction of sources of livelihoods during the forced evictions, led to long-term inability to afford education'.[107]

A particularly egregious example of forced evictions was a large-scale military operation carried out by Zimbabwean authorities in 2005. Operation Murambatsvina ('Restore Order') involved a campaign against allegedly illegal housing and commercial activities that cost some 700,000 individuals their homes, livelihoods, or both.[108] The government argued

[104] *Social and Economic Rights Action Center (SERAC) and Center for Economic and Social Rights* v. *Nigeria, Communication 155/1996, 27 October 2001*, ACommHPR, paras. 61–3 (footnotes omitted).

[105] See for instance, *Aksoy* v. *Turkey, Application No. 21987/93, 18 December 1996*, ECtHR; *COHRE* v. *Italy, Complaint No. 58/2009, 3 March 2010*, ECttSR; Aoife Nolan, 'Aggravated Violations' (2011) 11 *Human Rights Law Review*, 2, 343–61.

[106] AU Convention for the Protection and Assistance of Internally Displaced Persons in Africa, Kampala, 23 October 2009 (entered into force 6 December 2012), Art. 1b.

[107] For a report on the link between forced evictions and education, see in particular Amnesty International, *Left Behind: The Impact of Zimbabwe's Mass Forced Evictions on the Right to Education* (Amnesty International, 2011), 3. In a recent case, a Kenyan high court has recognised that the right to education was violated, in addition to other ESCR, because of a forced eviction. See *Ibrahim Osman* v. *Minister of State et al. (Garissa Eviction), Constitutional Petition No. 2 of 2011, High Court at Embu, Kenya.*

[108] Report of the UN Fact-Finding Mission to Zimbabwe, 17 July 2005, 7.

that the operation was justified as an urban clean-up.[109] Various commentators raised the question as to whether these alleged housing rights violations amounted to crimes against humanity under the Rome Statute, and several legal opinions concluded that crimes against humanity were indeed committed.[110] A UN Special Envoy on Human Settlements Issues in Zimbabwe, however, reported that the available evidence would make it 'difficult to sustain that crimes against humanity were committed'.[111] Given the uncertainties about the circumstances under which those responsible for forced evictions could be held individually responsible under international criminal law, the legal elements of the crime of deportation or forcible transfer needed to be assessed. The example of Operation Murambatsvina will be used to illustrate the main areas of legal controversies related to the qualification of forced evictions within the context of crimes against humanity.

As for all crimes against humanity, the conduct must meet the *chapeau* elements, that is it must be part of a widespread or systematic attack directed against any civilian population.[112] The UN envoy on Zimbabwe did not dispute that the massive evictions of Operation Murambatsvina constituted such an attack,[113] and the threshold elements could be established straightforwardly. Can the same be said about the other elements of the crime against humanity of deportation and forcible transfer?

### *4.3.1 The terms 'deportation' and 'forcible transfer'*

'Deportation' has been defined as the forced displacement of persons across international borders,[114] while 'forcible transfer' refers to displacement within the same state.[115] The Rome Statute affirms that it is not necessary for individuals to be transferred across an international

[109] Briefing by Minister Counsellor Zhou of the Zimbabwe High Commission, Pretoria, 7 July 2005. Cited in International Crisis Group, *Zimbabwe's Operation Murambatsvina: The Tipping Point?*, 3.

[110] Displacement Solutions, *Housing, Land and Property Rights and International Criminal Justice* (Displacement Solutions, 2012), 42; COHRE et al., 'Security Council Must Refer Zimbabwe Evictions to the International Criminal Court: Joint Media Release, May 2007', 23 May 2007.

[111] Report of the UN Fact-Finding Mission to Zimbabwe, 17 July 2005, 67.

[112] See Section 4.1.

[113] Report of the UN Fact-Finding Mission to Zimbabwe, 17 July 2005, 65–6.

[114] Charter of the IMT, Nuremberg, 8 August 1945, Art. 6(c).

[115] ILC, Draft Code of Crimes against the Peace and Security of Mankind 1996, *Yearbook of the International Law Commission*, vol. II, Part Two, 1996, Commentary on Art. 18(g), para. 3.

border.[116] A footnote in the ICC Elements of Crimes explains that 'deported or forcibly transferred' is interchangeable with 'forcibly displaced'.[117] Even though the statutes of the *ad hoc* tribunals did not include forcible transfer of population, both the ICTR and the ICTY have found that the forced transfer of populations within national borders constitutes a crime against humanity.[118] Given the number of internally displaced people[119] and the fact that violations of housing rights, such as forced evictions, most often take place within one and the same state, the absence of a requirement that international borders be crossed significantly enhances the prospects of the violation of the right to housing falling within the ambit of this crime against humanity.

Do housing rights violations as defined in human rights law amount to such transfers? They do if the following elements are met.

### *4.3.2 Expulsion or coercive acts from the area where present*

The crime requires that individuals be displaced by expulsion or coercive acts. 'The term "forcibly" is not restricted to physical force, but may include threat of force or coercion' to capture the full range of coercive pressures.[120] This is noteworthy in this discussion on ESCR violations because forced evictions can be carried out without the use of physical force. The UN special envoy in Zimbabwe was guarded against taking a stand on whether Operation Murambatsvina involved a transfer or not, since many individuals demolished their homes themselves because of pressure from the authorities. The International Crisis Group reported

[116] Rome Statute, Art. 7(1)d, referring to 'an area' rather than a state.

[117] ICC Elements of Crimes, note 13.

[118] *Prosecutor* v. *Krstić, IT-98-33-T, 2 August 2001*, ICTY, paras. 531–32; *Prosecutor* v. *Kupreškić, IT-95-16-T, 14 January 2000*, ICTY, para. 566. See also *Prosecutor* v. *Blagojević and Jokić, IT-02-60-T, 17 January 2005*, ICTY, paras. 602, 629, holding that forcible population displacements also form part of the category of other inhumane acts and that transfers within a state's borders may constitute persecution. For the history of the crime and early case law, see Triffterer (ed.), *Commentary on the Rome Statute*, 248 (Hall).

[119] It is estimated that 1 per cent of the world's population is internally displaced. Report of the Representative of the SG on the Human Rights of Internally Displaced Persons (Walter Kälin), A/HRC/10/13, 9 February 2009, para. 90.

[120] ICC Elements of Crimes, footnote 12. The definition of the term 'forcibly' in the Elements of Crimes takes over wording from the ICTR Akayesu decision interpreting the same term. *Prosecutor* v. *Akayesu, ICTR-96-4-T, 2 September 1998*, ICTR, para. 688. During the drafting, all but two states (Turkey and the UAE) supported the otherwise uncontroversial footnote. Statements Made in Plenary on the Report of the Working Group on the Rules of Procedure and Evidence and the Report of the Working Group on Elements of Crimes, PCNICC/2000/INF/4, 13 July 2000, 5, 65.

that those who did not pull down their structures fast enough were beaten by the police.[121] To constitute the crime against humanity of forced displacement, it is not required that physical force be involved in the forced eviction. Jurisprudence and the ICC Elements of Crimes confirm this interpretation. A transfer can occur even when people demolish their own homes out of fear or to salvage building materials. For instance, the ICTY in *Simić* held that '[t]he term "forced" is not limited to physical force; it may also include the "threat of force or coercion, such as that caused by fear of violence, duress, detention, psychological oppression or abuse of power against such person or persons or another person, or by taking advantage of a coercive environment"'.[122] The essential element is that the displacement is involuntary in nature: that 'the relevant persons had no real choice'.[123] What matters is the involuntary, coercive pressure to leave, and such pressure can undoubtedly originate from ESCR violations.

To constitute the crime against humanity of forced displacement, the individuals in question must have been transferred 'from the area where present'.[124] Victims of forced evictions do not necessarily always move far away from the homes or lands from which they were evicted. They may instead choose (or have no other option than) to remain close to their old homes where they would have access to work, education or their support networks. Would this affect the determination as to whether the forced evictions constitute the crime against humanity of forced displacement? The key to answering this question lies in the interpretation of the phrase 'from the area where present'. In the aftermath of Operation Murambatsvina, the UN envoy noted that some people remained close to or even on the territory of their former homes. According to her, this made it 'difficult to make a case for systematic forced expulsion'.[125]

There is scant literature on the meaning of an 'area', and the geographic distance from which victims must be transferred so as to fulfil this requirement is nowhere specified. The judicial interpretation of the

[121] International Crisis Group, *Zimbabwe's Operation Murambatsvina: The Tipping Point?*, 1.

[122] *Prosecutor* v. *Simić, IT-95-9, 17 October 2003*, ICTY, para. 125 (footnotes omitted); *Prosecutor* v. *Milošević, IT-02-54-T, Decision on Motion for Judgment of Acquittal, 16 June 2004*, ICTY, para. 75.

[123] *Prosecutor* v. *Simić, IT-95-9, 17 October 2003*, ICTY, para. 125 (footnotes omitted); *Prosecutor* v. *Milošević, IT-02-54-T, Decision on Motion for Judgment of Acquittal, 16 June 2004*, ICTY, para. 75.

[124] Rome Statute, Art. 7(2)d.

[125] Report of the UN Fact-Finding Mission to Zimbabwe, 17 July 2005, 65.

term 'area' is thus a matter that remains to be resolved by courts. When Pre-Trial Chamber II confirmed forcible transfer charges in the situation of Kenya, it specified that there were sufficient grounds to believe that people were displaced in and from various areas, such as the area of Turbo town, or 'the greater Eldoret area'.[126]

In human rights law, forced evictions can take place even if the victims stay exactly where they are. Individuals may be evicted from a flat and decide to sleep outside in the backyard of the same building. Even if victims are tolerated in the backyard, this hypothetical situation would still constitute a forced eviction. The claim that the same case would satisfy the requirement of transfer 'from the area where present' is, however, less certain. The ordinary meaning of the term 'from the area where present' requires that 'an area' – or 'a location'[127] – be left. The terms 'area' and 'location' can be used for relatively small-size units,[128] which implies that the distance between the original and the post-eviction location does not need to be large. The Latin word *locus* simply means 'place' (as in dis-placement), and the Latin origin of 'area' refers to 'a piece of ground',[129] rather than to larger geographic units such as 'a town' or 'a region'. A location or an area could therefore be as small as a street or a subdivision of a neighbourhood.

Thus, the crime of forcible transfer does require at least some geographic distance between the location of the homes or the land from where the persons were evicted and the place in which they ended up. The legislative development of the crime confirms that the object and purpose of the recognition of the crime is concerned with the forcible nature of having to leave one's home rather than the physical distance. In line with this conclusion, the ICTY Appeals Chamber in *Krnojelac* held that '[t]he prohibition against forcible displacements aims at safeguarding the right and aspiration of individuals to live in their communities and

[126] *Prosecutor* v. *Ruto, Kiprono Kosgey and Arap Sang, Decision on the Confirmation of Charges, 23 January 2012, Pre-Trial Chamber II, ICC-01/09-01/11*, ICC, paras. 251–4.

[127] ICC Elements of Crimes, Art. 7(1)d, element 1. Here, the word 'location' is used instead of 'area'.

[128] COHRE and Zimbabwe Lawyers for Human Rights, 'Operation Murambatsvina: A Crime against Humanity' (COHRE, ZLHR, May 2007), 30. Presumably, the authors considered that it was necessary to argue that an area is a unit of considerable size in order to argue that the individuals were 'lawfully present'. This interpretation should not be retained. It is not the size of the area that matters for the element of lawful presence. See Section 4.3.3.

[129] Oxford University Press, *Shorter Oxford English Dictionary* (Oxford University Press, 2007), 114–15.

homes without outside interference'.[130] Hence, even a short distance between the old and new locations could meet the requirement that people were transferred 'from the area where present'. In the vast majority of evictions, victims will have left an easily distinguishable 'area'. It is only in those cases of eviction where victims stay exactly at the same location that the eviction is difficult to qualify as the *actus reus* of a forcible transfer as a crime against humanity. In relation to the victims of Operation Murambatsvina, the issue only arises in respect to those individuals who did not move to other areas but instead stayed where they were. The requirement of transfer was met for those who, for instance, remained in Harare, but who left their location (e.g., by moving to a different 'location' within Harare). The existence of a transfer is, however, lacking for the victims who remained in the location of their former homes, staying, for example, on the same plot. Yet this finding is unsatisfactory. Those who stay behind may be the most vulnerable survivors and may have nowhere else to go, but they may not qualify as victims of the crime of forcible transfer. While human rights law prohibits forced eviction regardless of where people end up, the requirement of a transfer 'from the area' leads to disqualifying some evictions as forcible transfers despite the fact that they are carried out within one and the same broader attack against a civilian population in which other qualified forcible transfers occur.

While unsatisfactory, this limitation should not be overstated. The definitions of a 'transfer from an area' and of 'forced evictions' will, in the vast majority of cases, be congruent. OHCHR even includes the phrase 'movement from an area' within the definition of forced evictions,[131] indicating that most victims of evictions do leave the area in which they were originally present. In any event, even if some forced evictions are disqualified in the context of a widespread or systematic attack against a civilian population, those who did not leave the location may nevertheless have suffered other crimes against humanity such as inhumane acts or persecution. It thereby follows that attempts to prosecute the crime against humanity of forced displacement in relation to forced evictions should be done after it is ascertained whether some of the victims had to stay behind in the same location. In the

[130] *Prosecutor* v. *Krnojelac, IT-97-25-A, 17 September 2003*, ICTY, para. 218. This relationship between this international crime and housing rights was further studied by Guido Acquaviva, 'Displacement', in *Legal and Protection Policy Research Series* (UNHCR, 2011), 16.

[131] OHCHR, Forced Evictions and Human Rights, Factsheet No. 25, OHCHR, 1996, 6.

latter case, the accused might be convicted on the basis of crimes against those victims who left the area, but alternative charges may need to be considered if those who stayed behind should obtain a remedy.

### 4.3.3 *Lawfully present*

The crime of deportation or forcible transfer also requires the evictees to have been lawfully present in the area from which they were removed. The function of this element is to maintain a state's right to regulate entry into its territory. The requirement of lawful presence is usually straightforward as far as deportation across national borders is concerned, but it is delicate with regard to forcible transfers within national borders. Forced evictions often affect vulnerable members of society who may find themselves in a difficult legal situation even before the eviction. Many victims of Operation Murambatsvina, for instance, had established their residence unlawfully, and lacked valid leases, construction permits, permits for commercial activities or simply personal documentation. Does absence of such documents make their presence unlawful? The government of Zimbabwe argued that the victims were not lawfully present in the area because they did not have construction permits or were trading in the informal sector without valid authorisations.[132]

The ordinary meaning of the phrase 'lawfully present', the drafting history and other international instruments clearly indicate that the requirement refers to a general legal presence on the state's territory rather than to domestic law on residence or possession. The HRCttee concluded that national legislation may subject the entry of an alien to the state's territory to restrictions, provided they are in compliance with the state's international obligations. In *Celepli* v. *Sweden*, an alien was considered to be lawfully present within Sweden despite the fact that he was only allowed to stay in certain municipalities and did not fully comply with these restrictions.[133] If an individual is a national of the state on whose territory the forced eviction occurs, or if the individual has a legal right to be present anywhere in that particular state, the element of lawful presence is met even though the individual simultaneously carries out activities for which he or she may lack a valid permit.

[132] Zimbabwe, Response by the Government of Zimbabwe to the Report by the UN Special Envoy on Operation Murambatsvina/Restore Order, August 2005, para. 3.5.13.

[133] *Celepli* v. *Sweden, 26 July 1994, CCPR/C/51/D/456/1991*, HRCttee, para. 4.5.

Interpreting the element of lawful presence by reference to any practices illegal under domestic law is therefore erroneous. The ordinary meaning of lawful presence in an area is to be distinguished from the legal background of residence or an activity carried out.[134] It merely implies that the individuals must be lawfully present in that state's territory. Such an understanding can be confirmed from the drafting history of the provision on forcible transfers under the Rome Statute; delegations at the negotiations of the ICC Statute exclusively referred to the presence on state territory and were cautious not to have lawful expulsion from a state's territory accidentally caught by Art. 7.[135] This was the concern that led to the introduction of the 'lawful presence' criterion in Art. 7(2)d of the Rome Statute, but no delegation raised the issue with regard to internal transfers. This supports the claim that the legality of exploitation or occupation under domestic law could not have been the issue.[136] Reading this requirement differently would render the criminalisation of transfers within state borders meaningless since a state could simply invoke its domestic law to give a specific interpretation to key terms in an international treaty with the aim of shielding itself from responsibility. This is an approach that is evidently unsupported by general international law.[137]

### 4.3.4 *Without grounds permitted under international law*

International law sometimes permits the displacement of individuals from an area. The prosecution bears the burden of demonstrating the absence of any justification on grounds permitted under international law. There are abundant examples of justifications advanced for evictions,[138] often relating to promises of social or economic progress. How, then, can it be determined if displacement was carried out in accordance with international law? First, it is necessary to determine where, under international law, such grounds potentially exist. Human rights law is the most relevant branch to consider. If the forced evictions

[134] This point is also made by COHRE and Zimbabwe Lawyers for Human Rights, 'Operation Murambatsvina: A Crime against Humanity', 10.

[135] Report of the Preparatory Committee for the Establishment of the ICC, Official Records, March/April–August 1996, para. 95.

[136] Triffterer (ed.), *Commentary on the Rome Statute*, 250 (Hall).

[137] VCLT, Art. 27.

[138] For examples of justifications advanced by states, see Final Report of the Special Rapporteur on Freedom of Movement: Human Rights and Population Transfer (Awn Al-Khasawneh), E/CN.4/Sub.2/1997/23, 27 June 1997.

arose in a situation of armed conflict, it must further be examined whether the applicable rules of international humanitarian law (IHL) contain any grounds permitting the displacement.

#### 4.3.4.1 Human rights law

As mentioned, a state is generally allowed to deport aliens from its territory. The scope of lawful deportation of aliens is however limited under international law.[139] Human rights law also sets out instances where deportation of nationals is prohibited.[140] If the deportation does not fall within the restrictions imposed by human rights (and refugee law), then the removal across state borders would be for permissible reasons and the evictions do not fall within the definition of deportation as a crime against humanity.

In cases of displacement *within* state borders, human rights law implicitly provides for the right of every human being to be protected against arbitrary displacement from his or her home.[141] The prosecution will bear the burden to prove the absence of any justification under the applicable legal regimes. There is abundant jurisprudence on the exceptional circumstances in which evictions are permissible under international human rights law. To summarise, evictions within state borders

[139] The most relevant principle is the principle of non-refoulement, which prohibits removing an individual to places where his or her fundamental rights would be threatened. For references to treaties, see Guy Goodwin-Gill, *International Law and the Movement of Persons between States* (Clarendon Press, 1978).

[140] International Covenant on Civil and Political Rights, GA Res. 2200a (XXI), 999 UNTS 171, 16 December 1966 (entered into force 23 March 1976), Art. 12(4): 'No one shall be arbitrarily deprived of the right to enter his own country.' African Charter on Human and Peoples' Rights, Adopted June 27, 1981, 21 ILM 58 (1982), Art. 12(2); American Convention on Human Rights, 1144 UNTS 123, entered into force July 18, 1978, Art. 22(5); European Convention for the Protection of Human Rights and Fundamental Freedoms, as amended by Protocol Nos. 11 and 14, Rome, 4 November 1950 (entered into force with Protocol 14: 1 June 2010), Protocol 4, Art. 3; Guiding Principles on Internal Displacement, E/CN.4/1998/53/Add.2, 11 February 1998, Principle 6(1).

[141] This protection can be derived from a number of human rights safeguards. For instance, International Covenant on Economic, Social and Cultural Rights, GA Res. 2200a (XXI), 16 December 1966 (entered into force 3 January 1976), Art. 11(1) (right to housing); ICCPR, Art. 17 (freedom from unlawful or arbitrary interference with the home). See also Guiding Principles on Internal Displacement, E/CN.4/1998/53/Add.2, 11 February 1998, Principles 5–9. A right to be protected against arbitrary displacement is explicit in the African Convention for the Protection and Assistance of Internally Displaced Persons and in relation to indigenous and tribal peoples. See Kampala Convention, Art. 3. And ILO Convention No. 169 Concerning Indigenous and Tribal Peoples in Independent Countries, ILO Official Bulletin, Vol. LXXII (1989) Ser. A, No. 2 (entered into force 5 September 1991), Art. 16.

may be permissible on 'grounds permitted under international law' if, and only if, the following criteria – derived from the work of the CESCR, regional bodies and other entities – are cumulatively met. As such, evictions

- must have a legitimate purpose and the aim sought must be sufficiently serious to warrant the harm caused by the evictions;[142]
- must be proportional to the aim sought and the state must have evaluated all alternatives and taken appropriate steps to mitigate the harm caused;[143]
- must not be carried out using disproportionate force;[144]
- must not violate other human rights.[145] Since the prohibition of torture or cruel, inhuman or degrading treatment is absolute, evictions must never amount to inhuman or degrading treatment or torture. In *Selçuk and Asker* v. *Turkey*, the ECtHR found that the evictions in that particular case amounted to inhuman and degrading treatment. In such a case, the underlying motive for evictions is irrelevant.[146] Any evictions breaching the prohibition of torture or inhuman treatment are not justified under international law;

[142] This follows from the requirement that evictions are *prima facie* a violation of the right to housing. Evictions therefore require a legitimate purpose. See Note 97.

[143] Committee on Economic, Social and Cultural Rights, *General Comment 7 on the Right to Adequate Housing: Forced Evictions*, para. 14; Basic Principles and Guidelines on Development-Based Evictions and Displacement, A/HRC/4/18, Annex 1, 5 February 2007, para. 21. Relying on GC 4 of the CESCR, the ACHPR affirmed that forced evictions could only be justified in the 'most exceptional circumstances' and after 'all feasible alternatives' to eviction have been explored in consultation with the affected community. *Endorois Welfare Council* v. *Kenya, Communication 276/2003, 4 February 2010*, ACommHPR, para. 200. The ECtHR found the proportionality requirement to be infringed because the eviction order was ordered automatically and without considering the applicant's interests. *Gladysheva* v. *Russia, Application No. 7097/10, 6 December 2011*, ECtHR, paras. 93–7.

[144] The requirement that the use of force be proportionate is a general requirement of law enforcement. ICCPR, Arts. 6(1) and 9(1); Basic Principles on the Use of Force and Firearms by Law Enforcement Officials, Adopted by the 8th UN Congress on the Prevention of Crime and the Treatment of Offenders, 7 September 1990, in particular Principles 4 and 5; UN Code of Conduct for Law Enforcement Officials, GA Res. 34/169, 17 December 1979, Art. 3. See also Basic Principles and Guidelines on Development-Based Evictions and Displacement, A/HRC/4/18, Annex 1, 5 February 2007, para. 48.

[145] Committee on Economic, Social and Cultural Rights, *General Comment 4 on the Right to Adequate Housing*, para. 18; Committee on Economic, Social and Cultural Rights, *General Comment 7 on the Right to Adequate Housing: Forced Evictions*, para. 14.

[146] *Selçuk and Asker* v. *Turkey, Application Nos. 23184/94, 23185/94, 24 April 1998*, ECtHR, paras. 72–80.

- must be non-arbitrary and non-discriminatory.[147] The term 'arbitrary' has been interpreted in General Comment (GC) 16 of the HRCttee and by the ECtHR and extends to interference with the right to privacy provided for by law.[148] Even if a home was constructed without a valid permit, interference with the home is not automatically rendered lawful.[149] The ECtHR similarly held that the term 'home' under the ECHR extends to dwellings unlawfully established,[150] and the ECttSR repeatedly found forced evictions to be inconsistent with the conditions required by the European Social Charter even in cases where sites or dwellings were unlawfully occupied.[151] The protection of one's home does not automatically expire in cases where individuals have been away from their home, for instance, instance after having fled the region because of political instability.[152] The right to be free from arbitrary interference with the home also implies that a state must not provide military and logistic support to paramilitary troops carrying out unlawful forced evictions.[153]

[147] ICESCR, Art. 2(2). See also Principles on Housing and Property Restitution for Refugees and Displaced Persons (Pinheiro Principles), E/CN.4/2006/2 at 39, Sub-Commission on the Promotion of the Protection of Human Rights, 28 June 2005, Principles 3–5.

[148] Human Rights Committee, *General Comment 16 on the Right to Respect of Privacy, Family, Home and Correspondence, and Protection of Honour and Reputation*, 23 March 1988, A/43/40 (1988), para. 4. Forced transfers have repeatedly been found to amount to breaches of Art. 8 of the ECHR (respect for private and family life, home and correspondence). *Cyprus* v. *Turkey, Application No. 25781/94, 10 May 2001*, ECtHR Grand Chamber, 175; *Mentes and Others* v. *Turkey, Application No. 23186/94, 28 November 1997*, ECtHR Grand Chamber, para. 73. Or: *Akdivar et al.* v. *Turkey, Application No. 99/1995/605/693, 16 September 1996*, ECtHR Grand Chamber, para. 88.

[149] Concluding Observations, Israel, HRCttee, CCPR/C/79/Add.93, 18 August 1998, para. 24. The HRCttee considers the demolition of 'illegally' constructed Arab homes to conflict directly with the obligation of the state party to ensure without discrimination the right not to be subjected to arbitrary interference with one's home.

[150] *Buckley* v. *United Kingdom, Application No. 20348/92, 25 September 1996*, ECtHR, paras. 52–5, concluding that Art. 8 was applicable even if the residence was not lawfully established; *Chapman* v. *United Kingdom, Application No. 27238/95, 18 January 2001*, ECtHR Grand Chamber, paras. 68–70, holding the right applicable to a mobile home established in a plot of land despite the refusal of planning permission to station caravans on the applicant's land.

[151] *ERRC* v. *Bulgaria, Complaint No. 31/2005, 18 October 2006*, ECttSR, para. 57; *ERRC* v. *Italy, Complaint No. 27/2004, 7 December 2005*, ECttSR, paras. 42, 46; *ERRC* v. *Greece, Complaint No. 15/2003, 8 December 2004*, ECttSR, para. 51.

[152] *Khamidov* v. *Russia, Application No. 72118/01, 15 November 2007*, ECtHR, para. 127. In this case, a Russian family abandoned their home in Chechnya. The government unsuccessfully claimed that the police forces could therefore lawfully occupy the applicant's estate.

[153] *Ituango Massacres* v. *Colombia, Judgment (Preliminary Objections, Merits, Reparations and Costs), 1 July 2006*, IACtHR, para. 7.

- As with other human rights, procedural protection is an essential aspect of the right to housing. Evictions are only permitted under international law if procedural safeguards have been met.[154] International law does therefore not provide grounds for evictions that infringe on procedural guarantees. The UN special envoy in Zimbabwe concluded that Operation Murambatsvina clearly failed to comply with such safeguards,[155] and the Zimbabwean authorities did not have grounds under international law that would have permitted the forced evictions.

The prosecution needs to demonstrate that the conduct of the perpetrator(s) was not justified by showing that the evictions were incompatible with the criteria outlined above. Furthermore, the prosecution must analyse whether the evictions could be permitted under international law by virtue of limitations or derogations. As explained in Chapter 3, restrictive criteria apply for derogating or limiting ESCR.[156] In particular, limitations must be 'compatible with the nature of [the right], enacted solely for the purpose of promoting the general welfare in a democratic society',[157] and limitations to housing rights should not result in homelessness.[158] If a treaty with a limitations clause, such as the ICESCR, applies to a specific case of evictions in the context of a widespread or systematic attack against a civilian population, the prosecution is prudent to demonstrate that the state could not have limited the right to housing in such a way as to allow for reasons permitting the evictions under international law.

#### 4.3.4.2 International humanitarian law

If forced evictions take place in a situation of armed conflict, the prosecution will also need to show that there were no grounds under IHL permitting the evictions. In an international armed conflict, deportation *from* occupied territory is usually prohibited under conventional and customary international law.[159] It amounts to a grave breach, with the

154 Committee on Economic, Social and Cultural Rights, *General Comment 7 on the Right to Adequate Housing: Forced Evictions*, para. 15, listing specific procedural protections.

155 Report of the UN Fact-Finding Mission to Zimbabwe, 17 July 2005, 26 and Section 6.3.

156 See Section 3.2.1.3.

157 ICESCR, Art. 4.

158 Committee on Economic, Social and Cultural Rights, *General Comment 7 on the Right to Adequate Housing: Forced Evictions*, para. 16.

159 Convention (IV) Relative to the Protection of Civilian Persons in Time of War, TIAS No. 3365, 75 UNTS 287, 12 August 1949 (entered into force 21 October 1950), Arts. 49 and 147; Jean-Marie Henckaerts and Louise Doswald-Beck, (eds.), *Customary IHL*, 2 vols., vol. 1 (Cambridge University Press, 2005), Rules 129–32.

sole exception that 'the occupying power may undertake total or partial evacuation of a given area if the security of the population or imperative military reasons so demand'.[160] Displacement purely incidental to combat operations would be permissible where civilians, for instance, flee lawful bombardment by the enemy. With no exceptions, states may not deport or transfer, forcibly or not, parts of their own civilian population *into* a territory they occupy.[161] In a non-international armed conflict, it is prohibited to compel civilians to leave their own territory for reasons connected with the conflict unless the security of the civilians involved or imperative military reasons so demand.[162] Hence, in any armed conflict, internal displacement is only allowed in narrowly defined exceptional circumstances and on a temporary basis.[163]

In sum, permissible grounds for forced displacement are narrow, both in times of armed conflict as well as in times of peace. Where they are absent, it may be possible to argue that housing rights violations overlap with a crime against humanity.

The elements discussed above, including the absence of permissible grounds, need to be present in order to substantiate the claim that forced evictions can be qualified as a crime against humanity of forced displacement – provided of course that they take place in the context of a widespread or systematic attack against a civilian population. Cases of forced evictions meeting these requirements show that it is possible to find overlap between violations of the right to housing defined in human rights law and crimes against humanity giving rise to criminal responsibility. With reference to the case study referred to above, provided that the factual background of Operation Murambatsvina was correctly reported by the UN envoy, all but a very few victims of

160 GVA IV, Arts. 49 and 147.

161 Ibid., Art. 49; Protocol Additional to the Geneva Conventions of 12 August 1949, and Relating to the Protection of Victims of International Armed Conflicts, 1125 UNTS 3, 8 June 1977 (entered into force 7 December 1978), Art. 85(4)a.

162 Protocol Additional to the Geneva Conventions of 12 August 1949, and Relating to the Protection of Victims of Non-International Armed Conflicts, 1125 UNTS 609, 8 June 1977 (entered into force 7 December 1978), Art. 17(2); Henckaerts and Doswald-Beck (eds.), *Customary IHL*, vol. 1, Rules 129, 31, 32 are held to be applicable both in international armed conflict (IAC) and in armed conflict not of an international character (NIAC).

163 GVA IV, Art. 49; AP II, Art. 17; Guiding Principles on Internal Displacement, E/CN.4/1998/53/Add.2, 11 February 1998, Principles 5–8. See also *Prosecutor* v. *Simić, IT-95-9, 17 October 2003*, ICTY, note 218. For a comprehensive review of the prohibition of forced displacement in armed conflicts, see Mélanie Jacques, *Armed Conflict and Displacement* (Cambridge University Press, 2012).

evictions also qualify as victims of the crime of forcible transfer. Yet, in reality, the crimes in Zimbabwe have not been addressed, and 'despite existing frameworks, perpetrators continue to commit this crime with impunity'.[164]

Shortly before this book went to press, the ECCC issued an important decision which confirms the significance of the possible overlap between forcible population movements in the context of crimes against humanity and violations of ESCR. In August 2014, the ECCC delivered the first trial judgment of Case 002 after the ECCC ordered the division of Case 002 into a series of smaller trials in fall 2011, deciding to commence with the forced movement of population. The ECCC Trial Chamber justified this move by emphasising that '[t]he forced movement of population also affected a very broad cross-section of the Cambodian population at the time'.[165] In the 630-page judgment delivered in summer 2014, the trial chamber convicted the accused on the basis of forcibly transferring at least 2 million people.[166] Between approximately 2,000 and 20,000 people died due to the fact that they were already weakened from food shortages and 'forced to march to rural areas in the hottest time of the year and in the almost complete absence of food, water, medical care, accommodation or transportation'.[167] The judgment is highly significant for the arguments made in this chapter that forcibly transferring populations can go hand in hand with gross ESCR violations and can be successfully prosecuted as a crime against humanity. Of particular interest is the chamber's unequivocal rejection of the contention by the defence that forced transfer did not form part of customary international law at the time of the events between 1975 and 1979 because acts of forced transfer would not be as serious as other international crimes and because 'displacement for economic purposes was widely practiced prior to, during and immediately following the temporal jurisdiction of the ECCC' and could therefore not be considered a crime against humanity.[168] The chamber also convincingly dismissed the alternative argument made by

[164] Federico Andreu-Guzman, 'Forced Displacement', in *Transitional Justice and Displacement*, ed. Roger Duthie (Social Science Research Council, 2012), 233–53: 253.

[165] 'Severance of Proceedings Ordered in Case 002, Press Release, 22 September 2011', www.eccc.gov.kh/en/articles/severance-proceedings-ordered-case-002.

[166] *Noun Chea and Khieu Samphan*, Judgment, Case 002/19-09/2007/ECCC/TC, 7 August 2014, para. 520. The displacement was prosecuted under the heading of 'other inhumane acts' as the Law on the Establishment of the ECCC does not explicitly list forcible transfer as a crime against humanity (as was the case with the statutes of the *ad hoc* tribunals).

[167] Ibid., para. 459. See also para. 491.

[168] Ibid., paras. 452–3.

the defence that the food shortage and economic conditions in Phnom Penh were permissible grounds justifying the forced transfer.[169] The chamber held that the transfer was based on a 'pre-established plan and generalised policy' with little to no consideration for the socio-economic well-being and the dignity of the affected population.[170] Noting that the regime 'had control of all transportation routes ... which could have been used to allow supplies to come in' and that it refused to accept humanitarian assistance,[171] the chamber dismissed the argument of the defence that the transfer pursued 'a legitimate resettlement policy aiming to regenerate the economy and hence alleviate humanitarian conditions in Phnom Penh'.[172] The chamber added hypothetically that even if the justifications had been established, the transfer and the conditions in which it occurred failed to satisfy the requirement of proportionality.[173]

The judgment focused on two major population movements and the execution of military and civilian personnel on political grounds. Other abuses are to be considered in the subsequent trials pertaining to Case 002, which may lead to further developments of the case law.

## 4.4 Enslavement

This section discusses the link between the crime against humanity of enslavement and two separate, but related ESCR violations. The two ESCR violations discussed in relation to enslavement are, first, the right to work and, second, the right to just and favourable conditions of work. Under certain conditions, these violations of ESCR will be part of the factual ingredients of the crime against humanity of enslavement and can therefore be addressed through international criminal law. Outside the context of crimes against humanity, abusive labour practices can still constitute international crimes if they amount to slavery and related practices dealt with in Chapter 7.[174] Before it is possible to conclude that ESCR violations of the right to work and the right to just and favourable conditions of work can be part of the factual background of enslavement cases, it is necessary to spell out the basis on which forced labour constitutes a violation of the right to work and the right to just and favourable conditions of work.

[169] Ibid., paras. 525 and 535–40. [170] Ibid. para. 541. [171] Ibid., paras. 538–40.
[172] Ibid., para. 549. [173] Ibid., para. 550. [174] See Section 7.1.

### *4.4.1 Forced labour as a violation of the right to work and the failure to provide just and favourable conditions of work*

Forced labour is a violation of the right to work and the right to just and favourable conditions of work. In Art. 6 of the ICESCR, for instance, states recognise 'the right of everyone to the opportunity to gain his living by work he freely chooses or accepts'.[175] The reference to free acceptance of work means that (in the absence of permissible exceptions under general international law) forced labour is prohibited under the covenant,[176] complementing a wide range of other instruments prohibiting forced labour. The committee expressed concern about forced labour in relation to the right to work and the right to just and favourable conditions of work in GC 18,[177] as well as in more than thirty concluding observations, for the first time in 1994 in relation to debt bondage in Mali.[178]

Numerous other instruments protect individuals against forced labour as well as against unjust and unfavourable conditions of work. ILO Convention No. 29 prohibits forced labour except in narrowly defined exceptions.[179] A further treaty, ILO Convention No. 105, categorically prohibits states to make use of any form of forced labour as a means of political coercion, for purposes of economic development or re-education or as a means of labour discipline.[180] The ICCPR prohibits forced labour in a non-derogable provision and only allows for exceptions in cases of court-sanctioned labour, work or service, service of a military character (or national service required by law of conscientious objectors) or services exacted in cases of national emergency or calamity.[181] The Convention on

[175] ICESCR, Art. 6(1).

[176] Committee on Economic, Social and Cultural Rights, *General Comment 18 on the Right to Work*, 6 February 2006, E/C.12/GC/18, paras. 32–4. The same conclusion can be drawn from the ordinary meaning of the term opportunity and from Art. 5 of the Covenant prohibiting any activity aimed at the destruction of any of the rights or freedoms recognised in the Covenant. Matthew Craven, *The ICESCR* (Clarendon Press, 1995), 198. For the drafting history, see also 218–19; Nicolas Valticos, *International Labour Law* (Kluwer, 1979), 98.

[177] Committee on Economic, Social and Cultural Rights, *General Comment 18 on the Right to Work*, para. 6.

[178] Concluding Observations, Mali, E/C.12/1994/17, 21 December 1994, para. 8.

[179] ILO Convention No. 29 Concerning Forced or Compulsory Labour, 39 UNTS 55, 28 June 1930 (entered into force 1 May 1932). For the exceptions, see Section 4.4.2.

[180] ILO Convention No. 105 Concerning the Abolition of Forced Labour, 320 UNTS 291, 25 June 1957 (entered into force 17 January 1959), Art. 1.

[181] ICCPR, Art. 8. The list of permissible exceptions is similar to ILO Convention No. 29 (Forced Labour, 1930), Art. 2(2).

the Protection of the Rights of All Migrant Workers and Members of Their Families prohibits slavery and servitude as well as the forced labour of migrants or members of their families.[182] Regional instruments further emphasise the prohibition of compulsory labour.[183] In a case before a US district tribunal, it was undisputed, including by the defendants, that forced labour is a violation of international law.[184]

The institution of forced labour has both a particular impact on the right to work, and it is also undisputed that state obligations under the covenant and other instruments on ESCR are violated if just and favourable conditions of work are not provided. The ILO pioneered much of the contemporary legal framework on conditions of work, such as maximum hours of work, health and safety regulations.[185] In forced labour contexts, conditions of work most often fail to comply with elementary standards of what could be considered 'just and favourable', and it is this type of scenario that lends itself to demonstrate the overlap between enslavement and violations of the right to work and the right to just and favourable conditions.

An illustration of the possible overlap between the violations of ESCR and the crime of enslavement is provided by allegations concerning Burma/Myanmar and North Korea. The Irish Centre for Human Rights concluded that the Rohingya population, a minority in Burma/Myanmar, was a victim of enslavement.[186] Numerous reports documented that the social and economic rights of the Rohingyas are/were grossly violated, including the rights to work and to just and favourable

[182] International Convention on the Protection of the Rights of All Migrant Workers and Members of Their Families, GA Res. 45/158, 18 December 1990 (entered into force 1 July 2003), Art. 11.

[183] For a comprehensive overview of regional instruments, see Peter Robbins and Kevin Bales, 'No One Shall Be Held in Slavery or Servitude' (2001), 2 *Human Rights Review*, 2, 18–45. The youngest regional treaty, not yet included in the cited study, equally prohibits compulsory labour: Arab Charter on Human Rights (Revised), 22 May 2004 (entered into force 15 March 2008), Art. 10.

[184] *Roe et al* v. *Bridgestone, (Sd Ind.) 492 F Supp. 2d 988 (2007)*, USA, 1016–22. See also *Doe I.* v. *Unocal, 395 F.3d 932 (9th Cir. 2002)*, USA, 946, for the finding that forced labour violates international law. Although vacated, the opinion is cited for its authority that forced labour constitutes a violation of the law of nations.

[185] See for instance ILO Convention No. 155 Concerning Occupational Safety and Health and the Working Environment, 1331 UNTS 279, 1 August 1983 (entered into force 22 June 1981); ICESCR, Art. 7.

[186] Irish Centre for Human Rights, *Crimes against Humanity in Western Burma* (University of Ireland, 2010).

conditions of work.[187] The conclusion that such violations could amount to crimes against humanity is not new. In 2006, the Governing Body of the ILO recommended that the Security Council refer the situation to the ICC, estimating that the requirements of crimes against humanity might be proven in relation to the exaction of forced labour.[188] Previously, the ILO Commission of Inquiry on Myanmar reported that acts of enslavement could have been committed.[189] Already in 2009, the ILO shared documentation with the Prosecutor of the ICC.[190] A report by Harvard Law School also found that enslavement as a crime against humanity was being committed in Burma,[191] and reports of a UN special rapporteur indicate that the gross human rights violations were the result of a state policy and 'may entail categories of crimes against humanity'.[192] Similarly, a recent UN inquiry concluded that enslavement is also committed in North Korea because of the exaction of forced labour as a crime against humanity.[193]

### *4.4.2 The exercise of any or all of the powers attaching to the right of ownership over a person*

Where the threshold elements of crimes against humanity are met, enslavement 'means the exercise of any or all of the powers attaching to

[187] ILO, Report of the Commission of Inquiry under Article 26 of the Constitution of the ILO to Examine the Observance by Myanmar of the Forced Labour Convention, 1998, 219, Conclusions, noting that the government is in flagrant violation of the Convention. Two years later, the ILO Governing Body adopted a resolution noting ongoing forced labour. ILO Governing Body, Measures Recommended under Article 33 of the Constitution – Implementation of Recommendations of the Commission of Inquiry Entitled Forced Labour in Myanmar, 88th session, 2000; Report of the Special Rapporteur on the Situation of Human Rights in Myanmar (Tomás Quintana), A/HRC/10/19, 2009, para. 65.

[188] ILO Governing Body, Developments Concerning the Question of the Observance by the Government of Myanmar of the Forced Labour Convention, GB.297/8/2, November 2006, paras. 20–4.

[189] ILO, Report of the Commission of Inquiry under Article 26 of the Constitution of the ILO to Examine the Observance by Myanmar of the Forced Labour Convention, 1998, para. 543.

[190] International Labour Conference, Committee on the Application of Standards, Question of the Observance by the Government of Myanmar of the Forced Labour Convention, 98th session, 2009, para. 14.

[191] Harvard Law School Human Rights Clinic, *Crimes in Burma* (Harvard Law School, 2009), 101.

[192] Progress Report of the Special Rapporteur on the Situation of Human Rights in Myanmar (Tomás Quintana), A/HRC/13/48, 10 March 2010, para. 121.

[193] North Korea Inquiry, A/HRC/25/CRP.1, 7 February 2014, paras. 1048–9.

the right of ownership over a person and includes the exercise of such power in the course of trafficking in persons, in particular women and children'.[194] It is warranted to enquire what is meant by 'the exercise of any or all of the powers attaching to the right of ownership over a person', in particular whether this may cover forced labour. For the purposes of the Rome Statute, the ICC Elements of Crimes specify that this phrase means that '[t]he perpetrator exercised any or all of the powers attaching to the right of ownership over one or more persons, such as by purchasing, selling, lending or bartering such a person or persons, or by imposing on them a similar deprivation of liberty'.[195] The ICC Elements of Crimes thus make clear that the crime of enslavement is not limited to practices related to commercial activities, nor does it require physical deprivation of liberty or sexual exploitation.[196] This aspect is important and implies that the area of overlap between labour-related ESCR abuses and enslavement is potentially significant. The Pre-Trial Chamber I of the ICC held that the list on forms of deprivation of liberty was illustrative and that enslavement could be committed without any commercial dimension.[197] In the trial against Charles Taylor, a trial chamber of the SCSL also confirmed that abducting civilians to force them to carry loads, collect arms, perform domestic chores and find food amounted to the exercise of powers of ownership.[198] In a domestic case, the concept of ownership has equally been interpreted to refer to a factual situation. An Australian high court convicted a brothel owner who purchased five women from Thailand to work in debt bondage conditions. The court accepted that the concept of ownership can refer to a *de facto* condition, rather than the fact of holding legal title.[199]

Labour-related abuses amounting to international crimes may occur in various forms. Traditional slavery – often referred to as 'chattel slavery' – undoubtedly gives rise to criminal liability, including outside the context of crimes against humanity.[200] It is covered by the crime against humanity of enslavement where it is part of a widespread or systematic attack

[194] Rome Statute, Art. 7(2)c. [195] ICC Elements of Crimes, Art. 7(1)c.

[196] Schabas, *Commentary on the Rome Statute*, 161.

[197] *Prosecutor* v. *Katanga and Chui, Decision on the Confirmation of Charges, 30 September 2008, Pre-Trial Chamber I, ICC-01/04-01/07*, ICC, para. 431.

[198] *Prosecutor* v. *Taylor, SCSL-03-1-T, 26 April 2012*, SCSL, paras. 1663–754 (the legal conclusion can be found in para. 1753).

[199] *R* v. *Wei Tang [2006] VCC 637, Melbourne Criminal Court, Australia.*

[200] See Section 7.1 for slavery-related abuses independent of crimes against humanity.

against a civilian population.[201] The above-mentioned considerations imply that international law also addresses contemporary forms of slavery-like practices such as servitude, debt bondage, forced labour and human trafficking. But are these contemporary slavery-like practices that often also give rise to simultaneous ESCR violations covered by the crime against humanity of enslavement? It must be noted that the concept of slavery is distinct from forced labour,[202] and overlap between enslavement and work-related abuses is therefore not obvious. While slavery is clearly a form of enslavement, careful analysis is needed before a similar conclusion can be drawn for related practices.

In a first step, it must be examined whether a factual situation of labour-related abuses does not fall within one of the exceptions under international law before we can analyse whether the element of a 'similar deprivation of liberty' constituting the 'exercise of any or all of the powers attaching to the right of ownership' is met. Forced labour is defined in ILO Convention No. 29 as 'all work or service that is exacted from any person under the menace of any penalty and for which the said person has not offered himself [or herself] voluntarily'.[203] Permissible exceptions are limited. The exceptions are (i) compulsory military service; (ii) work forming part of an individual's normal civil obligations; (iii) prison labour; (iv) work necessary in cases of emergency; and (v) communal services of benefit to the community in question.[204] In armed conflict, domestic law and human rights law continue to prohibit forced labour, while IHL foresees an additional permissive exception for the tolerance of certain forms of labour, namely an occupying power can compel protected persons to complete certain forms of labour, but only if the individuals are older than eighteen years, and only if the work is necessary for the needs of the occupying army or for public utility services.[205]

[201] *Prosecutor* v. *Kunarac, Kovac and Vukovic, IT-96-23-A, 12 June 2002*, ICTY, para. 117; *Prosecutor* v. *Kunarac, Kovac and Vukovic, IT-96-23-T, 22 February 2001*, ICTY, para. 541.

[202] Slavery Convention, Geneva, 25 September 1926, as amended on 7 December 1953 (entered into force with amendments, 7 July 1955). Compare the wording of Arts. 2 and 5 of the convention. The High Contracting Parties undertake to bring about the complete abolition of slavery in all its forms, while forced labour may only be exacted in exceptional circumstances. See also Cherif Bassiouni, 'Enslavement' (1991) 232 *Journal of International Law and Politics*, 445–517: 468. That slavery and forced labour are separate concepts also follows from the ICCPR, which treats them in two separate paragraphs of the same provision. ICCPR, Art. 8.

[203] ILO Convention No. 29 (Forced Labour, 1930), Art. 2(1). [204] Ibid., Art. 2(2).

[205] GVA IV, Art. 51.

In a non-international armed conflict, AP II expressly protects the concept of just and favourable conditions of work for persons whose liberty has been restricted and requires that those made to work have the benefit of working conditions and safeguards similar to those enjoyed by the local civilian population.[206]

In the absence of permissible exceptions, does prohibited forced labour constitute the 'exercise of the powers attaching to the right of ownership'? For the purposes of the Rome Statute, a footnote to the first element of enslavement affirms that forced labour is indeed 'a similar deprivation of liberty' forming part of enslavement.[207] Jurisprudence and doctrine confirm that forced labour is included in the definition of enslavement. In the *Pohl* case, the Nuremberg tribunal insisted that compulsory labour formed part of the crime against humanity, whether or not the victim was ill treated.[208] The Tokyo tribunal also convicted a number of individuals of charges related to enslavement.[209] The difficulty with World War II jurisprudence is that the tribunals simultaneously dealt with forced labour as well as with deportation (to forced labour), and the definitional boundaries between these two crimes remained somewhat unclear. An exception is the *Flick* trial, in which the tribunal focused on 'slave-labour' rather than deportation thereto. Two of the defendants, Flick and Weiss, knowingly 'increased the production quota of freight cars which constitute military equipment within the contemplation of the Hague Convention'.[210] With the approval of Flick, Weiss took part 'in the procurement of a large number of Russian prisoners of war for work in the manufacture of such equipment'.[211] The reference to the Hague Convention of 1907 and its Regulations, however, indicates that the defendants' conduct would today be qualified a war crime, rather than a crime against humanity.

[206] AP II, Art. 5(1)(e).

[207] ICC Elements of Crimes, footnote 11: 'It is understood that such deprivation of liberty may, in some circumstances, include exacting forced labour or otherwise reducing a person to a servile status as defined in the Supplementary Convention on the Abolition of Slavery, the Slave Trade, and Institutions and Practices Similar to Slavery of 1956.'

[208] *United States of America* v. *Pohl et al., V TWC 958*, NMT, 970: 'Slaves may be well fed, well clothed, and comfortably housed, but they are still slaves if without lawful process they are deprived of their freedom by forceful restraint.'

[209] Neil Boister and Robert Cryer, *Documents on the Tokyo Tribunal* (Oxford University Press, 2008), 32–3.

[210] *United States of America* v. *Flick et al. (Opinion and Judgment), VI TWC 1187*, NMT, 1202.

[211] Ibid.

With the establishment of *ad hoc* tribunals and hybrid courts, the definition of enslavement has been clarified. The ICTY confirmed that contemporary understandings such as forced labour are included in the criminalisation of enslavement, including under customary international law: the appeals chamber referred to 'some destruction of the juridical personality' and endorsed the trial chamber's finding that factors indicating that enslavement was committed included, *inter alia*, elements of control, measures taken to prevent or deter escape, force, duration, abuse, the victim's vulnerability or forced labour.[212] The ICTY Chambers relied on the commentary of the ILC to the 1996 Draft Code, which lists servitude or forced labour as part of enslavement.[213] That forced labour is an established indicator of enslavement was further endorsed in the *Krnojelac* case as well as by the Trial and Appeals Chambers of the SCSL, and the UN inquiry in North Korea has followed this approach.[214]

In short, the exaction of forced labour outside permissible exceptions is 'a similar deprivation of liberty' constituting the 'exercise of any or all of the powers attaching to the right of ownership'. Whenever the *chapeau* requirements of crimes against humanity are met, the exaction of forced labour constitutes the crime of enslavement within the terms of Art. 7(1)c of the Rome Statute as well as under customary international law.

There are other forms of enslavement. The crime against humanity of enslavement also covers practices such as human trafficking. This is indirectly supported by the drafting history of the UDHR. The phrase 'no one shall be held in slavery or servitude' was explicitly meant 'to cover traffic in women, involuntary servitude and forced labour'.[215] Since trafficking in persons, 'in particular women and children', is explicitly mentioned in the ICC Elements of Crimes as a manner in which the powers of ownership over an individual can be exercised,[216] contemporary understandings of the concept of trafficking in human beings must fall within the term 'similar deprivation of liberty'. The ECtHR

212 *Prosecutor* v. *Kunarac, Kovac and Vukovic, IT-96-23-A, 12 June 2002*, ICTY, paras. 117–21.

213 ILC, Draft Code of Crimes against the Peace and Security of Mankind 1996, *Yearbook of the International Law Commission*, vol. II, Part Two, 1996, 48, Commentary to Art. 18.

214 *Prosecutor* v. *Krnojelac, IT-97-25-T, 15 March 2002*, ICTY, para. 353; *Prosecutor* v. *Sesay, Kallon and Gbao, SCSL-04-15-T, 2 March 2009*, SCSL, para. 160; *Prosecutor* v. *Sesay, Kallon and Gbao, SCSL-04-15-A, 26 October 2009*, SCSL, paras. 93–4; *Prosecutor* v. *Taylor, SCSL-03-1-T, 26 April 2012*, SCSL, paras. 46–50; North Korea Inquiry, A/HRC/25/CRP.1, 7 February 2014, paras. 1048–9.

215 Report of the Working Group on the Declaration of the Second Session of the Commission on Human Rights, E/CN.4/57, 10 December 1947, 8.

216 ICC Elements of Crimes, footnote 11.

supported the view that trafficking falls within the scope of the prohibition of slavery.[217] In order to interpret the definition of trafficking, recourse can be had to the widely ratified Protocol to Prevent, Suppress and Punish Trafficking in Persons, Especially Women and Children, which defines trafficking, including for purposes other than prostitution.[218] Several commentators note the surprising absence of jurisprudence on this form of enslavement despite abundant evidence of human trafficking.[219] As this section shows, this lack of case law cannot be explained by a lack of legal provisions.

There are further indications on the potential overlap between the crime against humanity of enslavement and ESCR violations, in particular in relation to acts of a sexual nature. ESCR violations in connection with acts of a sexual nature may constitute both enslavement and sexual slavery.

### *4.4.3 Sexual crimes*

The Rome Statute groups a number of crimes within the category of 'sexual crimes'. In previous statutes, rape was often the only explicitly listed 'sexual crime'.[220] The Rome Statute lists 'rape, sexual slavery, enforced prostitution, forced pregnancy, enforced sterilisation, or any other form of sexual violence'.[221] Any of these crimes can involve a range of gross human rights abuses, including violations of ESCR. If rape, enforced prostitution or other forms of sexual violence of comparable gravity are imputable to the state, then the state is almost certainly in violation of the right to health. In addition, sexual slavery and enforced prostitution are cognate to extreme violations of the right to work and to just and favourable conditions of work, either if actors imputable to the

217 *Rantsev* v. *Cyprus and Russia, Application No. 25965/04, 7 January 2010*, ECtHR, para. 282.

218 Protocol to Prevent, Suppress and Punish Trafficking in Persons, Especially Women and Children, Supplementing the UN Convention against Transnational Organized Crime, Art. 3.

219 Hall reports that there has been only one unsuccessful prosecution for this crime in Montenegro. Triffterer (ed.), *Commentary on the Rome Statute*, 247 (Hall), note 444. Also noting the lack of cases: Steven Ratner et al., *Accountability*, 3rd edn (Oxford University Press, 2009), 119.

220 See for instance ICTR Statute, Art. 3(g). The SCSL Statute, in line with the 1996 Draft Code, was the first to explicitly include other forms of sexual abuse. Agreement between the UN and the Government of Sierra Leone Pursuant to SC/Res/1315, Statute of the Special Court for Sierra Leone, 16 January 2002, Arts. 2 and 3.

221 Rome Statute, Art. 7(1)g.

state commit them or if the state fails to protect individuals from abuses. The Economic Community of West African States Community Court of Justice, for instance, condemned Niger for violations of the ACHPR because of its administrative and judicial authorities' failure to protect a young woman from sexual slavery.[222]

Three specific sexual crimes lend themselves for an examination of overlap between ESCR violation and crimes against humanity of a sexual nature.

#### 4.4.3.1 Sexual slavery and enforced prostitution

The crime of sexual slavery shares the same elements with the crime of enslavement analysed above. The only distinction is that sexual slavery additionally requires 'one or more acts of a sexual nature'.[223] The previous section on enslavement elucidated that forms of human trafficking may also amount to enslavement. If, in addition, an act of a sexual nature is forced upon the victim, for example, if the victim is trafficked for the purpose of compulsory sexual activity, the conduct could be qualified as sexual slavery. Sexual slavery is thus best understood as a special form of enslavement.[224] The SCSL has held that sexual slavery is 'a *jus cogens* prohibition in the same manner as slavery for the purpose of physical labour'.[225] That sexual slavery can involve – amongst a range of other human rights violations – extreme violations of the right to work was indicated by the Pre-Trial Chamber I of the ICC, which held that sexual slavery can encompass domestic servitude and other forced labour involving compulsory sexual activity.[226] In short, sexual slavery overlaps with ESCR violations in the same way as enslavement does, with the added requirement of an act of sexual nature being forced upon the victim.

Enforced prostitution is a separate sexual crime under the Rome Statute. However, the crime of sexual slavery encompasses conduct that used to be qualified as enforced prostitution, and it is today preferable to refer to 'sexual slavery' rather than 'enforced prostitution'. The latter concept is rooted in expectations of chastity and family honour and has

222 *Koraou* v. *Niger, Judgment No. Ecw/CCJ/Jud/06/08, 27 October 2008*, Economic Community of West African States Community Court of Justice.

223 ICC Elements of Crimes, Art. 7(1)g, sexual slavery.

224 Schabas, *Commentary on the Rome Statute*, 173. See generally Valerie Oosterveld, 'Sexual Slavery and the ICC' (2004) 25 *Michigan Journal of International Law*, 3, 605–51.

225 *Prosecutor* v. *Brima, Kamara and Kanu, SCSL-04-16-T, 20 July 2007*, SCSL, para. 705.

226 *Prosecutor* v. *Katanga and Chui, Decision on the Confirmation of Charges, 30 September 2008, Pre-Trial Chamber I, ICC-01/04-01/07*, ICC, para. 431.

been criticised for not adequately reflecting the nature of the crime.[227] In the context of this study, it is useful to know that the ICRC commentary to Art. 27 of the Fourth Geneva Convention – the normative root of the crime of enforced prostitution – confirmed the relationship between this crime and the right to health or work by noting that 'thousands of women were made to enter brothels against their will or were contaminated with venereal diseases'.[228] Today, such policies undoubtedly constitute failures to respect and protect ESCR such as the right to work and health and can be qualified as sexual slavery if committed in the context of a widespread or systematic attack directed against a civilian population.

#### 4.4.3.2 Forced marriage

Forced marriage is another sexual crime against humanity. In the trial against Charles Taylor, the SCSL extensively analysed forced marriage given that many victims of the Sierra Leone conflict were forced to become so-called 'bush wives' and had to cook, clean or perform other domestic labour for rebels who abducted them. These abusive practices clearly impacted on victims' enjoyment of a number of ESCR, such as their right to work or the right to education. If committed in the context of a widespread or systematic attack against a civilian population, should such conduct be charged as the crime of forced marriage? The problem with this offence is that forced marriage is a misnomer as it seems inappropriate to refer to the perpetrators as 'spouses'.[229] Yet, the trial chamber in *Taylor* highlighted that the forced conjugal association made it a practice that deserves to be prosecuted under a different heading than the other sexual crimes. The chamber said that the rape and the other sexual violence inflicted upon the victims amounted to sexual slavery while the forced domestic labour amounted to enslavement. Since the two were inflicted in conjunction and both were imposed through forced conjugal association, the chamber thought that forced marriage was the best classification. The chamber also held that it was preferable not to charge the experience as 'other inhumane acts', as this category of crimes against humanity does not capture the specific nature of the victimisation.[230]

[227] For an outline of the debate, see Oosterveld, 'Sexual Slavery and the ICC', 611–22 and especially note 31 with further references.

[228] Oscar Uhler et al., *Commentary, Fourth Geneva Convention* (ICRC, 1958), 205.

[229] *Prosecutor* v. *Taylor, SCSL-03-1-T, 26 April 2012*, SCSL, para. 426.

[230] Previously, the Appeals Chamber of the SCSL found that forced marriage was not predominantly inflicted as a sexual crime with the exercise of an ownership interest,

#### 4.4.3.3 Enforced sterilisation

Enforced sterilisation is a crime against humanity if committed in the context of a widespread or systematic attack directed against a civilian population.[231] Simultaneously, there is no doubt that enforced sterilisations and failures of a state to protect therefrom infringe the right to health. The CESCR held that the right to health in Art. 12 of the ICESCR encompasses the right to be free from interference such as non-consensual medical 'treatment',[232] as well as protection against the 'deliberate withholding or misrepresentation of information vital to health protection'.[233] Enforced sterilisations are often conducted without proper information or with no information provided at all.[234] The CESCR concluded that '[r]eproductive health means that women and men have the freedom to decide if and when to reproduce'.[235] Moreover, the committee has emphasised that a number of interrelated and essential elements are part of the right to health.[236] One of these elements is acceptability, which includes the requirement that 'all health facilities, goods and services must be respectful of medical ethics'.[237]

While the crime of enforced sterilisation can affect men and women, CEDAW contains a number of express provisions and specific jurisprudence that refer to the right to health of women and girls. The CEDAW Committee stated that '[s]tates parties should not permit forms of coercion, such as non-consensual sterilisation . . . that violate women's rights

but rather as the imposition of a forced conjugal association upon the victims, coercing them to perform a variety of conjugal duties, including forced domestic labour. *Prosecutor* v. *Brima, Kamara and Kanu, SCSL-2004-16-A, 22 February 2008*, SCSL, para. 190.

231 Enforced sterilisation can constitute genocide when committed with intent to destroy a particular group in whole or in part. Sterilisations can also constitute extermination or persecution, including sterilisations of targeted groups defined by socio-economic conditions.

232 Committee on Economic, Social and Cultural Rights, *General Comment 14 on the Right to the Highest Attainable Standard of Health*, 11 August 2000, E/CN.12/2000/4, para. 8.

233 Ibid., para. 34.

234 Center for Reproductive Rights and Poradna, *Body and Soul: Forced Sterilization and Other Assaults on Roma Reproductive Freedom in Slovakia* (CRP, 2003), 100.

235 Committee on Economic, Social and Cultural Rights, *General Comment 14 on the Right to the Highest Attainable Standard of Health*, para. 12.

236 Ibid.

237 Ibid., para. 12c; International Federation of Gynecology and Obstetrics, 'Ethical Issues in Obstetrics and Gynecology for the Ethical Aspects of Human Reproduction and Women's Health' (2006); CEDAW Committee, *General Recommendation No. 24, Women and Health*, 1999, A/54/38 at 5 (1999), para. 22.

to informed consent and dignity',[238] and confirmed their right to decide on the number and spacing of their children.[239] In the aftermath of World War II, Nazi doctors were convicted for the infamous sterilisation programme developed in the Third Reich. Dr Carl Clauberg, a Nazi gynaecologist, for instance, was found guilty of performing experimental sterilisations on approximately 700 women in concentration camps.[240] Since then, there have been no prosecutions for this crime against humanity, despite various reports alleging widespread practices of forced sterilisations. The Czech Ombudsman, for instance, suggested in 2005 that during the Communist period, authorities 'had embarked on what amounted to a programme of social engineering' by coercively sterilising women, most of them members of the Roma minority.[241] In 2009, the Czech Prime Minister expressed regret over forced sterilisations and expressed the view that 'it would be a mistake to assume that measures taken by the pre-1989 authorities towards the Roma minority were implemented by chance as opposed to being coordinated'.[242] A non-governmental organisation noted that there was a targeted campaign involving both offers of financial incentive and threats to withhold social welfare or take children into state care throughout the 1980s.[243] The Peruvian government reached a friendly settlement in a case before the Inter-American Commission on Human Rights (IACommHR), in which it was alleged that there were 'a large number of cases of women affected by a massive, compulsory, and systematic government policy to stress sterilization as a means for rapidly altering the reproductive behavior of

[238] CEDAW Committee, *General Recommendation No. 24, Women and Health*, para. 22.

[239] Ibid.

[240] *United States of America* v. *Brandt et al. (Medical Trial), II TWC 171*, NMT, 226, 38–39; Paul Weindling, *Nazi Medicine* (Palgrave, 2004). A trial for enforced sterilisations was also conducted in the Soviet Union in 1948 and by the British courts operating under Control Council Law No. 10. *United Kingdom* v. *Kramer et al.* (Belsen Trial), *Case No. 10, II Law Reports of Trials of War Criminals 1, 17 November 1945, British Military Court at Luneberg*, Courts in the British Zone of Control in Germany under Control Council Law 10, 11 and 25, allegations of enforced sterilisation and other medical experiments in Belsen and Auschwitz. A summary account of the experiments and the Soviet trial can be found in Danuta Czech, *Auschwitz Chronicle 1939–1945* (Holt, 1997).

[241] Otakar Motejl, *Final Statement in the Matter of Sterilisations Performed in Contravention of the Law and Proposed Remedial Measures* (Public Defender, 2005), 59. See also Concluding Observations, Czech Republic, CEDAW/C/CZE/CO/2, 25 August 2006, paras. 23–4.

[242] Rob Cameron, 'PM Expresses Regret over Roma Sterilization but Activists Say Practice Continues', *Czech Radio 7*, 24 November 2009.

[243] ERRC et al., 'Submission to the HRCttee, Implementation of the ICCPR in the Czech Republic', 16.

the population, especially poor, Indian, and rural women'.[244] To constitute a crime against humanity, the threshold elements of crimes against humanity would need to be proven, but the examples illustrate how overlap between this crime and ESCR violations can potentially arise.

The ICC Elements of Crimes contains two specifications of the definition of enforced sterilisation. In addition to the *chapeau* requirements of crimes against humanity, the following two elements determine whether a given conduct amounts to enforced sterilisation as a crime against humanity.[245]

**4.4.3.3.1 Deprivation of biological reproductive capacity** The perpetrator must have deprived one or more persons of their biological reproductive capacity. According to a footnote to the ICC Elements of Crimes, such deprivation has to be of a permanent nature.[246] This is a relevant consideration in order to demonstrate overlap between violations of the right to health and the crime of enforced sterilisation, as a defendant could try to argue that a deprivation of reproductive capacity is not permanent. A determination of the point at which surgical sterilisation would amount to permanent deprivation of reproductive capacity has been made by the CEDAW Committee. In a case where a Romani woman alleged that a public hospital had subjected her to coerced sterilisation, the Hungarian courts rejected her claims by holding that she had failed to prove permanent infertility, as the sterilisation could potentially be reversed by another surgical procedure.[247] The CEDAW Committee noted that sterilisation surgery is intended to be irreversible even if procedures to reverse it technically exist.[248] The deprivation of *natural* reproductive capacity was the test that established that the sterilisation had to be considered to be permanent.[249]

**4.4.3.3.2 Lack of justification or genuine consent** The definition of the crime of enforced sterilisation requires the sterilisation not to be justified for medical reasons and to be carried out without the genuine consent of the individual.

[244] *Chávez* v. *Peru, 22 October 2003, IACommHR Report No. 71/03*, IACommHR, para. 9.

[245] It should be noted that it is not required to prove any 'sexual violence' even if the crime is grouped together in the category of so-labelled 'sexual crimes'.

[246] ICC Elements of Crimes, footnote 19.

[247] *A. S.* v. *Hungary, 29 August 2006, CEDAW/C/36/D/4/2004*, CEDAW Committee, paras. 2.8, 4.2, 8.4.

[248] Ibid., para. 10.4. [249] Ibid., paras. 10.4, 11.4.

The case of the Romani woman mentioned above is a clear example of lack of justification and consent: when the patient was rushed to a public hospital, the physician informed her that a caesarean section was needed. While on the operating table, she was asked to sign a form as well as a handwritten note authorising her sterilisation. The sterilisation had been referred to in a medical term that was unknown to her.[250] The CEDAW Committee found a violation of her health rights and refuted the government's argument that she had genuinely consented to the procedure.[251]

Where perpetrators act on behalf of states and permanently sterilise individuals without their consent or without a medical justification, their conduct not only results in a violation of the victims' right to health, but may also amount to a crime against humanity if the *chapeau* elements of such crimes are met.

## 4.5 Persecution

The crime against humanity of persecution overlaps with a wide range of human rights abuses, including violations of ESCR. The essential element in determining the existence of persecution is the existence of discriminatory intent and not whether the human right violated belongs to ESCR, to civil and political rights, or to a combination thereof.

Persecution consists of the severe deprivation of fundamental rights on discriminatory grounds in the context of a widespread or systematic attack against a civilian population. The crime against humanity of persecution is a complex offence, and the boundaries of its scope are not yet fully resolved. Associating ESCR violations with the crime of persecution demands a critical look at the elements of this crime.

Paragraph (2)g of Art. 7 of the ICC Statute specifies that persecution 'means the intentional and severe deprivation of fundamental rights contrary to international law by reason of the identity of the group or collectivity'. There is no indication that the crime under customary international law would have a different meaning.

When persecution is committed, the following five groups of ESCR are often particularly affected:

First, we will see that the ICTY has held that the comprehensive destruction of homes, if committed with discriminatory intent, may

[250] Ibid., paras. 2.2–2.3. [251] Ibid., paras. 11.2–11.4.

constitute persecution. The destruction of homes often simultaneously meets the legal definition of forced evictions provided earlier.[252]

Second, violations of the right to food can overlap with persecution. The right to food is violated if a state takes measures that result in preventing access to adequate food.[253] If a government deliberately withholds food aid or otherwise prevents access to food to particular groups, the elements of this crime against humanity will warrant a closer examination. Situations that might fall into this category include that of the Rohingya refugees in Bangladesh or certain abuses in Sri Lanka or in Gaza. Bangladeshi authorities were alleged to be waging a campaign of food deprivation, expulsion and forced internment against the Rohingya refugees, who face critical levels of malnutrition and disease. In 2010, Physicians for Human Rights, a non-governmental organisation, claimed to have corroborated evidence of an active and coordinated state policy of obstructing humanitarian relief as well as a strict prohibition on delivering any food aid to the Rohingya refugees.[254] Authorities are also said to threaten villagers who do not turn in their Rohingya neighbours.[255] To this date, a persecution conviction based on the denial of humanitarian relief has never been rendered. Yet, the ICTY Trial Chamber indicated that the discriminatory deprivation of humanitarian assistance could give rise to a persecution conviction.[256] In Sri Lanka, the UN SG's Panel of Experts found credible allegations pointing 'to a widespread or systematic attack on the civilian population of the Vanni [region] ... This attack included ... deprivation of food and medicine' and 'credible allegations support a finding of the crime against humanity of persecution'.[257] The UN Fact Finding Mission on the Gaza Conflict concluded that 'the series of acts that deprive Palestinians in the Gaza Strip of their means of sustenance ... and water ... could lead a competent court to find that the crime of persecution, a crime against humanity, has been committed'.[258]

252 For the definition of forced evictions, see Section 4.3.

253 Committee on Economic, Social and Cultural Rights, *General Comment 12 on the Right to Adequate Food*, 12 May 1999, E/C.12/1999/5, para. 15.

254 Physicians for Human Rights, 'Stateless and Starving' (Physicians for Human Rights, 2010), 6, 7, 9, 11 and 5.

255 Ibid., 9 and note 12.

256 *Prosecutor* v. *Gotovina and Markač, IT-06-90-T, 15 April 2011*, ICTY, para. 1843. In the case at hand, the chamber found that no or limited evidence was received.

257 Report of the SG's Panel of Experts on Accountability in Sri Lanka, 31 March 2011, para. 251.

258 Final Report of the UN Fact Finding Mission on the Gaza Conflict, A/HRC/12/48, 15 September 2009, para. 1733.

Third, violations of the right to freely choose one's work and a violation of just and fair conditions of work can constitute the abuse that gives rise to persecution as a crime against humanity. The Irish Centre for Human Rights concluded that forced labour and other abuses directed at the Rohingyas in Burma not only amounted to enslavement, but that the forced labour also seemed to qualify as persecution given that the Rohingyas are targeted as an ethnic, racial and religious group.[259] The *Justice Trial* provides ample examples of persecution committed by way of what would today be considered violations of the Jews' right to freely choose their work: 'forms of racial persecution were universally practiced by governmental authority and constituted an integral part in the general policy of the Reich. We have already noted the decree by which Jews were excluded from the legal profession',[260] the tribunal observed. Whenever forced labour or discriminatory labour practices are instituted against a particular group, the elements of the crime against humanity of persecution merit scrutiny.

Fourth, persecution can be committed by violating the right to health. In Art. 12 of the ICESCR, states recognised the right of everyone to enjoy the highest attainable standard of physical and mental health. The CESCR provided a list of examples of violations contravening this obligation: 'violations of the obligation to respect are those state actions, policies or laws that contravene the standards set out in Art. 12 of the Covenant and are likely to result in bodily harm, unnecessary morbidity or preventable mortality'.[261] The wording of this paragraph of GC 14 does not, however, provide an exhaustive explanation of violations of the right to health. For instance, harm to mental health would have to be added to this formulation by virtue of the fact that it is unambiguously mentioned in Art. 12.[262] However, GC 14 usefully provides criteria to identify some undisputed violations of the right to health. Such undisputed violations would be abuses that are (i) a result of a state's actions, policies or laws incompatible with Art. 12; and (ii) likely to result in

[259] See also Irish Centre for Human Rights, *Crimes against Humanity in Western Burma*, 115ff, in particular 143 for the explicit mention of Arts. 6 and 7 of the ICESCR and the link to persecution of the Rohingyas.

[260] *United States of America* v. *Altstoetter et al.* (Justice Trial), *III TWC 954*, NMT, 1063.

[261] Committee on Economic, Social and Cultural Rights, *General Comment 14 on the Right to the Highest Attainable Standard of Health*, para. 50.

[262] It also does not have to be cumulative 'bodily harm, unnecessary morbidity and preventable mortality'. When the analysis concerns a single victim, it would lead to an absurd result if morbidity and mortality would both have to be demonstrated.

bodily harm, unnecessary morbidity and preventable mortality. The committee also noted that 'the denial of access to health facilities, goods and services to particular individuals or groups as a result of de jure or de facto discrimination' violates the right to health.[263]

A number of reports allege what, if true, would meet the requirements of violations of the right to health, as mentioned by the CESCR. Controversial reports argue that ever since the banning of the Chinese Falun Gong, a group with particular beliefs and rituals, the Chinese authorities in effect installed a policy to kill Falun Gong practitioners to harvest their organs.[264] These allegations are surrounded by controversy about the factual accuracy of the information on which they are based. Since there have been several court cases in Argentina and Spain concerning these allegations, it is warranted to raise the question of whether the alleged acts could fall within the scope of the crime of persecution.

In 2007, two Canadian investigators reported that organs are harvested from imprisoned Falun Gong practitioners.[265] Their report points to a gap in the total number of organ transplants compared to the number of available organ donors from official sources, including organs from prisoners sentenced to death.[266] The authors argue that the sharp increase in organ transplants parallels the increase in persecution of Falun Gong.[267]

[263] Committee on Economic, Social and Cultural Rights, *General Comment 14 on the Right to the Highest Attainable Standard of Health*, para. 50.

[264] David Matas and David Kilgour, 'Bloody Harvest' (2007); Subcommittee on Oversight and Investigations, House of Representatives, *Falun Gong: Organ Harvesting and China's Ongoing War on Human Rights. Statement of Kirk Allison, Medical School Minnesota*, 29 September 2006, 17–26, noting violations of the right of everyone to the enjoyment of the highest attainable standard of health. Allison also noted that the short time frame of on-demand transplantations could not be assured on a random death basis. Edward McMillan-Scott, former vice-president of the European Parliament, conducted a fact-finding mission to China and reported on evidence on organ harvesting. Edward McMillan-Scott, 'Secret Atrocities of Chinese Regime', *Yorkshire Post*, 13 June 2006.

[265] Matas and Kilgour, 'Bloody Harvest', 38.

[266] Ibid., 39. In 2005, the Chinese Deputy Health Minister admitted that organs of prisoners sentenced to death are harvested. Jane Maccartney, 'China to "Tidy Up" Trade in Executed Prisoners' Organs', *Times*, 3 December 2005.

[267] Matas and Kilgour, 'Bloody Harvest', 40–3. Not pronouncing themselves on the accuracy of these reports, two UN Special Rapporteurs requested Chinese authorities to adequately respond to the allegations. Communication of the Special Rapporteur on Freedom of Religion and Belief (Asma Jahangir) Sent to China, Jointly with the Special Rapporteur on the Question of Torture (Manfred Nowak), A/HRC/7/10/Add.1, 28 February 2008, paras. 40–1; see paras. 42–9 for the governmental response. The CAT Committee noted its concerns at reports of the increase in organ transplant operations coinciding with the beginning of the persecution of Falun Gong practitioners. Concluding Observations, China, CAT/C/CHN/CO/4, 21 November 2008, para. 18(C).

The 610 Office, an extrajudicial office created by Jiang Zemin, former president of People's Republic of China, is said to be in charge of the organ harvesting of Falun Gong prisoners.[268] If this is indeed the case, the involvement of the state could be shown to meet the first requirement of the CESCR criteria to establish whether the right to health has been violated, and the threshold element of crimes against humanity might also be established. Killing prisoners to harvest their organs is antithetical to the right to enjoyment of health and is clearly incompatible with states' ESCR obligations. Organ harvesting also leads to bodily harm and, in many cases, to death. In sum, such practices would constitute a flagrant violation of the right to health as enshrined in the ICESCR and other treaties.[269]

An Argentinian judge concluded in 2009 that a fully organised and systematically developed plan had been put into motion to persecute Falun Gong.[270] The judge issued international arrest warrants and mentioned that in his view, the issue of the case centred on 'persecution'.[271] The case was dismissed after the Chinese authorities requested the Argentinian government to intervene.[272] A temporarily assigned judge lifted the arrest warrants, and the file was closed in March 2010.[273] Three years later, a cassation court declared the closure null and void,[274] but, to date, the case has not yet resulted in a judicial assessment of the allegations. A similar case has also been brought in Spain against five Chinese officials. Charges were reportedly admitted

[268] Matas and Kilgour, 'Bloody Harvest', 85.

[269] Where applicable, the Arab Charter on Human Rights explicitly forbids organ harvesting as a violation of the right to health. Arab Charter on Human Rights, Art. 9.

[270] *Luo Gan y otros, Imposición de tortura, Caso No. 17.885/2005, Federal Criminal Court No. 9*, Argentina. The defendants are former president Jiang Zemin and Luo Gan (former Secretary of the Central Committee of the Communist party).

[271] Octavio Aráoz de Lamadrid, 'Speech of Judge de Lamadrid of Argentina, 13th Session of the Human Rights Council, 17 March 2010' (UN Forum on Human Rights in China). Technically, the jurisdictional basis for the case is torture under the Argentine criminal code and genocide. *Luo Gan y otros, Imposición de tortura, Caso No. 17.885/2005, Federal Criminal Court No. 9*, Argentina. The Argentinean criminal system had not yet provided for universal jurisdiction for crimes against humanity but the issues are framed as persecution.

[272] *Chinese Embassy, Letter to the Chancellor of Argentina, Posición del gobierno chino sobre el caso de falsas acusaciones presentadas por Falun Gong, 8 January 2010, Buenos Aires (on file with the author)*, Argentina.

[273] *Luo Gan y otros, Imposición de tortura, Caso No. 17.885/2005, Devuelve actuaciones, 3 March 2010 [Closing the Case], Fiscalía federal 3*, Argentina.

[274] *Luo Gan y otros, Causa No. 13.774, Recurso de casación, Sala III, 17 April 2013*, Argentina.

in late 2009,[275] but Spain subsequently restricted its legislation on universal jurisdiction to cases with a 'close link' to Spain. Although this legislative change was adopted after the cases were filed, the Spanish Supreme Court has applied them.[276] While it is for courts to determine the accuracy of the allegations and contingently the context in which they may have taken place, the examples illustrate that severe deprivations of the right to health may often justify a closer analysis to determine if they might simultaneously constitute persecution as a crime against humanity.

Fifth, persecution has been found to exist in relation to cultural rights abuses, based on findings that perpetrators destroyed educational and religious institutions of the targeted group or harassed those who practise their religion or culture. If such conduct is the result of the state failing to respect or protect rights, cultural rights such as the right to take part in cultural life, as well as the right to education, are simultaneously at stake. The 2014 UN inquiry on North Korea found that persecution takes place in North Korea *inter alia*, because the state vilifies those who practice their religion outside the state-controlled churches.[277] An additional example concerns the allegations of Tibetans that Chinese policies infringe their cultural rights.[278] In spring 2014, judges in Spain ordered international arrest warrants against five Chinese officials, but the Spanish legislature adopted further restrictions on the law that previously enabled Spanish courts to deal with extraterritorial allegations, forcing the dismissal of the case.[279]

Abuses of cultural rights, including the right to education, can be considered by criminal tribunals adjudicating persecution. In *Kordić*

275 Charlotte Cuthbertson, 'Spanish Judge Calls Top Chinese Officials to Account for Genocide', *Epoch Times*, 15 November 2009. See also *Jiang Zemin et al., Sentencia en el recurso de amparo Núm. 3382–2005, Stc 227/2007, 22 October 2007, (on file with the author), Constitutional Court*, Spain. In this decision (prior to the legislative changes in Spain), universal jurisdiction was affirmed; permitting investigation to proceed against China's ex-president, Jiang Zemin and Luo Gan, head of the Falun Gong Unit within the Chinese government.

276 *Auto 1566/2011, Recurso Casación 857/2011, 6 October 2011, Tribunal supremo*, Spain.

277 North Korea Inquiry, A/HRC/25/CRP.1, 7 February 2014, para. 1094.

278 The International Campaign for Tibet argues that the alleged abuses amount to cultural genocide. Given the controversies surrounding the concept of cultural genocide, the allegations are discussed in relation to persecution. International Campaign for Tibet, *60 Years of Chinese Misrule: Arguing Cultural Genocide in Tibet* (International Campagn for Tibet, 2012).

279 Ley Orgánica del Poder Judicial de España, con las modificaciones del articulo 23 (27 Febrero 2014), Ley Orgánica 6/1985.

*and Čerkez*, the destruction of religious and educational institutions of Bosnian Muslims led to convictions for persecution as a crime against humanity because the tribunal found that these institutions were destroyed on political, racial, ethnic or religious grounds and the destruction constituted a severe deprivation of fundamental rights.[280] While the destruction of a single educational institution would not be enough to constitute a severe deprivation of fundamental rights, the ICTY Trial Chamber in *Krnojelac* summarised that 'acts should not be considered in isolation but rather should be examined in their context and with consideration of their cumulative effect'.[281] Furthermore, systematic infringements of the right to education were a cornerstone of the persecutory policies of the Third Reich. In a report to Hitler, Himmler secretly wrote:

> A basic issue in the solution of these problems [avoiding that the non-German inhabitants of Poland would unite, and making the ethnic concepts of Poles, Ukrainians, Goralen and Lemken disappear] is the question of schooling and thus the question of sifting and selecting the young. For the non-German population of the East there must be no higher school than the four-grade elementary school. The sole goal of this school is to be: Simple arithmetic up to 500 at the most; writing of one's name; the doctrine that it is a divine law to obey the Germans and to be honest, industrious, and good. I do not think that reading should be required.[282]

Today, such policies not only blatantly violate the right to education,[283] but Himmler's memorandum also illustrates how such abuses can be an essential aspect of persecution and thus overlap with crimes against humanity.

When considering whether a violation of ESCR constitutes a severe deprivation of fundamental rights, the following indications serve to delineate those human rights violations that meet the 'severe deprivation' requirement of the crime of persecution.

280 *Prosecutor* v. *Kordić, Čerkez, IT-95-14/2-T, 26 February 2001*, ICTY, paras. 206–7.

281 *Prosecutor* v. *Krnojelac, IT-97-25-T, 15 March 2002*, ICTY, 434. The *ad hoc* tribunals have stressed that the persecutory abuses must be of similar gravity as other abuses amounting to crimes against humanity. Various discriminatory acts not individually rising to the requisite gravity may cumulatively qualify as persecution: *Prosecutor* v. *Kvočka, IT-98-30/1-T, 2 November 2001*, ICTY, para. 185. See also *Prosecutor* v. *Naletilić & Martinović, IT-98-34-T, 31 March 2003*, ICTY, para. 635.

282 *United States of America* v. *Greifelt et al. (RuSHA Case), V TWC 88*, NMT, 35, 'Reflections on the Treatment of Peoples of Alien Races in the East', Secret memorandum handed to Hitler by Himmler on 25 May 1940.

283 For instance, CRC, Art. 28 or ICESCR, Art. 13.

### 4.5.1 *Intentional and severe deprivation of fundamental rights*

The main difficulty with the definition of the offence is the delineation of the scope of a 'severe deprivation of fundamental rights'. This lack of clarity may create challenges of legality, but it should be noted that such difficulties exist whether defendants are indicted for violations of civil and political rights, ESCR or a combination thereof. Since ESCR belong to 'fundamental rights',[284] there is nothing in the definition of persecution that would restrict the scope of the offence to violations of civil and political rights. The ICTY emphasised that persecutory acts could include 'inter alia, those of a physical, economic, or judicial nature, that violate an individual's right to the equal enjoyment of his basic rights'.[285] In *Simić*, the trial chamber found that 'an insufficient supply of food and water, lack of space, unhygienic detention conditions, and an insufficient access to medical care are circumstances that may ... meet the *actus reus* of cruel and inhumane treatment as a persecutory act'.[286] Endorsed on appeal,[287] the trial chamber in *Krnojelac* emphasised that the *actus reus* of persecution can take many forms but that 'the test will only be met by gross or blatant denials of fundamental human rights'.[288]

Importantly, the ICTY warned that '[i]t would be contrary to the principle of legality to convict someone of persecution based on a definition found in international refugee law or human rights law'.[289] In the *Kupreškić* case, the defence argued that 'a broad definition' would be 'a violation of the principle of legality.'[290] The tribunal dismissed the challenge,[291] but agreed that 'not every denial of a human right may constitute a crime against humanity'.[292] What this cautionary note implies is not that human rights law is irrelevant. Rather, it is international criminal law that has to serve as the starting point for the content of the crime, while the specific terms of international criminal law often hinge on an understanding shaped by human rights law. In order to assess whether

284 Theodor Meron, 'On a Hierarchy of International Human Rights' (1986) 80 *American Journal of International Law*, 1, 1–23: 5, 'noting that there is no substantive or definable legal difference between the terms "fundamental rights" and "human rights"'.

285 *Prosecutor* v. *Tadić, IT-94-1-T, 7 May 1997*, ICTY, para. 710.

286 *Prosecutor* v. *Simić, IT-95-9, 17 October 2003*, ICTY, para. 97.

287 *Prosecutor* v. *Krnojelac, IT-97-25-A, 17 September 2003*, ICTY, para. 199.

288 *Prosecutor* v. *Krnojelac, IT-97-25-T, 15 March 2002*, ICTY, para. 434.

289 *Prosecutor* v. *Kupreškić, IT-95-16-T, 14 January 2000*, ICTY, para. 589.

290 *Prosecutor* v. *Kupreškić, Brief of the Defendants on Legal Trial Issues, IT-95-16-T, 19 November 1998*, ICTY, paras. 55–6.

291 *Prosecutor* v. *Kupreškić, IT-95-16-T, 14 January 2000*, ICTY, para. 616.

292 Ibid., para. 618.

there has been a 'severe deprivation of fundamental rights', the trial chamber in *Kupreškić* 'underscored that massive violations of civil and political rights often begin with violations of socioeconomic rights',[293] and affirmed that ESCR violations may fall within the ambit of the crime: 'Persecution can also involve a variety of other discriminatory acts, involving attacks on political, social, and economic rights.'[294]

In *Kupreškić*, the chamber cited several World War II cases of defendants convicted of persecution in the form of discriminatory economic acts,[295] deprivations of the rights to work and education or slave labour.[296] In the *Justice Trial*, defendants were convicted for adopting decrees expelling Jews from public services, educational institutions and many enterprises[297] – acts which would today easily be qualified as violations of the right to education and work and hence ESCR violations. In the *Flick* case, the tribunal suggested that there is a difference between acts against industrial property (which would not fall within the ambit of the crime) and acts against 'the dwellings, household furnishings, and food supplies of a persecuted people':[298]

> Under the basic law of many states the taking of property by the sovereign, without just compensation, is forbidden, but usually it is not considered a crime. A sale compelled by pressure or duress may be questioned in a court of equity, but, so far as we are informed, such use of pressure, even on racial or religious groups, has never been thought to be a crime against humanity. A distinction could be made between industrial property and the dwellings, household furnishings, and food supplies of a persecuted people. In this case, however, we are only concerned with industrial property.[299]

293 Mark Drumbl, 'Accountability for Property and Environmental War Crimes' (ICTJ, November 2009), 15.

294 *Prosecutor* v. *Kupreškić, IT-95-16-T, 14 January 2000*, ICTY, para. 615.

295 Ibid., para. 596 and accompanying notes. Particularly notable is the defendant Frick, convicted for 'having drafted, signed and administered many laws designed to eliminate Jews from German life and [the] economy'. See *United States of America, the French Republic, the United Kingdom of Great Britain and Northern Ireland, and the Union of Soviet Socialist Republics against Major War Criminals, Opinion and Judgment, in Nazi Conspiracy and Aggression (Red Series), 1 October 1946*, IMT, 126.

296 *Prosecutor* v. *Kupreškić, IT-95-16-T, 14 January 2000*, ICTY, para. 599 and note 874. The chamber notes the deprivation of the right to teach, to practise professions, to obtain education and to engage in business enterprises. *United States of America* v. *Von Weizsaecker et al.* (Ministries Case), *XIV TWC 308*, NMT, 471, 750.

297 *United States of America* v. *Altstoetter et al.* (Justice Trial), *III TWC 954*, NMT, 1063–4.

298 *United States of America* v. *Flick et al. (Opinion and Judgment), VI TWC 1187*, NMT, 1214.

299 Ibid., 1214–15. This was taken up in *United States of America* v. *Krauch et al. (IG Farben), VIII TWC 1081*, NMT, 1129–30. Discussed in *Prosecutor* v. *Kupreškić, IT-95-16-T, 14 January 2000*, ICTY, note 897.

The position in *Flick* is correct in principle: property as such and alone is not a legal interest protected by the prohibition of persecution, but human dignity and human life are. Only where the deprivation of property severely affects the fundamental rights related to human dignity and human life can a charge of persecution succeed.[300] Regrettably, however, the Nuremberg Military Tribunal (NMT) in *Flick* does not explore its own finding and fails to consider the possible links between the deprivation of property and abuses affecting 'the life and liberty of the oppressed peoples':[301]

> It may be that *incidental* to these persecutions the oppressed peoples lost their homes, household goods, and investments in industrial property but so far as we are aware the outcry by the other nations was against the *personal atrocities*, not the loss of possessions. We believe that the proof does not establish a crime against humanity recognized as such by the law of nations when defendants were engaged in the property transactions here under scrutiny.[302]

As mentioned, it is correct that property transactions as such do not amount to a crime against humanity. However, the tribunal failed to analyse why the deprivation of property *in casu* did not affect 'the life and liberty of the oppressed peoples'[303] (or, in contemporary language, constitute an intentional and severe deprivation of fundamental rights). It would have been more convincing if the binary distinction of industrial and personal property would not have been used. Rather, the decisive test

[300] See also the analysis in *Frick* on the *Funk* and *Seyß-Inquart* cases before the IMT:

> Likewise in the cases of Funk and Seyss-Inquart, anti-Semitic economic discrimination is cited as one of several facts from which it is concluded that he was a war criminal. But it nowhere appears in the judgment that [the] IMT considered, much less decided, that a person becomes guilty of a crime against humanity merely by exerting anti-Semitic pressure to procure by purchase or through state expropriation of industrial property owned by Jews.

*United States of America* v. *Flick et al. (Opinion and Judgment), VI TWC 1187*, NMT, 1215. This statement confirms that property transactions alone do not constitute persecution.

[301] Ibid., 1214–15. [302] Ibid., 1215 (emphasis added).

[303] Ibid., 1215. The tribunal's statement that the '[c]ompulsory taking of industrial property, however reprehensible, is not in that category' is too broad a conclusion and contradicts the NMT's (correct) statement that the effects of the deprivation on 'the life and liberty of the oppressed peoples' is the relevant test, rather than the type of property. The type of property must, however, be taken into account when analysing the next element of the crime, that is whether the deprivation of property was 'contrary to international law'.

is whether the deprivation of property constitutes a severe deprivation of fundamental rights. Today, a distinction based on the nature of property clearly has no basis in the elements of the crime of persecution, and the ICTY was correct not to rely on such a distinction. In the notes on the case, the UN War Crimes Commission observed that the tribunal left open the question whether offences against property 'which amount to an assault upon the *health and life* of a human being (such as the burning of [the victim's] house or depriving him of his food supply or his paid employment)' would constitute a crime against humanity.[304] The commission seemed to indicate that such a conclusion was likely because '[e]ven the examples quoted by the Prosecution in its Rebuttal statement, from the judgment of the International Military Tribunal, could refer to acts of economic deprivation of this more personal type'.[305] The commission furthermore enumerated examples of other defendants convicted of acts related to economic discrimination against the Jews.[306] Hence, where 'economic acts' personally and severely affect victims' fundamental rights, the *actus reus* of persecution can be established.

In addition, national tribunals convicted individuals of persecutory acts involving what would today be labelled as severe deprivations of ESCR. A case in point is *Eichmann*. The Israeli Supreme Court convicted the defendant of persecution for, *inter alia*, causing starvation.[307] In the Netherlands, Hans Albin Rauter, a Nazi Police leader, was convicted of issuing orders subjecting Jews to discriminatory treatment in economic and cultural aspects of life, facilitating their being detected and apprehended for slave labour and extermination.[308]

Having reviewed the cases related to World War II, the *Kupreškić* chamber went on to examine whether the destruction of homes and other personal property could amount to a severe deprivation of fundamental rights. Endorsed on appeal,[309] and based on the jurisprudence of the *Flick* case, it found that there could be certain types of property whose destruction may *not* have a severe enough impact on human rights, even if such a destruction was perpetrated on discriminatory grounds.

304 *United States of America* v. *Flick et al.* (Notes on the Case), *IX TWC 1*, NMT, 50–1 (emphasis in original).

305 Ibid., 50.

306 Ibid., 50–1. The Commission refers to Funk, Seyß-Inquart and Göring.

307 *The Attorney-General of Israel* v. *Eichmann, 36 ILR 277 (1968), 29 May 1962, Supreme Court*, Israel, 277–8.

308 *Prosecutor* v. *Rauter, No. 88, English Translation in XIV Law Reports of Trials of War Criminals 89, 12 January 1949, Special Court of Cassation*, Netherlands, 93.

309 *Prosecutor* v. *Kupreškić, IT-95-16-A, 23 October 2001*, ICTY, para. 254.

'However, the case at hand concerns the comprehensive destruction of homes and property'[310] and hence victims' livelihoods: 'The Trial Chamber therefore concludes that this act may constitute a gross or blatant denial of fundamental human rights, and, if committed on discriminatory grounds, it may constitute persecution.'[311] Rather than considering the type of human rights violation involved, the criteria to be used in determining whether an abuse could constitute persecution revolved around the question whether the abuse had a 'severe enough impact on the victim'.[312] The chamber explicitly cited the ICESCR as part of the 'set of fundamental rights appertaining to any human being, the gross infringement of which may amount, depending on the surrounding circumstances, to a crime against humanity'.[313] In *Kvočka*, the ICTY further concluded that 'jurisprudence from World War II trials found acts or omissions, such as denying bank accounts, educational or employment opportunities . . . constitute persecution'.[314] In *Blaškic*, the trial chamber confirmed that the crime of persecution encompasses a wide range of abuses, including acts targeting property and economic livelihoods.[315]

While clearly affirming that socio-economic or cultural abuses are relevant, the *Kupreškić* chamber, however, went on to opine that the current understanding of the crime may be more limited than what appears from the Nuremberg judgments. The trial chamber concluded that the IMT included, in the crime of persecution,

> acts which, at present, may not fall under the Statute of the [ICTY], such as the passing of discriminatory laws, the exclusion of members of an ethnic or religious group from aspects of social, political, and economic life, the imposition of a collective fine on them, the restriction of their movement and their seclusion in ghettos . . . Moreover . . . several individual defendants were convicted of persecution in the form of discriminatory economic acts.[316]

The chamber did not provide reasons why such acts may today no longer constitute persecution if the *chapeau* requirements of crimes against

310 *Prosecutor* v. *Kupreškić, IT-95-16-T, 14 January 2000*, ICTY, para. 631. 311 Ibid.
312 Ibid. 313 Ibid., para. 621 (emphasis omitted).
314 *Prosecutor* v. *Kvočka, IT-98-30/1-T, 2 November 2001*, ICTY, para. 186, also citing the same passage of the Ministries Case. See Note 288.
315 *Prosecutor* v. *Blaškić, IT-95-14-T, 3 March 2000*, ICTY, paras. 232–33. See also *Prosecutor* v. *Krnojelac, IT-97-25-T, 15 March 2002*, ICTY, para. 431 and *Prosecutor* v. *Krnojelac, IT-97-25-A, 17 September 2003*, ICTY, para. 185. See also *Prosecutor* v. *Tadić, IT-94-1-T, 7 May 1997*, ICTY, para. 707.
316 *Prosecutor v. Kupreškić, IT-95-16-T, 14 January 2000*, ICTY, para. 610 (footnotes omitted).

humanity were met. Moreover, the verb 'may' is inconclusive, and the chamber affirmed a few paragraphs later that it is 'bolstered in its conclusion that persecution can consist of the deprivation of a wide variety of rights'.[317] The safest interpretation of these ambiguous statements is simply that acts not deemed to be severe enough would be excluded from the crime. As mentioned above, persecution requires a 'severe deprivation of fundamental rights'. Passing discriminatory laws or discriminatory economic acts does not automatically meet this element. At the same time, such conduct will be included in the crime if, and only if, it constitutes a severe deprivation of fundamental rights. This interpretation has been confirmed and the statements in *Kupreškić* have been clarified in a subsequent case before the ICTY. The ICTY Trial Chamber corrected the impression that the contemporary definition of persecution would be different from the one employed by the World War II tribunals: some of the facts underlying the conviction of General Gotovina and Commander Markač concerned the adoption, by the Croatian authorities, of legislation that declared all abandoned property to be state property and provided no compensation to persons who '[took] part in the war against Croatia'.[318] This property legislation made it impossible or extremely difficult for the Serbs who had left the area to return and facilitated permanent transfer of ownership to Croats who settled into the abandoned properties.[319] The tribunal unequivocally found that 'the imposition of restrictive and discriminatory measures with regard to housing and property, considered in conjunction with deportation and other crimes against Krajina Serbs, constitutes persecution'.[320] Although Gotovina and Marcač were acquitted on appeal, the appeals chamber did not criticise these findings of the trial chamber.[321] In another subsequent ICTY case in which ESCR abuses were considered a 'blatant denial of fundamental rights' with a severe enough impact on victims to satisfy this element of persecution, detainees had poor sanitary conditions and 'little, if any, food, water or medical treatment'.[322]

[317] Ibid., para. 614.

[318] *Prosecutor* v. *Gotovina and Markač, IT-06-90-T, 15 April 2011*, ICTY, para. 2061.

[319] Ibid., for the full discussion of the legislation and the reasons for finding it discriminatory, see paras. 2061–99.

[320] Ibid., para. 1843.

[321] *Prosecutor* v. *Gotovina and Markač, IT-06-90-A, 16 November 2012*, ICTY. Gotovina and Markač were acquitted because the appeals chamber was of the opinion that a joint criminal enterprise was not proven, and, hence, that the liability of the accused was not established but not because of the qualification of the conduct as persecution.

[322] *Prosecutor* v. *Popović, IT-05-88-T, 10 June 2010*, ICTY, paras. 993–4.

Hence, what can be distilled from the jurisprudence is that the deprivation of fundamental rights can include a wide variety of rights, but only if such deprivation has a 'severe' impact on persons (as opposed to impacts solely on industries, for instance). The term 'severe deprivation of fundamental rights' is not confined to violations of civil and political rights. Violations of the rights to housing, education, food and work have already been classified in jurisprudence as constituting 'severe deprivation of fundamental rights' for the purpose of crimes against humanity.

### 4.5.2 *Contrary to international law*

To constitute persecution, the severe deprivation of fundamental rights must be 'contrary to international law'. This requirement merely affirms that right deprivations can sometimes be justified under international law. The prosecution must, therefore, positively establish that the deprivation of fundamental rights is in breach of international law and could not have been consonant with international law, for instance, by virtue of limitations, derogations or exceptions inherent to the definition of human rights. How limitations or derogations apply to ESCR has been described above where we saw that these concepts are defined narrowly.[323]

### 4.5.3 *By reason of the identity of the group or collectivity*

The severe deprivation of fundamental rights must have been inflicted 'by reason of the identity of the group or collectivity'. This specific discriminatory intent requirement is a key element of persecution. For the purposes of the Rome Statute, Art. 7(1)h contains the grounds on which persecution gives rise to criminal responsibility, namely on 'political, racial, national, ethnic, cultural, religious, gender . . ., or other grounds that are universally recognised as impermissible under international law'.[324] The list of impermissible grounds in the Rome Statute is longer than in previous instruments, and the addition of political and gender grounds is particularly significant. Moreover, Schabas points out that a case could be made that discrimination based on disability is another ground 'universally recognized as impermissible under international law'.[325] Indeed, with the adoption of the Convention on the Rights of Persons with Disabilities, and the ratification thereof by more than one

[323] See Section 3.2.1.3. [324] Rome Statute, Art. 7(1)h.
[325] Schabas, *Commentary on the Rome Statute*, 177.

hundred states, disability is a ground universally recognised as impermissible. In the context of a broader attack, severe deprivations of fundamental rights of people with a disability could therefore be considered persecution under the Rome Statute definition. These wider grounds potentially open the door for considerations of various ESCR violations because persons with disabilities or marginalised political groups or persons whose gender identity does not conform to the majority often face discrimination in the fields of work, education, health, social security or housing.

The discriminatory intent requirement is crucial for a finding of persecution. The violation of the right to food of the Rohingya population, for instance, can only be qualified as persecution if the Bangladeshi authorities deprive the Rohingyas of access to adequate food specifically for reasons of their identity. If the intent of Bangladeshi authorities is or was to dissuade refugees, whatever their identity, such violations of the right to food could not be captured by the concept of persecution.[326] Yet, in regard to the systematically extracted forced labour of the Rohingyas in Burma itself, the Irish Centre for Human Rights unambiguously concludes that 'the Rohingyas are the target for such treatment as a consequence of their ethnic, racial and religious make-up'.[327]

Demonstrating discriminatory intent does not pose more difficulties if the underlying deprivation of rights concerns ESCR than if the rights deprivation is primarily related to civil and political rights. On the contrary, the expanded list of impermissible grounds in the Rome Statute may make it even more likely that such a demonstration is successful for ESCR-type abuses given the manifold relationships between discrimination and educational, occupational or cultural opportunities.

### *4.5.4 In connection with any act referred to in this paragraph or any crime within the jurisdiction of the court*

At the ICC, the offence of persecution requires a connection 'with any act referred to in this paragraph or any crime within the jurisdiction of the Court'.[328] This element did not appear in the statutes of the *ad hoc* tribunals, and it is unsettled what it requires. Pocar warns that the

[326] It was speculated that Bangladeshi authorities feared an influx of further refugees because of upcoming elections in Burma in 2010. Physicians for Human Rights, 'Stateless and Starving', 9.

[327] Irish Centre for Human Rights, *Crimes against Humanity in Western Burma*, 115.

[328] Rome Statute, Art. 7(1)h.

connection requirement may imply in practice that 'policies of discrimination not specifically linked to war crimes, genocide or other crimes against humanity might go unpunished'.[329] Pocar's warning should not be overestimated, since the most plausible interpretation of the connection requirement is that the requirement is satisfied if persecutory acts are linked with another crime within the jurisdiction of the court. As Luban suggests, the ordinary meaning of the element indicates that the requirement is met if a crime is committed 'in connection with any act referred to *in other subsections of* [paragraph 1 of Art. 7]', that is, another crime against humanity.[330]

The restriction may be less burdensome than it seems at first, because the vast majority of persecutory acts could also be prosecuted as other crimes against humanity, such as 'other inhumane acts' under Art. 7(1)k.[331] While the interpretation of the connection element in the Rome Statute remains unsettled, customary international law on persecution clearly requires no such element. The ICTY in *Kupreškić* concluded that Art. 7(1)h of the Rome Statute is not 'consonant with customary international law'.[332] This indicates that tribunals or other bodies not bound by the Rome Statute, in applying domestic legislation on crimes against humanity, for instance, do not need to confine the crime of persecution to only those abuses that bear a connection to other crimes under the ICC Statute.

Against the background of this analysis, Arbour's conclusion that some ESCR violations can be recognised as the crime against humanity of persecution is correct.[333] While the scope of persecution deserves some further clarification, there is consensus that the type of human rights violation is not the decisive factor in determining the existence of persecution.

## 4.6 Apartheid

It is implausible that apartheid could ever be committed without violations of ESCR. Apartheid is a form of gross institutionalised discrimination and

329 Fausto Pocar, 'Persecution' (2008) 2 *Journal of National Security Law and Policy*, 365, 355–65: 364.

330 Luban, 'Crimes against Humanity', 103, note 68 (emphasis in the original).

331 This, in turn, may lead to circular reasoning because 'other inhumane acts' require 'similarity' with the other acts in Art. 7(1) of the Rome Statute. This seems to be an area where the Rome Statute lacks tidiness, but not one that would seem to endanger the prosecution of persecution related to ESCR violations.

332 *Prosecutor* v. *Kupreškić, IT-95-16-T, 14 January 2000*, ICTY, paras. 579–81.

333 Louise Arbour, 'Economic and Social Justice for Societies in Transition' (2007) 40 *New York University Journal of International Law and Politics*, 1, 1–28: 15.

a crime against humanity. The South African apartheid regime is notoriously well known for simultaneous repression in the sphere of civil and political rights intertwined with blatant discrimination in access to the enjoyment of ESCR.[334]

If discrimination in the field of housing, health, food, education or work takes place in the context of a broader attack against a civilian population and in the context of a racial regime,[335] the ESCR violations can be captured under the heading of apartheid if the requirements described below are met. This section discusses apartheid as a crime against humanity under the Rome Statute. Apartheid as an international crime that lies outside the context of crimes against humanity is addressed in Chapter 7.[336] It should also be noted that apartheid may constitute a war crime, if committed in armed conflict.[337]

The Rome Statute defines apartheid as 'inhumane acts of a character similar to those referred to in paragraph 1 [of Art. 7], committed in the context of an institutionalized regime of systematic oppression and domination by one racial group over any other racial group or groups and committed with the intention of maintaining that regime'.[338] The first element of Art. 7(2)h is that the acts must be 'inhumane acts of a character similar to those referred to in paragraph 1'.

### 4.6.1 *Inhumane acts of a character similar to those referred to in paragraph 1*

The *actus reus* of apartheid not only requires multiple inhumane acts, but the acts must be 'similar' to other conduct qualified as crimes against humanity. Since the ordinary wording of this provision alone does not lead to sufficient specificity, and given that the VCTL allows consideration of the other relevant rules of international law applicable in the

[334] For a general overview of the legal situation of human rights under apartheid, see John Dugard, *Human Rights and the South African Legal Order* (Princeton University, 1978); David Penna, 'Apartheid, the Law and Reform in South Africa' (1990) 37 *Africa Today*, 2, 5–21.

[335] In South Africa, the threshold elements of crimes against humanity were met since the attack constituted in the violent imposition of abuses against civilians pursuant to the regime's policy of racial segregation.

[336] See Section 7.3.

[337] For international armed conflict: AP I, Art. 85(4)c. Under the Rome Statute, apartheid could also amount to a war crime as an outrage on personal dignity, as well as humiliating and degrading treatment.

[338] Rome Statute, Art. 7(2)h.

relations between many (but not all) of the states parties to the Rome Statute,[339] it is legitimate to take into account the Apartheid Convention in order to interpret the terms of Art. 7(2)h of the Rome Statute and in order to consider how the Rome Statute definition can overlap with ESCR violations. The ILC, for instance, took the Apartheid Convention into account in its commentary on the crime against humanity of apartheid.[340] However, the question of whether the definition of apartheid in the Rome Statute is narrower than the one contained in Art. II of the Apartheid Convention arises, and the drafters of the Rome Statute may have legitimately departed from the definition contained in the Apartheid Convention.

Article II of the Apartheid Convention defines the crime by reference to a multitude of ESCR violations, such as 'measures calculated to prevent a racial group ... from participation in the political, social, economic and cultural life of the country, and the deliberate creation of conditions preventing the full development of such a group, in particular by denying [them] basic human rights and freedoms, including the right to work, the right to form recognized trade unions, the right to education', or by exploiting 'the labour of the members of a racial group'.[341] It must be noted that the status of the Apartheid Convention under customary law is doubtful.[342] It is thus safer to abstain from interpreting the Rome Statute definition of apartheid by invoking the definition of apartheid in the Apartheid Convention. An uncontroversial interpretation is one that considers that the examples listed in Art. II of the Apartheid Convention cannot automatically be assumed to constitute 'inhumane acts of a character similar to those referred to in paragraph 1'. Nevertheless, the acts listed in Art. II will in fact often be 'similar' to other acts of Art. 7(1),[343] and are also included in the crime of apartheid under the ICC Statute as long as one can show that the similarity requirement is met. Rather than arguing how ESCR violations are covered by the Apartheid Convention, one should also adduce arguments on how such conduct is similar to

339 VCLT, Art. 31(3)c.

340 ILC, Draft Code of Crimes against the Peace and Security of Mankind 1996, *Yearbook of the International Law Commission*, vol. II, Part Two, 1996, 49.

341 International Convention on the Suppression and Punishment of the Crime of Apartheid, GA Res. 3068 (XXVIII), 30 November 1973 (entered into force 18 July 1976), Art. II.

342 The Convention lacks the broad international support necessary to be considered customary international law. United Nations, 'Treaty Collection, Status of Treaties', http://treaties.un.org/Pages/ParticipationStatus.aspx.

343 ICC Elements of Crimes, Art. 7(1)j, Element 2.

other crimes against humanity. As Hall concludes, such a demonstration is possible:

> Although some may contend that some of the other acts listed in article II [of the Apartheid Convention], such as the denial of the right to work or to education, although, of course, very serious deprivations, are not of the same nature as the acts listed in article 7 para. 1, this contention overlooks the devastating impact on the lives of those denied these rights recognized by the Universal Declaration of Human Rights and guaranteed by the International Covenant on Economic, Social and Cultural Rights, and on the society deprived of the full potential of its members.[344]

### *4.6.2 In the context of 'an institutionalized regime of systematic oppression and domination by one racial group over another'*

To constitute apartheid, the conduct must also be committed in the context of an 'institutionalised regime'. This regime must be of 'systematic oppression and domination' 'by one racial group over another'.[345] The distinction between 'oppression' and 'domination' is unclear, but the ordinary meaning of both terms implies that the victim population cannot freely pursue their life plans and is discriminated against.

The most likely interpretative help to understand the term 'racial' is the UN Convention on the Elimination of All Forms of Racial Discrimination (CERD) that defines the concept in Art. 1(1) as 'any distinction, exclusion, restriction or preference based on race, colour, descent, or national or ethnic origin which has the purpose or effect of nullifying or impairing the recognition, enjoyment or exercise, on an equal footing, of human rights and fundamental freedoms in the political, economic, social, cultural or any other field of public life'.[346]

CERD is almost universally ratified,[347] and its first article can safely be considered a rule of international law applicable in the relations between the parties that shall be taken into account when interpreting the definition of apartheid in the Rome Statute.[348] The definition of the term 'racial discrimination' covers a wide range of discriminatory acts, including in the economic, social and cultural spheres. There is no indication that

344 Triffterer (ed.), *Commentary on the Rome Statute*, 264 (Hall).
345 Rome Statute, Art. 7(2)h.
346 International Convention on the Elimination of All Forms of Racial Discrimination, GA Res. 2106 (XX), 660 UNTS 195, 7 March 1966 (entered into force 4 January 1969), Art. 1(1).
347 177 states are parties to CERD, and no state has attached a reservation or declaration to Art. 1.
348 VCLT, Art. 31(3)c.

drafters at the Rome Conference wanted to give the term a more restrictive meaning than the one contained in the widely accepted CERD,[349] and this element poses no additional difficulties for the argument that apartheid overlaps with ESCR violations.

### 4.6.3 *The intention of maintaining that regime*

The next element of the crime of apartheid is the requirement of a specific intent to maintain the racial regime. This requirement paradoxically excludes acts by perpetrators who intend to replace an apartheid regime with something worse, or those seeking to replace it with just another apartheid regime.[350]

### 4.6.4 *Examples of ESCR violations that underlie the crime of apartheid*

The subsequent paragraphs present five groups of ESCR violations that are likely to overlap with the crime of apartheid. Examples from South Africa illustrate this area of overlap because there is consensus that the system in South Africa between 1948 and the early 1990s was one of apartheid.

First, forced evictions and a general decline of housing conditions go hand in hand with the commission of apartheid. As outlined previously, the CESCR found that forced evictions *prima facie* violate the right to housing.[351] Regional bodies, such as the ACommHPR, also repeatedly condemned forced evictions as a violation of human rights.[352] The committee described 'a general decline in living and housing conditions, directly attributable to policy and legislative decisions by States parties',

[349] This point also made by Triffterer (ed.), *Commentary on the Rome Statute*, 265 (Hall), note 565.

[350] This requirement also excludes all acts committed by perpetrators not seeking to implement a government. One of the reasons for the insertion of this criterion was the concern of the US government to have the ICC exercise jurisdiction over US nationals (such as members of white supremacist organisations that were not seeking to implement a government). Tim McCormack, 'Crimes against Humanity', in *The Permanent International Criminal Court*, ed. Dominic McGoldrick (Hart, 2004), 179–202: 199–200.

[351] For a detailed discussion of the legal criteria, see Section 4.3.4.1.

[352] *Social and Economic Rights Action Center (SERAC) and Center for Economic and Social Rights* v. *Nigeria, Communication 155/1996, 27 October 2001*, ACommHPR, paras. 60–1; *COHRE* v. *Sudan, Communication 296/05, 29 July 2010*, ACommHPR, paras. 157–68.

as inconsistent with obligations under the covenant,[353] and the 'right to live somewhere in security, peace and dignity'.[354]

In South Africa, both types of violations of the right to housing were the consequence of legislative and policy decisions of the oppressive regime. Mass evictions are integral to a system of apartheid.[355] Estimates indicate that more than 5 million black people were forcibly evicted.[356] Laws forced people to live in areas assigned to different races.[357] The Prevention of Illegal Squatting Act empowered the Minister of Native Affairs to displace black people.[358] Such practices would qualify as a violation of 'a general decline of housing conditions directly attributable to policy and legislative decisions by States parties'.[359] The so-called 'resettlement-villages' were, according to the World Health Organization (WHO), grossly insanitary and ill constructed.[360]

Second, discrimination in access to food is a common feature of apartheid. State policies discriminating in access to food violate the right to food.[361] The South African apartheid regime failed to respect the right to food by interfering with the access to food of black people

[353] Committee on Economic, Social and Cultural Rights, *General Comment 4 on the Right to Adequate Housing*, para. 11; Committee on Economic, Social and Cultural Rights, *General Comment 7 on the Right to Adequate Housing: Forced Evictions*, para. 11. Although the CESCR does not explicitly use the term 'violation', customary international law provides that a state violates international law if an act of that state is 'not in conformity with what is required of it by that obligation'. ILC Articles on State Responsibility, Annex to GA Res. 56/83, 12 December 2001, Art. 12.

[354] Committee on Economic, Social and Cultural Rights, *General Comment 4 on the Right to Adequate Housing*, para. 7.

[355] Susan Marks and Andrew Clapham, *International Human Rights Lexicon* (Oxford University Press, 2005), 219; Laurine Platzky and Cherryl Walker, *The Surplus People* (Ravan, 1985).

[356] Scott Leckie, 'Forced Evictions' (1994) 6 *Environment and Urbanization*, 1, 131–46: 132.

[357] For instance, Group Areas Act 1950, Act 41, 7 July 1950.

[358] Prevention of Legal Squatting Act 1951, Act 52, 6 July 1951.

[359] To date, South Africa has not ratified the ICESCR. The mentioned practices of the South African regime therefore merely constitute illustrations of violations of covenant rights, but the instrument continues to be inapplicable as treaty law. Since 1996, South Africa is a state party to the ACHPR, which, as mentioned, also protects the right to adequate housing. For the duration of South African apartheid, however, one would have to argue that the rights were part of customary international law at the time of the abuses since the treaty was only ratified after the end of apartheid.

[360] Halfdan Mahler, Address by the Director-General of the World Health Organization, Apartheid and Health, WHO, 1983, 23.

[361] Committee on Economic, Social and Cultural Rights, *General Comment 14 on the Right to the Highest Attainable Standard of Health*, para. 18.

evicted from the land used for producing food.[362] In a study on the right to food, Eide reported to the former UN Sub-Commission on Prevention of Discrimination and Protection of Minorities that 'apartheid [in South Africa] was a policy deliberately intended to create and maintain differences [in income and consumption between the rich (most of whom are White) and the poor (most of whom are Africans)]'.[363]

Third, the adoption of policies interfering with the underlying components of health on a discriminatory basis can constitute inhumane acts of apartheid. As mentioned, the CESCR considers policies interfering with components of health as a violation of the obligation to respect the right to health if they 'are likely to result in bodily harm, unnecessary morbidity and preventable mortality'.[364] Such was certainly the case with a number of policies of apartheid South Africa, such as the lack of medical attention to those tortured, which is another illustration of health rights violations in apartheid South Africa, or the deliberate refusal of ambulances legally reserved for white people to stop and provide medical attention to a black patient.[365] These policies most certainly also violated the right to health under the ACHPR.

The WHO, amongst others, initiated a number of studies on the health implications of apartheid, including to mental health.[366] The then WHO Director-General concluded that 'South Africa is a striking exception from the general trend for an inverse relationship between GDP and infant mortality rates ... There is no other explanation for this fact but the drastic, enforced inequalities in the apartheid society, amounting to a denial of access to adequate health care for the vast black majority.'[367] For instance, infectious and parasitic diseases produced some 70 deaths per 1,000 live births among coloured children

[362] Kofi Yakpo and FIAN, 'Agrarian Reform and the Right to Adequate Food in South Africa', ed. FIAN (FIAN, 2004), 12.

[363] Updated Study of the Rapporteur on the Right to Adequate Food and to Be Free from Hunger (Asbjørn Eide), E/CN.4/Sub.2/1999/12, 28 June 1999, para. 69.

[364] Committee on Economic, Social and Cultural Rights, *General Comment 12 on the Right to Adequate Food*, para. 50.

[365] South African Community Law Centre et al., 'Submission to the TRC Concerning the Relevance of Economic, Social and Cultural Rights to the Commission's Mandate, 18 March 1997', www.justice.gov.za/trc/hrvtrans/submit/esc6.htm.

[366] World Health Organization, *Health Implications of Apartheid in South Africa* (WHO, 1975); World Health Organization, Apartheid and Health, International Conference on Apartheid and Health, WHO, 1983, Vol. II.

[367] Mahler, Address by the Director-General of the World Health Organization, Apartheid and Health, WHO, 1983, 25.

within the first year of life, 28 times the mortality from the same cause suffered by white babies.[368]

Fourth, apartheid is known for discrimination in the field of cultural rights and particularly the right to education. 'The introduction or failure to repeal legislation which discriminates against individuals or groups on any of the prohibited grounds' is a violation of the right to education.[369] The CESCR explained that the failure to respect, protect and fulfil the 'essential features' (availability, accessibility, acceptability, adaptability) of the right to education amounts to a violation of this right.[370] Of particular relevance to this discussion is the obligation to fulfil the acceptability of education 'by taking positive measures to ensure that education is ... of good quality for all'.[371] The UNESCO Convention against Discrimination in Education lays down a definition of the concept of discrimination within the context of education and obligates every state party to abrogate any statutory provisions and any administrative instructions that involve discrimination in education.[372] The education system in South Africa was designed with openly discriminatory intent,[373] and there is no doubt that the South African apartheid education system would today be a pertinent example of a number of violations of the right to education under the ICESCR or, had it been committed in Europe, the First Protocol to the ECHR,[374] as well as the Charter of Fundamental Rights of the European Union.[375]

Fifth, the right to work can be severely affected in apartheid systems. The formal repeal or the suspension of legislation necessary for continued

[368] Ibid. No comprehensive infant mortality statistics existed for the black population.

[369] Committee on Economic, Social and Cultural Rights, *General Comment 13 on the Right to Education*, 8 December 1999, E/C.12/1999/10, para. 59.

[370] Ibid., para. 50. [371] Ibid.

[372] UNESCO Convention against Discrimination in Education, 14 December 1960 (entered into force 22 May 1962), Art. 3(a).

[373] Ad Hoc Working Group of Experts on Southern Africa, Report, E/CN.4/1989/8, 31 January 1989, paras. 399–413, concluding that there was *de jure* discrimination in education. Whereas education was free and compulsory for white children, it was neither free nor compulsory for black children. World Health Organization, Apartheid and Health, International Conference on Apartheid and Health, WHO, 1983, 30.

[374] European Convention for the Protection of Human Rights and Fundamental Freedoms, First Protocol, 20 March 1952 (entered into force 1 November 1998), Art. 2. The Grand Chamber of the ECtHR found a violation of the right to education in conjunction with discrimination, based on the fact that Roma children in the Czech Republic were disproportionately placed in special schools intended for children with mental deficiencies. See *D.H. and Others* v. *Czech Republic, Application No. 57325/00, 13 November 2007*, ECtHR Grand Chamber.

[375] Charter of Fundamental Rights of the European Union (200/C364/01), Art. 14.

enjoyment of the right to work or the denial of access to work to particular individuals or groups violates the right to work under the Covenant,[376] as well as under ILO conventions.[377] In South Africa, examples of the denial of access to work to particular groups included the criminalisation of the performance of any skilled work by black people in urban areas. The National Party reserved entire occupations in the manufacturing sector for whites.[378] In addition, trade union rights were severely restricted.[379]

Such abuses in the realm of people's access to ESCR can be subsumed under the definitions of the crime against humanity. The General Assembly of the United Nations (GA) qualified the practices of the South African regime before the country's transition as a crime against humanity.[380] There is, however, very limited case law on the crime of apartheid that would have tested the argument that discriminatory ESCR abuses can sometimes be addressed from the angle of apartheid as a crime against humanity under the Rome Statute or customary law. An unsuccessful attempt was made to prosecute Pik Botha, a former South African Minister of Foreign Affairs, for the crime of apartheid during a visit to Uruguay. The case was dismissed, and the court did not enter into the substance of the definition of apartheid.[381] More recently, a US court dismissed claims related to corporate complicity in the South African apartheid. The court argued that US domestic law did not allow for such claims for international law violations occurring abroad and it consequently did not examine whether discriminatory ESCR violations can be qualified as the crime against humanity of apartheid.[382]

Limited judicial experience with the crime should not prevent the conclusion that the elements of this crime against humanity allow for a number of acts to be subjected to the jurisdiction of criminal tribunals, clearly including acts related to violations of ESCR. In any event, the

376 Committee on Economic, Social and Cultural Rights, *General Comment 18 on the Right to Work*, para. 32.

377 For instance, ILO Convention No. 111 Concerning Discrimination (Employment and Occupation), 362 UNTS 31, 25 June 1958 (entered into force 15 June 1960), Art. 2.

378 Bantu Building Workers Act 1951, Act 27, 1951; Muriel Horrell, *Laws Affecting Race Relations in South Africa* (Institute of Race Relations, 1978).

379 The Industrial Conciliation Act of 1956 excluded Africans from formal trade union representation and the Native Labour Act of 1953 prohibited strike action by black people. Industrial Conciliation Act 1956, Act 28, 1956.

380 Apartheid as a Crime against Humanity, GA Res. 2202 A (XXI), 16 December 1966.

381 Triffterer (ed.), *Commentary on the Rome Statute*, 263 (Hall).

382 *Balintulo* v. *Daimler, 2013 09-2778-Cv(L) (2nd Cir. 2013)*, USA. See Section 8.2.4.2.

crime of apartheid is not limited to the history of South Africa.[383] Hall concludes that the

> wide number of acts which constitute 'the crime of apartheid', the broad definition of racial discrimination under international law . . ., and the significant number of states which have today institutionalised regimes of systematic oppression and domination by one racial group over at least one other racial group, means that the potential number of acts which would be subjected to the [ICC]'s jurisdiction is considerable.[384]

ESCR violations are a prominent feature of apartheid. This finding implies that there was no legal reason for the South African Truth and Reconciliation Commission not to analyse violations of ESCR as part of its investigations. The commission was established with the mandate of establishing 'as complete a picture as possible of the nature, causes and extent of gross violations of human rights' committed during apartheid, 'including the antecedents, circumstances, factors and context of such violations'.[385] Many have criticised the Commission's almost exclusive focus on civil and political rights abuses and argued that the picture presented by the commission failed to represent some of the most troubling of apartheid's injustices, namely the numerous violations of ESCR.[386]

Another crime against humanity that can overlap with ESCR violations is murder.

[383] The former UN Special Rapporteur for Palestine, John Dugard, stated in 2007 that 'elements of the Israeli occupation constitute forms of colonialism and of apartheid, which are contrary to international law'. Another special rapporteur, Richard Falk, similarly argued that 'the dual discriminatory structure of settler administration, security, mobility, and law as compared to the Palestinian subjugation seems to qualify the long Israeli occupation of the West Bank as an instance of apartheid'. Report of the Special Rapporteur on the Situation of Human Rights in the Palestinian Territories Occupied since 1967 (John Dugard), A/HRC/4/17, 29 January 2007, para. 62; Report of the Special Rapporteur on the Situation of Human Rights in the Palestinian Territories Occupied since 1967 (Richard Falk), A/HRC/16/72, 10 January 2011, para. 8.

[384] Triffterer (ed.), *Commentary on the Rome Statute*, 229 (Hall).

[385] Promotion of National Unity and Reconciliation Act 1995, Act 95-34, 26 July 1995, Chapter 2, Art. 3(1)a.

[386] Mahmood Mamdani, 'Amnesty or Impunity? A Preliminary Critique of the Report of the TRC of South Africa' (2002) 32 *Diacritics*, 3–4, 33–59: 37–8. See also South African Community Law Centre et al., 'Submission to the TRC Concerning the Relevance of Economic, Social and Cultural Rights to the Commission's Mandate, 18 March 1997', www.justice.gov.za/trc/hrvtrans/submit/esc6.htm.

## 4.7 Murder

A single act of murder can constitute a crime against humanity,[387] provided that the *chapeau* requirements for crimes against humanity are met. Because the term 'killing' is synonymous with 'causing death',[388] it is straightforward to consider that certain deprivations of ESCR could constitute murder.

The basic *actus reus* requirement for the commission of the crime of murder is that the perpetrator must have killed one or more persons.[389] Murder can be an international crime in three ways: as a crime against humanity, as a war crime or as genocide by killing. The war crime of murder/wilful killing is addressed in Chapter 5,[390] and genocide by killing is discussed in Chapter 6.[391] As a crime against humanity, the elements of crime do not require that the killing take place in armed conflict, nor must the victim have protected status under IHL (i.e., it is not necessary that the victim is wounded or sick, shipwrecked at sea, a prisoner of war or an individual not taking part in hostilities). Rather, the threshold elements of crimes against humanity must be met. Otherwise, the elements of murder as a crime against humanity and as a war crime are the same.[392] In some, but not all cases, the *ad hoc* tribunals have held that murder/wilful killing as a war crime has a broader mental element than murder as a crime against humanity,[393] but, as argued below, this distinction is unwarranted. Since murder as a war crime and as a crime against humanity otherwise share the elements, ESCR violations as murder will be elaborated in the chapter on war crimes. Here, suffice it to address the debate surrounding the possible difference between the mental element for murder as a crime against humanity and murder/wilful killing as a war crime in order to clarify the significance of this debate in relation to ESCR violations.

### 4.7.1 *The mental element of murder as a crime against humanity*

Existing case law is inconsistent with regard to the mental element of murder as a crime against humanity. In particular the early case law contained divergent views on whether premeditation is required for

[387] *Prosecutor* v. *Bemba, Decision on the Charges of the Prosecutor, 15 June 2009, Pre-Trial Chamber II, ICC-01/05-01/08-424*, ICC, para. 151.

[388] ICC Elements of Crimes, footnote 7. [389] ICC Elements of Crimes, Art. 7(1)a.

[390] See Section 5.2.1.1. [391] See Section 6.2.1.

[392] See also *Prosecutor* v. *Krnojelac, IT-97-25-T, 15 March 2002*, ICTY, para. 323; *Prosecutor* v. *Blagojević and Jokić, IT-02-60-T, 17 January 2005*, ICTY, 556.

[393] In particular: *Prosecutor* v. *Delalić, IT-96-21-T, 16 November 1998*, ICTY, para. 439.

murder as a crime against humanity,[394] and whether it is enough that a perpetrator is reckless. Today, it is accepted that premeditation is not required for murder as a crime against humanity, whether in customary law or in the Rome Statute.[395] This implies that killing by way of harming someone's enjoyment of ESCR does not need to be pre-planned.

With regard to reckless conduct, the position is less certain and is complicated by the fact that understandings of recklessness differ across jurisdictions. In national law, each jurisdiction has its own nuanced understanding of the mental requirements for the definition of murder.[396] The ambiguities in case law reflect the various conceptions of the subjective elements for a murder conviction before national courts. Undoubtedly, before the ICC or before another tribunal applying international criminal law, a high threshold of culpable mind is required for the purpose of a murder conviction as a crime against humanity. Causing death by depriving victims of food, water or medicine alone would, for instance, not suffice to constitute murder since this only describes the *actus reus*. The perpetrator must intend to engage in the conduct. It is submitted that such a mental element is present where an actor does not desire a harmful consequence, but foresees the possibility and takes the risk. While it is not necessary that the perpetrator has been aware that death would ensue in all certainty, he or she must have anticipated that death will occur in the ordinary course of events. The prosecutor must, therefore, in line with the intent requirements of Art. 30 of the Rome Statute, establish that the perpetrator meant to cause the consequence,

394 No premeditation was required in *Prosecutor* v. *Akayesu, ICTR-96-4-T, 2 September 1998*, ICTR, para. 589. Other ICTR Chambers required premeditation under the ICTR Statute, but not under customary international law, for example, in *Prosecutor* v. *Kayishema and Ruzindana, ICTR-95-1-T, 21 May 1999*, ICTR, para. 138. Most ICTY Chambers, but not all, have not required premeditation for murder as a crime against humanity. See for instance *Prosecutor* v. *Krnojelac, IT-97-25-T, 15 March 2002*, ICTY, para. 324. See Triffterer (ed.), *Commentary on the Rome Statute*, 186 (Hall).

395 Intent, required by Art. 30 of the Rome Statute, does not require that the perpetrator has 'thought through' the crime in advance, while premeditation does. There was a linguistic problem in the Statutes of the *ad hoc* tribunals, which used the French term of '*assassinat*' (requiring premeditation in French law), rather than '*meurtre*' (not requiring premeditation). The French version of the Rome Statute uses the term '*meurtre*' and thus does clearly not require the premeditation as for '*assassinat*' in French criminal law. Triffterer (ed.), *Commentary on the Rome Statute*, 184–5 (Hall); Antonio Cassese, *International Criminal Law*, 2nd edn (Oxford University Press, 2008), 61.

396 Triffterer (ed.), *Commentary on the Rome Statute*, 184 (Hall), noting the differences between mental elements for murder in domestic systems and the absence of discussion on these differences at the Rome Conference.

that is the death of the victim, or was aware that death would normally occur after depriving someone of food, water or essential medicine.[397]

The exact meaning of 'will occur in the ordinary course of events' in Art. 30(2)b of the Rome Statute has been interpreted in various cases. In *Bemba*, the ICC Pre-Trial Chamber II explained that 'the required standard of occurrence is close to certainty',[398] whereas the Pre-Trial Chamber I in *Katanga and Chui* only required that the perpetrator accepts an outcome, that is commits an *actus reus* with *dolus eventualis*/recklessness.[399] Based on the wording of 'will occur' (as opposed to, for instance, 'may occur'), Trial Chamber I stated in the *Lubanga* judgment that it accepted the higher standard used in *Bemba*.[400] At the same time, the trial chamber explained that the requisite mental standard 'means that the participants anticipate, based on their knowledge of how events ordinarily develop, that the consequence will occur in the future. This prognosis involves considerations of the concepts of "possibility" and "probability".'[401] In the same vein, Trial Chamber II recently confirmed this stance in the *Katanga* judgment, excluded the *dolus eventualis* and repeated that 'virtual certainty' is required.[402] At the same time, the chamber stressed that the certitude does not need to be absolute. Rather, the perpetrator must realise that the consequence will occur except if the course of events would take an unexpected turn.[403]

We can conclude from this that the difference of the mental element under the Rome Statute as opposed to the mental element under other sources is one of degree and not of kind. The Rome Statute requires a slightly higher standard of occurrence than a 'domestic' type of recklessness, where it is usually enough that a perpetrator simply accepts the possible outcome of death, but does not necessarily anticipate that death will almost certainly occur. Such a higher standard can obviously still be

397 Rome Statute, Art. 30.

398 *Prosecutor* v. *Bemba, Decision on the Charges of the Prosecutor, 15 June 2009, Pre-Trial Chamber II, ICC-01/05-01/08-424*, ICC, para. 362, also referring to 'virtual certainty', 'practical certainty', 'the consequence will follow, barring an unforeseen or unexpected intervention that prevents its occurrence'.

399 *Prosecutor* v. *Katanga and Chui, Decision on the Confirmation of Charges, 30 September 2008, Pre-Trial Chamber I, ICC-01/04-01/07*, ICC, note 329.

400 *Prosecutor* v. *Lubanga Dyilo, Judgment Pursuant to Article 74 of the Statute, 14 March 2012, Trial Chamber I, ICC-01/04-01/06-2842*, ICC, para. 1011.

401 Ibid., para. 1012.

402 *Prosecutor* v. *Katanga, Jugement rendu en application de l'article 74 du Statut, 7 March 2014, Trial Chamber II, N° ICC-01/04-01/07*, ICC, paras. 775–7.

403 Ibid.

met by conduct related to ESCR violations. It is easy to imagine scenarios in which it is 'practically certain' that, for instance, a person in detention will die if drinking water, live-saving medical treatment or food is withheld or if people under a perpetrator's control and with no option to sustain themselves are turned adrift when sufficient resources are available.

Throughout this study, the terms 'intent' and 'knowledge'[404] are interpreted to include 'wilfulness'.[405] If a perpetrator deprives an individual of food, medicine or water and he or she has knowledge that this will almost certainly cause the death of the person concerned, the mental element would be fulfilled, independently of how the same requirement would be understood in various national jurisdictions (such as recklessness, wilful blindness or *dolus eventualis*).

To prosecute a violation of ESCR as murder, it will be of utmost importance to assess the mental elements that the tribunal will apply. In cases of omission, when death is, for instance, caused by the failure to provide individuals with food or medical attention, it is traditionally more challenging to prove the mental element than if murder is committed by direct killing. Cases of individuals deprived of food, water or health care in custody are the classic examples in which omissions can be qualified as murder. This is because the existence of an obligation to act and causality are easier to establish for people deprived of liberty, whereas it is more difficult to show that a certain act or omission caused death if the individual was not under the absolute control of the perpetrator. But this does not imply that detention or other forms of custody are required to prove murder by deliberate failure to act, such as by withholding food, water or medicine. Both, acts or omissions causing the death of one or more individuals, can constitute the crime against humanity of murder, provided that the threshold requirements of crimes against humanity and the requisite *mens rea* are met. As mentioned, we will consider further examples on the interrelatedness of murder and ESCR violations in Chapter 5.

## 4.8 Extermination

Extermination shares important characteristics with the crime against humanity of murder, as well as with the crime of genocide. A more

404 Rome Statute, Art. 30.

405 See also Knut Dörmann et al., *Elements of War Crimes* (Cambridge University Press, 2003), 41.

detailed analysis of ESCR violations as extermination is contained in the chapter on genocide, since a sub-paragraph of the genocide definition specifically refers to genocide by deliberately inflicting conditions of life calculated to bring about physical destruction.[406] Here, it is sufficient to flag the specificities of the legal definition of extermination as opposed to genocide and as opposed to murder as a crime against humanity.

The jurisprudence has consistently held that the core elements of murder and extermination are the same, apart from the fact that killings must occur on a massive scale to qualify as extermination.[407] Numerous killings resulting from the deprivation from essential food, water, shelter or health care, for instance, will constitute extermination if committed with intent and knowledge and if inflicted in the context of a broader attack against a civilian population.

As far as the main difference from genocide is concerned, extermination as a crime against humanity does not require the genocidal *dolus specialis* to destroy a protected group. In addition, extermination also covers situations in which a group of individuals do not share the common characteristics that are required for genocide. The ICTR's jurisprudence in this regard is undisputed: the ICTR has held that for extermination, a targeted group could be any identifiable group, such as a neighbourhood.[408] Extermination could therefore be committed against groups identified by reason of their socio-economic status (for instance, where a policy targets the poor, people with disabilities, *campesinos*, etc.).

The Rome Statute expressly states that extermination 'includes the intentional infliction of conditions of life, *inter alia* the deprivation of access to food and medicine, calculated to bring about the destruction of part of a population',[409] and the same has been consistently affirmed by

[406] See Section 6.2.3.

[407] *Prosecutor* v. *Akayesu, ICTR-96-4-T, 2 September 1998*, ICTR, para. 591; *Prosecutor* v. *Ntakirutimana, ICTR-96-10-T and ICTR-96-17-T, 21 February 2003*, ICTR, para. 813; *Prosecutor* v. *Brđanin, IT-99-36-T, 1 September 2004*, ICTY, para. 388. See also ILC, Draft Code of Crimes against the Peace and Security of Mankind 1996, *Yearbook of the International Law Commission*, vol. II, Part Two, 1996, commentary to Art. 18. In *Krstić*, the ICTY Trial Chamber held that 'the definition should be read as meaning the destruction of a numerically significant part of the population concerned'. *Prosecutor* v. *Krstić, IT-98-33-T, 2 August 2001*, ICTY, para. 502. The ICTR held that a 'mass scale' but no numerical minimum must be reached. *Prosecutor* v. *Munyakazi, ICTR-97-36a-T, 5 July 2010*, ICTR, para. 506. Extermination must be aimed at a group rather than identified individuals. *Prosecutor* v. *Vasiljevic, IT-98-32-T, 29 November 2002*, ICTY, para. 227.

[408] *Prosecutor* v. *Kamuhanda, ICTR-95-54a-T, 22 January 2004*, ICTR, para. 694.

[409] Rome Statute, Art. 7(2)b.

the *ad hoc* tribunals,[410] as well as the ECCC.[411] As Bassiouni notes, 'this formulation . . . states that "extermination" does not merely occur when a perpetrator executes the material act of, for instance, firing a rifle or wielding a knife that directly results in the killing of another, but also when a perpetrator creates "conditions of life" amenable to mass killing'.[412] The *inter alia* implies that other socio-economic conditions, in addition to the deprivation of access to food and medicine, could be covered, as long as they are calculated to bring about massive deaths. In the context of extermination as a crime against humanity, illustrative examples listed in the case law include, for instance, 'imprisoning a large number of people and withholding the necessities of life which results in mass death [or] introducing a deadly virus into a population and preventing medical care which results in mass death'.[413] The ICC Pre-Trial Chamber I approved a charge of genocide by inflicting conditions of life calculated to bring about the death of the targeted group against Sudanese President Bashir.[414] In Cambodia, the *actus reus* of extermination arguably took place because perpetrators implemented 'a system of forced labour, state expropriation of foodstuffs and extreme restrictions on basic rights', and thereby subjected 'Cambodian civilians to famine conditions that would inevitably lead to death'.[415] Similar findings have been made by the UN Commission of Inquiry on Human Rights in the Democratic People's Republic of Korea.[416]

The difficulty of obtaining a conviction for extermination based on the infliction of extreme living conditions is the establishment of the requisite *mens rea*. This potentially complicates the qualification of ESCR violations as extermination. As Davidsson cautions,

> [i]t appears therefore that policies imposing economic hardship on a civilian population, including the creation of conditions conducive to malnutrition, disease, low life expectancy and high infant mortality

410 For instance, in *Prosecutor* v. *Kayishema and Ruzindana, ICTR-95-1-T, 21 May 1999*, ICTR, para. 146; *Prosecutor* v. *Stakić, IT-97-24-A, 22 March 2006*, ICTY, para. 259.

411 *Prosecutor* v. *Kaing Guek Eav (Duch), Judgment, Case 001/18-07-2007/ECCC/Tc, 26 July 2010*, ECCC, para. 335.

412 Bassiouni, *Crimes against Humanity*, 305.

413 *Prosecutor* v. *Kayishema and Ruzindana, ICTR-95-1-T, 21 May 1999*, ICTR, para. 146.

414 *Second Decision on the Prosecution's Application for a Warrant of Arrest against Al Bashir, 12 July 2010, Pre-Trial Chamber I, ICC-02/05-01/09*, ICC, paras. 38–40.

415 Randle DeFalco, 'Accounting for Famine' (2011) 5 *International Journal of Transitional Justice*, 1, 142–58: 150.

416 North Korea Inquiry, A/HRC/25/CRP.1, 7 February 2014, especially paras. 1117–27.

> could amount to extermination as a crime against humanity under the Rome Statute only if it can be shown that the perpetrators were aware that massive deaths would ensue as the natural consequences of their acts.[417]

Yet, even such foreseeability is not enough. The verb 'calculated' implies that the deprivation of access to basic socio-economic rights must have been intended as a mechanism to bring about the destruction of part of a population.[418] Proof of such a calculated causal relationship is challenging, but not impossible. In the example of Cambodia, DeFalco enumerates factual information showing that the requisite *mens rea* of extermination could be satisfied in relation to several alleged perpetrators. He points to available pieces of evidence establishing that leaders were aware of the deadly famine that surrounded them and that they utilised famine as a primary means to control the population or to provide the Communist Party of Kampuchea with 'surplus' rice.[419]

The chapter on genocide further analyses the points at which violations of the right to health or the prevention of access to food aid can be qualified as 'calculated to bring about the destruction of part of a population'.[420] The point here is that mass killings falling within this category of genocide will qualify as extermination even in the absence of the specific intent to destroy a protected group as long as the threshold elements of crimes against humanity are also met.

In addition to the crimes against humanity analysed so far, the remaining two crimes – torture and other inhumane acts – can overlap with ESCR violations in similar ways but without the requirement that the conduct causes death.

[417] Elias Davidsson, 'Economic Oppression' (2005) 23 *Netherlands Quarterly of Human Rights*, 2, 173–212: 195. Bassiouni regrets that the drafters of the ICTY, ICTR and ICC Statutes failed to specifically state that intentional killings included those situations in which the perpetrator knew or should have known that death would be the result of a given conduct. Bassiouni, *Crimes against Humanity*, 304–5.

[418] A UN report uses a lower standard and argues that it is sufficient that the perpetrator makes 'the calculated assessment that the infliction of the particular conditions of life will in the ordinary course of events result in mass killing, even though this might not be the perpetrator's subjective purpose'. North Korea Inquiry, A/HRC/25/CRP.1, 7 February 2014, note 1558.

[419] DeFalco, 'Accounting for Famine', 149–52.

[420] ICC Elements of Crimes, Art. 7(1)b, element 1. See also the interpretation of the term 'calculated' in the context of genocide in Section 6.2.3.

## 4.9 Torture

Torture is an exceptionally complex crime. It is defined slightly differently in a number of legal sources. Chapter 7 addresses the circumstances under which ESCR violations overlap with torture as a discrete crime,[421] and Chapter 5 deals with torture as a war crime.[422] Here, the specificity in the definition of torture as a crime against humanity is outlined and compared to other definitions of torture.

For the purposes of the ICC, torture as a crime against humanity is the 'intentional infliction of severe pain or suffering, whether physical or mental, upon a person in the custody or under the control of the accused; except that torture shall not include pain or suffering arising only from, inherent in or incidental to, lawful sanctions'.[423] In addition to the different contextual elements, there are two main specificities in the definition of torture as a crime against humanity as opposed to other definitions of torture:

First, at least under the Rome Statute, the crime against humanity of torture does not require the torture to have been committed for a specific purpose.[424] This means that it is not necessary for the accused to have attempted to attain a certain result or fulfilled a particular purpose by torturing the individual(s). The conclusion that there is absence of a prohibited purpose requirement is less certain under customary international law, and *ad hoc* tribunals have applied the prohibited purpose requirement, stating that their position reflected customary international law.[425] If a tribunal applies a prohibited purpose requirement, this means that the conduct harming the victim's ESCR must have been inflicted for a purpose such as obtaining information or a confession.

Second, the crime against humanity of torture does not require the involvement of a person acting in a public capacity. As with the prohibited purpose requirement, this conclusion is safe for the Rome Statute,[426] but also seems to be accurate for torture as a crime against humanity in customary international law. While the definition of torture contained in the UNCAT requires that torture be 'inflicted by, or at the instigation of, or with the consent or acquiescence of a . . . person acting in an official

[421] See Section 7.2. [422] See Section 5.2.1.1. [423] Rome Statute, Art. 7(2)f.

[424] ICC Elements of Crimes, footnote 14.

[425] *Prosecutor* v. *Bemba, Decision on the Charges of the Prosecutor, 15 June 2009, Pre-Trial Chamber II, ICC-01/05-01/08-424*, ICC, para. 195; *Prosecutor* v. *Kvočka, IT-98-30/1-T, 2 November 2001*, ICTY, para. 140; *Prosecutor* v. *Kunarac, Kovac and Vukovic, IT-96-23-A, 12 June 2002*, ICTY, para. 142.

[426] Rome Statute, Art. 7(2)e.

capacity',[427] the Rome Statute definition of torture as a crime against humanity lacks such a requirement.[428] The ICTY also found that the customary definition of torture as a crime against humanity does not contain a public official requirement,[429] contradicting its own previous case law.[430] For both of these requirements, the negotiation of the ICC Elements of Crimes provided states with the opportunity to express their views on the customary elements of torture as a crime against humanity. The conscious elimination of the prohibited purpose requirement and the absence of a public official element tend to strengthen the position that both elements are not required under customary international law. This implies that a non-state actor who intentionally inflicts severe pain or suffering to a person under his or her control, for instance, by depriving the victim of medical care, is committing torture, and such torture overlaps with an ESCR violation if the state fails to protect people against such abuses.

The Rome Statute further contains a control element for torture. Under the Rome Statute, victims of torture as a crime against humanity before the ICC must be 'under the control of the accused'.[431] Whereas UNCAT does not explicitly contain such an element, Burger and Danelius demonstrate that the history of UNCAT confirms that the victims must be understood to be persons who are under the factual power or control of the person inflicting the pain or suffering.[432] The two experts specify that this implicit requirement must be understood broadly to include any form of restraint and that it was intended to exclude such acts as use of armed force in conflicts.[433] This element certainly poses no problems in cases where individuals are deprived of liberty such as in cases of detention. The UN inquiry on North Korea, for

427 Convention against Torture and Other Cruel, Inhuman or Degrading Treatment or Punishment, GA Res. 39/46 (1984), 10 December 1984 (entered into force 26 June 1987), Art. 1().

428 Rome Statute, Art. 7(2)e.

429 *Prosecutor* v. *Kunarac, Kovac and Vukovic, IT-96-23-A, 12 June 2002*, ICTY, para. 148; *Prosecutor* v. *Kvočka, IT-98-30/1-T, 2 November 2001*, ICTY, para. 139.

430 *Prosecutor* v. *Delalić, IT-96-21-T, 16 November 1998*, ICTY, para. 494; *Prosecutor* v. *Krnojelac, IT-97-25-T, 15 March 2002*, ICTY, para. 188; *Prosecutor* v. *Furundžija, IT-95-17/1-T, 10 December 1998*, ICTY, para. 162; *Prosecutor* v. *Furundžija, IT-95-17/1-A, 21 July 2000*, ICTY, para. 111, requiring the public official element, but stating that this was an element of the crime of 'torture in a situation of armed conflict'.

431 Rome Statute, Art. 7(2)e.

432 Herman Burgers and Hans Danelius, *The United Nations Convention against Torture* (Nijhoff, 1988), 120–1.

433 Ibid., 121.

instance, extensively documented the deliberate starvation and deprivation of detainees in political prison camps and concluded that these amount to torture as a crime against humanity.[434]

Even when an individual is not deprived of liberty, he or she can be 'under the control' of the accused. For instance, as Rottensteiner persuasively explains, if access to a territory is completely controlled by enemy troops, the civilian population can be considered to be under the control of the forces regulating the entry of humanitarian relief, food, water or health care.[435] Such was arguably the case in some so-called safe areas in Bosnia[436] or in the last strip of rebel-held land in the North of Sri Lanka in 2009.[437]

The remaining offence of crimes against humanity analysed in this chapter concerns 'other inhumane acts'.

## 4.10 Other inhumane acts of a similar character intentionally causing great suffering, or serious injury to body or to mental or physical health

'Other inhumane acts of a similar character intentionally causing great suffering, or serious injury to body or to mental or physical health' are a crime against humanity.[438] The crime is not further defined, and its open-ended nature causes difficulties in determining the circumstances under which ESCR violations, or any abuses, would fall within the ambit of this provision.

This section provides an outline of the existing indications guiding the assessment of whether ESCR violations can amount to the crime of 'other inhumane acts'. Given the number of overlapping conceptual elements between the crime of 'other inhumane acts', torture and the grave breach of 'wilfully causing great suffering or serious injury to body or health', this section is best read in conjunction with the interpretation of these crimes.[439]

A provision on 'other inhumane acts' appeared in the Nuremberg Charter, Council Law No. 10, the Tokyo Charter, the Nuremberg

434 North Korea Inquiry, A/HRC/25/CRP.1, 7 February 2014, para. 1053.

435 Christa Rottensteiner, 'The Denial of Humanitarian Assistance' (1999) 81 *International Review of the Red Cross*, 555–82: 574.

436 Ibid.

437 Report of the SG's Panel of Experts on Accountability in Sri Lanka, 31 March 2011, para. 176.

438 Rome Statute, Art. 7(1)k. See also Note 432.

439 See Section 4.9 and Section 5.2.1.4.

Principles and the statutes of the *ad hoc* tribunals.[440] None of these texts contained an exhaustive list of prohibited conduct. The crux of this crime is that the category of 'other inhumane acts' was introduced to catch up with the imagination of future perpetrators,[441] while the interpretation of the crime must comply with the requirements of criminal law, in particular the principle of legality. As a compromise, the ILC 1996 Draft Code restricted the scope of the crime to 'other inhumane acts which severely damage physical or mental integrity, health or human dignity, such as mutilation and severe bodily harm'.[442] The ICTY followed this approach in the *Tadić* case,[443] and the wording of the provision in the Rome Statute resonates with the objective to restrict the scope, while abstaining from providing an exhaustive list of acts, in order to conserve a residual category of crimes against humanity. The Rome Statute provides a somewhat more restrictive definition than the ICTY Statute by requiring the acts to be 'of a similar character intentionally causing great suffering, or serious injury to body or to mental or physical health'.[444] The crime of other inhumane acts remains open ended, and the same is true for the eventual defence claim that the interpretation of the crime is in violation of the principle of strict construction.[445] This is true whether a case mostly relates to civil and political rights or to ESCR violations, and the problem of legality is no more acute for the latter category.

In addition to the threshold requirements of all crimes against humanity and for the purposes of the Rome Statute, the conduct must meet the following criteria.

440 See Nuremberg Charter, Art. 6(c); Control Council Law No. 10, Punishment of Persons Guilty of War Crimes, Crimes against Peace and against Humanity, 20 December 1945, Art. II(1)a; Charter of the International Military Tribunal for the Far East, 19 January 1946, Art. 5(c); ILC, Principles of International Law Recognized in the Charter of the Nuremberg Tribunal and in the Judgment of the Tribunal, with Commentaries, *Yearbook of the International Law Commission*, 1950, vol. II, 1950, Principle 6(c); ICTR Statute, Art. 3(i); ICTY Statute, Art. 5(i).

441 Confirming this point, see *Prosecutor* v. *Kupreškić, IT-95-16-T, 14 January 2000*, ICTY, para. 563.

442 For the development of this provision, see Triffterer, (ed.), *Commentary on the Rome Statute*, 230–4 (Boot). The ICTY Appeals Chamber held that 'other inhumane acts' were part of customary law and that convictions for this offence do not violate the principle of legality. *Prosecutor* v. *Stakić, IT-97-24-A, 22 March 2006*, ICTY, para. 315.

443 *Prosecutor* v. *Tadić, IT-94-1-T, 7 May 1997*, ICTY, para. 729.

444 Rome Statute, Art. 7(1)k.

445 Vincent Sautenet, 'Crimes against Humanity and the Principles of Legality' (2000) 7 *Murdoch Electronic Journal of Law*, 1: para. 28.

### 4.10.1 Other inhumane acts of a similar character

The first element is that acts must be 'inhumane' and 'of a similar character' to the other acts listed in the first paragraph of article 7 of the Rome Statute.

As the ICC Pre-Trial Chamber has expressed it, inhumane acts are serious violations of 'the basic rights pertaining to human beings, drawn from the norms of international human rights law, which are of a similar nature and gravity to the acts referred to in article 7(1) of the Statute'.[446]

An ICTY Trial Chamber in *Kupreškić* held that the interpretation of 'other inhumane acts' shall be done in light of international standards such as those laid down in the UDHR and the two UN Covenants of 1966 in order to identify a set of basic rights appertaining to human beings, 'the infringement of which may amount, depending on the accompanying circumstances, to a crime against humanity'.[447] The chamber thus explicitly refers to the ICESCR. It also confirmed the existence of a close relationship between the crime of 'other inhumane acts' and the understanding of the prohibition of torture, inhuman or degrading treatment in human rights law,[448] and the arguments presented for these crimes thus apply *mutatis mutandis.*

'Other inhumane acts' are among the charges pressed by the ICC Prosecutor in the *Situation in Uganda*, where the arrest warrants refer to 'serious bodily injury and suffering upon civilian residents of an internally displaced persons' camp'.[449] At the time of writing, the specific factual background of the individual charges against the Ugandan rebels is not public, but it is likely that socio-economic abuses figure among the alleged conduct given that such abuses have been the concern of several reports.[450]

Considering the ordinary meaning of the elements of the crime and the fact that the ICTY referred to standards contained in the UDHR as well as in both Covenants – and this statement has remained unchallenged – the notion of 'other inhumane acts' is in no way limited to the infringement

[446] *Prosecutor* v. *Katanga and Chui, Decision on the Confirmation of Charges, 30 September 2008, Pre-Trial Chamber I, ICC-01/04-01/07,* ICC, para. 448.

[447] *Prosecutor* v. *Kupreškić, IT-95-16-T, 14 January 2000,* ICTY, para. 566.

[448] Ibid.

[449] *Arrest Warrant for Kony, as Amended on 27 September 2005, 27 September 2005, Pre-Trial Chamber II, ICC-02/04-01/05,* ICC, counts 22 and 9; *Arrest Warrant for Otti, 8 July 2005, Pre-Trial Chamber II, ICC-02/04,* ICC, counts 22 and 9; *Arrest Warrant for Ongwen, 8 July 2005, Pre-Trial Chamber II, ICC-02/04,* ICC, count 29.

[450] See, for instance, Chris Dolan, *Social Torture* (Berghahn Books, 2009). Or Phuong Pham et al., *Forgotten Voices* (ICTJ, Berkeley Human Rights Center, 2005), 22.

of civil and political rights. The chamber emphasised the criterion of seriousness of the acts,[451] and there is no indication in the wording of the provision or in case law that the phrase might not cover socio-economic abuses. Indeed, in his memorandum on the Nuremberg Principles, the UN Secretary-General mentioned in 1949 that the deprivation of means of sustenance is an act that this phrase might cover.[452] In contrast to extermination charges, massive death is not required. This implies that devastating, but not deadly, cases of undernourishment resulting from a deliberate hindrance of access to food can potentially be addressed by this provision.

Similarity requires that the acts are similar in kind and gravity to the other acts listed as crimes against humanity.[453] The ordinary meaning of the phrase 'of a similar character' implies that such acts not only refer to acts such as direct killings or arbitrary imprisonment, but also to persecution or apartheid, because these form part of the provision that defines crimes against humanity on an equal footing with the other prohibited acts.

The case law of the *ad hoc* tribunals has offered little guidance on how to determine similarity.[454] The ICTR Trial Chamber stated that similarity 'should be determined on a case-by-case basis'.[455] Since the crime of forcible transfer of population was not yet explicitly listed in the ICTY Statute, the ICTY has considered the forced removal of people to be tantamount to other inhumane acts amounting to crimes against humanity.[456] The Special Panels in East Timor provided more examples of acts found to constitute other inhumane acts: cutting off a man's ear and making him eat it;[457] holding victims for four days and repeatedly punching, kicking and beating them with sticks and rifle butts;[458] severe

451 *Prosecutor* v. *Kupreškić, IT-95-16-T, 14 January 2000*, ICTY, para. 566.

452 The Charter and the Judgment of the Nuremberg Tribunal, Memorandum Submitted by the SG, A/CN.4/5, 1949, 67.

453 ICC Elements of Crimes, footnote 30.

454 For further analysis, see Triffterer (ed.), *Commentary on the Rome Statute*, 231 (Boot).

455 *Prosecutor* v. *Musema, ICTR-96-13-T, 27 January 2000*, ICTR, para. 233; *Prosecutor* v. *Bagilishema, ICTR-95-1a-T, 7 June 2001*, ICTR, para. 92.

456 For instance, *Prosecutor* v. *Milošević, IT-02-54-T, Decision on Motion for Judgment of Acquittal, 16 June 2004*, ICTY, para. 52; *Prosecutor* v. *Krajišnik, IT-00-39-T, 27 September 2006*, ICTY, paras. 722–32.

457 *Prosecutor* v. *Cardoso Fereira, 04/2001, 05 April 2003*, Special Panels for Serious Crimes – East Timor, para. 402. Cases cited in Triffterer (ed.), *Commentary on the Rome Statute*, 230 (Boot).

458 *Prosecutor* v. *Pedro, 01/2001, 14 April 2005*, Special Panels for Serious Crimes – East Timor, para. 8.

beating;[459] and striking victims with machetes and stones and leaving them for dead.[460] In addition to these examples of direct physical violence mentioned in the case against Ena, the panel added that 'a large number of cattle belonging to the villagers were stolen', but it did not explicitly qualify these acts as 'other inhumane acts'.[461] Given the impact for victims' socio-economic well-being, the stealing of cattle possibly constituted a violation of the right to be free from hunger. The defendants' militia was allegedly institutionally attached to the Indonesian armed forces,[462] and the conduct may therefore possibly have been attributable to a state. Even if the panel did not elaborate on the relationship between the possible deprivation of food and the crime against humanity, similarity with other prohibited acts could have been established, if, for instance, the theft of the livestock resulted in the starvation of victims. In addition to similarity with other acts, the crime requires that the perpetrator must intentionally cause great suffering or serious injury.

### *4.10.2 Intentionally causing great suffering, or serious injury to body or to mental or physical health*

The ICTY interpreted language very similar to the phrase 'great suffering, or serious injury to body or to mental or physical health' in the context of grave breaches of the Geneva Conventions. It can be expected that an interpretation of the terms 'great suffering' and 'serious injury' in the context of Art. 7(1)k of the Rome Statute or under customary international law would be done similarly. The ICTY found that the subjection of the detainees at the Čelebići camp to inhumane living conditions constituted 'great suffering or serious injury to body or to health': the factual background that led the ICTY to reach this conclusion was the deprivation of the individuals of adequate food, water, medical care, sleeping facilities and sanitation.[463] In *Kupreškić*, the facts included the

[459] *Prosecutor* v. *Mendes Correia, 19/2001, 9 March 2004*, Special Panels for Serious Crimes – East Timor, para. 51.

[460] *Prosecutor* v. *Ena, 05/2002, 23 March 2004*, Special Panels for Serious Crimes – East Timor, paras. 42–6 (factual background), para. 92 (qualification).

[461] Ibid., para. 46.

[462] Tapol (Indonesia Human Rights Campaign), 'Analysis of Army Documents from East Timor', www.etan.org/et/1998/november/15-21/15analys.htm.

[463] *Prosecutor* v. *Delalić, IT-96-21-T, 16 November 1998*, ICTY, paras. 1092, 1096 (food), 1100 (water), 1105 (medical care), 1108 (sleeping facilities), 1111 (sanitation) and 1119

burning of homes and the killing of livestock in order to deprive the people living in the area of their most precious assets, with economic, but also emotional and cultural significance.[464] Similarly, the ECCC Trial Chamber convicted defendants of inhumane acts committed in the context of detention, *inter alia*, because of the 'lack of adequate food, hygiene and medical care'.[465] Although a number of cases dealt with 'other inhumane acts', the Special Panels in East Timor did not provide additional guidance as to when socio-economic matters would be considered inhumane acts. The panels affirmed that holding victims in a small room in unhygienic conditions without proper sanitation facilities, food or water constituted inhumane acts,[466] but the same was denied in a different case in which the tribunal found no evidence of great suffering or serious harm.[467]

As with other crimes studied in this book, the demonstration of overlap between a crime against humanity and ESCR violations is already apparent in early cases: a clear case that met the test of great suffering or serious harm was the very first trial before the NMT. As is well known, the US tribunal convicted fifteen defendants of 'other inhumane acts' that can today be conceptualised as violations of the right to health, water, food or bodily integrity. The tribunal considered more than twelve series of horrendous Nazi medical experiments, such as a study making inmates drink chemically modified sea water, while others would get no water at all, to be crimes against humanity.[468]

Despite some interpretative challenges associated with the crime of 'other inhumane acts', it can be concluded in all safety that the type of

for the conclusion that these deprivations amounted to great suffering, or serious injury to body or to health.

464 *Prosecutor* v. *Kupreškić, IT-95-16-T, 14 January 2000*, ICTY, para. 336.

465 *Prosecutor* v. *Kaing Guek Eav (Duch), Judgment, Case 001/18-07-2007/ECCC/Tc, 26 July 2010*, ECCC, para. 372.

466 *Prosecutor* v. *Gouveia Leite, 04a/2001, 7 December 2002*, Special Panels for Serious Crimes - East Timor, para. 161 (factual background) and para. 162 (qualification). The Panel found that 'this submission to inhumane conditions made the victims to suffer serious bodily or mental harm'.

467 In *Cardoso*, the Panel examined almost identical factual conditions as in *Leite*, but considered that the socio-economic conditions of detention did not constitute other inhumane acts, essentially because there was no evidence that the conditions led to serious bodily or mental harm and because there was no element of a crime distinct from the other crimes against humanity charged against the accused. *Prosecutor* v. *Cardoso Fereira, 04/2001, 05 April 2003*, Special Panels for Serious Crimes - East Timor, para. 415 (legal qualification), para. 397 (factual background).

468 *United States of America* v. *Brandt et al. (Medical Trial), II TWC 171*, NMT, 198, 214-17.

human rights violation underlying the offence is not the decisive criterion, but rather the inhumanity of the act and its similarity to other crimes against humanity. There is absolutely no element indicating that ESCR violations could not amount to 'other inhumane acts', and this is clearly confirmed in case law.

## 4.11 Conclusion

Many of the existing definitions of crimes against humanity, under certain circumstances, encompass violations of ESCR. We reviewed how ESCR violations are not solely an issue of international human rights law, but can simultaneously amount to crimes against humanity as defined in international criminal law.

Current international law on crimes against humanity contains a complex set of conditions and elements that must be met before any abuse is to be qualified as a crime against humanity. In particular, the threshold elements of crimes against humanity imply that only abuses within a specific context can qualify. Even where the conduct meets the elements of crimes of the underlying offences discussed in this chapter, such conduct can only be a crime against humanity when committed as part of a widespread or systematic attack directed against a civilian population. At the same time, careful analysis of the definitional elements of crimes against humanity and their interpretation in light of their context and their object and purpose gives us a nuanced picture that incorporates a range of abuses in the realm of survivors' ESCR. Even the early Nuremberg cases confirm such interrelatedness, and it is almost trite to argue how the Nazi regime, for instance, would today be considered in violation of the right to health or work. It is thus unwarranted to conclude *a priori* that violations of ESCR should not be a matter for tribunals and other actors dealing with the legacy of crimes against humanity. It remains open to debate, for instance, why the UN envoy to Zimbabwe was given a legal opinion summarily concluding that the events in Zimbabwe did not constitute such crimes or why the prosecutor of the ECCC did not press charges to examine famine under the Khmer Rouge. Even more important is the understanding that institutional mechanisms intended to prevent the commission of crimes against humanity must not limit their monitoring to civil and political rights but should also pay attention to abuses in the realm of ESCR. These latter abuses often precede and underlie crimes that not only shock the conscience of humanity, but leave a legacy that weighs heavily on societies for decades to come.

This leads us to consider whether a similar conclusion can be reached for war crimes – a group of crimes that can only arise in the context of an armed conflict.

# 5

# Four groups of war crimes and the forgotten trial of Gauleiter Greiser

Many abuses in armed conflict can be understood as violations of ESCR, particularly where states fail to respect rights, such as by directly interfering with the enjoyment of people's access to housing, food, education or health, or where states fail to protect persons within their jurisdiction from abuses by non-state actors.[1] The destruction of homes, the looting of crops or livestock and the denial of humanitarian relief are all too familiar occurrences in times of armed conflicts. In Timor Leste, for instance, the Commission for Reception, Truth and Reconciliation concluded that Indonesian armed forces and local militias looted virtually all of the country's medical equipment. Moreover, 'hundreds of thousands of people were rounded up . . . and herded like cattle from their homes or places of shelter onto trucks and boats bound for West Timor'.[2] More recently, the ICC Prosecutor opened an investigation, *inter alia*, to examine whether the looting of hospitals in Mali amounted to the war crime of pillage.[3] Denial of access to water can prove equally or more deadly than a massacre by firearms,[4] and the same is true for the wilful hindrance of humanitarian assistance,[5] or for attacks on health-care facilities, personnel and vehicles and impediments to the wounded and sick reaching health-care services.[6] As a nutritionist of the ICRC explains, the lack of access to food during armed conflicts exacts a heavy toll on human life and often results from adverse human agency, rather than from exogenous environmental circumstances:

1 Part of the text and material in this chapter previously appeared in Evelyne Schmid, 'War Crimes Related to Violations of ESCR' (2011) 71 *Heidelberg Journal of International Law*, 3, 523–41.
2 Truth and Reconciliation in Timor-Leste Commission for Reception, *Chega!* (CAVR, 2005), Chapter 7.9, para. 4, and Chapter 7.3, para. 423.
3 ICC Office of the Prosecutor, 'Situation in Mali: Article 53(1) Report' (ICC, 2013), para. 163.
4 Ameur Zemmali, 'Water in Times of Armed Conflict' (1995) *International Review of the Red Cross*, 308, 550–64: 550.
5 See for instance Alex De Waal, *Famine Crimes* (International African Institute, 1997).
6 ICRC, 'Health Care in Danger' (ICRC, 2011).

> Most famines, especially those which kill, occur during armed conflicts. There is a very simple explanation: apart from those climatic and economic factors which generally give rise to famines, the loss of access to food resources is largely the result of intentional acts. These are mainly of two kinds: i) acts which directly or indirectly deprive the population of its own resources and of the means to adapt, for instance displacement of the population, restrictions on production activities, the severance of lines of communication and the pillaging and destruction of resources; ii) acts which prevent access to food from being restored, such as those banning the provision of food aid, the transfer of resources and the creation of employment.[7]

Tribunals have dealt with such adverse human agency when adjudicating war crimes cases. As mentioned in the introductory chapter, the IMT has already convicted war criminals for conduct that human rights lawyers today would qualify as violations of ESCR. The conviction of Hans Frank, the leading Nazi legal advisor and Governor-General of Poland, is the most notable case in this regard. Frank not only knowingly promoted the undernourishment of the Polish population but also planned the spread of lethal diseases among Jews and forcibly recruited labourers by ordering that only factories working for German interests could distribute food ration cards. Frank also gave orders to remove Polish citizens from their homes so that the homes could be given to Germans and ruthlessly intended to destroy the Polish culture and intelligentsia.[8] Defendant Frick was punished because he 'drafted, signed and administered many laws designed to eliminate Jews from German life and economy'.[9] Defendants Funk and Seyß-Inquart participated in the Nazi programme of 'economic discrimination against the Jews'.[10]

Post-World War II tribunals convicted other defendants for war crimes and crimes against humanity because they deprived detainees of food, sanitation, water or health care or because they conducted gruesome medical experiments.[11] Eichmann was convicted for

[7] Alain Mourey, 'Famine and War' (1991) 31 *International Review of the Red Cross*, 285, 549–57.

[8] *United States of America, the French Republic, the United Kingdom of Great Britain and Northern Ireland, and the Union of Soviet Socialist Republics against Major War Criminals, Opinion and Judgment, in Nazi Conspiracy and Aggression (Red Series), 1 October 1946*, IMT, 123–6.

[9] Ibid., 126. [10] Ibid., 132 (Funk) and 155 (Seyß-Inquart).

[11] In early cases, tribunals did not yet separate war crimes from crimes against humanity. Relevant cases on medical experiments and the deprivation of detainees of food, sanitation, medical care or water are discussed in the chapter on crimes against humanity (in Section 4.10) as well as in this chapter in Section 5.2.1.4.

starvation.[12] Had human rights instruments existed in that era, the defendants' contribution to these policies as senior state officials would have engaged the responsibility of the German state for infringing access to the right to freedom from hunger and the rights to education and housing.[13] The defendants' conduct engaged the individual criminal responsibility of perpetrators for war crimes and gave rise to violations of ESCR attributable to a state, thus demonstrating overlap between ESCR violations and the definitions of war crimes in some of the earliest cases of international criminal law.

This chapter examines the circumstances under which the existing definitions of war crimes under international law can encompass and relate to violations of ESCR. The core of the chapter examines four groups of punishable acts that constitute war crimes and that can overlap with ESCR violations: (i) war crimes against persons, (ii) war crimes against property, (iii) war crimes consisting in the use of prohibited methods of warfare and (iv) war crimes consisting in the use of prohibited means of warfare.

But before we embark on this analysis, there is a case that deserves special treatment. The very first individual convicted according to the principles underpinning the IMT Charter was Arthur Greiser, the Nazi *Gauleiter* (territorial leader) of the Warthegau in western Poland. Though often overlooked in the literature for historic and historiographic reasons,[14] his trial provides ample and disturbing illustrations of how war crimes, crimes against humanity and genocide can overlap with abuses depriving people of access to their ESCR.

The Supreme National Tribunal of Poland convicted Greiser of international crimes but did not differentiate between the underlying offences in the same way as modern international criminal law is structured.[15] It is

[12] *The Attorney-General of Israel* v. *Eichmann, 36 ILR 5 (1968), 24 July 1996, District Court of Jerusalem, Israel.*

[13] Many of the defendants' acts could have been attributed to the German state under the law of state responsibility. See ILC Articles on State Responsibility, Annex to GA Res. 56/83, 12 December 2001, especially Art. 4.

[14] For an excellent biography, see Catherine Epstein, *Arthur Greiser* (Oxford University Press, 2010). Epstein thinks that the trial was overlooked because of the Cold War (the verdict was rendered by the Supreme National Tribunal of Poland), as well as because of linguistic reasons and the tendency of historians to downplay the role of individual perpetrators, but not for the fact that many of the abuses affected ESCR.

[15] *Prosecutor* v. *Greiser, Case No. 74, XIII Law Reports of Trials of War Criminals 70, 7 July 1946, Supreme National Tribunal, Poland,* 74. The Genocide Convention had not yet been adopted at that time, but the judgment refers to 'a totalitarian genocidal attack on the rights of small and medium nations to exist, and to have an identity and culture of their own'. Ibid., 114.

therefore warranted to discuss the case of Arthur Greiser separately, rather than under the heading of a specific war crime. The tribunal classified the relevant abuses as falling within the umbrella charge of 'exceeding the rights accorded to the occupying authority by international law, and in particular violating ... the Hague Regulations'.[16] The abuses that relate to victims' enjoyment of ESCR can, therefore, be seen as war crimes, even though the trial is also relevant for the understanding of crimes against humanity and genocide.

The UN War Crimes Commission summarised Greiser's trial as well as most of the expert evidence leading to the defendant's conviction. The trial report of the charges of which Greiser was found guilty reads like a catalogue of abuses that can be viewed as ESCR violations: Greiser implemented a process of 'Germanisation' that included the 'systematic destruction of Polish culture',[17] 'allotting to the Germans to the detriment of the Polish population easier conditions of life and better material comforts on the grounds that such were "*nur für Deutsche*" (for Germans only)'.[18] Greiser was the first to force Jews into a ghetto, in the knowledge that living conditions were terrible.[19] He was also personally responsible for setting 'the limits within which the Polish language might be used in the territories over which he had authority'.[20]

The victims' enjoyment of what we today conceptualise as ESCR was most strikingly curtailed by Greiser's introduction of the *Polenstatut*. This set of regulations was found to have

> completely deprived the Poles of all rights to real property ..., deprived the Poles of the right to choose their employment, fixed their conditions of employment and wages, of the scale of nourishment, terms of health and other social services for the Poles at a considerably lower level than that for the Germans; ... forbade their taking any part in cultural life or sport, and compulsorily limited the education of Polish children to its elementary stages only.[21]

Greiser's trial today stands as a sharp reminder that international crimes can be committed by conduct affecting people's ESCR. It should serve as an interpretative aid as we understand the meaning of various specific offences in contemporary international criminal law,[22] and, in

[16] Ibid., 71. [17] Ibid., 84. [18] Ibid., 86. [19] Ibid., 72, 107. [20] Ibid., 93.

[21] Ibid., 73.

[22] Mark Drumbl has traced the trial's unjustifiably limited jurisprudential legacies in Mark Drumbl, 'The Trial of Arthur Greiser in Poland', in *The Hidden Histories of War Crimes Trials*, ed. Kevin Heller and Gerry Simpson (Oxford University Press, 2013), 411–29.

particular, as we consider whether some of the definitions of war crimes are capable of accommodating claims related to ESCR violations.

When considering whether conduct amounts to a war crime, we must – as with crimes against humanity – take into account certain contextual elements; namely, war crimes can only occur in the context of armed conflicts.

## 5.1 Preliminary steps: human rights law on ESCR and war crimes

To demonstrate that the same factual situation can sometimes at the same time be described as a violation of ESCR and as a war crime, it must first be verified whether and how human rights law continues to apply in armed conflict. As already suggested in Chapter 3,[23] there can only be ESCR violations in armed conflict if human rights law continues to apply. Second, we shall briefly consider the relationship between human rights law, IHL and international criminal law related to war crimes in order to ascertain how a situation may simultaneously give rise to a human rights violation and a war crime.

As far as the first step is concerned, it is widely accepted that human rights law continues to apply in situations of armed conflict and occupation. This position not only follows from the ordinary wording of derogation clauses in human rights law, but has also been confirmed on three different occasions before the ICJ as well as by the Permanent Court of Arbitration,[24] and, with very few exceptions, states and highly qualified publicists share it.[25] In the *Wall Advisory Opinion*, the ICJ specifically held that the main treaty source of ESCR on the global level, the ICESCR,

[23] See Section 3.2.1.3.

[24] *Legality of the Threat or Use of Nuclear Weapons, Advisory Opinion of 8 July 1996*, ICJ, 240; *Case Concerning Armed Activities on the Territory of the Congo (DRC* v. *Uganda), 19 December 2005*, ICJ, para. 220; *Legal Consequences of the Construction of a Wall in the Occupied Palestinian Territory, Advisory Opinion of 4 July 2004*, ICJ, 178; *Ethiopia's Claim No. 5, Partial Award, Civilians Claims, 17 December 2004, Eritrea-Ethiopia Claims Commission*, Permanent Court of Arbitration, paras. 26–8.

[25] Theodor Meron, 'Human Rights', in *Contemporary Issues in International Law*, ed. Thomas Buergenthal (Engel, 1984), 1–21; Louise Doswald-Beck and Sylvain Vité, 'International Humanitarian Law and Human Rights Law' (1993) 33 *International Review of the Red Cross*, 293, 95–105. The United States and Israel are the only states fundamentally rejecting this position. For a defence of this view, see Michael Dennis, 'Application of Human Rights Treaties Extraterritorially in Times of Armed Conflict and Military Occupation' (2005) 99 *American Journal of International Law*, 1, 119–41.

applies in armed conflict.[26] This conclusion is also supported by the ILC's Draft Articles on the Effect of Armed Conflict on Treaties, which stipulate that human rights treaties continue in operation during armed conflict.[27] In the case of occupied territories, questions arise concerning the ways ESCR interact with the principle of continuity of the legal system, that is, the customary rule that the occupier must not induce long-term changes in the institutional or legal structures of the occupied territory.[28] This rule does not, however, conflict with the basic obligations relevant to this study. Most experts convened by the ICRC for a recent study on occupation and other forms of administration of foreign territory 'shared the ICJ's view that foreign forces are bound by the ICESCR in exercising the powers available to them as an occupying power'.[29] Some of the experts emphasised how the flexibility of the ICESCR was 'particularly important during a period of occupation since it would permit the implementation of the ICESCR to be adjusted to the realities of the situation'.[30] They explained how the normative framework of the ICESCR usefully complements the IHL principles of occupation law.[31] Where there is no discrepancy between the respective norms of human rights law and IHL, we do not have to dismiss the relevance of one of the two bodies of law by reference to the principle of *lex specialis*.[32] It would be wrong to assume that human rights law is displaced by IHL as the solely relevant body of law. Rather, the relationship between norms of human rights law and those of IHL must be examined in relation to specific norms, rather than 'at a macroscopic level'.[33] The

[26] *Legal Consequences of the Construction of a Wall in the Occupied Palestinian Territory, Advisory Opinion of 4 July 2004*, ICJ, para. 112.

[27] ILC, Draft Articles on the Effects of Armed Conflicts on Treaties, Annex to the ILC's report to the GA (A/66/10, para. 100), 2011, Art. 3, 7.

[28] Convention (IV) Respecting the Laws and Customs of War on Land and Regulations, The Hague, 18 October 1907 (entered into force 26 January 1910), Art. 43.

[29] ICRC and Tristan Ferraro, *Occupation and Other Forms of Administration of Foreign Territory: Report of Expert Meetings* (ICRC, 2012), 12.

[30] Ibid., 64. [31] Ibid., 65.

[32] *Case Concerning Armed Activities on the Territory of the Congo (DRC* v. *Uganda), 19 December 2005*, ICJ, para. 178, where the ICJ suggests assessing the lawfulness of the Ugandan conduct against both the laws of military occupation and international human rights law.

[33] Robert Cryer, 'The Interplay of Human Rights and Humanitarian Law' (2009) 14 *Journal of Conflict and Security Law*, 3, 511–27: 514. This view is shared in Gilles Giacca, 'Economic, Social, and Cultural Rights in Armed Conflict and Other Situations of Armed Violence' (Graduate Institute of International Studies and Development, 2013), 183. See also Gilles Giacca, *ESCR in Armed Conflict* (Oxford University Press, 2014).

questions studied in this chapter are what the ICJ termed 'matters of both these branches of international law',[34] human rights law and IHL. The relevant provisions related to ESCR and IHL do not conflict with each other,[35] and we can therefore examine both bodies of law.

When a state is involved in an armed conflict abroad, there is a question of the extent to which the ICESCR applies extraterritorially. Together with academic commentators, the UN Committee on ESCR (CESCR) has interpreted the convention to mean that 'all individuals within [a state's] territory *or* under its jurisdiction' fall under the scope of the ICESCR.[36] For situations of occupation, the ICJ concluded twice that the obligations of an occupying power extend to occupied territories.[37]

States thus continue to be bound by obligations related to ESCR also in armed conflict, because human rights law continues to apply to the territory or a person under the jurisdiction of the controlling state. Consequently, such obligations can also be violated in times of armed conflict.

In the second preliminary step, it is necessary to consider how a situation may simultaneously be understood as a human rights violation and a war crime. It cannot be stressed enough that only very few violations of human rights amount to international crimes. To constitute a

[34] *Legal Consequences of the Construction of a Wall in the Occupied Palestinian Territory, Advisory Opinion of 4 July 2004*, ICJ, para. 106. Cited affirmatively in *Case Concerning Armed Activities on the Territory of the Congo (DRC* v. *Uganda), 19 December 2005*, ICJ, para. 216.

[35] For a recent in-depth analysis of this complementary relationship between ESCR protections in human rights law and IHL, see Giacca, 'Economic, Social, and Cultural Rights in Armed Conflict and Other Situations of Armed Violence' (Graduate Institute of International Studies and Development, 2013), 181. See also Sylvain Vité, 'Occupation and ESCR' (2008) 90 *International Review of the Red Cross*, 871, 629–52: 651; ICRC and Ferraro, *Occupation and Other Forms of Administration of Foreign Territory: Report of Expert Meetings*, Part I, 3B.

[36] Committee on Economic, Social and Cultural Rights, *General Comment 1 on Reporting by States Parties*, 24 February 1989, E/1989/22, para. 3 (emphasis added); Maastricht Principles on Extraterritorial Obligations of States in the Area of Economic, Social and Cultural Rights, Adopted by a Group of Experts Convened by Maastricht University and the International Commission of Jurists, 21 September 2011. For more analysis, see Malcolm Langford et al., *The Extra-Territorial Scope of ESCR* (Cambridge University Press, 2012); Fons Coomans and Rolf Künnemann, *Extraterritorial Obligations in the Area of ESCR* (Intersentia, 2012); Elizabeth Mottershaw, 'ESCR in Armed Conflict' (2008) 12 *International Journal of Human Rights*, 3, 449–70.

[37] *Legal Consequences of the Construction of a Wall in the Occupied Palestinian Territory, Advisory Opinion of 4 July 2004*, ICJ, para. 112. Cited affirmatively in *Case Concerning Armed Activities on the Territory of the Congo (DRC* v. *Uganda), 19 December 2005*, ICJ, para. 216.

war crime, conduct must violate a rule of IHL protecting important values, and violations of this rule must have been criminalised as war crimes.[38] If we are to determine what constitutes a war crime that can overlap with ESCR violations, then we must start with those IHL rules that protect concepts similar to those under human rights law related to ESCR and verify whether their violation constitutes a war crime. In times of armed conflict, the destruction of homes, for instance, is covered by rules of IHL, which are criminalised as war crimes (such as the prohibition of population transfers), as well as by human rights law on ESCR (which prohibits arbitrary forced evictions).

It must be noted that some conduct constitutes a war crime in IAC alone, some in NIAC alone and some in all conflicts. The various types of armed conflicts must carefully be distinguished to determine the applicable law and there is a vast body of literature on the definition of an armed conflict and its type.[39] The number of war crimes in NIAC is smaller than in IAC. Furthermore, states did not entrust the ICC with jurisdiction over all war crimes existing in international law.[40] As a special type of war crimes in IAC, the four Geneva Conventions of 1949 criminalise certain conduct as so-called grave breaches.[41] In 1977, states codified further grave breaches that imposed criminal responsibility.[42] Grave breaches are a category of war crimes applicable in IAC only, and the Geneva Conventions and AP I

[38] *Prosecutor* v. *Tadić, Decision on the Defence Motion for Interlocutory Appeal on Jurisdiction, IT-94-1-Ar72, 2 October 1995*, ICTY, para. 94. The ICTY Appeals Chamber employed the following test to ascertain war crimes: (i) whether the violation infringes a rule of IHL; (ii) whether the rule is customary in nature or the conditions of a treaty have been met; (iii) the violation is serious, that is, there are grave consequences for the victim; (iv) the violation entails individual criminal responsibility. For an analysis of these criterion, see Cryer, 'The Interplay of Human Rights and Humanitarian Law', 514–16. On the general characteristics of war crimes, see also Yoram Dinstein and Mala Tabory (eds.), *War Crimes* (Nijhoff, 1996), 2.

[39] For a short overview of the qualification of armed conflicts with further references, see, for instance, Otto Triffterer (ed.), *Commentary on the Rome Statute* (Beck, 2008), 290–3 (Cottier).

[40] Notable omissions from the Rome Statute are the criminalisation of attacks on demilitarised zones, attacks against works or installations containing dangerous forces and the non-inclusion of provisions relating to the use of prohibited weapons in NIAC. Rome Statute of the International Criminal Court, 2187 UNTS 90, 17 July 1998 (entered into force 1 July 2002). The latter omission was partially corrected at the 2010 Kampala Review Conference. See Section 5.2.4.

[41] Geneva Conventions, Arts. 50/51/130/147 respectively.

[42] Protocol Additional to the Geneva Conventions of 12 August 1949, and Relating to the Protection of Victims of International Armed Conflicts, 1125 UNTS 3, 8 June 1977 (entered into force 7 December 1978), Art. 85.

establish a regime of mandatory collaboration in the repression of such breaches.[43]

In the past, the notion of war crimes was confined to crimes committed in the context of international armed conflicts.[44] Since 1994 (the adoption of the Statute of the ICTR) and especially the jurisprudence of the ICTY, however, it is accepted that war crimes (but not grave breaches) also exist in NIAC.[45] The adoption of the Rome Statute and national implementing legislation consolidated the view that there is criminal responsibility under international law for war crimes committed in NIAC.

With the adoption of Art. 8 of the Rome Statute, states granted the ICC jurisdiction over a long list of war crimes. Because of its length and the similarity between different offences, the list of war crimes included in the Rome Statute is confusing. This chapter therefore regroups war crimes so that similar crimes can be discussed together. For example, 'wilful killing' and 'murder' are separate crimes in the Rome Statute but will be discussed together here.[46] Readers should bear in mind that each category of war crimes under the Rome Statute has specific thresholds pertaining to the nature of the conflict.[47]

The general requirements for all war crimes are the existence of a situation of armed conflict,[48] and a nexus between the conduct of the

[43] States must enact legislation necessary to provide effective penal sanctions, search for persons alleged to have committed grave breaches and prosecute or extradite them. See also Section 8.2.2.1.

[44] An exception of a treaty with war crimes applicable in NIAC was the Second Protocol to the Hague Convention of 1954 for the Protection of Cultural Property in the Event of Armed Conflict, The Hague, 26 March 1999 (entered into force 9 March 2004), Art. 15.

[45] Statute of the International Tribunal for Rwanda, Annex to S/Res/955, 8 November 1994, Art. 4, providing for jurisdiction over violations of Common Article 3 of the Geneva Conventions and AP II. The ICTY famously held that its jurisdiction extended to war crimes in NIAC *Prosecutor* v. *Tadić, Decision on the Defence Motion for Interlocutory Appeal on Jurisdiction, IT-94-1-Ar72, 2 October 1995*, ICTY, para. 119.

[46] The classification of war crimes used in this chapter is an adaptation of the way the German Code of Crimes against International Law regroups war crimes.

[47] The Rome Statute technically distinguishes two types of NIAC. Articles 8(2) (c) and (d) apply to all NIAC, while Arts. 8(2) (e) and (f) only apply to NIAC that reach a threshold similar to the threshold of AP II but modified by the *Tadić* Jurisdiction Appeal (control over territory is not required, nor that one of the parties be governmental, but the conflict must be 'protracted'). It is, however, difficult to conceive that the ICC would prosecute crimes in a 'non-protracted' NIAC, and there may thus be no significance to this technical distinction. In any event, the ICC Pre-Trial Chamber II treated the two thresholds as if they were the same. *Prosecutor* v. *Bemba, Decision on the Charges of the Prosecutor, 15 June 2009, Pre-Trial Chamber II, ICC-01/05-01/08-424*, ICC, para. 232.

[48] For an overview of the definition of an armed conflict for the purpose of the Rome Statute, see Triffterer (ed.), *Commentary on the Rome Statute*, 291 (Cottier).

alleged perpetrator and such conflict.[49] The perpetrator must have been aware of factual circumstances that established the existence of an armed conflict,[50] and the victim or the property must have been protected under IHL. Protected persons, and thus potential victims of war crimes, are those individuals who are covered by one or more of the Geneva Conventions of 1949 or their 1977 protocols, namely the wounded and sick, prisoners of war and civilians who do not or no longer directly take part in hostilities. Not all civilians are automatically protected persons, but victims must be neutral or linked to the other side of the conflict.[51]

Now that we have briefly surveyed how human rights law on ESCR applies during conflict and the basic requirements of war crimes, we can examine specific war crimes and how they relate to ESCR violations.

## 5.2 Particular war crimes offences and ESCR violations

### 5.2.1 *War crimes against persons*

#### 5.2.1.1 Wilful killing

Murder or wilful killing is a war crime in both IAC and NIAC.[52] The objective elements of this war crime are that the perpetrator caused the death of a protected person, and the death resulted from an act or omission contrary to the law of armed conflicts. The term 'killing' is

[49] ICC Elements of Crimes, ICC-ASP/1/3, 9 September 2002, Art. 8, para. 2(a)(i), para. 4. This element is repeated for all war crimes and has also been applied by the *ad hoc* tribunals. *Prosecutor* v. *Kunarac, Kovac and Vukovic, IT-96-23-A, 12 June 2002*, ICTY, para. 58.

[50] Knowledge of armed conflict does not imply a requirement for a legal evaluation by the perpetrator. ICC Elements of Crimes, Art. 8 (introduction).

[51] ICC Elements of Crimes, Art. 8, para. 2(c)(1)-1, para. 2. For an overview, see Knut Dörmann et al., *Elements of War Crimes* (Cambridge University Press, 2003), 19. For grave breaches (but not for other war crimes), victims must be 'in the hands of' the party that is committing the grave breach. The expression 'in the hands of' is used broadly and is not restricted to a physical sense. Usually this means that victims must be in occupied territory or otherwise under the control of the party committing the conduct. In a teleological but controversial approach, the ICTY held that allegiance to a party to the conflict was the critical test (rather than nationality). *Prosecutor* v. *Tadić, IT-94-1-A, 15 July 1999*, ICTY, para. 166.

[52] The Rome Statute and the Geneva Conventions stipulate that wilful killing in the context of an IAC constitutes a grave breach. Rome Statute, Art. 8, para. 2(a)(i). Geneva Conventions Arts. 50/51/130/147. In NIAC, the term murder is employed, but the content of the two crimes is understood in the same manner. Rome Statute, Art. 8, para. 2(c)(i). See also Art. 3 common to the Geneva Conventions and Protocol II, Art. 4.2(a). *Prosecutor* v. *Delalić, IT-96-21-T, 16 November 1998*, ICTY, para. 422.

equivalent to the term 'causing death'.[53] Thus, as this crime is defined, if the perpetrator meant to cause death or must have been aware that death would occur in the ordinary course of events,[54] conduct such as reducing food or water rations or medical care is criminalised.

Multiple authorities have confirmed that this crime can be committed either by act or by omission,[55] including before the ICC.[56] The fact that the ICC Pre-Trial Chambers have recognised omission liability for this war crime is significant for the interpretation of other crimes under the Rome Statute as well. The ICC Statute in Art. 8 only employs the term 'acts' (rather than the term 'conduct'), but Art. 30 on mental elements refers to 'conduct',[57] that is acts and omissions. Omission liability seems unproblematic at the very least for grave breaches adjudicated before other tribunals,[58] but the Rome Statute does not contain an explicit provision on omissions, except in relation to command responsibility.[59] A draft provision on omissions was not included in the final text of the Rome Statute,[60] and the issue remains

[53] ICC Elements of Crimes, footnote 2.

[54] Triffterer (ed.), *Commentary on the Rome Statute*, 305–6 (Cottier). Intent can be inferred if death is the foreseeable consequence of an omission. The term wilfully should be considered as synonymous with 'intentional' and therefore follows the rule of the mental element laid down in Art. 30 of the Rome Statute. On this point, see also William Schabas, *Commentary on the Rome Statute* (Oxford University Press, 2010), 214. Negligence is not enough, but recklessness probably is. On the interpretation of the requirement that death will/might occur in the ordinary course of events, see Section 4.7.1.

[55] *Prosecutor* v. *Delalić, IT-96-21-T, 16 November 1998*, ICTY, para. 424; *Prosecutor* v. *Akayesu, ICTR-96-4-T, 2 September 1998*, ICTR, para. 589.

[56] *Prosecutor* v. *Katanga and Chui, Decision on the Confirmation of Charges, 30 September 2008, Pre-Trial Chamber I, ICC-01/04-01/07*, ICC, para. 287; *Prosecutor* v. *Bemba, Decision on the Charges of the Prosecutor, 15 June 2009, Pre-Trial Chamber II, ICC-01/05-01/08-424*, ICC, para. 183.

[57] A similar problem was disused in Blaškić before the ICTY. The ICTY Appeals Chamber interpreted the term acts in Art. 7(3) of the ICTY Statute to mean act or omission. See *Prosecutor* v. *Blaškić, IT-95-14-A, 29 July 2004*, ICTY, paras. 663–4.

[58] AP I, Art. 86 provides for omission liability for grave breaches resulting from 'a failure to act when under a duty to do so'. Equating acts and omissions was standard in the Nuremberg case law, and, with very few exceptions (most notably French law), most domestic legal systems recognise liability for 'commission by omission' where there is a legal duty to act. For a discussion, see Michael Duttweiler, 'Liability for Omission' (2006) 6 *International Criminal Law Review*, 1, 1–61.

[59] Rome Statute, Art. 28.

[60] Preparatory Committee Draft Statute for the ICC, A/CONF.183/2/Add.1, 14 April 1998, 54–5, Art. 28 in square brackets. This article would have explicitly stated that a person may be criminally responsible for an omission under specific circumstances. For a summary of the inconclusive history of draft Art. 28, see Schabas, *Commentary on the Rome Statute*, 476–7.

unsettled. In any event, the absence of an explicit provision on omission liability should not mean that the equation of acting and omitting a legally required act is never possible under the Rome Statute. As commentators have noted, general principles of criminal law would seem to allow the equation of omissions with active conduct if the defendant was under a legal duty to act, including for the purpose of the ICC Statute.[61] The fact that the ICC Pre-Trial Chambers have recognised that the war crime of killing under the Rome Statute can be committed by omission indicates that the ICC might accept omission liability for other crimes under the ICC Statute as well – an issue which will have to be considered in future case law.[62]

Prosecutors must prove causation between the defendant's conduct and the result (the death of the victim).[63] In the *Los Palos* case, the Dili District Court has interpreted identical language in the United Nations Transitional Administration in East Timor (UNTAET) regulation as in the Rome Statute. It held that 'the perpetrator's act be a substantive cause of the victim's death'.[64]

[61] Duttweiler, 'Liability for Omission'; Robert Cryer, 'Liability', in *The Permanent International Criminal Court: Legal and Policy Issues*, ed. Dominic McGoldrick, Peter Rowe and Eric Donnelly (Hart, 2004), 233–62.

[62] In practice, separating acts from omissions is not always straightforward. It is often possible to describe conduct that primarily appears to consist of omissions as active conduct (e.g., the failure to allow access to humanitarian aid is often combined with active conduct blocking such access). For cases of 'pure omissions', it is suggested that liability for the commission of a crime by omission should be recognised when a defendant was under a legal obligation to act (derived from any applicable rules of law), the defendant had the capacity to avoid the result or consequence which must have been caused by the omission, and the result or consequence is imputable to the defendant. It is more doubtful whether other forms of omission liability exist in international criminal law. In any event, tribunals should not recognise instigations by omission as this would impermissibly expand the notion of instigation to situations in which the principal already had the requisite *mens rea* to commit a crime and only made its execution dependant on an external circumstance (i.e., the omission of the defendant). On instigation by omission liability, see also *Prosecutor* v. *Karadžić, Preliminary Motion on Lack of Jurisdiction Concerning Omission Liability, IT-95-05/J8-Pt, 25 March 2009*, ICTY. And on aiding and abetting by omission, see Christopher Gosnell, 'Damned If You Don't: Liability for Omissions in International Criminal Law', in *The Ashgate Research Companion to International Criminal Law: Critical Perspectives*, ed. William Schabas, et al. (Ashgate, 2012).

[63] Unhelpfully and circularly, one of the ICC Pre-Trial Chambers has required that 'the death must result from the act of murder'. *Prosecutor* v. *Bemba, Decision on the Charges of the Prosecutor, 15 June 2009, Pre-Trial Chamber II, ICC-01/05-01/08-424*, ICC, para. 132.

[64] *Prosecutor* v. *Marques and Nine Others (Los Palos Case), 9/2000, 11 December 2001*, Special Panels for Serious Crimes – East Timor, para. 644.

Crucially, causing death is possible by way of depriving victims of food, water, shelter or other essential socio-economic items. Hart and Honoré, writing on causation, explain: 'The notion of causing death is not of course confined to crude cases where the actor initiates changes in the victim's body by introducing some foreign element; it also extends to cases where the actor shortens the victim's life by depriving him of something needed by his organism for survival.'[65] Similarly, Bassiouni writes that state practice views murder as including the creation of life-endangering conditions highly likely to result in death.[66]

The CESCR has held that '[t]he denial of access to food to particular individuals or groups . . ., the prevention of access to humanitarian food aid in internal conflicts or other emergency situations' by states or entities insufficiently regulated by states constitute violations of the right to food.[67] If such conduct causes death and if causality can be established, the unlawful denial of humanitarian relief, for instance, can constitute the war crime of wilful killing or murder.[68] In this scenario, the same facts give rise to an ESCR violation as well as a war crime. The denial of access to food, health care or drinking water, for instance, can cause the death of protected persons and may therefore constitute the war crime of wilful killing. Therefore, the ICRC commentary includes the deprivation of detainees with essential goods such as food rations in the examples of conduct criminalised under this war crime.[69] A striking but little-known illustration of the way in which failure to ensure minimal access to food, water, clothing, sanitation and health care results in war crimes convictions for killings can be found in the trial of Junsaburo Toshino and others before the American Military Commission in Yokohama. Toshino was the guard commandant aboard one of the Japanese ships used to house prisoners of war during World War II – vessels described as 'hell ships'. The deadly conditions on board were documented in evidence: many prisoners died as a consequence of the intentional denial of food, water and the most elementary sanitation or medical attention. A prisoner noted in his diary, and affidavits attest, that the lack of drinking water was due not to a shortage of water, but to Toshino's order to the

[65] Herbert Hart and Tony Honoré, *Causation*, 2nd edn (Clarendon, 1985), 240.

[66] Cherif Bassiouni, *Crimes against Humanity* (Kluwer, 1999), 301–2.

[67] Committee on Economic, Social and Cultural Rights, *General Comment 12 on the Right to Adequate Food*, 12 May 1999, E/C.12/1999/5, para. 19.

[68] Christa Rottensteiner, 'The Denial of Humanitarian Assistance' (1999) 81 *International Review of the Red Cross*, 555–82: 564.

[69] Oscar Uhler et al., *Commentary, Fourth Geneva Convention* (ICRC, 1958), 597.

guards commanding them to drive the prisoners away from the ship's galley before they could get the water.[70]

Of course, these examples of wilful killings equally constitute violations of the right to life, and hence violations of the ICCPR.[71] The possibility to qualify some abuses simultaneously as violations of ESCR as well as of civil and political rights also arises for other examples mentioned in this study. However, killings without bloodshed tend to be overlooked, especially if they are a result of socio-economic conditions inflicted, for instance, by way of depriving victims of access to humanitarian relief. It is worth making it explicit how they resemble a massacre by firearms or machetes from a legal standpoint. We shall revisit this point in the concluding chapter.[72]

#### 5.2.1.2 Unlawful deportation or transfer

Forcibly moving a civilian population for reasons related to a conflict can constitute a war crime. This offence extends to NIAC.[73] There is considerable overlap between the elements of this war crime and the crime against humanity of deportation or forcible transfer. Depending on the context, as well as the location and nationality of the victims, acts of deportation and transfer can be classified a war crime or a crime against humanity.[74] As we saw in the chapter on crimes against humanity, forcible population movements frequently go hand in hand with ESCR violations, particularly forced evictions.[75] The unlawful deportation or transfer of a civilian population constitutes a group of complex war crimes that differ according to the type of conflict and protect slightly different groups of persons. These differences are analysed by other

[70] *United States of America* v. *Toshino et al., Case No. 154, 4 May 1948, US Military Commission at Yokohama, USA*, 23.

[71] International Covenant on Civil and Political Rights, GA Res. 2200a (XXI), 999 UNTS 171, 16 December 1966 (entered into force 23 March 1976), Art. 6. A case in point is *Lantsova* v. *Russia, 26 March 2002, CCPR/C/74/D/763/1997*, HRCttee. The HRCttee concluded that Russia had violated the right to life after a prisoner died because of grossly inadequate food and medical attention.

[72] See Section 9.2.1. [73] Rome Statute, Art. 8, para. 2(e)(viii). AP I, Art. 85(4)a.

[74] Contrary to the crime against humanity, the war crime of deportation or transfer does not require the lawful presence of residence. The ICTY has nevertheless held that the element of lawful presence was also part of the war crime. *Prosecutor* v. *Blagojević and Jokić, IT-02-60-T, 17 January 2005*, ICTY, para. 595; *Prosecutor* v. *Krnojelac, IT-97-25-T, 15 March 2002*, ICTY, para. 473, concluding that the content of the underlying offence does not differ whether perpetrated as a war crime or as a crime against humanity. On lawful presence, see Section 4.3.3.

[75] See Section 4.3.

authors.[76] Here, the focus is limited to the examination of how violations of ESCR are related to deportations and forcible transfers as war crimes.

As with the crime against humanity, criminal offences for forcible population displacements do not require that the displacement involve physical force.[77] Rather, displacement is made forcible by the absence of genuine choice on the part of the individuals displaced.[78] Disruption of access to supplies and services, education, water or food is often the underlying factor that makes the transfer forced. Intentionally destroying food crops, household items or infrastructure to force civilians to move to government-controlled areas is a known practice in NIAC.[79] This war crime covers deprivations of ESCR that are deliberately inflicted to provoke the displacement of civilians; transfers that are a side effect of other conduct do not meet the qualification.

In NIAC, an additional mental element narrows the area of overlap between ESCR violations and the war crime of forcible transfer, namely Art. 8(2)(e)(viii) of the Rome Statute proscribes '*ordering* the displacement of the civilian population for reasons related to the conflict, unless the security of the civilians involved or imperative military reasons so demand'.[80] The term 'ordering' implies that it is not enough that the acts result in population displacement; removing the civilians must have been a specific aim of the conduct,[81] and coercion without an order does not suffice.[82] It is, however, not necessary that an order of displacement is publicly addressed to the population.[83] It is of course possible that such an order relates to people's access to ESCR. Imagine, for instance, that a perpetrator orders the removal of persons and dispatches representatives who threaten the inhabitants by claiming that all water supplies will be cut.[84]

76 Dörmann et al., *Elements of War Crimes*, 277ff and 472ff; Theodor Meron, 'Deportation of Civilians', in *Broadening the Frontiers of Human Rights*, ed. Donna Gomien and Asbjørn Eide (Scandinavian University Press, 1993), 201–18.

77 See Section 4.3.1.

78 Uhler et al., *Commentary, Fourth Geneva Convention*, 278–9.

79 See, for instance, Jordan Paust, 'The Human Rights to Food, Medicine and Medical Supplies' (1998) 31 *Vanderbilt Journal of Transnational Law*, 3, 617–40: 622.

80 Rome Statute, Art. 8, para. 2(e)(viii) (emphasis added).

81 Triffterer (ed.), *Commentary on the Rome Statute*, 497 (Zimmermann).

82 This element is contested by Jan Willms, 'Without Order, Anything Goes?' (2009) 91 *International Review of the Red Cross*, 875, 547–65. Willms argues that there is no order requirement under customary international law.

83 An order within the chain of command would suffice.

84 A report alleged that Israeli authorities sent a representative to the village of Al-Nu'man in the south-east of Jerusalem to encourage the villagers to leave their village as the Israeli government would cut water and electricity supplies to the village to force the population

The ICTY has confirmed, in the *Krajišnik* judgment, that the creation of severe living conditions can constitute the underlying conduct of forcible transfer. The tribunal found that discriminatory dismissals from employment and cutting off water or electricity were aimed at, and succeeded in, making it practically impossible for most Muslims and Croats to remain in municipalities controlled by Serb forces.[85] The trial chamber found that the victims, who were not taking active part in the hostilities at the relevant time, were displaced against their will.[86] State failure to prevent and correct discriminatory dismissals from employment constitutes a violation of the right to work,[87] cutting off water has been interpreted as a violation of the right of everyone to an adequate standard of living[88] and the same was held of the provision of electricity.[89] The connection between deprivations of basic access to ESCR and forcible transfers has also been recognised in the *Popović* judgment, in which the trial chamber held that enclaves in the former Yugoslavia had been intentionally deprived of food, water, shelter and humanitarian relief so that people would leave the area. The trial chamber highlights that '[t]he wish of some Bosnian Muslims to leave the enclave in the months preceding the fall of Srebrenica, does not negate the forcible nature' of the transfer.[90] Rather, '[i]t was the consequence of a deliberate plan ... culminating in a military attack and the creation of disastrous conditions which compelled the entire population to abandon their homes'.[91] In sum, the factual background leading to forcible transfers of protected

to leave. Grazia Careccia and John Reynolds, *Al-Nu'man Village: A Case Study of Indirect Forcible Transfer* (Al-Haq, 2006), 10, 20. *In casu*, the situation in Al-Nu'man is governed by the Fourth Geneva Convention, rather than by the more limited rules of NIAC.

85 *Prosecutor* v. *Krajišnik, IT-00-39-T, 27 September 2006*, ICTY, para. 729.

86 Ibid., para. 732.

87 International Covenant on Economic, Social and Cultural Rights, GA Res. 2200a (XXI), 16 December 1966 (entered into force 3 January 1976), Arts. 6(1) and 2(2). See in particular *Dogan* v. *Netherlands, 10 August 1988, 1/1984, CERD/C/36/D/1/1984*, CERD Committee, para. 9.3, finding a violation of the petitioner's right to work after a Dutch court upheld a dismissal without considering the alleged discrimination by the employer.

88 Human Rights and Access to Safe Drinking Water and Sanitation, A/HRC/RES/15/9, 6 October 2010 (adopted without a vote), para. 3. See also The Human Right to Water and Sanitation, GA Res. 64/292, 3 August 2010; Committee on Economic, Social and Cultural Rights, *General Comment 15 on the Right to Water*, 20 January 2003, E/C.12/2002/11, paras. 21, 42.

89 For a recent example on electricity, see *CESCR*, Concluding Observations, Afghanistan, E/C.12/Afg/CO/2-4, 7 June 2010, para. 35.

90 *Prosecutor* v. *Popović, IT-05-88 T, 10 June 2010*, ICTY, para. 920; see also the discussion in paras. 227–41 on restrictions to humanitarian access in the enclaves.

91 Ibid.

persons in armed conflict or occupation can sometimes qualify as ESCR violations and simultaneously constitute a war crime.

IHL contains some exceptions that note when ordering the displacement of civilians is lawful. As outlined in Chapter 4, it is lawful to displace civilians, first, if the security of the population requires their displacement and, second, if imperative military necessity so demands.[92] There are narrow conditions under which these exceptions may be invoked,[93] and these exceptions never apply to the deportation or transfer of the occupying power's own population *into* the occupied territory.[94] Minimum humanitarian standards must be safeguarded during the evacuation 'to the greatest practicable extent'.[95] The minimum standards that must be safeguarded include many socio-economic considerations such as proper accommodation, conditions of hygiene, health and nutrition.[96] If an actor acting on behalf of a state deliberately fails to provide food during the displacement, for instance, the state is most likely violating the obligation under the ICESCR to ensure the satisfaction of, at the very least, the minimum essential level required to be free from hunger.[97] The conditions under which removals take place can in themselves transform an otherwise lawful transfer into a criminal offence. In the *Krupp* case, the tribunal confirmed that 'deportation becomes illegal . . . whenever generally recognized standards of decency and humanity are disregarded'.[98]

#### 5.2.1.3 Collective punishment

The Hague Regulations, the Geneva Conventions, AP I and AP II and customary international law prohibit collective punishments in both types of armed conflict.[99] The ICC has not been given jurisdiction over

[92] See Section 4.3.4.2.

[93] Convention (IV) Relative to the Protection of Civilian Persons in Time of War, TIAS No. 3365, 75 UNTS 287, 12 August 1949 (entered into force 21 October 1950), Art. 49. Protected persons must not be displaced outside the bounds of the occupied territory except if such is unavoidable. Only a given area must be evacuated and it must be temporary until the hostilities in the area have ceased. In addition, minimum humanitarian standards must be safeguarded and the protecting power shall be informed of any such transfers.

[94] Ibid. [95] Ibid. [96] Ibid.

[97] Committee on Economic, *General Comment 12 on the Right to Adequate Food*, para. 17.

[98] *United States of America* v. *Krupp et al., IX TWC 1327*, NMT, 144.

[99] Convention (III) Relative to the Treatment of Prisoners of War, 12 August 1949, TIAS No. 3364, 75 UNTS 135, Art. 87; Hague Convention and Regulations (1907), Art. 50; GVA IV, Art. 33.; AP I, Art. 75(2)d; AP II, Art. 4(2)b; ILC, Draft Code of Crimes against the Peace and Security of Mankind 1996, *Yearbook of the International Law Commission*, vol. II, Part Two, 1996, Art. 20(f)ii.

this prohibition.[100] Although the status of collective punishment as a war crime in customary international law is doubtful,[101] the ICTR and SCSL Statutes contain a provision on collective punishments,[102] which implies that it is warranted to include them within the scope of this study.[103]

The commentary of the ICRC clarifies that the offence refers to 'penalties of any kind inflicted on persons or entire groups of persons . . . for acts that [they] have not committed'.[104] Collective penalties may simultaneously constitute violations of ESCR and vice versa. The Third Geneva Convention specifically includes a provision prohibiting collective disciplinary measures affecting food.[105] The ICRC commentary also refers to Art. 89 of the Third Convention, which prohibits any disciplinary punishments 'dangerous to the health of prisoners of war'.[106] During the Iran-Iraq war, for instance, a special mission dispatched by the UN Secretary-General reported that prisoners of war suffered collective punishment measures in the form of deprivation of food or water.[107]

In the *Delalić* case, the ICTY stated that assigned residence under Art. 78 of the Fourth Geneva Convention is a measure that may never be taken on a collective basis.[108] State actors who collectively assign residence during an armed conflict will in most cases forcibly evict people from their homes and hence violate the right to housing.[109] Collective

[100] Darcy reports that states 'involved in annexation or occupation of "foreign" territory' opposed the inclusion of collective punishments in the list of war crimes. Shane Darcy, 'Collective Punishment' (2010) 8 *Journal of International Criminal Justice*, 1, 29–51: 18.

[101] See ibid. Darcy agrees that the conventional prohibitions of collective punishment under IHL have crystallised into customary international law. However, the prohibition has not (yet) been criminalised as a war crime. For the contrary view, see *Prosecutor* v. *Hass and Priebke, Sentenza N. 322, 22 July 1997, Military Tribunal of Rome (First Instance), Italy*, affirming the customary nature of the offence; Jean-Marie Henckaerts and Louise Doswald-Beck (eds.), *Customary IHL*, 2 vols., vol. 1 (Cambridge University Press, 2005), rule 103. The Appeals Chamber of the SCSL elaborated a (vague) list of the elements of collective punishment as a war crime in *Prosecutor* v. *Fofana and Kondewa, SCSL-04-14-A, 28 May 2008*, SCSL, para. 224.

[102] ICTR Statute, Art. 4(b); Agreement between the UN and the Government of Sierra Leone Pursuant to SC/Res/1315, Statute of the Special Court for Sierra Leone, 16 January 2002, Art. 3(b).

[103] See Section 3.2.2. [104] Uhler et al., *Commentary, Fourth Geneva Convention*, 225.

[105] Convention (III) Relative to the Treatment of Prisoners of War, 12 August 1949, TIAS No. 3364, 75 UNTS 135, Art. 26.

[106] Jean De Preux et al., *Commentary, Third Geneva Convention* (ICRC, 1960), 200.

[107] Prisoners of War in Iran and Iraq, Report of a Mission Dispatched by the Secretary-General, S/16962, 22 February 1985, para. 273.

[108] *Prosecutor* v. *Delalić, IT-96-21-T, 16 November 1998*, ICTY, para. 578.

[109] Committee on Economic, Social and Cultural Rights, *General Comment 7 on the Right to Adequate Housing: Forced Evictions*, 13 December 1997, E/1997/4, para. 3.

evictions related to an armed conflict may thus constitute the war crime of collective punishment. The SCSL convicted the accused in the *CDF* case of collective punishment, *inter alia*, because they commanded the burning of homes and the pillage of food, livestock and medical drugs to punish the population for their support of, or failure to actively resist, opposing forces.[110] At least some of this conduct seems attributable to the state of Sierra Leone,[111] and some of the same behaviour can thus straightforwardly also be described as an ESCR violation. The link between the prohibition of collective punishment and violations of ESCR is also made by the CESCR. General Comment (GC) 14 holds that limiting access to health services as a punitive measure during armed conflict constitutes both a violation of the right to health, as well as a violation of IHL.[112]

#### 5.2.1.4 Other war crimes against persons

A group of other war crimes against persons also demonstrate overlap with ESCR violations. The overlapping war crimes of torture, inhumane treatment, physical mutilation and outrages upon personal dignity all encompass conduct that touches upon ESCR, such as the right to health of persons protected under IHL.

*Torture or inhumane treatment*, including biological experiments, constitutes a grave breach in IAC and a war crime in NIAC.[113] Both torture and inhumane treatment are war crimes.[114] Torture (but not inhumane treatment) as a war crime must be inflicted for a certain purpose, such as obtaining information or a confession, punishment, intimidation or coercion or for any reason based on discrimination of any kind.[115] That experimentation on detainees not only constitutes torture but also the failure to respect or protect the right to health is

[110] *Prosecutor* v. *Fofana and Kondewa, SCSL-04-14-T, 2 August 2007*, SCSL, paras. 176–81.

[111] One of the accused, Norman, was the former Defence Minister of Sierra Leone, and his conduct is easily attributable to the state. ILC Articles on State Responsibility, Art. 4.

[112] Committee on Economic, Social and Cultural Rights, *General Comment 14 on the Right to the Highest Attainable Standard of Health*, 11 August 2000, E/CN.12/2000/4, para. 34.

[113] Rome Statute, Art. 8, para. 2(a)(ii). Arts. 50/51/130/147 Geneva Conventions. *Prosecutor* v. *Delalić, IT-96-21-T, 16 November 1998*, ICTY, para. 443.

[114] For torture as a crime unrelated to armed conflict and crimes against humanity, see Section 4.9.

[115] ICC Elements of Crimes, Art. 8, para. 2(c)(i)-4. It is not required that the prohibited purpose is the sole reason for the conduct. *Prosecutor* v. *Delalić, IT-96-21-T, 16 November 1998*, ICTY, para. 471. The requirement of a prohibited purpose also exists under customary international law. Note, however, that the requirement of the involvement of a person acting in official capacity is not part of the elements of torture as a war crime or as a crime against humanity. See also Section 4.9.

straightforward, at least if the experiments themselves are attributable to the state, or if the state does nothing to prevent third parties from conducting such experiments. Medical personnel providing assistance in torturous interrogation or medical experiments related to an armed conflict risk convictions for involvement in torture, inhumane treatment or other war crimes.[116] Various World War II trials convicted individuals of torture related to non-consensual medical experimentation.[117] Today, such experiments can easily be conceptualised as an interference with the right of everyone to the highest attainable standard of health – a violation of ESCR.

Note that medical or scientific experiments could also constitute the separate war crime of *physical mutilation*.[118] According to researchers, Japanese soldiers were involved in a horrific instance of 'medical' experimentation during World War II in a covert research laboratory established in Manchuria. The Japanese allegedly experimented with biological weapons and tried them on prisoners and civilians. People were deliberately infected with diseases, were subjected to vivisection without anaesthesia or were deprived of food, water or clothing to determine the length of time until death. Plague was allegedly spread in eastern China when rodents and infected fleas were airdropped.[119] However, the Tokyo trials did not examine evidence on these crimes. Bert Röling, the Dutch judge at the Tokyo trials, recounts the withholding of evidence from the tribunal and explains how he came to believe that the United States wanted to 'profit undisturbed from the criminal Japanese activity' by using the data for their own purposes.[120] The omission of these

[116] For an overview of the IHL rules governing medical treatment in armed conflict in armed conflict, see Sigrid Mehring, 'The Rights and Duties of Physicians in Armed Conflict' (2010) 103 *Militair Rechtelijk Tijdschrift*, 205–21.

[117] *United States of America* v. *Brandt et al. (Medical Trial), II TWC 171*, NMT; *United States of America* v. *Aihara, Case No. 290, 2 May 1949, US Military Commission at Yokohama, USA*. On the Nazi experiments and the *Brandt* trial, see also George Annas and Michael Grodin (eds.), *Nazi Doctors* (Oxford University Press, 1992). For cases related to experimental sterilisations, see Chapter 4, Note 232.

[118] Rome Statute, Art. 8, para. 2(b)(x). In NIAC, physical mutilation is criminalised in Rome Statute, Art. 8, para. 2(c)(i) and further elaborated also in para. e(xi).

[119] John Powell, 'Japan's Germ Warfare: The US Cover-Up of a War Crime' (1980) 12 *Bulletin of Concerned Asian Scholars*, 4, 2–17; Edward Drea, *Researching Japanese War Crimes Records* (Nazi War Crimes and Japanese Imperial Government Records Interagency Working Group, 2006), 4. See also Neil Boister and Robert Cryer, *The Tokyo Tribunal* (Oxford University Press, 2008), 63–4.

[120] Bernard Röling and Antonio Cassese, *The Tokyo Trial and Beyond* (Polity Press, 1993), 48–9.

shocking allegations from the Tokyo trials may have contributed to the perception that war crimes tribunals are mostly concerned with extra-judicial executions or waging aggressive war rather than with 'public health in reverse'[121]. In any event, it was not the nature of the human rights violations that prevented these crimes from making it onto the radar screen of the Tokyo tribunal; instead, they were ignored for unpleasant political reasons. Later, twelve of those responsible were brought to trial in the little-known *Khabarovsk War Crime Trials* in the Soviet Union in 1949.[122]

Let us consider a few other situations that may be covered by the war crime of torture or inhumane treatment. Deliberately violating the right to be free from hunger during armed conflict will often be inhumane. As Paust wrote on Sri Lanka, starvation 'seems necessarily inhumane because it involves unnecessary and lingering death and suffering',[123] and the same is true when governments intentionally withhold medicine from areas controlled by rebels.[124] Housing rights violations resulting from a failure to prevent the destruction (by private citizens) of a Romani settlement has been qualified by the Committee against Torture (CAT Committee) to amount to cruel treatment.[125] The committee implied that Israel may inflict cruel or inhuman treatment on the Palestinian inhabitants of the houses that it demolishes.[126] In July 2010, the ACommHPR concluded that forced evictions in Darfur not only violated the right to housing, but rose to violations of the right to integrity of the person and prohibition on cruel, inhuman or degrading treatment (CIDT).[127] Moreover, it qualified the destruction of homes, livestock and farms and poisoning of water sources such as wells, as a violation of the right to the highest attainable standard of health.[128] In the latter two examples, IHL is or was applicable to these situations alongside human rights law, and the conduct has a nexus to the armed conflict. The same factual conduct

[121] Powell, 'Japan's Germ Warfare: The US Cover-Up of a War Crime', 2.

[122] Jing-Bao Nie, 'The West's Dismissal of the Khabarovsk Trial as Communist Propaganda: Ideology, Evidence and International Bioethics' (2004) 1 *Journal of Bioethical Inquiry*, 1, 32–42.

[123] Paust, 'The Human Rights to Food, Medicine and Medical Supplies', 630.

[124] Ibid., 634, mentioning that the Sri Lankan government intentionally withheld medical supplies from areas controlled by the rebels, in contravention to ICESCR, Art. 12.

[125] *Dzemajl et al.* v. *Yugoslavia, 2 December 2002, CAT/C/29/D/161/2000*, CAT Committee.

[126] Concluding Observations, Israel, CAT/C/ISR/CO/4, 23 June 2009, para. 33; Concluding Observations, Israel, HRCttee, CCPR/C/ISR/CO/3, 3 September 2010, para. 17.

[127] *COHRE* v. *Sudan, Communication 296/05, 29 July 2010*, ACommHPR, para. 159.

[128] Ibid., para. 212.

appears to give rise to a violation of ESCR as well as criminal responsibility under the offence of inhumane treatment as a war crime.

Similarly, the crime of *wilfully causing great suffering or serious injury to body or health* can be committed by way of depriving protected persons of adequate food, sanitation, clothing or health care.[129] The Appeals Chamber of the ICTY upheld the conviction of Mucić for cruel treatment and wilfully causing great suffering or serious injury to body or health because the accused failed to provide the detainees with adequate food, water, health-care and toilet facilities in the Čelebići prison camp.[130] Two surviving members of the Khmer Rouge Central Committee currently stand trial for similar war crimes. According to the Closing Order for Case 002 before the ECCC, the conditions of detention of protected persons, 'including the overcrowded living conditions and the lack of adequate sanitation, medicine, food or clothing', amounted to the infliction of serious physical or mental suffering or injury.[131] Other less well-known cases before the Hong Kong War Crimes Tribunal dealt with food deprivation, refusal of medical care and adequate shelter in detention camps during World War II.[132]

The infliction of such inhumane conditions that cause great suffering or serious injury can in some circumstances simultaneously be qualified as violations of ESCR. If the direct interference with access to the rights in question is attributable to the state, that state is obliged by virtue of its international legal obligations to respect the right of everyone to be free from hunger,[133] or the right of everyone to the highest attainable standard of physical and mental health.[134] In relation to the right to be free from hunger, the ICESCR emphasised that 'a state claiming that it is

[129] Rome Statute, Art. 8, para. 2 (a)(iv). GVA Conventions Arts. 50/51/130/147. In NIAC, the crime is not listed as a separate war crime, but almost all of the same conduct is covered by the war crime of inhumane treatment (with the unlikely exception of serious injuries which would not at the same time cause severe pain or suffering).

[130] *Prosecutor* v. *Delalić, IT-96-21-A, 20 February 2001*, ICTY, para. 744.

[131] *Prosecutor* v. *Khieu Samphan, Nuon Chea, Ieng Sary and Ieng Thirith, Closing Order, Case 002, 15 September 2010*, ECCC, paras. 1502–5. (On this case, see also Section 4.3.)

[132] See for instance *Prosecutor* v. *Kennosuke, Case No. Wo235/999, 24 February 1947, Hong Kong Military Court for the Trial of War Criminals (British Military Court No. 7), United Kingdom*, convicted for the mismanagement of places of detention resulting in overcrowding, starvation and refusal of medical attention and consequential sufferings and deaths. Or *Prosecutor* v. *Hideo, Shiro and Yoshio, Case No. Wo235/1029, 9 June 1947, Hong Kong Military Court for the Trial of War Criminals (British Military Court No. 7), United Kingdom*, convicted for exposing prisoners of war to 'utter lack of food amounting to a deliberate policy of starvation'.

[133] ICESCR, Art. 11(2). [134] ICESCR, Art. 12.

unable to carry out its obligation for reasons beyond its control therefore has the burden of proving that this is the case'.[135] In the case of the Čelebići prison camp, the trial chamber held that it 'cannot, as a matter of fact, accept the assertion made by the Defence that the conditions in the Čelebići prison-camp were the result of the lack of resources available at the time'.[136] Since the camp was run by units of the Bosnian Ministry of the Interior, at least part of the relevant time, attribution to the state of Bosnia and Herzegovina seems conceivable,[137] permitting the conclusion that ESCR were violated. In sum, wilfully starving protected persons in armed conflict may not only constitute a violation of ESCR, but can also amount to the war crime of wilfully causing great suffering.

Committing *outrages upon personal dignity* is a war crime with identical substantive meaning both in IAC and in NIAC. Human dignity is at the core of IHL and human rights law, and a wide range of acts and omissions are therefore potentially constitutive of this war crime. In *Katanga*, the ICC Pre-Trial Chamber affirmatively cited the HRCttee stating that conduct such as leaving infants without care after killing their guardians constituted outrages upon personal dignity.[138] If a state actor leaves young children without care, the state may violate the obligation to take special measures of protection and assistance on behalf of children and therefore violates victims' ESCR.[139] The concept of dignity can be 'outraged' in countless ways, including by depriving protected persons of the most basic ESCR, such as clothing, essential food or care for people with disabilities.[140]

Moreover, conflict-related violations of the right to freely choose or accept one's work may under some circumstances be qualified as *sexual war crimes*, such as sexual slavery and enforced prostitution, or as the war crime of *compelling service in hostile forces*. In addition, *recruiting children* under the age of fifteen is a war crime in both NIAC and IAC.[141] If a

[135] Committee on Economic, Social and Cultural Rights, *General Comment 12 on the Right to Adequate Food*, para. 17.

[136] *Prosecutor* v. *Delalić, IT-96-21-T, 16 November 1998*, ICTY, para. 1118.

[137] ILC Articles on State Responsibility, Art. 10.

[138] *Prosecutor* v. *Katanga and Chui, Decision on the Confirmation of Charges, 30 September 2008, Pre-Trial Chamber I, ICC-01/04-01/07*, ICC, para. 370.

[139] ICESCR, Art. 10; Convention on the Rights of the Child, GA Res. 44/25 (1989), 20 November 1989 (entered into force 2 September 1990), Art. 20.

[140] Christopher McCrudden, 'Human Dignity' (2008) 19 *European Journal of International Law*, 4, 655–724: 670.

[141] Rome Statute, Art. 8, para. 2(b)(xxvi), for IAC and Art. 8, para. 2(e)(vii), for NIAC. In IAC, only the conscription or enlistment of children into *national* armed forces constitutes a crime. In contrast, in the case of NIAC, it extends to all armed forces.

government conscribes children into its armed forces, this state may well fail to respect children's ESCR, in particular the right to education.[142] If armed opposition groups recruit children with impunity, the state may be violating the right to education by failing to protect children from the disruption of their education. In the situation of Mali, the ICC Prosecutor is currently gathering information on allegations that newly recruited children received army training in schools in violation of IHL.[143]

### *5.2.2 War crimes against property*

Violations of ESCR can also go hand in hand with war crimes related to the destruction and appropriation of property.

#### 5.2.2.1 Pillage

Pillage is one of the oldest war crimes and it has identical elements both in IAC and in NIAC.[144] For the purposes of the Rome Statute, the ICC Elements of Crimes require that (i) the perpetrator appropriated certain property, (ii) he or she intended to deprive the owner of the property and to appropriate it for private or personal use and (iii) the owner did not consent to the appropriation.[145] Pillage charges based on these elements have been confirmed against Katanga and Chui.[146] The ICC later acquitted Chui based on the judges' finding that the evidence was insufficient to prove beyond reasonable doubt that the accused had authority over the combatants alleged of pillaging.[147] In early 2014, Katanga was found guilty of pillage as well as murder, attacks against civilians and destruction of property.[148] We will discuss his case further below.

Outside the ICC, the war crime of pillage is not restricted to personal or private purposes. The majority of World War II prosecutions that

142 ICESCR, Art. 13. CRC, Art. 28. See also Triffterer (ed.), *Commentary on the Rome Statute*, 467 (Cottier) on the relationship between forced recruitment and disruption of education.

143 ICC Office of the Prosecutor, 'Situation in Mali: Article 53(1) Report', paras. 120–4.

144 Rome Statute, Arts. 8, para. 2(b)(xvi) and 8, para. 2(e)(v). The pillage of cultural property is further criminalised by the second protocol to the 1954 Hague Convention on Cultural Property.

145 ICC Elements of Crimes, Arts. 8, para. 2(b)(xvi) and 8, para. 2(e)(v).

146 *Prosecutor* v. *Katanga and Chui, Decision on the Confirmation of Charges, 30 September 2008, Pre-Trial Chamber I, ICC-01/04-01/07*, ICC, paras. 327–38.

147 *Prosecutor* v. *Ngudjolo, Judgment Pursuant to Article 74 of the Statute, 18 December 2012, Trial Chamber II, ICC-01/04-02/12*, ICC, para. 503.

148 *Prosecutor* v. *Katanga, Jugement rendu en application de l'article 74 du Statut, 7 March 2014, Trial Chamber II, N° ICC-01/04-01/07*, ICC.

condemned acts of pillage precisely concerned property appropriated to further the Axis war effort. A case in point is the case against Röchling. Röchling was a civilian convicted of war crimes, 'because, with a view to increasing the war potential of the Third Reich, he exploited to the highest possible degree the foundries of the occupied countries . . ., and caused a great deal of material belonging to the industries of the occupied countries . . . to be taken away'.[149]

Tribunals adjudicating pillage charges under customary international law or national law do not have to follow the purpose restriction of the ICC Statute.[150] Rather, the Hague Regulations delineate the scope of a belligerent's right of lawful requisition and seizure.[151] To conclude whether an appropriation of property constitutes pillage, one must verify if the relevant IHL rules defining when such appropriation is unlawful have been infringed. In situations of occupation, Arts. 52–4 of the Hague Regulations allow an occupier to demand certain requisitions in kind and services, but only within strict limits.[152] First, requisitions for the needs of the (occupying) army are allowed. This, however, only allows for the day-to-day needs of the army, and selling requisitioned goods is generally prohibited.[153] Second, movable state or private property, which is by its very nature capable of military use, may be taken.[154] However, the preparatory works of Art. 53 of the Hague Regulations confirm that it is illegal to appropriate property simply because it can be converted into money.[155] Third, the occupying power must safeguard the capital of these properties and administer them in accordance with the rules of *usufruct*, that is the occupier may benefit from the property but must not damage

149 *France* v. *Röchling et al., 25 January 1949, in XIV TWC 1061, Appendix B, Superior Military Government Court*, Courts in the French Zone of Control in Germany under Control Council Law No. 10, 1140.

150 The ICTY did not restrict the offence to appropriations for private or personal use. *Prosecutor* v. *Hadžihasanović, IT-01-47-T, 15 March 2006*, ICTY, para. 52. The SCSL concluded that the ICC restriction to personal private purposes did not reflect customary international law. *Prosecutor* v. *Brima, Kamara and Kanu, SCSL-04-16-T, 20 July 2007*, SCSL, para. 754; *Prosecutor* v. *Fofana and Kondewa, SCSL-04-14-T, 2 August 2007*, SCSL, para. 160; *Prosecutor* v. *Taylor, SCSL-03-1-T, 26 April 2012*, SCSL, para. 452.

151 Arts. 52–55 Hague Regulations. See also James Stewart, *Prosecuting the Pillage of Natural Resources* (Open Society Institute, 2010).

152 Strictly speaking, these exceptions only apply to military occupiers, but it is reasonable to expect that the same exceptions can also be invoked in NIAC. Ibid., 21. See, however, *Prosecutor* v. *Sesay, Kallon and Gbao, SCSL-04-15-T, 2 March 2009*, SCSL, para. 982.

153 *United States of America* v. *Krupp et al., IX TWC 1327*, NMT.

154 Hague Regulations, Art. 53.

155 Conférence de Bruxelles, Actes de la conférence de Bruxelles, Hayez, 1874, 121.

or destroy it.[156] Where these limitations are not respected, the appropriation of property is unlawful.

There are important links between pillage and violations of ESCR. Pillage overlaps with various ESCR violations if the pillage is, for instance, perpetrated by the armed forces of the government who interfere with people's access to ESCR, or if the state fails to protect civilians from the deprivation of access to adequate food, work or other rights by other actors, such as members of paramilitary groups. In the *Armed Activities (DRC* v. *Uganda)* case, the ICJ concluded that Uganda had not taken the necessary measures to prevent pillage in the DRC. The court ruled that, as the occupying power, Uganda should have taken action to stop the pillage not only by members of its armed forces, but also by private persons in the region.[157] A UN report on abuses in the DRC illustrates how the pillage of natural resources went hand in hand with violations of ESCR, lowering people's standard of living.[158]

Contrary to the war crime of excessive property destruction, the wording of the relevant provisions does not require that pillage be committed excessively.[159] Zimmermann, however, posits that 'items of marginal value would not be subject to the jurisdiction [of the ICC]', because war crimes are crimes of concern to the international community as a whole.[160] Even when property may seem of 'marginal value' at first sight, care must be taken to assess its practical value for victims, particularly if the property played an important role in victims' enjoyment of ESCR, such as adequate food, water or shelter, including as the underlying determinants of health. The theft of even just a few pots and a livestock may have left the victim without the necessary means to bring water to her household, and the livestock may have been the survivor's only available source of protein. In some contexts, stealing kitchen gear can be an inexpensive but highly effective strategy to displace people. The ICC Pre-Trial Chamber confirmed that 'the [ICC] Elements of Crimes do

156 Hague Regulations, Art. 55. Eyal Benvenisti, 'Water Conflicts' (2003) 97 *American Journal of International Law*, 4, 860–72: 869. Benvenisti argues that Iraq's freshwater resources qualify as public immovable property, so that the rules of *usufruct* apply.

157 *Case Concerning Armed Activities on the Territory of the Congo (DRC* v. *Uganda), 19 December 2005*, ICJ, para. 248.

158 OHCHR, Report of the Mapping Exercise Documenting the Most Serious Violations of Human Rights and International Humanitarian Law Committed within the Territory of the DRC between March 1993 and June 2003, OHCHR, 2010, paras. 726–7.

159 Uhler et al., *Commentary, Fourth Geneva Convention*, 226.

160 Triffterer (ed.), *Commentary on the Rome Statute*, 409 (Zimmermann).

not require the property to be of a certain monetary value'.[161] While the chamber concluded that cases of petty property expropriation might not fall under the scope of the crime, it also stressed that the determination of the seriousness of the violation must be made 'in light of the particular circumstances of the case'.[162] The ICTY Trial Chamber in *Gotovina* also used this approach and stressed that 'a case-by-case assessment is necessary to determine whether such acts involve grave consequences for the victims'.[163] Importantly, the recent evolution of the case law on pillage demonstrates that judges now recognise the gravity of the theft of cattle and 'ordinary' household items. In a welcome development in the recent *Katanga* judgment, Trial Chamber II emphatically pointed out that kitchen items, furniture, food, iron sheets, cattle and other goods can be essential for the daily life of survivors and are thus of great value in the specific context of the case.[164] The ICC will have further opportunities to address allegations of pillage in the case against the Congolese rebel leader Ntaganda as well as in the situation of Mali, where the Prosecutor currently investigates the looting of food reserves, shops and hospital equipment.[165]

The crime of pillage not only covers the looting of personal property, but also criminalises more complex forms of exploitation, although tribunals have to date only confirmed this hypothesis in *obiter dicta*.[166] While Charles Taylor was convicted of aiding and abetting pillage in Sierra Leone, the trial chamber based its finding on the traditional looting of personal property rather than the more complex forms of pillaging diamonds and other natural resources that characterised the conflict in

[161] *Prosecutor* v. *Bemba, Decision on the Charges of the Prosecutor, 15 June 2009, Pre-Trial Chamber II, ICC-01/05-01/08-424*, ICC, para. 317.

[162] Ibid.; *Prosecutor* v. *Delalić, IT-96-21-T, 16 November 1998*, ICTY, para. 1154. The *Delalić* Trial Chamber dismissed a charge of pillage because the amount was not of 'sufficient monetary value'. Schabas supports the view that the rationale was jurisdictional, rather than based upon a requirement with respect to the definition of pillage. Schabas, *Commentary on the Rome Statute*, 242.

[163] *Prosecutor* v. *Gotovina and Marcač, IT-06-90-T, 15 April 2011*, ICTY, para. 1672 (note omitted).

[164] *Prosecutor* v. *Katanga, Jugement rendu en application de l'article 74 du Statut, 7 March 2014, Trial Chamber II, N° ICC-01/04-01/07*, ICC, paras. 953–7.

[165] *Second Arrest Warrant Decision for Ntaganda, 13 July 2012, Pre-Trial Chamber II, ICC-01/04-02/06*, ICC, para. 59; ibid.; ICC Office of the Prosecutor, 'Situation in Mali: Article 53(1) Report', paras. 114–16.

[166] *Prosecutor* v. *Taylor, SCSL-03-1-T, 26 April 2012*, SCSL, para. 453. The Trial Chamber states that the crime of pillage 'covers both organised or systematic appropriation and the isolated acts of individuals', citing *Prosecutor* v. *Brima, Kamara and Kanu, SCSL-04-16-T, 20 July 2007*, SCSL, para. 754, and *Prosecutor* v. *Delalić, IT-96-21-T, 16 November 1998*, ICTY, para. 590.

West Africa.[167] Nevertheless, van den Herik and Dam-De Jong convincingly argue that the war crime addresses various forms of illegal exploitation of natural resources.[168] Even though the definition of this war crime – particularly in the Rome Statute – is not without difficulties,[169] the crime is addressed to all persons in situations of armed conflict and covers all kinds of property, making it a potentially useful tool to deal with the linkages between natural resource exploitation, armed conflict and violations of ESCR.

#### 5.2.2.2 Destruction and appropriation of property

Excessive and unlawful destruction and appropriation of protected property not justified by military necessity is a separate war crime.[170] Both in IAC and in NIAC, the destruction and appropriation must be extensive to constitute a war crime. Different types of property enjoy distinct standards of protection under IHL, depending on the type of property involved and whether the property is situated in an occupied territory.[171] In NIAC, the war crime included in Art. 8(2)(e)(xii) of the Rome Statute is based on the wording of the customary Art. 23(g) of the Hague Regulations.

In an occupied territory, Arts. 53 and 147 of GVA IV prohibit destruction of property belonging to private or public authorities. Art. 43 of the Hague Regulations requires the occupying authorities to exercise their powers with a view to the interest of the local population of the area, thus including the socio-economic well-being of the population living in the

167 *Prosecutor* v. *Taylor, SCSL-03-1-T, 26 April 2012,* SCSL, paras. 1957 (money), 8 (food), 62 (property from shops). The exploitation of diamond mines was, however, used to establish that Taylor aided and abetted crimes by providing assistance, and because his acts had a substantial effect on the perpetration of the crimes. Ibid., para. 6142 (summary of findings), for the individual factual findings, see paras. 5876–7, 5951, 5993, 6060–1, 6106.

168 Larissa van den Herik and Daniëlla Dam-De Jong, 'Revitalizing the Antique War Crime of Pillage' (2011) 22 *Criminal Law Forum*, 3, 237–73.

169 In particular, the Rome Statute limitation to 'private or personal use' restricts the scope of the crime because government officials looting the state's natural resources in NIAC can escape accountability if they can claim that they did not personally enrich themselves. Furthermore, concessions over natural resources are often granted with the consent of the owner, making it impossible to establish an intention to deprive the owner of the property. Ibid., 262–3.

170 Rome Statute, Arts. 8, para. 2(a)(iv) and 8, para. 2(b)(xiii) (IAC) and 8, para. 2(e)(xii) (NIAC).

171 For a detailed overview, see Dörmann et al., *Elements of War Crimes*, 81–95. Military necessity can only be invoked to justify property destruction and appropriation if the underlying rule of IHL explicitly provides for it. Triffterer (ed.), *Commentary on the Rome Statute*, 312 (Dörmann); Uhler et al., *Commentary, Fourth Geneva Convention*, 391.

territory. In the words of an Israeli high court, 'a territory held in belligerent occupation is not an open field for economic or other exploitation'.[172] Failure to comply with this rule can lead to a conviction for war crimes. In his capacity as the Minister of Economics and President of the central bank, Walther Funk was involved in the seizure of vast amounts of gold reserves, funds, oil and other products from the territories occupied by the Nazis.[173] Funk participated in a meeting in which Göring emphasised that these policies would be enforced without consideration given to the well-being of the population of the occupied areas:

> God knows, you [representatives of the Reich in the occupied territories] are not sent out there [to the occupied areas] to work for the welfare of the people in your charge, but to get the utmost out of them so that the German people can live ... It makes no difference to me in this connection if you say that your people will starve. Let them do so, as long as no German collapses from hunger.[174]

Based on such blatant infringements of the law of occupation, the IMT qualified Funk's participation 'in the economic exploitation of occupied territories' as war crimes and crimes against humanity.[175]

Another relevant court case is the *Hostage* trial before the NMT. General Rendulic was accused of wanton destruction of private and public property, in particular based on allegations that he ordered

> the complete destruction of all shelter and means of existence in, and the total evacuation of the entire civilian population of, the northern Norwegian province of Finmark ... For no compelling military reasons, and in literal execution of instructions to show no sympathy to the civilian

[172] *Jamiat Askaan* v. *Commander of the IDF Forces in the Area, HCJ 393/82 (Unofficial Translation by Hamoked, Centre for the Defence of the Individual), 28 December 1983, High Court of Justice*, Israel, para. 13. Confirmed in *Yesh Din* v. *IDF Commander in the West Bank et Al, High Court of Justice, HCJ 2164/09, ILDC 1820 (Unofficial Translation by Yesh Din), 26 December 2011, High Court of Justice*, Israel, para. 8.

[173] *United States of America, the French Republic, the United Kingdom of Great Britain and Northern Ireland, and the Union of Soviet Socialist Republics against Major War Criminals, Opinion and Judgment, in Nazi Conspiracy and Aggression (Red Series), 1 October 1946*, IMT, 133.

[174] The full translation of the speech is reproduced in *United States of America* v. *Von Weizsaecker et al.* (Ministries Case), *XIII TWC 1*, NMT, Prosecution Exhibit 3239, 799–800.

[175] *United States of America, the French Republic, the United Kingdom of Great Britain and Northern Ireland, and the Union of Soviet Socialist Republics against Major War Criminals, Opinion and Judgment, in Nazi Conspiracy and Aggression (Red Series), 1 October 1946*, IMT, 133–4.

> population, the evacuated residents were made to witness the burning of their homes and possessions and the destruction of churches, public buildings, food supplies, barns, livestock, bridges, transport facilities, and natural resources of an area in which they and their families had lived for generations. Relatives and friends were separated, many of the evacuees became ill from cold and disease, hundreds died from exposure or perished at sea in the small boats and fishing smacks used in the evacuation, while still others were summarily shot for refusing to leave their homeland – in all, the thoroughness and brutality of this evacuation left some 61,000 men, women, and children homeless, starving, and destitute.[176]

The tribunal observed that there was 'evidence in the record that there was no military necessity for this destruction and devastation'.[177] Subjectively, however, the tribunal concluded that 'the conditions as they appeared to the defendant at the time were sufficient, upon which he could honestly conclude that urgent military necessity warranted the decision made'.[178] Heller rightly criticises the tribunal for 'effectively transforming military necessity into a purely subjective test'.[179] Today, tribunals scrutinise the defence of military necessity for such policies much more stringently. Indeed, Trial Chamber II of the SCSL recently found Charles Taylor guilty of aiding and abetting the widespread destruction of civilian property by burning homes in Sierra Leone.[180] In that case, the burning of civilian homes was even qualified as 'acts of terrorism', since its primary purpose was to terrorise the civilian population.[181]

It is apparent that the conduct criminalised by the war crime of destruction or appropriation of civilian property not only has serious consequences for the population's enjoyment of ESCR, but can itself also be, or relate to, a violation of ESCR. The existence of a potential relationship between violations of the right to an adequate standard of living, including the right to housing, and criminal responsibility for war crimes has been suggested by the CESCR.[182] The UN Fact Finding Mission on

176 *United States of America* v. *List et al. (Hostage Case), XI TWC 1230*, NMT, 770.
177 Ibid., 1296. 178 Ibid., 1297.
179 Kevin Heller, *The Nuremberg Military Tribunals* (Oxford University Press, 2011), 311.
180 *Prosecutor* v. *Taylor, SCSL-03-1-T, 26 April 2012*, SCSL, para. 6959 (for factual findings concerning the burning of homes, see paras. 684, 716, 772 or 788).
181 Ibid., paras. 684, 710, 716, 740 (also concerns the destruction of other property), 788, 808, 841, 860.
182 Concluding Observations, Israel, E/C.12/1/Add.90, 26 June 2003, para. 26. The CESCR mentions that to the extent that expropriations are incompatible with IHL, they may give raise to individual criminal responsibility.

the Gaza Conflict, moreover, reported that the destruction of the last operating flour mill in the Gaza Strip, as well as the destruction of other food production, water installations, sewage treatment and housing had no military justification. The Mission therefore concluded that the destruction amounted to war crimes and simultaneously violated human rights provisions regarding the right to adequate food.[183]

### 5.2.2.3 Attacking cultural property

Intentionally attacking cultural property is another war crime relevant to the present analysis.[184] Cultural property is defined in the 1907 Hague Regulations, the UNESCO Convention, the 1954 Hague Convention, its second protocol and in AP I.[185] This war crime constitutes a *lex specialis* to the general protection of civilian objects from unlawful direct attacks.[186] By virtue of the second protocol to the 1954 Hague Convention and customary international law, this war crime extends to NIAC, and states must extradite or prosecute alleged perpetrators.[187]

The ICTY has convicted persons on charges of destruction of cultural property in the historic centre of Dubrovnik. The ICTY held that the entire old town of Dubrovnik constituted protected cultural property, because it was included in the list of UNESCO and had no military objectives in its vicinity.[188] The ICC Prosecutor furthermore argues

[183] Final Report of the UN Fact Finding Mission on the Gaza Conflict, A/HRC/12/48, 15 September 2009, para. 50. An early precedent of similar, but less explicit, reasoning can be found in the Report on the Situation of Human Rights in Kuwait under Iraqi Occupation (Walter Kälin), E/CN.4/1992/26, 16 January 1992. The report notes that ESCR were violated (paras. 240, 246–7) and that such violations may be qualified as crimes (para. 254) and that appropriation and excessive destruction of property, as well as pillage were committed (paras. 224–35).

[184] Rome Statute, Art. 8, para. 2(b)(ix), and Art. 8, para. 2(e)(iv). Convention for the Protection of Cultural Property in the Event of Armed Conflict, 249 UNTS 216, 14 May 1954 (entered into force 7 August 1956), Art. 28; Second Protocol to the Hague Convention on Cultural Property in Armed Conflict, Art. 15. AP I, Art. 85. The Rome Statute only criminalises the destruction of *immovable* cultural property, although the destruction of movable cultural property falls under the general protection of civil objectives.

[185] For an excellent overview of relevant treaty provisions, see Roger O'Keefe, 'Cultural Property', in *The Handbook of International Humanitarian Law*, ed. Dieter Fleck (Oxford University Press, 2008), 433–74: 436–42.

[186] Ibid., 435.

[187] Second Protocol to the Hague Convention on Cultural Property in Armed Conflict, Art. 15; Henckaerts and Doswald-Beck (eds.), *Customary IHL*, vol. 1, rule 38.

[188] *Prosecutor* v. *Strugar, IT-01-42-T, 31 January 2005*, ICTY, para. 446; *Prosecutor* v. *Jokić, IT-01-42/1-S, 18 March 2004*, ICTY, paras. 23, 113.

that some of the attacked objects in Afghanistan and in Mali are protected objects 'dedicated to religion, education, art, science or charitable purposes or historic monuments'.[189]

The destruction of cultural property by actors attributable to a state often violates the right to take part in cultural life,[190] particularly given that access to the physical infrastructure plays an important (physical and symbolic) role in the exercise of cultural life.[191] This war crime is not solely concerned with the physical destruction of cultural property, but the criminalisation of this offence expresses the international community's condemnation of conduct that offends other people's participation in cultural life. Consider the case against Kurtović before the Bosnia War Crimes Chamber. In that case, a Bosniak commander destroyed a Catholic shrine and mistreated Catholic prisoners of war and civilians detained in the church by ramming religious paintings into their heads and making them eat pages of the Bible. This conduct was qualified both as the infliction of great suffering and as the deliberate damaging of an establishment designated for religious purposes.[192] It is not difficult to argue that officials responsible for such conduct simultaneously engage their state's responsibility for cultural rights violations.

The Rome Statute includes buildings dedicated to education in the scope of the war crime of intentionally directing attacks against cultural property, both in IAC and in NIAC.[193] Directing attacks against educational buildings constitutes a war crime provided that the buildings are not military objectives. The commission of this crime will often simultaneously hamper the right to education,[194] a right that domestic courts

189 Rome Statute, Art. 8, para. 2(e)(iv). ICC Office of the Prosecutor, 'Report on Preliminary Examination Activities' (ICC, 2013), para. 31; ICC Office of the Prosecutor, 'Situation in Mali: Article 53(1) Report', paras. 109–13.

190 ICESCR, Art. 15(1)a.

191 Kerstin Odendahl, *Kulturgüterschutz* (Mohr Siebeck, 2005), 205. Odendahl writes that 'participation in cultural life includes access to and contact with cultural property' (translation by the author). Elsa Stamatopoulou, *Cultural Rights in International Law* (Nijhoff, 2007), 162, concluding that the inaccessibility of sacred sites is a justiciable aspect of the right to take part in cultural life. Instruments of soft law also emphasise the right to access to and participation in cultural life. See Cultural Rights: Fribourg Declaration, Interdisciplinary Institute for Ethics and Human Rights of the University of Fribourg, 7 May 2007, Art. 5.

192 *Prosecutor* v. *Kurtović, X-Kr-06/299, 30 April 2008, First Instance,* Bosnia War Crimes Chamber, paras. 2, 11; *Prosecutor* v. *Kurtović, X-Krž-06/299, 25 March 2009, Appellate Panel of the Section I for War Crimes,* Bosnia War Crimes Chamber, para. 108.

193 Rome Statute, Art. 8, para. 2(b)(ix) and e(iv). For the drafting history, see Schabas, *Commentary on the Rome Statute*, 236–7.

194 UNESCO, *Education under Attack* (UNESCO, 2007).

have found applicable just as other ESCR in times of armed conflict.[195] In 2011, the ECtHR declared admissible a case alleging that Russia was responsible for violating the right to education because Russia would have destroyed and looted schools and libraries during the conflict in Abkhazia and South Ossetia.[196] More recently, a Nigerian NGO called for international criminal accountability for attacks on schoolchildren and educational buildings allegedly committed by the armed group Boko Haram and explained that these attacks are 'also an attack on [children's] right to education' and are leading 'to dramatic decreases in school attendance rates'.[197]

Even where no individuals are injured or killed in an attacked educational building, the ICC is mandated to prosecute attacks directed against educational buildings. The explicit inclusion of educational buildings in the list of protected cultural property is a welcome innovation of the Rome Statute. Prosecutors should take this crime into account, particularly if one considers the widespread targeting of schools in conflict states and the effects such attacks have on children's right to education. In cases where educational buildings are not covered by the protection of cultural property, they are *prima facie* protected by the prohibition of attacking civilian objects and unlawfully destroying enemy property.[198] It was estimated that 80 per cent of school buildings in Afghanistan were in ruins, many of them having been targeted in attacks.[199] Although the availability of physical buildings is only one aspect of children's access to education, there is a strong link between the destruction of educational buildings and the lack of access to education, particularly for girls, children living in rural areas and children with disabilities.[200]

[195] See in particular *Sentencia C- 376/10, Demanda de inconstitucionalidad contra el artículo 183 de la Ley 115 de 1994 'Por la cual se expide la ley general de educación', 19 May 2010, Constitutional Court*, Colombia.

[196] *Georgia* v. *Russia (No. 2), Application No. 38263/08, Admissibility Decision of 13 December 2011*, ECtHR, paras. 34–5. See also Chapter 7, Note 52 and accompanying text.

[197] 'Nigeria: Abducted Schoolgirls - SERAP Seeks UN Intervention', *Guardian*, 25 April 2014.

[198] *Prosecutor* v. *Kordić, Čerkez, IT-95-14/2-A, 17 December 2004*, ICTY, para. 92.

[199] Asian Development Bank, 'Afghanistan: Comprehensive Needs Assessment in Education' (ADB, 2002), 2.

[200] Save the Children, 'The Future Is Now: Education for Children in Countries Affected by Conflict' (Save the Children, 2010), 7. For a comprehensive overview of interlinkages between the protection of educational facilities during armed conflicts and the right to education, see Kristin Hausler et al., *Education in Armed Conflict* (British Institute of International and Comparative Law, Education Above All, 2012).

### 5.2.3 *War crimes consisting in the use of prohibited methods of warfare*

#### 5.2.3.1 Prohibited attacks

Intentionally directing *attacks against civilians* not taking part in hostilities violates the fundamental principle of IHL, the principle of distinction. Civilians are those who do not participate in hostilities, and they are protected against direct attacks, unless and for such time as they directly participate in hostilities. Directing attacks against civilians is a war crime in both types of armed conflicts.[201]

Directing attacks against *civilian objects*[202] is explicitly defined as a war crime in IAC.[203] The Rome Statute does not contain a war crimes provision criminalising direct attacks against civilian objects in NIAC,[204] but criminalises the *destruction of 'the property of an adversary* unless such destruction . . . is imperatively demanded by the necessities of the conflict'.[205]

Food, water installations or agricultural areas are *prima facie* civilian objects. They may only be attacked if they are used 'as sustenance *solely* for the members of its armed forces' or 'if not as sustenance, then in direct support of military action, provided, however, that in no event shall actions against these objects be taken which may be expected to leave the civilian population with such inadequate food or water as to cause its starvation or force its movement'.[206] As the ICRC commentary

201 AP I, Art. 85; Rome Statute, Arts. 8, para. 2(b)(i) and 8, para. 2(e)(i). In the Rome Statute, the crime is defined slightly differently than the grave breach contained in Art. 85 of AP I. The Rome Statute requires that the attacks be 'intentionally directed' rather than 'wilfully'. However, the ICRC Commentary mentions that 'wilfully' stands for 'consciously and intent'. The two expressions of the mental element should thus be considered the same. See also Note 54. Yves Sandoz et al., *Commentary on the Additional Protocols* (Nijhoff, 1987), 994. This reasoning applies to other similarly worded war crimes. See further Triffterer (ed.), *Commentary on the Rome Statute*, 326 (Dörmann).

202 AP I, Art. 52 (constituting customary international law). There is abundant literature on the concept of military versus civilian objectives. See, for instance, Yoram Dinstein, *The Conduct of Hostilities* (Cambridge University Press, 2004), Part IV; Marco Sassòli, 'Targeting', in *New Wars, New Laws?*, ed. David Wippman and Matthew Evangelista (Transnational, 2005), 181–210: Chapter 7.

203 Rome Statute, Art. 8, para. 2(b)(ii).

204 Civilian objects are, of course, also protected in NIAC, although the violation of this norm is not criminalised as a war crime.

205 Rome Statute, Art. 8, para. 2(e)(xii) (emphasis added).

206 AP I, Art. 54 (emphasis added). Paragraph 5 of Art. 54 contains a derogation provision, allowing a party to derogate from the prohibition, but only in the defence of this party's national territory.

convincingly explains, 'agricultural areas or drinking water installations are hardly likely to be used solely for the benefit of armed forces'.[207] Hence, food or water for the benefit of both civilians and combatants must not be attacked. Moreover, even if farmlands or crops are exclusively destined for those taking part in hostilities, they may never be attacked, destroyed, removed or rendered useless if such would cause starvation or forced relocation.

*Disproportionate attacks* are a war crime applicable in IAC. It is a grave breach to launch an indiscriminate attack affecting the civilian population or civilian objects in the knowledge that such attack will cause excessive loss of life, injury to civilians or damage to civilian objects.[208] The Rome Statute requires a higher threshold. The loss of life, injury or damage must not just be excessive, but '*clearly* excessive in relation to the concrete and direct *overall* military advantage anticipated'.[209]

In addition, directing an *attack against* personnel, installations, material, units or vehicles involved in *humanitarian assistance* is a war crime in both types of armed conflict.[210] Such attacks can simultaneously constitute an interference with access to food, water, clothing, sanitation or health and therefore also amount to a violation of ESCR. That such could be the case was alluded to in the report of the International Commission of Inquiry on Côte d'Ivoire.[211]

#### 5.2.3.2 Starvation

Intentionally starving civilians is prohibited in both types of armed conflict.[212] Intentional starvation of civilians as a method of warfare by depriving them of objects indispensable to their survival, including by wilfully impeding relief, is also a war crime in IAC under the Rome Statute.[213] A proposal to include the same crime in the Rome Statute

207 Sandoz et al., *Commentary on the Additional Protocols*, 657.

208 AP I, Art. 85(3)b.

209 Rome Statute, Art. 8, para. 2(b)(iv) (emphasis added). AP I, Art. 57 requires only concrete and direct military advantage anticipated.

210 Rome Statute, Arts. 8, para. 2(b)(iii) and 8, para. 2(e)(iii).

211 Report of the International Commission of Inquiry on Côte d'Ivoire, A/HRC/17/48, 14 June 2011, para. 93. The relevant conduct is described in paras. 83–7.

212 AP I, Art. 54; AP II, Art. 53. Custom proscribes 'any attack upon means of subsistence which serves solely the civilian population.' Antonio Cassese, 'The Geneva Protocols of 1977' (1984) 3 *UCLA Pacific Basin Law Journal*, 55–118: 91.

213 Rome Statute, Art. 8, para. 2(b)(xxv).

provisions applicable to NIAC was not retained,[214] and this exclusion severely narrows the potential of this war crime to address violations of the right to freedom from hunger or the right to water before the ICC. The fact that the list of war crimes in the Rome Statute does not include intentional starvation inflicted in NIAC does not, however, prevent that customary international law could evolve to criminalise starvation in internal conflicts.[215] Moreover, several states have legislation classifying starvation as a war crime in any armed conflict and they may consequently convict alleged perpetrators for this crime, including if the conduct took place in NIAC.[216] In addition, the UN Security Council has affirmed individual responsibility for those who impede food and medical relief in NIAC.[217] That customary law today criminalises starvation as a method of war in NIAC is also the view of UN experts.[218]

Historically, starvation was considered a lawful way of forcing surrender.[219] Despite the development of commonly accepted rules of war in the Hague Regulations, the US military court in the *High Command* case after World War II condoned the Nazi siege of Leningrad that resulted in the deaths of more than 1 million Russians.[220] Doubtful

[214] Preparatory Committee Draft Statute for the ICC, A/CONF.183/2/Add.1, 14 April 1998, 21. At the African regional level, a draft protocol to grant criminal jurisdiction to the African regional court would include starvation as a method of warfare in NIAC. See African Union Draft Protocol on Amendments to the Protocol on the Statute of the African Court of Justice and Human Rights, Meeting of Government Experts and Ministers of Justice/Attorneys General on Legal Matters, 7–15 May 2012, Addis Ababa, Exp/Min/IV/Rev.7, Art. 28D(e)(xvi).

[215] For some authors, starvation in NIAC is already criminalised under customary international law today. Triffterer (ed.), *Commentary on the Rome Statute*, 459 (Cottier), stating that 'the deliberate starvation of civilians also appears to constitute, today, a war crime under customary international law'.

[216] Jean-Marie Henckaerts and Louise Doswald-Beck (eds.), *Customary IHL*, 2 vols., vol. 2 (Cambridge University Press, 2005), Practice relating to rule 53.

[217] Bosnia and Herzegovina, S/RES/787, 16 November 1992, para. 7; Somalia, S/RES/794, 3 December 1992, para. 5. Note that in both cases, the SC is referring to 'the deliberate impeding of the delivery of food and medical supplies to the civilian population', similar to the wording in the Rome Statute for the war crime in IAC. Over time, starvation in NIAC is likely to evolve to a war crime under customary international law to the extent that it is not already criminalised implicitly by other provisions. See on this point Note 221.

[218] Report of the SG's Panel of Experts on Accountability in Sri Lanka, 31 March 2011, para. 247.

[219] Lieber Code, US War Department, General Orders No. 100, 24 April 1863, Art. 17.

[220] *United States of America* v. *Van Leeb et al.* (High Command Case), *XI TWC 462*, NMT, 563: 'The propriety of attempting to reduce it by starvation is not questioned. Hence, the cutting off of every source of sustenance from without is deemed legitimate.'

even in World War II,[221] this position is today not only clearly outlawed but also criminalised at least in IAC. AP I prohibits attacking, destroying, removing or rendering useless objects indispensable to the survival of the civilian population for the purpose of denying them for their sustenance value to the population, whether in order to starve out civilians, to cause them to move away or for any other motive.[222] Note that the intentional deprivation of indispensable objects as a method of warfare suffices; death is not necessary. Article 14 of AP II prohibits starvation in NIAC. The ICRC commentary to AP II notes that no measure of military necessity justifies the starvation of civilians.[223] Starvation is nevertheless only a war crime if used as a *method* of warfare. This excludes starvation as a result of mismanagement.[224]

It is not difficult to argue that the right to an adequate standard of living can be violated in such a way as to constitute the war crime of starvation. The most basic content of the right to an adequate standard of living is the right to be free from hunger.[225] The definition of starvation applies not only to the deprivation of food and water,[226] but also to

[221] The tribunal's conclusion seems doubtful since the conduct could already at that time have been said to violate the principle of distinction contained in the Hague Regulations. The 1919 Report of the Commission on Responsibility set up after World War I listed deliberate starvation of civilians as a violation of the laws and customs of war subject to criminal prosecution. See Report of Commission to Determine War Guilt, in 14 *American Journal of International Law* 95–154 (1920), 6 May 1919, 114. In this regard, see also Leila Sadat Wexler, 'International Criminal Law Comes of Age' (1997) 8 *Criminal Law Forum*, 3, 461–505: 468–9. Sadat concludes that '[t]he *von Leeb* holding ... is contradicted by Art. 54 of [AP I] ... The reader is left wondering ... whether the *von Leeb* court really got it right in 1945.' Even if the *von Leeb* Court would have been correct back in 1945, Fenrick posits that 'it is not unreasonable to hope that ... customary law on this particular point is now somewhat more humane'. William Fenrick, 'Some International Law Problems Related to Prosecutions before the International Criminal Tribunal for the Former Yugoslavia' (1995) 6 *Duke Journal of Comparative and International Law*, 103–25: 110.

[222] AP I, Art. 54. Yoram Dinstein, 'Siege Warfare', in *Humanitarian Law of Armed Conflict: Essays in Honour of F. Kalshoven*, ed. Astrid Delissen and Gerard Tanja (Nijhoff, 1991), 145–52: 148.

[223] Sandoz et al., *Commentary on the Additional Protocols*, 1457; *Perišić and Others, 24 April 1997, District Court of Zadar, Croatia.*

[224] What Marcus terms 'second-degree famine crimes' is not covered by the war crimes provisions. David Marcus, 'Famine Crimes' (2003) 97 *American Journal of International Law*, 2, 245–81: 272.

[225] ICESCR, Art. 11(2).

[226] For a discussion on how the right to water and sanitation relates to the war crime of starvation, see Mara Tignino, 'The Right to Water and Sanitation in Post-Conflict Peacebuilding' (2011) 36 *Water International*, 2, 241–9: 244, and Mara Tignino, *L'eau et la guerre* (Bruylant, 2011), 81–3.

other essential objects. Art. 54 of AP I lists agricultural areas for the production of foodstuffs, crops, livestock, drinking water installations and irrigation works. The term 'such as' indicates that this list is illustrative.[227] Other objects such as clothing, medical supplies or objects required to process food also appear to be covered.[228] The OHCHR concluded that cutting off electricity sources may amount to the deprivation of objects indispensable for the survival of civilians, especially of hospital patients, who would die if electricity supplies are stopped for too long.[229] 'Wilfully impeding relief supplies' is included in the crime, and relief supplies are not limited to foodstuffs and drinking water, but may include a wide range of objects, from clothing, shelter, medical and sanitary supplies to tools. This supports the view that necessities other than food and water are covered by the criminalisation of starvation.

The obstruction of humanitarian relief illustrates important links between ESCR and the war crime of starvation. The provision of assistance is subject to certain conditions.[230] But where impartial and non-discriminatory humanitarian relief is hampered as a method of war, as international law experts have argued is the case in Syria,[231] the

[227] Triffterer (ed.), *Commentary on the Rome Statute*, 461 (Cottier), pointing out that dictionaries suggest that the meaning of 'starvation' is not limited to the fact of having too little food, but, more generally, to have insufficient supply of essential commodities or necessary things to live.

[228] Ibid., 460 (Cottier).

[229] OHCHR, Report of the Mapping Exercise Documenting the Most Serious Violations of Human Rights and International Humanitarian Law Committed within the Territory of the DRC between March 1993 and June 2003, OHCHR, 2010, para. 330. A similar point on electricity is made in one of the first reports in which a UN rapporteur documented ESCR violations during an armed conflict. Report of the Special Rapporteur on the Situation of Human Rights in Iraq (Max van der Stoel), E/CN.4/1995/56, 15 February 1995, para. 46.

[230] Relief must be humanitarian, impartial and neutral. The concerned government must consent to the assistance, but such consent must not be denied arbitrarily. GVA IV, Art. 59; AP I, Art. 70; AP II, Art. 18. Relief may only be withheld if there are 'serious reasons for fearing' that consignments may be diverted to the enemy. The sole purpose of humanitarian assistance must be to prevent and alleviate human suffering. *Military and Paramilitary Activities in and against Nicaragua (Nicaragua* v. *USA), (Merits), 27 June 1986*, ICJ, para. 243. See also Hans-Joachim Heintze and Andrej Zwitter, *Humanitarian Assistance* (Springer, 2011), 8–31; Joakim Dungel, 'Humanitarian Assistance in Internal Armed Conflicts: Respecting Sovereignty, Neutrality and Legitimacy: Practical Proposals to Practical Problems' (2004) *Journal of Humanitarian Assistance*, http://sites.tufts.edu/jha/archives/838; Amrei Müller, *ESCR and IHL* (Nijhoff, 2013), 239–70.

[231] UN Special Rapporteurs, Deprival of Food, Water, Shelter and Medical Care – A Method of War in Syria, and a Crime against Humanity, Joint press release, 6 February 2014; 'There Is No Legal Barrier to UN Cross-Border Operations in Syria', *Guardian*, 28 April 2014.

responsible individuals not only commit a war crime, but the state on whose account the individuals act is likely to also violate the human rights obligation to take steps, or at least not to create obstacles, to ensure that the population has access to essential goods and services.[232] The UN SG's panel of experts on accountability in Sri Lanka supposed in 2011 that starvation was a serious violation of Common Article 3 for which criminalisation is also available in NIAC. The experts concluded that allegations of starvation due to the denial of humanitarian relief as a war crime were credible,[233] and such conduct also engages Sri Lanka's state responsibility under the ICESCR.[234] In 2014, a group of five UN Special Rapporteurs concluded that the deprivation of basic necessities of life in the Syrian conflict amounts to the crime of starvation.[235]

At the Preparatory Commission for the ICC, the United States commented their own proposal for the elements of this crime that '[a]s with murder, the *actus reus* for this offence could be the failure to fulfil a lawful duty: for example, feeding prisoners under one's care. This offence does not impose or imply a duty of care that does not otherwise exist in international law.'[236] This comment correctly summarises the conditions for the *actus reus* by omissions, such as the deprivation of objects indispensable to the survival of the population. Since human rights law related to ESCR continues to apply during armed conflict and IHL itself establishes obligations to provide food to vulnerable populations in armed conflict,[237] state actors are obliged to take steps to ensure that individuals under their control are not starving. Failure to do so may under extreme circumstances give rise to individual liability.[238]

232 Vité, 'Occupation and ESCR', 639.

233 Report of the SG's Panel of Experts on Accountability in Sri Lanka, 31 March 2011, para. 247.

234 ICESCR, Arts. 2, 11, 12. See also the strongly worded Concluding Observations, Sri Lanka, E/C.12/LKA/CO/2-4, 9 December 2010, paras. 28–9.

235 UN Special Rapporteurs, Deprival of Food, Water, Shelter and Medical Care – A Method of War in Syria, and a Crime against Humanity, Joint press release, 6 February 2014.

236 USA: Draft Elements of War Crimes, PCNICC/1999/DP.4/Add.2, 4 February 1999, 18.

237 Buckingham provides a useful overview of the relevant norms of IHL related to food. Donald Buckingham, 'A Recipe for Change' (1994) 6 *Pace International Review*, 285–321: 299.

238 Cottier similarly submits 'that a qualified failure to fulfil a duty under [IHL] may also amount to depriving civilians of objects indispensable to their survival. For instance, an occupying power may fail to ensure food and medical supplies to civilian population within occupied territories'. Triffterer (ed.), *Commentary on the Rome Statute*, 463 (Cottier).

### 5.2.4 War crimes consisting in the use of prohibited means of warfare

IHL also prohibits the use of means of warfare (weapons) that cause superfluous injury or unnecessary suffering or are inherently indiscriminate.[239] Certain weapons are banned *per se*. The prohibition of poison or poisonous weapons is one of the oldest such rules and includes the poisoning of water or food supplies.[240]

There is no doubt that the use of prohibited means of warfare has extremely serious health impacts. Under the ICESCR, a government is under an obligation to respect the right to health, food or water of the population under its jurisdiction. For instance, mining a territory or spraying a region with chemicals designed to kill or injure by the effect of such poison may well violate the ICESCR and simultaneously give rise to a war crime.[241] Under the Rome Statute, the war crime of employing prohibited gases, liquids, materials or devices also covers weapons that are not *designed* to cause unnecessary suffering, but that are nevertheless known to release a substance that 'causes death or serious damage to health in the ordinary course of events, through its asphyxiating or toxic properties'.[242] This expansion prevents perpetrators from excusing their conduct as a side effect of the armed conflict – an excuse that is often invoked when people's ESCR are affected during conflict. Those who are involved in the use of prohibited weapons may also incur criminal liability for a war crime, which further illustrates that the same factual situation can give rise to an ESCR violation and simultaneously fall within the ambit of international criminal law.

## 5.3 Conclusion

This chapter explored a considerable area of overlap between the substantive definitions of ESCR violations, rooted in international human

[239] Henckaerts and Doswald-Beck (eds.), *Customary IHL*, vol. 1, rules 70–86. Under the Rome Statute, using weapons calculated to cause unnecessary suffering could only be prosecuted as a war crime once states draft an annex to the Rome Statute listing the prohibited weapons. Rome Statute, Art. 8, para. 2(b)(xx).

[240] The prohibition of poison or poisonous weapons is a well-accepted norm of customary law. *Legality of the Threat or Use of Nuclear Weapons, Advisory Opinion of 8 July 1996*, ICJ, para. 80. States at the 2010 Review Conference of the ICC Statute considered that the prohibition was part of customary international law applicable in NIAC. Amendments to Art. 8 of the Rome Statute, the Review Conference of the Rome Statute of the ICC, Rc/Res.5, 10 June 2010 (not yet entered into force), eighth preambular paragraph.

[241] Rome Statute, Art. 8, para. 2(b)(xx). But see Note 239.

[242] Rome Statute, Art. 8, para. 2(b)(xviii). ICC Elements of Crimes, Art. 8, para. 2(b)(xviii).

rights law, and the material elements of many war crimes. This allowed us to consider that violations of the right to housing, food, education, work, health or other ESCR during an armed conflict are often within the realm of international criminal law, and we saw how the trial of Arthur Greiser is an early confirmation of this phenomenon. In particular, war crimes such as killing, deportation or transfer, torture and inhumane treatment, pillage or starvation illustrate how the same factual conduct can give rise to a state's violation of ESCR and to criminal responsibility for war crimes.

An analysis of the definitions of international crimes would not be complete without an exploration of genocide, which is the topic of the following chapter.

# 6

# Genocide and the battles Raphael Lemkin did not lose

On 9 December 1948, a day before the General Assembly adopted the Universal Declaration of Human Rights (UDHR), it passed the Genocide Convention and ensured that extreme ESCR violations are covered by this instrument. The Genocide Convention provides the accepted legal definition of genocide, sets out rules of cooperation and prevention and is the first international instrument to envisage a permanent international criminal court.[1] The crime of genocide is solidly rooted in customary international law[2] and is undoubtedly part of *jus cogens*.[3] The term 'genocide' was coined by Raphael Lemkin, a Polish lawyer who dedicated his life to the elaboration and implementation of international law preventing and punishing genocide. As early as in 1933, Lemkin had proposed that the League of Nations elaborate a convention making the extermination of human groups a crime.[4] During World War II, Lemkin fled to the United States and published an influential book, *Axis Rule in Europe*, in which he analysed the decrees penalising the use of the Polish language and promoting the destruction of cultural monuments and treasures, the distribution of food on racial grounds, the use of Poles for slave labour and the settlement of Germans on Polish land. He felt

[1] Convention on the Prevention and Punishment of the Crime of Genocide, GA Res. 260 (III) A, 9 December 1948 (entered into force 12 January 1951), Art. VI.

[2] *Reservations to the Convention on the Prevention and Punishment of the Crime of Genocide, Advisory Opinion of 28 May 1951*, ICJ, 23, emphasising that 'the principles underlying the Convention are principles which are recognized by civilized nations as binding on States, even without any conventional obligation'. *Prosecutor* v. *Musema, ICTR-96-13-T, 27 January 2000*, ICTR, para. 151. The *Musema* Trial Chamber stated that '[t]he Genocide Convention is undeniably considered part of customary international law'.

[3] *Application of the Convention on the Prevention and Punishment of the Crime of Genocide (Bosnia and Herzegovina* v. *Serbia and Montenegro), 26 February 2007*, ICJ, para. 161, confirming that the norm prohibiting genocide is 'assuredly a peremptory norm of international law'.

[4] Raphael Lemkin, *Les actes constituant un danger général considerés comme delits de droit des gens* (Pedone, 1933), Part B, 'Persécution des collectivités de race, de confession ou sociales (actes de barbarie)'.

strongly that these measures were taken out of a desire to destroy essential foundations of the life of Poles, Jews or Czechs. He explained:

> By 'genocide' we mean the destruction of a nation or of an ethnic group. This new word, coined by the author to denote an old practice in its modern development, is made from the ancient Greek word *genos* (race, tribe) and the Latin *cide* (killing), thus corresponding in its formation to such words as tyrannicide, homicide, infanticide, etc. Generally speaking, genocide does not necessarily mean the immediate destruction of a nation, except when accomplished by mass killings of all members of a nation. It is intended rather to signify a coordinated plan of different actions aiming at the destruction of essential foundations of the life of national groups, with the aim of annihilating the groups themselves. The objectives of such a plan would be disintegration of the political and social institutions, of culture, language, national feelings, religion, and the economic existence of national groups, and the destruction of the personal security, liberty, health, dignity, and even the lives of the individuals belonging to such groups. Genocide is directed against the national group as an entity, and the actions involved are directed against individuals, not in their individual capacity, but as members of the national group.[5]

This citation hints at the central relationship between abusive socio-economic and cultural policies and the definition of genocide. This chapter examines this relationship. The analysis will allow us to conclude that the legal definition of genocide can be met when states commit extreme violations of ESCR. Lemkin's book and his thinking were influential in the adoption of the Genocide Convention, even though we shall see that the legal definition of genocide that was finally adopted in 1948 is narrower than the one Lemkin proposed. The Genocide Convention defines the crime as a series of acts committed with the 'intent to destroy, in whole or in part, a national, ethnical, racial or religious group'.[6] This definition has been reproduced in various statutes of international criminal tribunals as well as in national legislation.[7]

The finding of overlap between ESCR violations and genocide is complicated by two related issues around which this chapter is centred. First, the *dolus specialis* of the *chapeau* of the genocide definition is the

[5] Raphael Lemkin, *Axis Rule* (Carnegie Endowment for International Peace, 1944), 79 (footnote omitted).

[6] Genocide Convention, Art. II.

[7] Bassiouni therefore concluded that genocide is a 'single instrument crime'. Cherif Bassiouni, *Introduction* (Transnational, 2003), 139. The same definition appears in the ICTY Statute, Art. 4, and the ICTR Statute, Art. 2.

distinguishing and most demanding element of the crime.[8] Because of the requirement of specific genocidal intent, many mass human rights breaches colloquially called 'genocide' are in fact often other types of crimes against humanity.[9] Second, the perpetrator must intend to *destroy* a protected group. The interpretation of the verb 'to destroy' narrows the extent to which violations of ESCR are covered by the definition of genocide. Case law suggests that tribunals and other bodies only qualify abuses as genocide if the principal perpetrator's intent concerns the 'physical or biological destruction' of a protected group[10] rather than the destruction solely of cultural or social characteristics. Despite the unwillingness of tribunals to extend the definition of genocide beyond the 'physical or biological' destruction of a group, some of Lemkin's original thinking on the economic, social and cultural aspects of genocide remains more relevant than scholars and tribunals have so far acknowledged. Lemkin did not lose all his legal battles in relation to socio-economic and cultural dimensions of genocide. We will explore the implications of this finding in some detail.

The history of the law of genocide indicates that the lawyers who first used the term 'genocide' always considered what we now understand are violations of ESCR to be an important part of the law of genocide. A first such indication can be found in the memorandum prepared by Justice Robert Jackson shortly after he had read Lemkin's *Axis Rule in Europe*. In his memo to the delegates at the international conference of military trials in 1945, Jackson explains that genocide could be proven if there is evidence of means and methods such as '(1) underfeeding; (2) sterilization and castration; (3) depriving [victims] of clothing, shelter, fuel, sanitation, medical care; (4) deporting them for forced labor; (5) working them in inhuman conditions'.[11] A year later, Sir David Maxwell-Fyfe, the British deputy chief prosecutor at Nuremberg, cross-examined Freiherr

[8] ILC, Report to the General Assembly, A/51/10, 6 May–26 July 1996, 44.

[9] Genocide can be considered a special form of crimes against humanity – they are cognate concepts. See, for instance, ILC, Seventh Report of the Rapporteur on the Draft Code of Crimes against the Peace and Security of Mankind (Doudou Thiam), A/CN.4/419 & Corr.1 and Add.1, 1989, para. 30. Thiam included genocide within the definition of crimes against humanity.

[10] *Application of the Convention on the Prevention and Punishment of the Crime of Genocide (Bosnia and Herzegovina v. Serbia and Montenegro), 26 February 2007*, ICJ, para. 344: 'The Court concludes that the destruction of historical, religious and cultural heritage cannot be considered to be a genocidal act.'

[11] Robert Jackson, *Report to the International Conference on Military Trials* (US Government Printing Office, 1949), 68.

von Neurath, a former German diplomat, and reminded him that the charges against him included genocide, 'which we say is the extermination of racial and national groups, or, as it has been put in the well-known book of Professor Lemkin, "a co-ordinated plan of different actions aiming at the destruction of essential foundations of the life of national groups with the aim of annihilating the groups themselves"'.[12] In contemporary human rights law, the notion of 'essential foundations of the life' can today be translated as extreme abuses of ESCR alongside civil and political rights' denials.

Lemkin's original view of genocide was very focused on abuses that could today be qualified as ESCR violations: the first example of genocidal conduct Lemkin mentions is 'racial discrimination in feeding'.[13] He continues with 'endangering of health' by depriving groups of 'elemental necessities for preserving health and life. This latter method consists, for example, of requisitioning warm clothing and blankets in the winter and withholding firewood and medicine.'[14] Only after that does Lemkin mention direct mass killings.[15] Lemkin's holistic view of genocide did not make its way into positive law in its entirety. In particular, he lost the battle to include much of what he conceptualised as cultural genocide. However, it is uncontroversial that even the narrow interpretation of genocide, limited to physical or biological destruction, covers violations of ESCR. In fact, case law recognised early on that 'this new type of crime' had economic, social and cultural connotations. The Supreme National Tribunal of Poland, for instance, convicted Amon Göth, commandant of the forced labour camp near Kraków, of genocide prior to the adoption of the Genocide Convention. The court found that the 'economic, social and cultural connotations' of genocide were abusive policies underlying the 'machinery set in operation by the German authorities, for the gradual elimination and final extermination of the Jewish nation'.[16] Because these policies were intimately connected with the intent of wholesale extermination of Jews and Poles, the extermination 'had all the characteristics of genocide in the biological meaning of this term'.[17]

Despite the fact that the drafters of the genocide definition did not include the full spectrum of Lemkin's broad view of genocide, certain

[12] *Prosecutor* v. *von Neurath, in Nazi Conspiracy and Aggression (Red Series): Proceedings, 25 June 1946, XVII TWC 37*, IMT, 61.

[13] Lemkin, *Axis Rule*, 83. [14] Ibid. [15] Ibid.

[16] *Prosecutor* v. *Göth, Case No. 37, VII Law Reports of War Criminals 1, 5 September 1946, Supreme National Tribunal, Poland*, 8.

[17] Ibid., 9.

violations of cultural rights are also covered by the legal definition of genocide. Unfortunately, the labels used in the literature are more confusing than clarifying. Legal scholars often repeat that only 'physical' and 'biological' genocide are covered, while 'cultural genocide' was intentionally excluded by the drafters.[18] But it would be wrong to conclude that no violations of cultural rights are covered by the law of genocide. *De lege lata*, attacking 'only' cultural or sociological characteristics to annihilate the elements that give a distinct identity to a protected group would not suffice today to constitute the *actus reus* of genocide.[19] Lemkin felt strongly that five sub-categories of cultural genocide, prepared in the Secretariat Draft of the Genocide Convention, should be included,[20] but he did not win this fight.[21] The debate on cultural genocide met with opposition from states concerned about interference in what they considered exclusive domestic affairs: the protection of minorities, indigenous peoples and immigrants.[22] However, we shall see that conduct aimed at destroying the specific cultural characteristics of a group can nevertheless constitute evidence of the intent to destroy. Aspects of cultural genocide are therefore further addressed below in the section on the mental element of genocide. Moreover, the most serious cultural rights violations can be subsumed under the *actus reus* of genocide where brutal assimilation policies, for instance, of indigenous groups, are inflicted with the requisite

18 Hirad Abtahi and Philippa Webb, *Genocide Convention* (Nijhoff, 2008), 1499, reprinting UN Doc. A/C.6/S.R. 83. Another attempt to convince states to consider cultural genocide failed in the context of the declaration on the rights of indigenous peoples. Draft United Nations Declaration on the Rights of Indigenous Peoples, Sub-Commission on Prevention of Discrimination and Protection of Minorities, Resolution 1994/45, E/CN.4/Sub.2/1994/56, 28 October 1994, Art. 7.

19 *Application of the Convention on the Prevention and Punishment of the Crime of Genocide (Bosnia and Herzegovina* v. *Serbia and Montenegro), 26 February 2007*, ICJ, para. 344, considering that the destruction of historical, cultural and religious heritage cannot be considered to fall within the categories of acts of genocide.

20 Secretariat Draft, First Draft of the Genocide Convention, UN Doc. E/447, 1947. The five sub-categories of 'cultural genocide' were '(a) forcible transfer of children to another human group, or (b) forced and systematic exile of individuals representing the culture of a group, or (c) prohibition of the use of the national language even in private intercourse, or (d) systematic destruction of books printed in the national language or of religious works or prohibition of new publications or (e) systematic destruction of historical or religious monuments or their diversion to alien uses, destruction or dispersion of documents and objects of historical, artistic or religious value and of objects used in religious worship.'

21 With the exception of the inclusion of the underlying act of forcibly transferring children from one group to another, see Section 6.2.5.

22 For an overview of the drafting history, see William Schabas, *Genocide*, 2nd edn (Cambridge University Press, 2009), 207–21.

intent to destroy and where these policies constitute one of the underlying acts, such as 'causing serious bodily or mental harm to members of the group' or 'forcibly transferring children of the group to another group'.[23]

To examine what exactly was excluded from Lemkin's conception of genocide, the analysis has to be started with the subjective elements of genocide, because the definition of genocide hinges upon the perpetrator's mental plan.[24]

## 6.1 The *mens rea* of genocide

The demanding *mens rea* requirements of genocide are what stigmatise this crime above and beyond other crimes. The *mens rea* is also the area where most of the legal controversies of genocide lie. The extent to which ESCR violations are covered by the definition of the crime of genocide is largely defined by the interpretation of the *mens rea* of the crime, which is why this part of the analysis is the core of this chapter.

The subjective requirements of genocide exist at two levels. First, the perpetrator must present the *mens rea* of at least one of the prohibited acts of genocide listed in the sub-paragraphs of the genocide definitions. Second, the perpetrator must have the specific genocidal intent to destroy in whole or in part a protected group as such (the '*chapeau* intent' or *dolus specialis*).[25] The two groups of *mens rea* elements must not be confused. The *mens rea* for the underlying genocidal acts is easier to establish than the *mens rea* of the *chapeau*.

### 6.1.1 *The* mens rea *of the underlying genocidal acts*

The knowledge and intent requirements of the 'general' *mens rea* for genocide, that is the mental elements for the underlying acts, are met if

[23] For further references, see Study on International Criminal Law and the Judicial Defence of Indigenous Peoples' Rights (Bartolomé Clavero Salvador), E/C.19/2011/4, 8 February 2011, particularly para. 6.

[24] A standard criminal law analysis of the requirements of a crime usually starts with the *actus reus* of the crime. But because genocide is structurally similar to an attempt crime, it is preferable to start with the *mens rea*, thus proceeding in the same way as one would analyse an attempt. On this point, see also Kai Ambos, *Der allgemeine Teil des Völkerstrafrechts* (Duncker & Humblot, 2002), 411, viewing genocide as a 'goal-oriented crime'.

[25] See also *Decision on the Prosecution's Application for a Warrant of Arrest against Omar Hassan Ahmad Al Bashir, 4 March 2009, Pre-Trial Chamber I, ICC-02/05-01/09*, ICC, para. 139, finding that the general subjective element that must cover any genocidal act consists of the Art. 30 intent and knowledge requirement.

the perpetrator is reckless or if (s)he acts with intent in the form of *dolus eventualis*.[26] Where a genocidal offence requires a result,[27] the perpetrator must have intended this result or was aware that the result would occur in the ordinary course of events. A perpetrator who is reckless about the consequences of his or her conduct satisfies the requisite *mens rea* requirement for the underlying acts. This is an important point for the argument made in this book, as it implies that intent and knowledge with regard to the underlying genocidal act can be met when the perpetrator is involved in violations of ESCR, such as food deprivations, and recklessly accepts the consequences. Schabas provides an example of a configuration of the knowledge requirement met by *dolus eventualis*/ recklessness:

> Although there is as yet no case law on this subject, it is relatively easy to conceive of examples of recklessness within the context of genocide. A commander accused of committing genocide by 'inflicting on the group conditions of life calculated to bring about its physical destruction', and who was responsible for imposing a restricted diet or ordering a forced march, might argue that he or she had no knowledge that destruction of the group would indeed be the consequence. An approach to the knowledge requirement that considers recklessness about the consequences of an act to be equivalent to full knowledge provides an answer to such an argument.[28]

Two sub-paragraphs contain additional *doli speciales*. Sub-paragraphs (c) and (d) (conditions of life and prevention of births) require that the infliction of dire conditions of life be *calculated* to bring about the physical destruction of the protected groups, and that the measures be *specifically intended* to prevent births, respectively. The *mens rea* of deliberately inflicting conditions of life requires that the perpetrator

[26] Ambos, *Der allgemeine Teil des Völkerstrafrechts*, 412. This finding must not be confused with the requirements of the *chapeau* intent, which clearly requires more than recklessness. Marcus mistakenly implies that Schabas wrote about recklessness concerning the *chapeau* intent. David Marcus, 'Famine Crimes' (2003) 97 *American Journal of International Law*, 2, 245–81: 263.

[27] Only sub-paragraphs (a), (b) and (e) require a result. See Section 6.1.2.1.3.

[28] Schabas, *Genocide*, 254. Prof. Schabas here only addresses the general *mens rea* for the *underlying* genocidal acts (intent and knowledge). As far as sub-paragraph (c) is concerned, it is necessary that the perpetrator 'calculated' that the conditions of life would bring about destruction. It is difficult to conceive of a case in which a reckless imposition of such conditions of life could be reconciled with the additional mental element of 'calculation' The example is, however, perfectly convincing for sub-paragraphs (a), (b) and (e).

*calculated* the imposition of these conditions to be a *principal* mechanism to destroy the group as opposed to conduct ancillary to another mechanism.[29]

Apart from the *mens rea* for the underlying offence, it is necessary – and generally more challenging – to prove the special intent contained in the *chapeau* of the definition of genocide.

### *6.1.2 The special intent of the* chapeau *and its elements*

The special intent (*dolus specialis*) of the *chapeau* of the definition of genocide requires that the perpetrator must have the particularly aggravated objective to 'destroy, in whole or in part, a national, ethnical, racial or religious group, as such'.[30] Where this special intent is lacking, the act remains a crime, but does not constitute genocide.

That said, negligent genocide does not exist, as the crime presumes that the underlying acts are inflicted with the *dolus specialis* to destroy the group. Proposals to include negligent or 'second-degree' genocide in the 1948 convention had been rejected early in the drafting,[31] and massive suffering and death caused, for instance, by incompetent trade policies or resulting as an effect from anti-insurgency campaigns such as the faminogenic military practices of the Ethiopian Dergue are not covered by the crime of genocide.[32] The non-existence of negligent genocide does, however, not imply that all ESCR-related abuses are excluded from the definition, but means that the violations of ESCR must be inflicted with the genocidal objective to destroy a protected group. The special intent of the *chapeau* has a number of elements, and it is the requisite intent 'to destroy' that is the most decisive element to identify the scope of the area of overlap between ESCR violations and the definition of genocide. The intent to destroy is also the focus of Lemkin's battles during the elaboration of the legal definition of genocide.

[29] Ibid., 291. Some authors and national legislation, in the view of this study's author mistakenly, consider that 'calculated' is an objective element. See Note 66.

[30] Rome Statute of the International Criminal Court, 2187 UNTS 90, 17 July 1998 (entered into force 1 July 2002), Art. 6.

[31] Secretariat Draft, First Draft of the Genocide Convention, UN Doc. E/447, 1947, 25.

[32] Nevertheless, domestic courts in Ethiopia convicted the former ruler Mengistu Haile Mariam and numerous other officials of the Dergue regime of genocide. BBC, 'Profile: Mengistu Haile Mariam', http://news.bbc.co.uk/2/hi/africa/6171927.stm.

### 6.1.2.1 'To destroy'

**6.1.2.1.1 Physical/biological destruction v. destruction of the social unit** The interpretation of the 'intent to destroy' remains fraught with controversy and confusion. The verb 'destroy' can be understood either as limited to the 'physical or biological' destruction of the members of the group or relating to the dissolution of the group as a social or cultural community. Lemkin's views on the intent to destroy were broad. In his view, genocide starts with the perpetrators' intent to destroy the economic life or the linguistic and cultural characteristics of a group, culminating in physical destruction as the ultimate stage.[33] Lemkin's understanding that genocide extends to all forms of destruction of a group as a social entity was not retained to the full extent, although his view is supported by the case law of the German courts, as well as the writings of a number of commentators.[34] For better or worse, the currently accepted legal definition of genocide is narrower than Lemkin's original notion. But even assuming that this limited view will not evolve in the future, the intent to destroy, if correctly interpreted, includes ESCR violations. Genocidal intent is present where perpetrators intend to wipe out the existence of the group, whether in gas chambers or by denying them access to ESCR essential for subsistence.

**6.1.2.1.2 The decisions of tribunals on the meaning of 'to destroy'** The majority of court decisions and publicists adhere to the 'physical and biological' conception of group destruction.[35] *De lege lata*, this position is

[33] Lemkin, *Axis Rule*, 87–9; Raphael Lemkin, 'Genocide' (1947) 41 *The American Journal of International Law*, 1, 145–51: 147.

[34] The German *Bundesverfassungsgericht* considers that not only the physical, but also the social existence of groups is protected. *In Re Jorgić, 2 Bvr 1290/99, 12 December 2000, Federal Constitutional Court*, Germany, para. (III)(4)(a)(aa). For further references, see Gerhard Werle, *Principles*, 2nd edn (Asser Press, 2009), 278, note 172. The ECtHR accepted that the German court's interpretation of the special intent requirement of genocide could reasonably be regarded as consistent with the essence of that offence. *Prosecutor* v. *Jorgić, 26 September 1997, Oberlandesgericht Düsseldorf*, Germany, para. 108. See also Hans-Heinrich Jescheck, 'Die internationale Genocidium-Konvention vom 9. Dezember 1948 und die Lehre vom Völkerstrafrecht' (1954) 66 *Zeitschrift für die gesamte Strafrechtswissenschaft*, 2, 193–217: 213. Jescheck writes that the *dolus specialis* 'also includes the destruction of the group as a social unit with its otherness and uniqueness' (translation by the author).

[35] For a short overview of how the term has been interpreted, see also Larissa van den Herik, 'The Meaning of the Word Destroy and Its Implications for the Wider Understanding of the Concept of Genocide', in *The Genocide Convention: The Legacy of 60 Years*, ed. Harmen van der Wilt, et al. (Nijhoff, 2012), 51–8.

correct, but requires one important clarification because it is understood differently by different authors and even in decisions within the same tribunal.

The prevailing answer of tribunals has been that the contemporary legal definition of genocide requires that the perpetrator seek the *physical or biological destruction* of a protected group. It does not suffice when the perpetrator aims at destroying the protected group's social identity or their cultural or political characteristics. Thus, the intended destruction of the social and cultural identity of a group is insufficient to prove the requisite 'intent to destroy'. The ICTY Trial Chamber summarised this position in *Krstić*, finding that in customary law the definition of genocide is limited to the physical or biological destruction of a protected group: an 'enterprise attacking only the cultural or sociological characteristics of a human group in order to annihilate these elements which give to that group its own identity distinct from the rest of the community would not fall under the definition of genocide'.[36] Judge Shahabuddeen partially dissented to the appeals judgment endorsing the trial chamber's view,[37] but subsequent decisions have not adopted his approach.[38] The ICJ also took the view in the *Genocide Case* that the perpetrator's intent must relate to the 'physical or biological destruction' of the group.[39] With the exception of transferring children to another group, the perpetrator's intent must be to achieve physical or biological destruction. But what exactly is to be understood as 'physical or

[36] *Prosecutor* v. *Krstić, IT-98-33-T, 2 August 2001*, ICTY, para. 580. Endorsed by the Appeals Chamber in *Prosecutor* v. *Krstić, IT-98-33-A, 19 April 2004*, ICTY, para. 25.

[37] *Prosecutor* v. *Krstić, IT-98-33-A, 19 April 2004*, ICTY, Partially dissenting opinion of Judge Shahabuddeen, in particular para. 49. Shahabuddeen considered that only the intent attached to a genocidal act needs to be physical or biological. Otherwise it is enough, in his view, if the perpetrator intends to destroy the intangible characteristics binding together a collection of people as a social unit.

[38] The *Blagojević* trial judgment echoed Shahabuddeen's dissent, but was later overturned. *Prosecutor* v. *Blagojević and Jokić, IT-02-60-T, 17 January 2005*, ICTY, para. 659; *Prosecutor* v. *Blagojević and Jokić, IT-02-60-A, 9 May 2007*, ICTY, para. 123. The other decision echoing Shahabuddeen's view is *Prosecutor* v. *Krajišnik, IT-00-39-T, 27 September 2006*, ICTY, para. 854. Other subsequent decisions and reports have not adhered to his approach. *Arrest Warrant for Al Bashir, 4 March 2009, Pre-Trial Chamber I, ICC-02/05-01/09*, ICC, Separate and Partly Dissenting Opinion of Judge Ušacka, para. 62; Report of the International Commission of Inquiry on Darfur to the SG, Pursuant to SC Resolution 1564 of 18 September 2004, 25 January 2005, paras. 506, 518.

[39] *Application of the Convention on the Prevention and Punishment of the Crime of Genocide (Bosnia and Herzegovina v. Serbia and Montenegro), 26 February 2007*, ICJ, para. 344.

biological' destruction, and how much of Lemkin's broad concept of genocide is accepted as positive law?

**6.1.2.1.3 Identifying consensus on the terms physical and biological destruction and how such destruction relates to ESCR violations** The terms 'physical' and 'biological' are remnants from language that appeared in square brackets in the first draft of the Genocide Convention prepared by the Secretariat on behalf of the SG. The Secretariat divided acts of genocide into 'physical', 'biological' and 'cultural' categories.[40] Except for the transferring of children to another group, the acts listed under the bracketed heading of 'cultural genocide', understood as 'destroying the specific characteristics of the group', were ultimately not retained in the final version of the convention.[41] Since the exclusion of all but one acts of 'cultural genocide', the ILC has categorically affirmed that genocide is the 'material destruction of a group either by physical or biological means, not the destruction of the national, linguistic, cultural or other identity of a particular group'.[42] It is important to note, however, that the headings 'physical' and 'biological' genocide were both deleted from the final text of the Genocide Convention. With the exception of sub-paragraph (c), the terms 'physical' and 'biological' do not appear in the final wording and their precise meaning remains ambiguous for at least two reasons. First, the transfer of children to another group can hardly be considered a case of 'biological' destruction, but necessarily relates to cultural destruction.[43] The ILC gave no reasons why it considered that the transfer of children would constitute

40 Secretariat Draft, First Draft of the Genocide Convention, UN Doc. E/447, 1947.

41 At first, both the UN Secretariat Draft as well as the Ad Hoc Committee Draft submitted to the Commission on Human Rights contained cultural genocide: ibid., Art. I (II)3. The Ad Hoc Committee Draft defined it as 'any deliberate act committed with the intent to destroy the language, religion, or culture of a national, racial or religious group on grounds of the national or racial origin or the religious belief of its members'. Ad Hoc Committee Draft, Second Draft Genocide Convention, Prepared by the Ad Hoc Committee of ECOSOC, E/AC.25/SR.1 to 28, Art. III.

42 ILC, *Yearbook of the International Law Commission*, 1991, A/CN.4/SER.A/1991/Add. 1 (Part 2), 102, para. 4; ILC, Report to the General Assembly, A/51/10, 6 May–26 July 1996, 46, para. 12. In the explanation provided by the ILC, the terms physical and biological qualify the underlying offences, but the point made by the ILC supposedly addresses the question of the special intent of the *chapeau*.

43 The Secretariat Draft also categorised the transfer of children as a form of cultural genocide. Secretariat Draft, First Draft of the Genocide Convention, UN Doc. E/447, 1947, Art. I(II)3. See also Note 130.

'biological genocide'.[44] Second, the difference between 'physical' and 'biological' destruction is less clear than it seems at first sight. The term 'biological' may be redundant if what is required is ultimately the annihilation of members of the group.

Be this as it may, the terms 'physical' and 'biological' are not particularly helpful to clarify the meaning of intent 'to destroy'. Given that they do not appear in the wording of the Genocide Convention or in the Rome Statute and are used differently by different authors and court decisions, they should not be relied upon to interpret the definition of genocide. The three labels 'physical', 'biological' and 'cultural' destruction hide several related but distinct debates, namely how intent can be inferred, whether transferring children is a case of biological or cultural genocide and whether the ethnic cleanser intends to displace or to destroy a group.[45] Given these controversies, there is a risk that Lemkin's lost battle in relation to the destruction of the language, religion or culture of protected groups will be taken to mean that only certain extreme violations of civil and political rights would be covered by the contemporary legal definition of genocide.[46] Rather than relying on the terms of physical and biological genocide, the safest route to interpret the genocide definition for the purposes of this study is to start with the analysis of the ordinary wording of the text – the context of the provision as well as the object and purpose of the instrument – rather than the drafters' use of ambiguous labels.[47] The verb 'to destroy' means to 'put out of existence', to 'deprive of life'.[48] The ordinary meaning of the verb 'to destroy', understood in light of its context and the object and purpose of the

[44] ILC, Report to the General Assembly, A/51/10, 6 May–26 July 1996, 46, para. 12.

[45] Kress provides a striking illustration of the problem that the labels 'physical or biological' are sometimes used in very different ways. Kress criticises the use of the terms 'physical or biological' in the *Blagojević* trial judgment, in which the judges argue that 'the physical or biological destruction of the group is the likely outcome of a forcible transfer when this transfer is conducted in such a way that the group can no longer reconstitute itself'. *Prosecutor* v. *Blagojević and Jokić, IT-02-60-T, 17 January 2005*, ICTY, para. 666. Kress points out that this use of the terms physical or biological conceals the substantial digression from the concept of physical/biological group destruction. Claus Kress, 'Genocide' (2006) 6 *International Criminal Law Review*, 4, 461–502: 488.

[46] See also Evelyne Schmid, 'Genocide & Socio-Economic Rights: A Response' (25 March 2012), www.intlawgrrls.com/2012/03/genocide-socio-economic-rights-response.html.

[47] Vienna Convention on the Law of Treaties, 1155 UNTS 331, 23 May 1969 (entered into force 27 January 1980), Art. 31. This point is also made by William Schabas, *Genocide*, 1st edn (Cambridge University Press, 2000), 230.

[48] Oxford University Press, *Shorter Oxford English Dictionary* (Oxford University Press, 2007), 661.

Genocide Convention, undoubtedly includes the possibility that perpetrators intend to destroy a group by way of depriving them of food, water, sanitation, shelter and other essential access to ESCR.

The ordinary meaning of the verb 'to destroy' also implies that the correct, albeit restrictive, interpretation seems to be that the intent must be to 'annihilate', 'extinguish' or 'wipe out' the members of the group – in other words, to cause their death, directly or indirectly. One important clarification must, however, be made. Genocidal intent to destroy covers slow and indirect victimisation that certainly includes denying access to ESCR. Boas, Bischoff and Reid have interpreted the term 'to destroy' to mean both, the 'immediate and/or direct death of the victims' as well as the 'eventual disappearance of the group'.[49]

This conception introduces a temporal element differentiating between the intention of the perpetrator to destroy the protected group immediately or eventually. This temporal dimension can convincingly be inferred from the context of the term 'to destroy'. Several of the underlying acts do not immediately destroy a group, such as preventing births within the group. Ultimately, Boas, Bischoff and Reid's emphasis on the fact that both the intent of immediate and slow destruction are covered is accurate and provides a reliable and easier understanding of the requisite intent to destroy than do references to physical and biological genocide.[50] That 'long-term' and indirect destruction is covered has also been consistently affirmed by publicists and tribunals.[51] Rather than emphasising the confusing terms 'physical' and 'biological', it is preferable to clarify the predominant view in light of the temporal extension of the 'intent to destroy': as the ICTR explained in *Akayesu*, all 'methods of destruction by which the perpetrator does not immediately kill the members of the group, but which, ultimately, seek their physical destruction' may constitute genocidal acts,[52] and may consequently attract genocidal intent. Kress correctly points out that the verb 'destroy' must 'not be reduced to the physical destruction of the members of the group as it exists *at the time of the overall genocidal campaign*, but must extend to all possible

[49] Gideon Boas et al., *Elements of Crimes* (Cambridge University Press, 2008), 164.

[50] This also seems to be the view of Kress, 'Genocide', 487.

[51] *Prosecutor* v. *Göth, Case No. 37, VII Law Reports of War Criminals 1, 5 September 1946, Supreme National Tribunal, Poland*, 8, referring to the 'gradual elimination and final extermination of the Jewish nation' through the establishment of economic, social and cultural policies leading to such destruction.

[52] *Prosecutor* v. *Akayesu, ICTR-96-4-T, 2 September 1998*, ICTR, para. 505.

results of overall campaigns which take the form of a pattern of one or more prohibited acts'.[53]

In sum, there is consensus that genocidal intent is present where the perpetrator aims for the material destruction of the group both if immediate or longer-term destruction is intended. Even if tribunals have been unwilling to consider the intent to destroy as anything lesser than 'physical or biological' destruction, ESCR violations are covered by the narrow confines of the contemporary legal understanding of the genocidal intent to destroy.

As mentioned, the fact that not all aspects of Lemkin's conceptualisation of genocide were retained in positive law has sometimes led commentators to conclude that genocidal intent can only be inferred from large-scale extrajudicial executions, but not from other types of abuses. For some, abuses such as forcible displacement and other potential violations of the right to housing can only be covered by the definition of genocide if intent to sociologically or culturally destroy a group would be included in genocidal intent.[54] These conclusions are overly broad and have no basis in the text of the definition, nor its object and purpose, and they are not supported by the case law. A perpetrator intending to displace, starve or otherwise deprive a protected group of essential access to ESCR has the requisite *dolus specialis* of genocide if he or she intends, by his or her conduct, to destroy the group in whole or in part. It does not matter if the perpetrator summarily executes members of the group or denies them of access to essential food, health, water, sanitation or life-saving health care.

Of course, in practice, the relevant question for indirect and 'slow' abuses is that of the circumstances under which intent to destroy can be inferred from conduct that does not immediately result in the annihilation of members of the protected group. This question has so far been dealt with most prominently in relation to forcible population displacement/ethnic cleansing. Forcible population displacement goes hand in hand with severe housing rights violations where a state fails to

53 Kress, 'Genocide', 487 (emphasis added).

54 For instance, Cécile Tournaye, 'Genocidal Intent' (2003) 52 *International and Comparative Law Quarterly*, 2, 447–62: 453–4. Tournaye seems to assume that forcible transfer is necessarily a 'sociological' form of group destruction and never inflicted with the intent to physically or biologically destroy a group: 'The issue is whether genocide only covers an intent to physically or biologically destroy a group, or whether it also encompasses a "sociological" or cultural destruction of the group, which would allow acts such as forcible transfer to be included among the acts whose goal is the destruction of a group as such.'

respect or protect rights. While more challenging from an evidentiary standpoint, a perpetrator who decides to displace people rather than executing them can have genocidal intent to destroy. The genocide definition requires evidence to know with what objective the perpetrator displaced members of the protected group before the special intent of genocide can be inferred.[55] The displacement alone cannot suffice to establish the special intent, but it is perfectly conceivable that the perpetrator intends to displace people with the objective of achieving their material destruction over time. As the SG explained in his report to the draft Genocide Convention: 'Physical destruction is inevitable when people are driven from their homes and forced to travel long distances in a country where they are exposed to starvation, thirst, heat, cold and epidemics.'[56]

During the drafting of the Genocide Convention, Syria expressed the view that 'any measure directed towards forcing members of a group to leave their homes should be regarded as constituting genocide'.[57] The drafters rejected this proposal. As with Lemkin's lost battle on the full scope of what he wished to include as cultural genocide, the rejection of the Syrian proposal must not be equated with the view that housing rights violations would be irrelevant for the genocide definition. Rather, the significance of the exclusion of the Syrian proposal is that displacement alone 'does not concern the destruction of human groups'[58] and thus cannot alone satisfy the intent requirement. The ruling in *Stakić* summarises the status of the law on this point by emphasising that the 'mere dissolution' of the protected group is insufficient.[59] Housing rights violations and other forms of displacement can only meet the definition of genocide if they are intended to destroy the physical existence of the group. For instance, the perpetrator might believe that the group will freeze or starve to death if evicted from their homes, as the SG suggested.[60]

The most expansive view on the inference of genocidal intent from housing rights abuses is contained in the *Blagojevic* trial judgment, which was later reversed. The trial chamber mentioned that the special intent requirement of genocide was met because the perpetrators intended the

[55] *Application of the Convention on the Prevention and Punishment of the Crime of Genocide (Bosnia and Herzegovina* v. *Serbia and Montenegro), 26 February 2007*, ICJ, para. 190.

[56] Secretariat Draft, First Draft of the Genocide Convention, UN Doc. E/447, 1947, 24.

[57] Abtahi and Webb, *Genocide Convention*, 1490, A/CA.6.SR.82.

[58] Ibid., 1490–2, A/CA.6.SR.82.

[59] *Prosecutor* v. *Stakić, IT-97-24-T, 31 July 2003*, ICTY, para. 519, drawing a distinction between 'physical destruction' and 'mere dissolution of a group'.

[60] See Note 56.

forcible transfer of Bosnian Muslims of Srebrenica, and the manner in which it was carried out, to cause serious mental harm to the victims. The trial chamber essentially inferred the *dolus specialis* from the perpetrator's knowledge that the transfer occurred.[61] The appeals chamber disagreed.[62] Unsurprisingly, the appeals chamber noted that the *dolus specialis* cannot be inferred only from the fact that the perpetrator knew that the underlying acts were occurring. But it would be wrong to conclude from this that displacement or other ESCR-related abuses could never be committed with intent to destroy a protected group. If a perpetrator kills a large number of members of a protected group with firearms, that conduct by itself also does not constitute genocide. The correct position is that proof of intentional displacement, mental harm or death by firearms alone all cannot automatically satisfy the special intent requirement of genocide, but such proof can nevertheless be a piece of evidence that, in combination with other evidence, may lead a court to infer genocidal intent.[63] Housing rights violations or the dissolution of a group as a social and cultural entity can thus be relevant to infer genocidal intent.[64]

Another case in which displacement and concomitant housing rights abuses were discussed is *Brđanin*. The view held by the ICTY in this case should be rejected. In that case, the trial chamber said that displacement was not done with genocidal intent to destroy because enough resources, including firearms, would have been available to kill the group.[65] This reasoning implies that the ICTY considers that genocidal intent to destroy by means of displacement could only be present where perpetrators had no other means at their disposal. This approach is unconvincing. Perpetrators can have rational motives to pursue their genocidal intent by means of displacing people from their homes, even when they have resources to directly kill them. Displacement may be cheaper to

[61] *Prosecutor* v. *Blagojević and Jokić, IT-02-60-T, 17 January 2005*, ICTY, para. 666.

[62] *Prosecutor* v. *Blagojević and Jokić, IT-02-60-A, 9 May 2007*, ICTY, para. 123.

[63] *Decision on the Prosecution's Application for a Warrant of Arrest against Omar Hassan Ahmad Al Bashir, 4 March 2009, Pre-Trial Chamber I, ICC-02/05-01/09*, ICC, para. 145. The chamber correctly considers that ethnic cleansing may result in genocide if genocide's objective elements are committed with the intent to destroy.

[64] *Prosecutor* v. *Karadžić and Mladić, Review of the Indictments Pursuant to Rule 61 of the Rules of Procedure and Evidence, Case Nos. IT-95-5-R61 and IT-95-18-R61, 11 July 1996*, ICTY, para. 94, finding that 'the massive deportations may be construed as the first step in a process of elimination'; *Prosecutor* v. *Krstić, IT-98-33-T, 2 August 2001*, ICTY, para. 580. Endorsed by the ICJ in *Application of the Convention on the Prevention and Punishment of the Crime of Genocide (Bosnia and Herzegovina* v. *Serbia and Montenegro), 26 February 2007*, ICJ, para. 344.

[65] *Prosecutor* v. *Brđanin, IT-99-36-T, 1 September 2004*, ICTY, para. 978.

implement and less likely to attract the same level of attention as massacres. Perpetrators may psychologically prefer to 'send people to the desert' to die rather than to execute them. Moreover, victims are likely to die in different places, thus dispersing the physical bodies, avoiding the need for perpetrators to hide the bodies in a mass grave. Perpetrators could also claim that the group left voluntarily, in order to increase their safety or to rejoin family members, and would be aware that these 'excuses' would not be available if proofs of mass executions became evident. The ICTY's assumption that genocidal perpetrators necessarily employ their resources with a preference for outright killing is wholly unconvincing and illustrates the predominant view that considers everything other than extrajudicial killings as a mark of subsidiary criminality.

Additionally, the specific intent requirement of genocide must not be confused with the realisation of the factual consequences of the perpetrator's implementation of his or her intent. As mentioned, only three of the sub-paragraphs ((a), (b) and (e)) require a result. The *dolus specialis* of the *chapeau* is independent, whether or not the conduct undertaken by the perpetrator is factually adequate to achieve the destruction of the protected group. The determination of intent to destroy is solely interested in whether the mental plan of the perpetrator was to inflict one or several of the underlying offences with the intent to destroy even if the aim of destruction is ultimately not achieved.[66] In this regard, it is useful to consider the German notion of a *Zieldelikt*, a goal-oriented crime characterised by the perpetrator's intent to infringe upon the legally protected interests.[67]

That the realisation of the factual consequence is not required to prove the *dolus specialis* of genocide is important for the argument that ESCR violations can be used to infer genocidal intent. Tribunals have

[66] But see Kress, 'Genocide', 481. Kress believes that 'calculated' is not a subjective element but refers to the objective capability of the conduct to bring about physical destruction. The German and Swiss legislation refer to 'conditions of life capable of destroying the group' ('*Lebensbedingungen, die geeignet sind, die Gruppe ganz oder teilweise zu vernichten*'). See also Report of the International Commission of Inquiry on Darfur to the SG, Pursuant to SC Resolution 1564 of 18 September 2004, 25 January 2005, para. 518, 'likely to bring about destruction'. The view to consider 'calculate' as an objective element is unpersuasive because the ordinary wording of 'calculated' refers to the perpetrator's mental plan. This is confirmed by the drafting history. Proposals to replace 'calculated' with the objective notion of 'is likely to cause' in the drafting of the Genocide Convention were rejected. Abtahi and Webb, *Genocide Convention*, 1989, A/C.6/238, Amendment proposed by the delegation of Uruguay.

[67] Kai Ambos, 'Intent to Destroy' (2009) 91 *International Review of the Red Cross*, 876, 833–58: 3, with further references.

sometimes confused the special intent requirement for genocide with the requirement of a result – thereby implicitly and mistakenly restricting the scope of the argument that ESCR abuses not (or not directly) resulting in death can be covered by the genocide definition.[68] Paragraph (a) (the underlying offence of killing) requires that victims die; paragraph (b) (the offence of creating serious bodily or mental harm) and paragraph (e) (the offence of forcibly transferring children) require proof of actual death, harm or transfer. For these underlying acts, the perpetrator must have intended this result or been aware that the result would occur in the ordinary course of events. Paragraphs (c) and (d) (conditions of life and prevention of births), in contrast, do not require any result, and the special intent of the *chapeau* requires intention to destroy, but no actual result. Even where the result of destruction does not materialise (or there is insufficient evidence to prove causality between the alleged perpetrator's conduct and the result), a perpetrator who intends to destroy a protected group by forcibly evicting members from their homes – calculating, for instance, that the heat will lead to their destruction – has the necessary genocidal intent to fulfil the offence if he or she intentionally commits one of the underlying acts. The perpetrator may miscalculate the weather conditions, or members of the group may survive because neighbouring communities or relief organisations assist them. Genocidal intent does not require proof that the perpetrator chose the most efficient or even a merely adequate method to accomplish his or her objective.[69] The conduct and the achievement of a result must not be confused with the *dolus specialis*. This point is well summarised in the *Akayesu* trial decision:

> Contrary to popular belief, the crime of genocide does not imply the actual extermination of group in its entirety, but is understood as such

[68] *Prosecutor* v. *Akayesu, ICTR-96-4-T, 2 September 1998*, ICTR, para. 518. The chamber explains: 'special intent is the key element of an intentional offence, which (is an) offence [*sic*] characterized by a psychological relationship between the physical result and the mental state of the perpetrator' (footnote omitted). The trial chamber seems to confuse the special intent requirement of the *chapeau* with the requirement of a result in two of the underlying offences (killing and mental and serious bodily or mental harm). For every intentional offence requiring a result, the perpetrator's intent must also cover the result, whether or not the offence also has a *dolus specialis*. Also note the confusing statement in para. 498 defining special intent as 'the specific intention, required as a constitutive element of the crime, which demands that the perpetrator clearly seeks to produce the act charged'. This definition is unsatisfactory as all intentional criminal offences require the intent of the perpetrator to produce the offence charged.

[69] Confirmed in *Prosecutor* v. *Krstić, IT-98-33-A, 19 April 2004*, ICTY, para. 32.

> once any one of the [underlying genocidal] acts . . . is committed with the specific intent to destroy 'in whole or in part' a national, ethnical, racial or religious group.[70]

The determination of the genocidal intent must thus be kept separate from the conduct element. Unfortunately, judgments on this point are confusing, including the judgment by the ICJ in the *Genocide Case.*[71] Where ESCR violations are involved, the real question should be how genocidal intent can be proven, rather than *a priori* concluding that everything other than massacres by firearms or gas chambers could not constitute genocide. From the very first genocide conviction before an international tribunal (the *Akayesu* case before the ICTR), it was accepted that the special intent 'can be inferred from a certain number of presumptions of facts', such as 'the general context of the perpetration of other culpable acts systematically directed against that same group', or 'the scale of atrocities committed, their general nature, . . . [or] the fact of deliberately and systematically targeting victims on account of their membership of a particular group, while excluding the members of other groups'.[72] Of course, where the underlying offences do result in immediate physical destruction, the genocidal intent will be easier to establish than in those cases in which a perpetrator calculates that slowly inflicting ESCR violations upon a group will ultimately lead to the group's destruction. In the absence of a confession, the mental plan of the perpetrator is rarely completely evident. In practice, the demanding subjective requirements to prove a plan for material destruction make the crime of genocide difficult, but certainly not impossible, to prove in general and for ESCR-related conduct in particular.

#### 6.1.2.2 In whole or in part

The perpetrator must intend to destroy a group as a whole or in part. The special and socially constructed meaning of some members of the group

[70] *Prosecutor* v. *Akayesu, ICTR-96-4-T, 2 September 1998,* ICTR, para. 497.

[71] *Application of the Convention on the Prevention and Punishment of the Crime of Genocide (Bosnia and Herzegovina* v. *Serbia and Montenegro), 26 February 2007,* ICJ, para. 190, mentioning that destruction of a group is not an automatic consequence of displacement. Factually, this statement is true, but it is misplaced because the objective achievement of the destruction is not required to determine the *dolus eventualis.* Similarly, an ICTY Trial Chamber analysed the objective likelihood of physical destruction resulting from forcible displacement to determine the perpetrator's special intent to destroy. *Prosecutor* v. *Blagojević and Jokić, IT-02-60-T, 17 January 2005,* ICTY, para. 666.

[72] *Prosecutor* v. *Akayesu, ICTR-96-4-T, 2 September 1998,* ICTR, para. 523.

has been found to imply that the perpetrator intended to destroy a sufficiently substantial part of a group.[73] These considerations apply identically to cases focusing on ESCR abuses and therefore do not need further elaboration here.

#### 6.1.2.3 Protected groups and the significance of the exclusion of economic groups

The prohibition of genocide protects four specific groups, namely national, ethnical, racial or religious groups. *De lege lata*, this list is exhaustive. The intended destruction of other groups (such as groups defined on the basis of socio-economic status, occupation or political views) does not constitute genocide unless the group would simultaneously fall within one of the enumerated categories of groups. Attempts to protect other groups under the definition of genocide have repeatedly failed.[74] A considerable number of national jurisdictions, however, extended the protection of the genocide prohibition to social, political and other groups.[75] The significance of the exclusion of economic and social groups deserves to be contemplated.

On the one hand, the narrow list of protected groups has the effect of excluding many violent persecutions from the definition of genocide. This is regrettable if one considers that victims belonging to certain groups are dealt with differently than others in a similar position. For instance, the Soviet persecution of (perceived) rich peasants – an economic group – does not constitute genocide under the contemporary definition of the term.[76] Although there is clearly no requirement that the

[73] *Prosecutor* v. *Krstić, IT-98-33-A, 19 April 2004*, ICTY, para. 16, finding that '[t]he elimination of the Muslim population of Srebrenica, despite the assurances given by the international community, would serve as a potent example to all Bosnian Muslims of their vulnerability and defenselessness in the face of Serb military forces'; *Prosecutor* v. *Jelisic, IT-95-10-T, 14 December 1999*, ICTY, para. 82, considering that a limited number of persons selected for the impact that their disappearance would have upon the survival of the group as such can suffice.

[74] William Schabas, *Commentary on the Rome Statute* (Oxford University Press, 2010), 144.

[75] Schabas mentions Ethiopia, Bangladesh, Panama, Costa Rica, Peru, Slovenia and Lithuania. Ibid., 141. More recently, Switzerland has also modified its criminal code to include social and political groups. Code pénal suisse, 21 December 1937 (avec modifications du 18 juin 2010), RO 54 781, Art. 264. France even includes any type of group in the definition of genocide: Nouveau Code pénal français, version consolidée au 20 décembre 2013, Art. 211.

[76] See also Schabas, *Genocide*, 166. This is not to say that the Soviet policy of forced collectivisation in Ukraine did not constitute genocide, to the extent that the targeted group was the Ukraine nation, thus a national group.

perpetrator of genocide belongs to a group other than the victims, the policies of the Khmer Rouge to attack fellow Cambodians sharing the nationality, ethnicity, race and religion of the perpetrators with the intent of forcing social changes also does not seem to be covered by the definition of genocide due to the exclusion of social groups.[77] On the other hand, the exclusion of economic and social groups from the definition of genocide has no bearing on the argument made in this chapter that genocide can be committed by way of violating ESCR. The significance of the exclusion of these groups should not be misunderstood to mean that measures affecting economic or social rights could not constitute genocide. Rather, the drafters' deliberate exclusion of economic and social groups from the definition 'merely' implies that the intent to destroy must relate to one of the protected groups, whether or not the underlying offences consist of extrajudicial executions, deliberate starvation or any other conduct. Importantly, the exclusion of economic groups is not a battle lost by Lemkin. Lemkin did not suggest that economic groups should be listed among the protected groups. Such a proposal was made by the United States.[78] Lemkin himself never intended to mean that the destruction of economic groups, such as a decline of certain professions following economic policies,[79] should amount to genocide. What he meant was that the underlying offences could be committed by the deliberate destruction of the foundations of the economic life of a protected group.[80] In short, Lemkin did not lose the battle to include aspects of 'economic genocide' within the scope of the accepted legal definition of genocide, and the exclusion of economic groups does not bar the argument that violations of economic rights can amount to genocide.

[77] The ECCC only charged acts committed against the Cham and Vietnamese minorities as genocide. See *Prosecutor* v. *Khieu Samphan, Nuon Chea, Ieng Sary and Ieng Thirith, Closing Order, Case 002, 15 September 2010*, ECCC. For a contrary view, see Hurst Hannum, 'Cambodian Genocide' (1989) 11 *Human Rights Quarterly*, 1, 82–138.

[78] Genocide: Draft Convention (E/794): Amendment to Article 2/United States of America, A/C.6/214, 4 October 1948.

[79] When the United States suggested adding economic groups to the list of protected groups under the Genocide Convention, other delegations felt that this would lead to the result that 'certain professions, when threatened by economic measures which were required in the interest of the country, might invoke the convention'. The Netherlands: Statement Made in the Continuation of the Consideration of the Draft Convention on Genocide, 74th Meeting, A/C.6/SR.74, 14 October 1948, 100.

[80] Lemkin, *Axis Rule*, 85–6. This point is also made by Schabas, *Genocide*, 166.

#### 6.1.2.4 As such

The words 'as such' clarify the special intent requirement and require that the victims be targeted *because* they belong to a protected group, rather than because of their personal characteristics or conduct.[81]

### 6.1.3 *The contextual element in the Rome Statute*

Compared to the Genocide Convention, the non-binding ICC Elements of Crimes contain an additional contextual element: the ICC Elements of Crimes suggest that the ICC will only prosecute genocide where there is a 'manifest pattern of similar conduct'.[82] The historical roots of genocide, as well as its role as a crime stigmatised above and beyond any other international crime, would seem to indicate that such a contextual element is implicit in other definitions of genocide as well. If not a legal element of the crime, a manifest pattern of similar conduct would be an indicator to infer intent.[83]

Since the proof of intent under the Rome Statute requires that the perpetrator be aware that a circumstance exists,[84] the *mens rea* for genocide should be construed to imply that the perpetrator was aware of the systemic dimension of a genocidal plan or policy.[85] In any event, if we are to infer genocidal intent from extreme failures to respect or protect ESCR, such a contextual element would almost naturally be present since the finding of an ESCR violation requires the determination of responsibility of the state. The deliberate deprivation of essential access to ESCR with a view to bringing about conditions of life leading to the destruction of a group are necessarily inflicted on a large scale and by a

81 Guénaël Mettraux, *International Crimes* (Oxford University Press, 2005), 231. The perpetrator may simultaneously be driven by other motivations. *Prosecutor* v. *Niyitegeka, ICTR-96-14-A, 9 July 2004*, ICTR, para. 53.

82 ICC Elements of Crimes, ICC-ASP/1/3, 9 September 2002, Genocide. The ICC Pre-Trial Chamber I has applied the contextual element in *Decision on the Prosecution's Application for a Warrant of Arrest against Omar Hassan Ahmad Al Bashir, 4 March 2009, Pre-Trial Chamber I, ICC-02/05-01/09*, ICC, para. 121.

83 See also Lemkin, *Axis Rule*, 79, mentioning that genocide is intended to 'signify a coordinated plan of different actions'.

84 Rome Statute, Art. 30(3).

85 Claus Kress, 'Genocidal Intent' (2005) 3 *Journal of International Criminal Justice*, 3, 562–78: 572–3. For a useful overview of the debate, see Antonio Cassese, 'The Policy Element', in *The Genocide Convention Sixty Years after Its Adoption*, ed. Christoph Safferling and Eckart-Alexander Conze (Asser, 2010), 133–40.

multitude of individuals in pursuance of a policy with the support or at least the acquiescence of the authorities.[86]

So far, we have analysed the relationship between ESCR violations and genocidal intent to destroy. Genocidal intent to destroy a protected group must be combined with the intentional commission of at least one of five genocidal acts, the *actus reus*.

## 6.2 *Actus reus*

International law criminalises five acts of genocide, and this list is exhaustive. They are as follows:

(a) Killing members of the group;
(b) Causing serious bodily or mental harm to members of the group;
(c) Deliberately inflicting on the group conditions of life calculated to bring about its physical destruction in whole or in part;
(d) Imposing measures intended to prevent births within the group;
(e) Forcibly transferring children of the group to another group.[87]

Perpetrators can commit genocide by acts and omissions. Genocide by omission requires that the perpetrator had a legal obligation and capacity to act, but intentionally chose not to do so.[88]

This section shows that all five genocidal acts can be committed by way of violating ESCR. They constitute genocide independently of whether the *dolus specialis* of the *chapeau* is also inferred from ESCR violations or from other abuses.

### *6.2.1 Killing*

Killing means causing the death of at least one member of the protected group.[89] As explained in Chapter 5 on war crimes, the *actus reus* of killings can be committed by way of violating people's access to essential ESCR.[90] The difference between the *actus reus* of killing as genocide and killing as a war crime is that the victim of a genocidal killing must be a member of a national, racial, ethnical or religious group, rather than a person protected

[86] This view is shared by Cassese, 'The Policy Element', 139.
[87] Genocide Convention, Art. II. Rome Statute, Art. 6.
[88] *Prosecutor* v. *Rutaganira, ICTR-95-1c-T, 14 March 2005*, ICTR, para. 68; *Prosecutor* v. *Blaškić, IT-95-14-T, 3 March 2000*, ICTY, para. 284, on aiding and abetting by omission.
[89] ICC Elements of Crimes, Genocide by killing, first element and footnote 2. Mettraux, *International Crimes*, 236.
[90] See Section 5.2.1.1.

under IHL. But as with war crimes, the term 'causing death' can be applied to cases where victims do not die because of attacks by firearms, machetes or gas chambers, but because, for instance, of the withholding of essential access to food, water or medicine. A pertinent example of this *actus reus* is the medical blockade of Bougainville in May 1990. Papua New Guinea imposed a total blockade on the island, which resulted in the killing of numerous inhabitants in need of medical attention.[91] If the other elements of genocide have also been met – as it has been argued[92] – it is possible to qualify the medical blockade as a case of genocide by killing.

### *6.2.2 Causing serious bodily or mental harm*

The next underlying offence requires serious bodily or mental harm. Causing serious *bodily* harm is understood as harm that 'seriously injures the health, causes disfigurement or causes serious injury to the external, internal organs or senses'.[93] Serious *mental* harm on the other hand 'may include, but is not necessarily restricted to, acts of torture, rape, sexual violence or inhuman or degrading treatment'.[94] This relatively vague language is best understood as harm that leads to 'a grave and long-term disadvantage to a person's ability to lead a normal and constructive life',[95] although the harm (both mental and bodily) need not be permanent or irremediable.[96] The relationship between ESCR-related abuses and serious bodily or mental harm is similar to the one between ESCR and 'other inhumane acts' as crimes against humanity,[97] the war crimes of torture or inhuman treatment or wilfully causing great suffering or serious injury to body or health.[98] The Israeli district court in the *Eichmann* case concluded that serious bodily and mental harm as a genocidal act was caused by 'enslavement, starvation, deportation and persecution, confinement to ghettos, to transit camps and to concentration camps',[99] that is, abuses pertaining to people's enjoyment of basic ESCR.

91 *Sarei* v. *Rio Tinto Plc, Original Complaint (September 2000)*, USA, para. 12.
92 Ibid., para. 212. The complainants moreover argued that the inhabitants of the island are racially distinct from the people of New Guinea and therefore constitute a protected group.
93 *Prosecutor* v. *Kayishema and Ruzindana, ICTR-95-1-T, 21 May 1999*, ICTR, para. 109.
94 ICC Elements of Crimes, Genocide by causing serious harm, first element, footnote 3.
95 *Prosecutor* v. *Krstić, IT-98-33-T, 2 August 2001*, ICTY, para. 42.
96 *Prosecutor* v. *Akayesu, ICTR-96-4-T, 2 September 1998*, ICTR, para. 502.
97 See Section 4.10. 98 See Section 5.2.1.4.
99 *The Attorney-General of Israel* v. *Eichmann, 36 ILR 5 (1968), 24 July 1996, District Court of Jerusalem*, Israel, para. 199. Cited approvingly in *Prosecutor* v. *Akayesu, ICTR-96-4-T, 2 September 1998*, ICTR, para. 503.

### 6.2.3 Deliberately inflicting on the group conditions of life calculated to bring about its physical destruction

Paragraph (c) is the genocidal act that presents the most significant overlap with ESCR violations. Indeed, the paragraph on deliberately inflicting conditions of life calculated to bring about the physical destruction in whole or in part would be inconceivable without the policies that human rights lawyers today consider violations of the rights to food, water, housing and health. ESCR abuses are thus strongly rooted within the contemporary confines of genocide. The Secretariat Draft of the Genocide Convention included conditions of life 'which, by lack of proper housing, clothing, food, hygiene and medical care, or excessive work or physical exertion are likely to result in the debilitation or death of the individuals', as well as 'deprivation of all means of livelihood, by confiscation of property, looting, curtailment of work, denial of housing and of supplies otherwise available to the other inhabitants of the territory concerned'.[100] Although the enumeration of examples was not retained in the Genocide Convention, a list of similar examples was included in the ICC Elements of Crimes: based on the language appearing in the *Eichmann* judgment,[101] the ICC Elements of Crime define 'conditions of life' to include 'deliberate deprivation of resources indispensable for survival, such as food or medical services, or systematic expulsion from homes'.[102] Given the contextual element of genocide, these abuses must almost necessarily constitute violations of ESCR, because the state or an organisation is required to implement such policies on a large scale. The fact that these abuses are the only explicitly listed examples given for this genocidal act is remarkable and emphasises the importance of the criminalisation of such extreme abuses of ESCR.

The ICRC Commentary to AP I mentions that starvation could not 'only' be a war crime: 'an action aimed at causing starvation . . . could also be a crime of genocide'.[103] Commentators made the uncontroversial suggestion that 'famine is a low-cost and low-technology method of genocide'.[104] In his seminal article on food and international criminal

[100] Secretariat Draft, First Draft of the Genocide Convention, UN Doc. E/447, 1947.

[101] *The Attorney-General of Israel* v. *Eichmann, 36 ILR 5 (1968), 24 July 1996, District Court of Jerusalem*, Israel, 340.

[102] ICC Elements of Crimes, footnote 4.

[103] Yves Sandoz et al., *Commentary on the Additional Protocols* (Nijhoff, 1987), 654.

[104] Sigrun Skogly, 'Crimes against Humanity' (2001) 5 *International Journal of Human Rights*, 1, 58–80: 70.

law, David Marcus points out that '[a]ssuredly, genocide law includes the *actus reus* elements of famine crimes'.[105]

Other authorities point to the strong relationship between ESCR violations and sub-paragraph (c) of the genocide definition. The Guatemalan Commission for Historical Clarification considered gross violations of the right to food and qualified the razing of food supplies of indigenous villagers as genocide.[106] Lemkin also called the Ukrainian *Holodomor* ('death by hunger') as genocide. As the BBC reports, millions of Ukrainians starved to death in the early 1930s when Stalin launched a forced collectivisation campaign. Farmers were forced to live and work in collective farms, and their estimated yields were increased by an unrealistic 150 per cent. About a quarter of the Ukraine's population was wiped out within a few years.[107] Lemkin's views on Stalin's controversial policy of enforced collectivisation remained largely unknown until 2008, when a brief speech by Lemkin was discovered. In this speech from 1953, Lemkin unequivocally qualifies the *Holodomor* 'as the classic example of Soviet genocide, its longest and broadest experiment [of] the destruction of the Ukrainian nation'.[108] Lemkin continues:

> [I]t was to eliminate that nationalism, to establish the horrifying uniformity of the Soviet state that the Ukrainian peasantry was sacrificed . . . A famine was necessary for the Soviet and so they got one to order, by plan, through an unusually high grain allotment to the state as taxes. To add to this, thousands of acres of wheat were never harvested, were left to rot in the fields.[109]

Scholars believe that Lemkin did not make his view on the genocidal nature of the Soviet famine more public because he did not want to endanger Soviet support for the adoption and later ratification of the Genocide Convention; thus, he may have 'soft-peddled' the Soviet Union's genocidal activities under Stalin.[110] In any event, *de lege lata*, it

105 Marcus, 'Famine Crimes', 262.

106 Comisión para el Esclarecimiento Histórico, 'Guatemala: memoria del silencio' (Asociación Americana para el Avance de las Ciencia, 2000), Conclusiones, paras. 116–8.

107 'Ukraine Demands "Genocide" Marked', *BBC News*, 25 November 2005.

108 Raphael Lemkin, 'Soviet Genocide in the Ukraine', in *Holodomor: Reflections on the Great Famine of 1932–1933 in Soviet Ukraine*, ed. Lubomyr Luciuk and Lisa Grekul (Kashtan, 2008), 235–44: 236, 239.

109 Ibid., 239.

110 Steven Jacobs, 'Lemkin and the Holodomor', in *Holodomor: Reflections on the Great Famine of 1932–1933 in Soviet Ukraine*, ed. Lubomyr Luciuk and Lisa Grekul (Kashtan, 2008), 159–70: 167.

is difficult to argue that the victims of atrocities in Ukraine fall within the genocide definition.[111] At the same time, it is easy to see how violations of the right to be free from hunger relate to the underlying act of causing serious bodily or mental harm to members of the group.

Links between the underlying determinants of the right to health and the *actus reus* of genocide have been studied by Helen Fein, a historical sociologist and genocide scholar. Fein shows how in the Warsaw Ghetto, starvation and disease were induced by elevated vulnerability following deportation and enforced concentration in overcrowded camps – illustrating how the right to food and adequate shelter are indispensable requirements for public health.[112] She shows how the overcrowding, overwork and exhaustion, the denial of drinking water and the consequent epidemics and diseases induced by these conditions led to what she calls 'genocide by attrition',[113] a form of imposing conditions of life calculated to bring about the physical destruction of a group.

The *ad hoc* tribunals also repeatedly affirmed that conditions 'such as lack of proper housing, clothing, hygiene, excessive work, physical exertion,'[114] or 'subjecting a group of people to a subsistence diet, systematic expulsion from homes and the reduction of essential medical services below minimum requirements' are relevant for this genocidal act.[115] The ICC has confirmed that serious violations of the right to water, food or housing such as through the contamination of water pumps, displacement or hindrance of humanitarian relief can fall within paragraph (c) of the genocide definition.[116] Under human rights law, this

[111] The special genocidal intent would be difficult to establish and one would have to argue that the targeted group was a national or ethnic group. See also Note 76.

[112] Helen Fein, 'Genocide by Attrition' (1997) 2 *Health and Human Rights*, 2, 10–45: 12.

[113] Ibid., 31.

[114] *Prosecutor* v. *Akayesu, ICTR-96-4-T, 2 September 1998*, ICTR, para. 503; *Prosecutor* v. *Kayishema and Ruzindana, ICTR-95-1-T, 21 May 1999*, ICTR, paras. 115–6; *Prosecutor* v. *Rutaganda, ICTR-96-3-T, 6 December 1999*, ICTR, para. 52; *Prosecutor* v. *Stakić, IT-97-24-T, 31 July 2003*, ICTY, para. 517; *Prosecutor* v. *Brđanin, IT-99-36-T, 1 September 2004*, ICTY, para. 691.

[115] *Prosecutor* v. *Akayesu, ICTR-96-4-T, 2 September 1998*, ICTR, para. 506.

[116] *Second Decision on the Prosecution's Application for a Warrant of Arrest against Al Bashir, 12 July 2010, Pre-Trial Chamber I, ICC-02/05-01/09*, ICC, paras. 34–8. Note that the Pre-Trial Chamber I at first considered that 'the contamination of wells and other water sources by the government of Sudan was not a core feature of the conduct'. *Decision on the Prosecution's Application for a Warrant of Arrest against Omar Hassan Ahmad Al Bashir, 4 March 2009, Pre-Trial Chamber I, ICC-02/05-01/09*, ICC, para. 93. In her partially dissenting opinion, Judge Ušacka correctly emphasised that policies affecting the right to water, food or shelter must be assessed 'in light of the harshness of the surrounding terrain'. Ibid., Partially dissenting opinion, para. 99.

conduct can be qualified as a violation of the right to water.[117] The right to water is violated when there is 'arbitrary or unjustified disconnection or exclusion from water services, discriminatory or unaffordable increases in the price of water or pollution and diminution of water resources affecting human health'.[118]

Housing rights violations *qua* deliberately inflicting on the group conditions of life calculated to bring about its physical destruction are entangled with the question of whether 'ethnic cleansing' can be subsumed under the genocide definition. Ethnic cleansing is not a legal term, but can be understood as targeted forced evictions, that is an abuse that includes housing rights violations.[119] As mentioned above, 'systematic expulsion from homes' is part of the examples listed in the ICC Elements of Crimes of the acts prohibited by paragraph (c) and therefore constitutes genocide provided the mental elements are met, that is the expulsions are *calculated* as a principal mechanism to bring about the physical destruction of at least a segment of a protected group.

The remaining two underlying acts of genocide involve measures to prevent birth and the transfer of children.

### *6.2.4 Imposing measures intended to prevent births*

The early case law on the imposition of measures intended to prevent births focused on forced sterilisation *qua* genocide.[120] Such measures to prevent birth can easily be considered as violations of reproductive health rights,[121]

[117] See Chapter 5, Note 88.

[118] Committee on Economic, Social and Cultural Rights, *General Comment 15 on the Right to Water*, 20 January 2003, E/C.12/2002/11, para. 44.

[119] Ethnic cleansing is best defined as rendering an area ethnically homogenous by using force or intimidation to remove persons of given groups from the area. Letter of the SG to the President of the Security Council [Evidence of Grave Breaches in the Former Yugoslavia], S/25274, 9 February 1993, para. 55.

[120] *Prosecutor* v. *Hoess, Case No. 38, VII Law Reports of Trials of War Criminals 11, 29 March 1947, Supreme National Tribunal, Poland; United States of America* v. *Greifelt et al. (RuSHA Case), V TWC 88,* NMT, 122. In both cases, Nazis were found responsible for sterilisations *qua* genocide. Charter 77 dissidents in Czechoslovakia alleged that Czechoslovakia carried out a genocidal policy of sterilisation of Roma women. Reprinted in Otakar Motejl, *Final Statement in the Matter of Sterilisations Performed in Contravention of the Law and Proposed Remedial Measures* (Public Defender, 2005), 24–5.

[121] ICESCR, Art. 12(1). Committee on Economic, Social and Cultural Rights, *General Comment 14 on the Right to the Highest Attainable Standard of Health*, 11 August 2000, E/CN.12/2000/4, para. 50. See also Section 4.4.3.3 on enforced sterilisation as a crime against humanity.

but the possible area of overlap between ESCR and this genocidal act is broader than the permanent deprivation of reproductive capacity through sterilisation. The ordinary meaning of 'imposing measures intended to prevent births within the group' includes any measures inflicted with intent to prevent births, such as forced birth control, obstacles to marriage and the segregation of the sexes.[122] The explanatory report to the Secretariat Draft of the Genocide Convention noted that segregation of the sexes could 'be induced by various causes such as compulsory residence in remote places, or the systematic allocation of work to men and women in different localities',[123] thus involving violations of the right to freely choose one's work as well as possibly housing rights violations, violations of the right to protection and assistance to the family[124], as well as various abuses of civil and political rights. Forced separation can be a measure imposed to prevent births within the group,[125] and a possible violation of housing rights.

There are convincing arguments for considering that extreme violations of the right to food could also fall under paragraph (d). Although there is no case law on this point, inflicting severe malnutrition can be used as a measure to prevent births, because women do not menstruate if malnourished – and intentionally inflicting malnutrition can thus constitute a form of 'birth control through famine'.[126] It was calculated that a projected 570,000 births did not take place because of famine in Cambodia.[127] As mentioned, it is doubtful that all the Cambodian victims could be qualified as a protected group under the law of genocide, but in cases where victims are targeted because of their membership in a protected group and victimised with intent to destroy, severe violations of the right to food inflicted with intent and knowledge would constitute the genocidal imposition of measures to prevent birth.

[122] A narrower wording proposed by the Soviet delegation was rejected. See also ILC, Report to the General Assembly, A/51/10, 6 May–26 July 1996, 46, note 125. Citing Nehemiah Robinson, *The Genocide Convention* (Institute of Jewish Affairs, 1960), 64. Discussed in Schabas, *Genocide*, 198.

[123] Abtahi and Webb, *Genocide Convention*, 234.

[124] ICESCR, Art. 10.

[125] *Prosecutor* v. *Rutaganda, ICTR-96-3-T, 6 December 1999*, ICTR, para. 53. Noting that no evidence was provided, the ICJ did, however, not analyse this any further. *Application of the Convention on the Prevention and Punishment of the Crime of Genocide (Bosnia and Herzegovina* v. *Serbia and Montenegro), 26 February 2007*, ICJ, para. 355.

[126] On this point, see Jeannette Smyth, 'Correspondence' (2003) 97 *American Journal of International Law*, 4, 899–900: 900.

[127] Judith Banister and Paige Johnson, *After the Nightmare: The Population of Cambodia* (Center for International Research, 1993), 90. See also Ben Kiernan, *The Pol Pot Regime* (Yale University Press, 1996), 226, reporting estimates that 90 per cent of women under the Pol Pot regime stopped menstruating, which drastically diminished birth rates.

Unlike paragraphs (a), (b) and (e), paragraph (d) does not require the realisation of a result, nor is it required that the measures be 'calculated' to prevent births. Ancillary and unsuccessful measures are therefore covered.[128]

### 6.2.5 *Forcibly transferring children*

Paragraph (e) prohibits forcibly transferring children of the protected group to another group. The inclusion of this sub-paragraph indicates that 'physical or biological' destruction cannot have been the entire scope of genocide that the drafters had in mind.[129] While the perpetrator must have intent to destroy the physical existence of the group, this sub-paragraph provides additional confirmation that the materialisation of such a result of destruction is not required. Although rejecting the inclusion of the other acts drafted under the heading of 'cultural genocide', the drafters agreed to maintain an act of genocide that can only be understood as protecting the cultural or sociological existence of a protected group.[130] When children, especially of young age, are transferred from one group to another, their own group will have no means to preserve their cultural identity but their physical existence may not be threatened. One can easily conceive this as a denial of the children's right to take part in their culture,[131] and aspects of their right to education, because the children's parents will be prevented from choosing schools in conformity with their own convictions.[132]

An Australian commission of inquiry concluded in 1997 that the Australian practice of forcible transfer of indigenous children to non-indigenous families and schools was 'an act of genocide, aimed at wiping out indigenous families, communities and cultures, vital to the precious and inalienable heritage of Australia'.[133]

[128] See Schabas, *Genocide*, 198, 201.

[129] Ibid., 201, noting that the provision was adopted with little substantive consideration.

[130] ILC, Report to the General Assembly, A/51/10, 6 May–26 July 1996, 46, mentioning that the forcible transfer of children would have particularly serious consequences for the future viability of the group as such. The ILC categorises this *actus reus* as 'biological genocide'. See also Kress, 'Genocide', 484. This categorisation is unconvincing, given that the biological survival of a group is not necessarily endangered. The transferred children of the protected group may be able to procreate amongst themselves.

[131] ICESCR, Art. 15. [132] ICESCR, Art. 11(3).

[133] Human Rights and Equal Opportunity Commission of Australia, *Bringing Them Home: Report of the National Inquiry into the Separation of Aboriginal and Torres Strait Islander Children from Their Families* (Federal Attorney General, 1997). The conclusion on

## 6.3 Conclusion

Albeit with delay, the international community honoured Raphael Lemkin for his success to achieve a multilateral treaty defining genocide and outlawing it as an international crime.[134] The legacy of Lemkin's relentless efforts transpires every aspect of the genocide definition. When it comes to the economic, social and cultural aspects of genocide, however, his legacy has not yet been widely recognised. The fact that Lemkin lost some battles during the negotiations of the Genocide Convention must not be misunderstood to mean that violations of ESCR would be irrelevant for the existing definition of genocide. The main battle lost by Lemkin concerns the requisite elements for the 'intent to destroy'. While Lemkin would have preferred that the intent to destroy the cultural and social existence of a group suffices to establish genocidal intent, we saw that tribunals have required that the perpetrator intends to destroy the physical existence of the protected group. Yet, it would be erroneous to conclude that such intent to destroy could not be inferred from ESCR violations. Rather, we saw that ESCR violations are as 'suitable' as other human rights violations to provide the factual background from which the demanding *mens rea* of genocide can potentially be inferred. We also saw that the rejection of the American proposal to include economic groups in the list of protected groups does not support a conclusion that no aspects of 'economic genocide' would have been retained in positive law. On the contrary, we saw that the inclusion of the sub-paragraph relating to the deliberate infliction of conditions of life calculated to bring about the physical destruction of a protected group means that the genocide definition would be inconceivable without the policies that human rights lawyers today consider violations of the rights to food, water, housing or health.

To summarise, this chapter has shown that the definition of genocide overlaps with ESCR violations in essentially two ways. First, it is legally possible to infer genocidal intent to destroy a protected group from ESCR abuses that are aimed at the physical annihilation of the group, including if the intention is to lead to 'slow deaths' and debilitation over a significant time horizon. Second, and independent of how the intent

genocide was cited approvingly by an Australian domestic court in *Nulyarimma v. Thompson [1999], FCA 1192, Federal Court*, Australia, paras. 5–11.

134 Message of the Secretary-General Kofi Annan Honoring Raphael Lemkin, Press release, SG/SM/7842, 13 June 2001.

requirement is proven, all the five prohibited acts of genocide can be inflicted by way of ESCR violations.

To constitute genocide, the abuses must be inflicted with a particularly aggravated *mens rea* requirement, namely the intent to physically annihilate the protected group in whole or in part. While inferring genocidal intent from a massacre by firearms is often easier from the evidentiary standpoint, intent to destroy a group by depriving them of food, water, sanitation, just and favourable conditions of work or other ESCR is nevertheless covered by the definition of genocide. This *dolus specialis* is a significantly higher standard than the mental requirements for other international crimes. In addition, the types of protected groups are narrowly defined. Many, if not most, shocking large-scale abuses do not meet the definition of genocide, and this is true whether or not ESCR violations are involved. Even if government officials know that their policies create large-scale famine among a group, unless they intend to destroy the group in whole or in part, these ESCR violations will not constitute genocide, but they are likely to remain punishable as crimes against humanity that may be 'no less serious and heinous than genocide'.[135]

[135] Report of the International Commission of Inquiry on Darfur to the SG, Pursuant to SC Resolution 1564 of 18 September 2004, 25 January 2005, para. 522. See also Payam Akhavan, *Reducing Genocide to Law* (Cambridge University Press, 2012), arguing that it is not advisable to view genocide as 'the ultimate crime'. Rather, other international crimes may be on an equal footing with genocide and equally entail serious legal consequences. On this point, see also van den Herik, 'The Meaning of the Word Destroy and Its Implications for the Wider Understanding of the Concept of Genocide', 58.

# 7

# Torture, slavery and other crimes overlapping with ESCR violations

In addition to war crimes, crimes against humanity and genocide, international criminal law contains many other offences that can overlap with ESCR violations. Consider, for example, the following situation:

> Pakistani newspapers printed chilling photographs of at least a dozen brick kiln workers posing shirtless outside the Lahore Press Club. Each of the workers displayed a large, diagonal scar above the left hip. They had sold their kidneys to pay off debts to kiln owners, and earn freedom for themselves or close family members. The workers were protesting against the lack of official attention to their plight, and that of thousands others like them.[1]

The International Labour Organization (ILO) estimates 'that 20.9 million people are victims of forced labour globally, trapped in jobs into which they were coerced or deceived and which they cannot leave',[2] many of them in debt bondage, a slavery-related practice. It is straightforward to argue that the practice of debt bondage in many cases constitutes a failure of states to protect the socio-economic rights of those abused. However, it will often be impossible to qualify such conduct as one of the international crimes so far analysed, whether because of the absence of an armed conflict (war crimes), because of the lack of a systematic or widespread attack on a civilian population (crimes against humanity) or because there is no intent to destroy a national, ethnic, racial or religious group (genocide).

The present chapter therefore examines the overlaps between ESCR violations and other international crimes. Debt bondage, for instance, is the subject of treaties with provisions that obligate states to criminalise the practice domestically. Are any of these provisions capable of accommodating claims related to conduct qualified by human rights lawyers as ESCR violations? In addition to debt bondage and other slavery-related offences,

[1] 'Pakistan: Focus on Kidney Sales by Bonded Labourers', *IRIN*, 7 April 2005.
[2] ILO, 'Global Estimate of Forced Labour 2012: Results and Methodology', 1 June 2012, 13.

we will consider a range of other conduct that is the subject of international criminal law, such as aggression, terrorist offences and the laundering of proceeds of crime or corruption. The list of relevant crimes is compiled according to criteria elaborated on in Chapter 3, which defined the scope of the study.[3] Given the high number of international crimes in addition to the three most prominent ones addressed so far, analysis of the various instruments will be unavoidably short. We shall briefly scrutinise examples illustrating the type of situations in which there is significant overlap between ESCR violations and the definition of a crime. The point is that for each of the examined crimes, some situations that violate ESCR can be addressed through the criminal provisions of the analysed treaties. We will start with the crimes for which the largest amount of information relevant to the research question was available.

## 7.1 Slavery-related practices

Contemporary slavery-related practices are criminal offences that can overlap with ESCR violations even outside the context of crimes against humanity or war crimes. We saw in Chapter 4 that contemporary forms of enslavement can fall within the scope of the crime against humanity and simultaneously violate the right to work and the right to just and favourable conditions of work, if the high threshold of crimes against humanity is met.[4] The purpose of this section is to address those international offences that are independent of crimes against humanity, but are related to contemporary slavery-related practices.

Before undertaking this analysis, the terminology deserves clarification. 'Contemporary slavery-related practices' encompass diverse but related legal concepts. The legal definitions of criminal conduct addressed in the dozens of relevant instruments[5] differ in four dimensions. First, the treaties differ based on the identity of potential victims (women, children, migrants, anyone). Second, conventions can be distinguished by the type of purpose requirements. Some conventions only address exploitation in prostitution; the more recent instruments include a range of other purposes, such as forced labour, servile forms of

[3] See Section 3.2.2.1. [4] See Section 4.4.

[5] Instruments include the Slavery Convention, Geneva, 25 September 1926, as amended on 7 December 1953 (entered into force with Amendments 7 July 1955). Or the Supplementary Convention on the Abolition of Slavery, the Slave Trade, and Institutions and Practices Similar to Slavery, 226 UNTS 3, 7 September 1956 (entered into force 30 April 1957).

'marriage', debt bondage or domestic servitude.[6] Third, some instruments only criminalise transnational conduct, while others apply to conduct that takes place entirely within one jurisdiction. Fourth, the thorny issue of how to treat the consent of the concerned individual is another element distinguishing the numerous conventions.[7] Because of the definitional variety, readers should bear in mind that the law applicable to concrete cases will differ from one situation to another and must be carefully assessed in accordance with those treaties ratified by the state in question.

All types of slavery-related practices are closely tied to ESCR abuses.[8] Given these links, it is possible to establish overlap between ESCR violations and conduct which states must criminalise by virtue of an international instrument with penal provisions. In particular, criminalised slavery-related practices overlap with violations of the right to work and the right to just and favourable conditions of work. Reference is made to Section 4.4.1 for the definition of violations of these two rights. Overlap between violations of these two rights or any other ESCR (such as the right to health or the right to an adequate standard of living), on the one hand, and conduct which states must criminalise by virtue of an international instrument, on the other, exists where the following two conditions are simultaneously met: first, a state violates one or several ESCR, for instance, by failing to protect the right to just and favourable conditions of work or the person's right to an adequate standard of living. Second, the same factual situation which gives rise to the ESCR violation displays conduct that falls under the definition of one of the following

[6] See in particular the Supplementary Slavery Convention, Art. 1, defining 'servile status' as including debt bondage, forced marriage or child exploitation and a range of other institutions and practices.

[7] For an overview, see David McClean, *Transnational Organized Crime* (Oxford University Press, 2007), 321–2.

[8] Commentators showed various links between ESCR and contemporary forms of slavery, but the literature has so far not examined whether there is overlap between the legal definitions of criminalised slavery-related conduct and violations of ESCR. Yasmine Rassam, 'Contemporary Forms of Slavery' (2004) 23 *Penn State International Law Review*, 3, 809–55. Rassam argues that the fight against slavery should be by adopting what she calls an 'economic and social rights-based approach'. In her view, the current regime fails to address the basic needs of enslaved persons, and she therefore advocates for new codification. Her complaints are well founded, but she does not consider the possibility that her concerns would be attenuated if existing instruments on ESCR were fully implemented. Ratner notes that slavery-related abuses are neglected despite the wide range of international conventions. Steven Ratner et al., *Accountability*, 3rd edn (Oxford University Press, 2009), 119, writing that '[t]his neglect ... is ironic in light of the many modern guises of slavery perpetrated against tens of millions of victims today'.

slavery-related practices that states must criminalise by virtue of an international instrument with penal characteristics. Such overlap exists in respect of the following three practices: slavery proper, the sale of children and human trafficking/migrant smuggling.

### *7.1.1 Slavery*

The concept of slavery proper refers to the exercise of ownership over a person who is treated like property and who consequently lacks autonomy. 'Chattel slavery' is no longer a widespread concern today, but there are many contemporary abuses that fall under the definition of slavery. In debt bondage (also called bonded labour), an individual works to repay a loan, but his or her work is not reasonably assessed and is not applied towards the liquidation of the debt. This can result in desperate situations like the one suffered by the Pakistani kiln workers described above. Debt bondage is the most common form of modern slavery and fits squarely under that definition.[9] Case law confirms that the definition of slavery does not require the slave holder to hold a legal title of ownership of the victim. As mentioned in Chapter 4, an Australian high court convicted a brothel owner who 'purchased' women from Thailand to work in debt bondage conditions. The court accepted that the concept of ownership can refer to a factual condition, rather than legal title.[10] This finding is significant as it makes it more likely that ESCR violations can be addressed by conventions suppressing slavery. Operating from 2008–2011, the Truth and Justice Commission of Mauritius was mandated specifically to document 'indentured labour' as a practice of slavery.[11] Similarly, the Economic Community of West African States Court of Justice recognised forced underage 'marriage' and the subsequent exploitation and loss of autonomy suffered by the victim as constituting slavery.[12] The European Court of Human Rights (ECtHR) confirmed that 'servitude' means an obligation to provide one's services that is imposed by the use of coercion and is 'to be

[9] Supplementary Slavery Convention, Art. 1(a). A delegation of the ACommHPR found in 1996 that it was still possible to find slaves in Mauritania. See *Malawi African Association et al.* v. *Mauritania, Communications 54/91, 61/91, 98/93, 164/97, 196/97 and 210/98, 11 May 2000*, ACommHPR, para. 134.

[10] *R* v. *Wei Tang [2006] VCC 637, Melbourne Criminal Court*, Australia. See Section 4.4.2.

[11] Truth and Justice Commission Act, 22 August 2008, Art. 4. The commission issued its report in late 2011.

[12] *Koraou* v. *Niger, Judgment No. Ecw/CCJ/Jud/06/08, 27 October 2008*, Economic Community of West African States Community Court of Justice, paras. 72–89.

linked' with the concept of slavery.[13] In all these forms of slavery, victims will very often also be victims of ESCR, in particular where states passively tolerate slavery.[14] The brick kiln workers, for instance, are likely victims not only of ESCR violations but also of slavery – and the state in which they find themselves incurs international obligations to criminalise the practice. In addition to relying on human rights instruments, the plight of the brick kiln workers could thus potentially be alleviated by implementing the criminal provisions of instruments suppressing debt bondage and by invoking the cooperation rules of such instruments.

### 7.1.2 *Involvement in the sale of children*

The sale of children; offering, delivering or accepting a child for the purpose of sexual exploitation; organ transfer; forced labour; false adoption; and child pornography, all fall under mandatory criminalisation provisions of the (first) Optional Protocol to the Convention on the Rights of the Child (OP-CRC).[15] It is easy to see that states may become responsible for violating children's right to be protected from economic exploitation, to health, to education, to an adequate standard of living or to the protection of families, if states passively tolerate the sale of children or related practices.[16] By virtue of international law, states parties to the OP-CRC must criminalise these practices, including conduct that takes place entirely within a single jurisdiction.[17]

### 7.1.3 *Trafficking in persons and migrant smuggling*

States have also agreed to criminalise a range of offences related to trafficking in persons, and these offences overlap with ESCR violations.

[13] *Siliadin* v. *France, Application No. 73316/01, 26 July 2005*, ECtHR, para. 124.

[14] *Koraou* v. *Niger, Judgment No. Ecw/CCJ/Jud/06/08, 27 October 2008*, Economic Community of West African States Community Court of Justice, para. 85, concluding that Niger was responsible 'for any form of human rights violations of the applicant founded on slavery because of its tolerance, passivity, inaction and abstention with regard to this practice'.

[15] Optional Protocol to the Convention on the Rights of the Child on the Sale of Children, Child Prostitution and Child Pornography, GA Res. 54/263, 25 May 2000 (entered into force 18 January 2002), Art. 4(1).

[16] See in particular Convention on the Rights of the Child, GA Res. 44/25 (1989), 20 November 1989 (entered into force 2 September 1990), Arts. 24, 32, 4, 6.

[17] Optional Protocol to the Convention on the Rights of the Child on the Sale of Children, Child Prostitution and Child Pornography, GA Res. 54/263, 25 May 2000 (entered into force 18 January 2002), Art. 4.

The international legal framework against trafficking and migrant smuggling falls short in some areas,[18] but it is capable of addressing conduct that violates ESCR and benefits from the fact that many states have ratified the relevant instruments with penal characteristics. The term 'trafficking' entered international law with the adoption of the 1949 Convention for the Suppression of the Traffic in Persons. This Convention remains applicable today and obliges state parties to punish any person who procures, entices or leads away, for purposes of prostitution, another person.[19] More recently, the UN Convention against Transnational Organized Crime (UNTOC) Protocol to Prevent, Suppress and Punish Trafficking in Persons provides for mandatory criminal sanctions including for trafficking unrelated to prostitution.[20] The Trafficking Protocol thus expands the possible use of slavery-related instruments for the purpose of addressing ESCR violations. To protect sovereignty, states have agreed that the rules of cooperation apply only if trafficking is transnational or where it is perpetrated by an organised group.[21] However, states have a mandatory obligation to criminalise trafficking in domestic legal systems even when there is no organised group involved and the conduct is not of a transnational nature.[22] The Council of Europe Convention on Action against Trafficking in Human Beings equally requires that all forms of human trafficking be criminalised, whether national or transnational, whether or not connected with organised crime.[23]

[18] The legal framework tends to ignore victims who do not match certain stereotypes, such as desperate white females forced into prostitution, stripped of agency. McClean, *Transnational Organized Crime*, 18. See also Note 24.

[19] Convention for the Suppression of the Traffic in Persons and of the Exploitation of the Prostitution of Others, GA Res. 317(IV), 2 December 1949 (entered into force 25 July 1951), Art. 1.

[20] Protocol to Prevent, Suppress and Punish Trafficking in Persons, Especially Women and Children, Supplementing the UN Convention against Transnational Organized Crime, Art. 5.

[21] Ibid., Art. 4.

[22] UN Convention against Transnational Organized Crime, GA Res. 55/383, 15 November 2000 (entered into force 29 September 2003), Art. 5. Article 3 of UNTOC does not limit the scope of the convention in domestic prosecutions to transnational offences because Art. 3(1) foresees that this limitation only applies 'except as otherwise stated herein'. Art. 34(2) states that '[t]he offences established in accordance with Arts. 5, 6, 8 and 23 of this Convention shall be established in the domestic law of each State Party independently of the transnational nature or the involvement of an organized criminal group as described in article 3, paragraph 1, of this Convention'.

[23] Council of Europe Convention on Action against Trafficking in Human Beings, Warsaw, 16 May 2005 (Partly entered into force), Art. 2.

Migrant smuggling is addressed in the second protocol supplementing UNTOC. The Protocol against the Smuggling of Migrants by Land, Sea and Air requires states to criminalise the 'procurement, in order to obtain, directly or indirectly, a financial or other material benefit, of the illegal entry of a person into a State Party of which the person is not a national or a permanent resident'.[24] Under this Protocol, acts committed outside the context of transnational crime still attach criminalisation: this view is confirmed by the drafting history and supported by an interpretative note attached to Art. 6 of the Migrants Smuggling Protocol, stating that the transnational element and the involvement of an organised criminal group are not to be considered elements of those offences for criminalisation purposes.[25] This means that conduct taking place within one jurisdiction is covered and must be criminalised by states within their domestic legal system – therefore widening possible avenues to address some ESCR violations through the use of treaties with penal characteristics.

It is not difficult to see how victims of the criminal offences of human trafficking and migrant smuggling can simultaneously be victims of ESCR violations. For instance, perpetrators of trafficking or migrant smuggling reportedly often force migrants to work until their debt is paid by family members.[26] If the state fails to take measures to protect individuals against such abuse, or if state actors are directly involved in abuses of the right to freely choose one's work, this conduct both violates the migrants' ESCR,[27] and falls within the scope of the offences of the Migrants Smuggling

[24] Protocol against the Smuggling of Migrants by Land, Sea and Air, Supplementing the UN Convention against Transnational Organized Crime, GA Res. 55/25, 15 November 2000 (entered into force 28 January 2004), Art. 6. In reality, the distinction between migrant smuggling and trafficking is blurred and based upon stereotypes of 'helpless, virtuous victims on the one side and foolish or greedy adventurers, complicit in their own misfortune, on the other'. Anne Gallagher, 'Human Rights and Human Trafficking: Quagmire or Firm Ground? A Response to James Hathaway' (2009) 49 *Virginia Journal of International Law*, 4, 790–848: 792.

[25] Report of the Ad Hoc Committee on the Elaboration of a Convention against Transnational Organized Crime on the Work of Its First to Eleventh Sessions, A/55/383/Add.1, 3 November 2000, para. 59. See also McClean, *Transnational Organized Crime*, 391–2.

[26] Richard Hoffman, 'Effective Countermeasures against the Trafficking in Human Beings and Smuggling of Migrants', in *122nd International Training Course Reports* (UN Asia and Far East Institute for the Prevention of Crime and the Treatment of Offenders, 2004), 82.

[27] Such as International Covenant on Economic, Social and Cultural Rights, GA Res. 2200a (XXI), 16 December 1966 (entered into force 3 January 1976), Arts. 7, 11 or 2. See also the International Convention on the Protection of the Rights of All Migrant Workers and Members of Their Families, GA Res. 45/158, 18 December 1990 (entered into force 1 July 2003).

Protocol. In such cases, it is possible to invoke the use of the treaties of criminal law in order to help address the ESCR abuses.

## 7.2 Torture

Another offence that encapsulates ESCR violations is torture: a separate crime, distinct in scope and context from torture as a war crime or as a crime against humanity.

Torture has long been considered as a serious crime by states and was first criminalised at the international level as a war crime and as a crime against humanity. Torture as a 'free-standing' crime has not been included in any of the statutes of the international criminal tribunals, but two hybrid tribunals – the Extraordinary Chambers in the Courts of Cambodia (ECCC) and the Special Panels of the Dili District Court – have or had jurisdiction over the crime of torture as a discrete crime.[28] Under customary international law, torture as a 'free-standing' crime incurs today criminal responsibility.[29]

To examine whether torture may be committed by way of violating ESCR, it must first be noted that the definition of torture varies according to the legal source, making it a complex offence. This means that the situations in which torture overlaps with ESCR violations are different for torture under UN Convention against Torture (UNCAT) than for torture as a war crime or as a crime against humanity. The UNCAT obligates state parties to criminalise torture in their national legal systems,[30] as well as to take measures as may be necessary to establish

[28] Law on the Establishment of the Extraordinary Chambers, with Inclusion of Amendments as Promulgated on 27 October 2004 (Ns/Rkm/1004/006), Art. 3; UN Transitional Administration in East Timor, UNTAET Regulation No. 2000/15, 6 June 2000, section 7. This provision lacks the requirement of the involvement of a person acting in official capacity.

[29] The view that torture is a crime under customary international law is supported by the fact that the prohibition of torture is non-derogable, part of *jus cogens* and because of the widespread ratification of UNCAT and the abundant state practice of criminalising torture. See also Ratner et al., *Accountability*, 122; Robert Cryer, *An Introduction to International Criminal Law and Procedure* (Cambridge University Press, 2007), 3. Against this view, see Paola Gaeta, 'International Criminalization of Prohibited Conduct', in *The Oxford Companion to International Criminal Justice*, ed. Antonio Cassese (Oxford University Press, 2009), 63–74: 69.

[30] Convention against Torture and Other Cruel, Inhuman or Degrading Treatment or Punishment, GA Res. 39/46 (1984), 10 December 1984 (entered into force 26 June 1987), Art. 4.

its jurisdiction over offences of torture.[31] If the alleged offender is found on the territory of a state party to UNCAT, that state is obliged to either extradite the person or submit the case to its competent authorities for the purpose of prosecution.[32] The definition of torture in UNCAT has three elements: the conduct must involve 'severe physical or mental pain or suffering'; it must be inflicted for a prohibited purpose, such as obtaining information or to intimidate the victim; and a person acting in an official capacity must inflict, instigate or acquiesce to the conduct or consent to it.[33] Contrary to the definition of torture as a war crime or a crime against humanity, torture under UNCAT thus requires that a person in official capacity participates in the treatment.[34] The prohibited purpose requirement and the requirement of severe pain or suffering are the same for torture as for 'free-standing' crime and for torture as a war crime, but not as a crime against humanity.[35]

For torture, the severity of the pain or suffering has to be assessed on a case by case basis.[36] The scope of torture is relatively 'shapeless'[37] and encompasses a wide range of acts and omissions, including ESCR violations. To date, many international tribunals and supervisory bodies interpreted the prohibition of torture *and* cruel, inhuman or degrading treatment or punishment (CIDT) to include certain socio-economic conditions. CIDT is characterised by less severe pain or suffering than torture and does not attach the same legal consequences: International law prohibits torture as well as CIDT, but only torture is an international crime.[38] The difference between the level of severe pain or suffering

[31] Ibid., Art. 5. [32] Ibid., Art. 7. [33] Ibid., Art. 1.

[34] See also ICC Elements of Crimes, ICC-ASP/1/3, 9 September 2002, Art. 7(1)f, Art. 8, para. 2(a)(ii)-1, Art. 8, para. 2(c)(i)-4. Overruling previous case law, the ICTY held that under customary law, for torture as a discrete crime there was no requirement for involvement of a person acting in official capacity: *Prosecutor* v. *Kunarac, Kovac and Vukovic, IT-96–23-A, 12 June 2002*, ICTY, para. 148. Nevertheless, the short explanation provided in *Kunarac* does not displace the apparently correct view of the majority of authorities: torture as a discrete international offence under customary law does have a requirement for public involvement. On this point, see also Section 4.9.

[35] See Sections 4.9 and 5.2.1.4.

[36] *Prosecutor* v. *Brđanin, IT-99–36-A, 3 April 2007*, ICTY, para. 251. This finding is uncontroversial and applies to all sources.

[37] *Prosecutor* v. *Naletilić, IT-98–34-A, 3 May 2006*, ICTY, para. 299. Cited affirmatively in *Prosecutor* v. *Brđanin, IT-99–36-A, 3 April 2007*, ICTY, para. 251; Ahcene Boulesbaa, *The Convention on Torture* (Nijhoff, 1999), 36.

[38] UNCAT. Article 4 refers only to torture, but not to CIDT. States have chosen not to attach the same legal attributes to CIDT as they did to torture.

required for torture versus for CIDT is one of gravity.[39] Human rights bodies such as the Human Rights Committee (HRCttee) or the ECtHR do not need to distinguish torture from CIDT to find a violation of the relevant instrument. This makes it difficult to determine if the higher threshold for torture was met in cases in which human rights bodies dealt with socio-economic conditions, and it thus complicates the assessment of how the crime of torture can overlap with ESCR violations.

At the same time, we can safely conclude that the crime of torture encompasses ESCR-related abuses that go beyond the level of pain or suffering found to constitute CIDT because the difference in the level of pain or suffering required for torture as compared to CIDT is one of gravity. Meanwhile, an explicit decision in this sense has yet to be made by international judicial authorities. Given the fine line distinguishing the required levels of pain or suffering for CIDT and torture, it is thus relevant to analyse CIDT even if CIDT does not constitute an international crime. In other words, treatment similar to CIDT constitutes torture if it was considered more severe and if it was inflicted for a prohibited purpose and with the involvement of a person acting in an official capacity.

Two landmark cases of the European Commission of Human Rights (ECommHR) provide guidance on the thresholds of the requisite level of pain or suffering.[40] In the *Ireland* v. *United Kingdom* case, the ECommHR held that inhuman treatment includes at least treatment deliberately causing severe suffering, whether mental or physical.[41] The ECommHR also interpreted the notion of CIDT in the *Greek Case*. The ECommHR concluded that 'treatment or punishment of an individual may be said to be degrading if it grossly humiliates him [or her] before others or drives him [or her] to act against his will or conscience'.[42]

[39] See *Ireland* v. *United Kingdom, Application No. 5310/71, 18 January 1978*, ECtHR, para. 167: 'In the Court's view, this distinction [between torture and CIDT] derives principally from a difference in the intensity of the suffering inflicted.' Unlike torture, there is also no reference to a prohibited purpose or the involvement of a person acting in official capacity.

[40] The definitions of torture and CIDT in human rights law complement and assist the interpretation of the relevant provisions under both the UNCAT and customary international law. *Prosecutor* v. *Delalić, IT-96-21-T, 16 November 1998*, ICTY, para. 534, concluding that the case law of the ECtHR was relevant to assess the seriousness of an act to determine if it was inhuman.

[41] *Ireland* v. *United Kingdom, Application No. 5310/71, 18 January 1978*, ECtHR, para. 167.

[42] *'Greek Case', Application Nos. 3321/67, 3322/67, 3323/67, 3344/67, Report Adopted on 15 April 1970, Yearbook of the European Convention on Human Rights, Vol. 12 (1972)*, ECommHR, 186.

No permanent injury is required,[43] and mental harm is explicitly covered.[44]

Let us look more closely at the cases in which socio-economic abuses were found to constitute CIDT. The clearest examples of overlap between ESCR-related abuses and CIDT occur in the context of detention. In 1976 already, the ECommHR found that withholding adequate food, drinking water and medical care from detainees constituted inhuman treatment.[45] The HRCttee decided a similar case and reached the same conclusion.[46] In *Dybeku* v. *Albania*, the ECtHR found that detention conditions and the medical treatment provided by the Albanian prison system were grossly inadequate. The court unanimously found that the treatment constituted CIDT because Albania failed to ensure that the applicant was detained in conditions protecting the person's mental health.[47] The more recent case of *Vasyukov* v. *Russia* is illustrative of numerous cases in which the ECtHR or the HRCttee have found violations of the prohibition of CIDT due to the state's failure to secure the health and well-being of detainees or to provide them with adequate medical care: the ECtHR found a violation of the prohibition of torture and inhuman or degrading treatment or punishment because the authorities failed to comply with their responsibility to ensure adequate medical assistance during detention.[48]

Human rights bodies also confirmed that CIDT can be committed by depriving a person of their ESCR outside the context of detention, where the responsibility of the state is more challenging to establish than for individuals in custody. The first such indication that socio-economic deprivations can amount to CIDT dates from 1979. In *Crutzescu* v.

[43] *Prosecutor* v. *Kvočka, IT-98-30/1-T, 2 November 2001*, ICTY, para. 148.

[44] UNCAT, Art. 1. Ibid., para. 149.

[45] *Cyprus* v. *Turkey, Application Nos. 9780/74 and 6950/75 (Report of the Commission 10 July 1976)*, ECommHR, para. 405. See also *Ireland* v. *United Kingdom, Application No. 5310/71, 18 January 1978*, ECtHR, para. 96. In the latter case, it was not entirely clear to what extent the detainees were deprived of nourishment and whether or not they were offered food but refused to take it. The ECtHR discussed various treatments inflicted in combination.

[46] *Mukong* v. *Cameroon, 10 August 1994, CCPR/C/51/D/458/1991*, HRCttee, paras. 9.3–9.4. The applicant was deprived of food, sanitation facilities and clothing.

[47] *Dybeku* v. *Albania, Application No. 41153/06, 18 December 2007*, ECtHR, para. 38.

[48] *Vasyukov* v. *Russia, Application No. 2974/05, 5 April 2011*, ECtHR, paras. 61–2 with further references. For the HRCttee, see *Mukong* v. *Cameroon, 10 August 1994, CCPR/C/51/D/458/1991*, HRCttee (lack of sanitation, food, clothing and a bed. Or: *Lantsova* v. *Russia, 26 March 2002, CCPR/C/74/D/763/1997 (2002)*, HRCttee (lack of medical attention, ventilation, food and hygiene).

*Germany*, an unreported admissibility decision of the ECommHR, the commission dealt with the complaint of a war veteran who had asked for an increase in his invalidity rent, claiming that, given his health condition, the social security benefits did not allow him an adequate standard of living. The commission held that it was conceivable that the lack of social security could amount to CIDT, but that, in the case at hand, the situation presented by the claimant was not serious enough to constitute CIDT. The ECommHR did not specify the requisite level of seriousness that would have to be met, but implied that more serious deprivations should be considered CIDT.[49] More recently, the ECtHR held that living conditions of impoverished migrants in Greece amounted to CIDT,[50] and Belgium violated the prohibition of torture and CIDT because it transferred an individual to Greece and knowingly exposed him to living conditions that amounted to degrading treatment.[51] The ECtHR currently faces the opportunity to further clarify its case law on the relationship with socio-economic abuses and torture or CIDT: in 2011, the ECtHR declared admissible an interstate case in which Georgia alleges, *inter alia*, that Russia violated the prohibition of torture and CIDT based on allegations that civilians had not been given bedding, blankets, basic nutrition, water, electricity and adequate sanitation during the armed conflict between Georgia and Russia in 2008.[52]

Courts and supervisory bodies have further concluded that expulsions to foreign states may be contrary to the prohibition of torture or ill treatment when an individual is suffering from a serious illness and if proper care was not provided in the recipient state,[53] in other words,

[49] *Crutzescu* v. *Germany, Application No. 8247/78, Unreported Admissibility Decision of 4 July 1979 (on file with the author)*, ECommHR. Discussed in Antonio Cassese, 'Inhuman and Degrading Treatment' (1991), 2 *European Journal of International Law* 1, 141–5, note 8.

[50] *M.S.S.* v. *Belgium and Greece, Application No. 30696/09, 21 January 2011*, ECtHR Grand Chamber, para. 264.

[51] Ibid., para. 368.

[52] *Georgia* v. *Russia (No. 2), Application No. 38263/08, Admissibility Decision of 13 December 2011*, ECtHR, paras. 28–9.

[53] *Tanko* v. *Finland, Application No. 23634/94, Admissibility Decision of 19 May 1994*, ECommHR: 'The Commission does not exclude that a lack of proper care in a case where someone is suffering from a serious illness could in certain circumstances amount to treatment contrary to Article 3.' See also *D.* v. *United Kingdom, Application No. 30240/96, 2 May 1997*, ECtHR, paras. 48–53, concluding that deportation of a terminally ill patient to St Kitts, where no appropriate treatment would have been available, constitutes CIDT. Another relevant case is *C.* v. *Australia, 28 October 2002, CCPR/C/76/D/900/1999*, HRCttee, paras. 8.4–9. The HRCttee concludes that the applicant's irreversible mental illness developed as a result of the protracted period of immigration detention and that Australia violated the prohibition of torture and CIDT of the ICCPR because authorities

when the person's right to health was at stake. CIDT was also found to encompass non-consensual medical interference, which constitutes a violation of the right to health if attributable to the state.[54]

In addition, the right to housing is also relevant for the assessment of whether a situation amounts to CIDT. The ECtHR found the destruction of homes to constitute CIDT. In *Selçuk and Asker* v. *Turkey*, the ECtHR categorised the housing rights violations as acts of inhuman treatment, in particular because the petitioners had lived in the village all their lives and their homes had been destroyed by security forces, forcing them to leave their village.[55] Similarly, in 2002, the CAT Committee found that the violent evictions of Roma from their dwellings constituted CIDT, based on the government's failure to protect the community from abuses by non-state actors.[56] Housing demolitions and forced evictions have also been linked to the prohibition of CIDT by the HRCttee,[57] and by the African Commission on Human and Peoples' Rights (ACommHPR).[58]

The negotiation of the prohibition of torture in the ICCPR confirms that the drafters considered ESCR considerations to be relevant in the decision whether the requisite level of severe pain or suffering has been reached. The annotations to the draft covenants show that states were careful to avoid stating that the term 'treatment' would cover degrading situations that arose solely from socio-economic conditions, but they did

failed to take steps to ameliorate the claimant's mental condition. The committee also held that given the lack of available treatment in Iran, Australia would breach the ICCPR if the patient was to be deported.

54 Human Rights Committee, *General Comment 28 on Equality of Rights between Men and Women*, 29 March 2000, CCPR/C/21/Rev.1/Add.10, para. 11: forced sterilisation is a practice that constitutes torture or CIDT. It has moreover been argued that the failure by the US government to protect detainees in US custody against torture in the 'enhanced interrogation programme' constituted simultaneously a violation of their right to health as well as the crime of torture. Physicians for Human Rights, 'Experiments in Torture' (Physicians for Human Rights, 2010), 9.

55 *Selçuk and Asker* v. *Turkey, Applications No. 23184/94; 23185/94, 24 April 1998*, ECtHR, paras. 76–80.

56 *Dzemajl et al.* v. *Yugoslavia, 2 December 2002, CAT/C/29/D/161/2000*, CAT Committee, para. 10. The evictions, followed by the destruction and the burning of the dwellings, were carried out by private individuals. The CAT Committee held Yugoslavia to account because the authorities acquiesced in the conduct.

57 The HRCttee has repeatedly expressed concern that Israel's practice of demolishing property, housing and civilian infrastructure such as hospitals, schools, farms or water plants falls within the scope of CIDT. See, for instance, Concluding Observations, Israel, HRCttee, CCPR/C/ISR/CO/3, 3 September 2010, para. 17.

58 *COHRE* v. *Sudan, Communication 296/05, 29 July 2010*, ACommHPR, para. 157. The ACommHPR concluded that forced evictions in Darfur not only violated right to housing, but rose to violation of right to integrity of the person and the prohibition of CIDT.

not imply that treatment touching upon the victim's ESCR should be excluded from the scope of the definition of torture: the drafters' concern was to ensure that only *treatment* attributable to individual perpetrators would be covered by the definition, as opposed to situations resulting from 'general economic and social factors'.[59]

Against this background, it is possible to conceive situations of ESCR violations that qualify as torture and thus fall within the scope of this international crime. At the same time, courts and supervisory bodies have provided limited guidance on the requisite level of seriousness that would lead them to find that ESCR-related abuses fall under the definition of torture. It is particularly disappointing that in a number of cases, tribunals and supervisory organs simply held that the case at hand did not present the requisite level of seriousness (whether for torture or CIDT), but did not advance reasons for their conclusion.[60] Be this as it may, the wording of Art. 1 of the UNCAT, the object and purpose of safeguarding the inherent dignity of the human person, as well as indications from the drafting history and existing case law allow the conclusion that torture can be committed by conduct that simultaneously gives rise to a violation of ESCR, provided that this conduct reaches the required level of severity and meets the purpose and official capacity requirement. Concluding otherwise would be erroneous, based on the untenable assumption that inflicting severe pain or suffering is not possible where a person's access to food, health care, housing or other ESCR are infringed upon.[61]

## 7.3 Apartheid

Apartheid is both a crime against humanity under the Rome Statute and criminalised in the Convention on the Suppression and Punishment of the Crime of Apartheid, a treaty that establishes a range of state

59 Manfred Nowak, *CCPR Commentary*, 2nd edn (Engel, 2005), 159–60. Nowak cites the Annotations on the Text of the Draft Covenants on Human Rights, A/2929, 1 July 1955, 31.

60 See the excellent case note by Cassese, 'Inhuman and Degrading Treatment', analysing a 1990 inadmissibility decision of the ECommHR which dealt with a destitute complainant whose heating was cut off in winter. See also *O'Donnell* v. *South Dublin County Council, Record No. 2006/1904 P, 22 May 2007, High Court, Ireland*, where disabled members of a Traveller family argued that their housing situation rose to CIDT. The court did not find that the suffering reached the level required for CIDT within the scope of Art. 3 of the ECHR.

61 For empirical work on the relationship between ESCR and torture and other violence, see Thomas McCarthy and World Organisation against Torture, *Attacking the Root Causes of Torture* (OMCT, 2006).

obligations to prevent, suppress and punish socio-economic abuses amounting to apartheid.[62] The Convention lacks the support necessary to be considered customary law.[63] However, in the relationship between state parties to the treaty, ESCR violations also can overlap with the crime of apartheid outside the context of crimes against humanity. Whereas the crime against humanity requires the specific threshold elements of a widespread or systematic attack, as well as similarity between the inhumane acts of apartheid with other conduct qualified as a crime against humanity,[64] no such requirement is included in the Apartheid Convention. The Apartheid Convention defines the crime of apartheid as 'inhuman acts committed for the purpose of establishing and maintaining domination by one racial group of persons over any other racial group of persons and systematically oppressing them'.[65] As we saw previously, there can be significant overlap between apartheid and violations of ESCR, and reference is therefore made to Chapter 4, where the relationship between the crime of apartheid and ESCR has been analysed.[66] The analysis applies *mutatis mutandis* with additional potential for overlap because the crime of apartheid under the Apartheid Convention does not require evidence of the threshold elements of crimes against humanity or of similarity to other crimes against humanity.

## 7.4 Aggression

It is furthermore possible to identify overlap between the crime of aggression and ESCR violations. The International Military Tribunal (IMT) in Nuremberg stated that aggression is not only an international

[62] International Convention on the Suppression and Punishment of the Crime of Apartheid, GA Res. 3068 (XXVIII), 30 November 1973 (entered into force 18 July 1976), Arts. III and IV.

[63] Although the convention has 107 state parties, the outspoken opposition by non-parties makes it difficult to argue that widespread and representative state practice considers the definition of apartheid in the convention a crime under customary international law. It must be noted, however, that the prohibition of apartheid itself is clearly part of customary law. See *Barcelona Traction, Light and Power Company Limited (Belgium* v. *Spain), 2nd Phase, 5 February 1970*, ICJ, para. 34.

[64] Rome Statute of the International Criminal Court, 2187 UNTS 90, 17 July 1998 (entered into force 1 July 2002), Art. 7(2)h. See Section 4.6.

[65] Apartheid Convention, Art. II, with a long list of policies and practices constituting apartheid.

[66] See Section 4.6.

crime, but 'the supreme international crime'.[67] States have strong and divergent views about the rules pertaining to the legitimate use of force in international law. Only in 2010 did states agree to empower the ICC to adjudicate on the crime of aggression, after the absence of any prosecutions for this crime since the end of the post-World War II trials.[68] Once the amendments to the Rome Statute have entered into force,[69] the ICC will be competent to exercise jurisdiction over the crime of aggression, defined for the purpose of the Rome Statute as 'the planning, preparation, initiation or execution, by a person in a position effectively to exercise control over or to direct the political or military action of a State, of an act of aggression which, by its character, gravity and scale, constitutes a manifest violation of the Charter of the United Nations'.[70]

Finding overlap between the crime of aggression and violations of ESCR is constrained by the fact that human rights law only rarely applies extraterritorially while aggression is directed at a state other than the one of the perpetrator. A violation of ESCR can only be found to exist where the state on whose behalf the aggressing perpetrator acts has a binding obligation related to ESCR. This would be unproblematic where the perpetrator's criminal conduct would affect ESCR within the jurisdiction of his own state. However, it is difficult to conceive that people's access to ESCR could be affected already at the stage of the perpetrator's planning or preparing of an act of aggression, that is, before the conduct acquires an extraterritorial dimension. Later on, at the stage of initiating or executing an act of aggression, it is likely that the conduct affects people's access and enjoyment of ESCR, but the conduct will be extraterritorial. As the wording of the new Art. 8*bis* of the Rome Statute and other definitions of aggression indicate, the criminalisation of aggression is designed to protect the 'sovereignty, territorial integrity or political

[67] *United States of America, the French Republic, the United Kingdom of Great Britain and Northern Ireland, and the Union of Soviet Socialist Republics against Major War Criminals, Opinion and Judgment, in Nazi Conspiracy and Aggression (Red Series), 1 October 1946*, IMT, 86.

[68] In the meantime, states did agree on a definition of aggression for the relations between states (but not for criminal purposes). Definition of Aggression, GA Res. 3314, 14 December 1974, which is an authoritative interpretation of the UN Charter.

[69] Ratification by thirty states is necessary before the ICC can exercise jurisdiction over aggression. Amendments to the Rome Statute of the International Criminal Court on the Crime of Aggression, the Review Conference of the Rome Statute of the ICC, Rc/Res. 6, 11 June 2010 (not yet entered into force). By virtue of Art. 15*bis* and *ter*, the ICC shall not exercise jurisdiction over aggression before 2017.

[70] Ibid.

independence of *another state*'.[71] Because the initiation or execution of an act of aggression is by definition conduct with extraterritorial effects, there can only be overlap between the definition of the crime and ESCR violations if we affirm the extraterritorial applicability of relevant provisions of human rights law. While the extent of extraterritorial applicability of human rights law is controversially discussed,[72] there is consensus that the right to self-determination recognised in Art. 1 of the ICESCR (as well as the identically worded Art. 1 of the ICCPR) expressly sets out extraterritorial obligations of state parties. Art. 1(3) of the ICESCR obliges states to respect and promote the right to self-determination including in respect of territories other than their own.[73]

Aggression is hardly consistent with people's access and enjoyment of the right to self-determination. The execution of acts of aggression can lead to large-scale destruction in the targeted country in the case of invasion, attack or bombardment or to serious economic hardship in the case of blockades. The right holders of the right to self-determination are 'peoples'.[74] Given that the inhabitants of a state can under certain circumstances be considered a 'people',[75] the right to self-determination is violated if the inhabitants of a state are either 'deprived of their own means of subsistence' or if the act of aggression interferes in people's right to freely pursue their economic, social and cultural development.[76]

[71] Amendments to Art. 8 of the Rome Statute, the Review Conference of the Rome Statute of the ICC, Rc/Res. 5, 10 June 2010 (not yet entered into force), Art. 8*bis* (emphasis added).

[72] See Chapter 5, Notes 36 and 37. For a recent overview of the debate, see Karen DaCosta, *The Extraterritorial Application of Selected Human Rights Treaties* (Nijhoff, 2012).

[73] See also the non-binding Maastricht Principles on Extraterritorial Obligations of States in the Area of Economic, Social and Cultural Rights, Adopted by a Group of Experts Convened by Maastricht University and the International Commission of Jurists, 21 September 2011, Principle 32(c). And Malcolm Langford, 'A Sort of Homecoming', in *Universal Human Rights and Extraterritorial Obligations*, ed. Mark Gibney and Sigrun Skogly (University of Pennsylvania Press, 2010), 168–9. In its landmark case on self-determination, the HRCttee argued that the facts of the case fall under Art. 27 ICCPR (protection of minorities). *Ominayak and the Lubicon Lake Band* v. *Canada, 10 May 1990, CCPR/C/38/D/167/1984*, HRCttee, para. 32.2. Article 2 of the OP-ICESCR allows the CESCR to decide cases based on alleged violations of the right to self-determination in conjunction with another covenant right. Optional Protocol to the International Covenant on Economic, Social and Cultural Rights, GA Res. 63/117, 63 UN GAOR Supp. (No. 49), 10 December 2008 (entered into force 5 May 2013), Art. 2.

[74] ICESCR, Art. 1.

[75] See *East Timor (Portugal* v. *Australia), 30 June 1995*, ICJ, 106, concluding that the population of East Timor had the right to self-determination.

[76] Human Rights Committee, *General Comment 12 on the Right to Self-Determination*, 13 March 1984, HRI/GEN/1/Rev.6.

In this scenario, the factual conduct of the act of aggression criminalised in international law simultaneously gives rise to a violation of the right to self-determination as an extraterritorial violation of ESCR. In contrast to other crimes, this area of overlap remains difficult to establish in practice because the contours of the right to self-determination are less clearly understood than other rights discussed in this study. This difficulty does not, however, diminish the conclusion that it is possible to relate the crime of aggression with violations of ESCR.

## 7.5 Terrorist offences

Under certain circumstances, a violation of ESCR can also constitute a terrorist offence criminalised by international law. A range of conventions criminalise specific acts of terrorism, such as hijacking airplanes, taking hostages or laying explosives. The General Assembly is working towards the adoption of a comprehensive convention against terrorism.[77] Identifying the common denominator of the definitions of terrorist acts in the long list of relevant conventions, the Appeals Chamber of the Special Tribunal for Lebanon claimed that the definition of terrorism in customary international law contained the following elements: the perpetration or threatening of a criminal act, the intent to spread fear among the population or to coerce an authority to take some action and a transnational element.[78] The decision of the Special Tribunal for Lebanon is controversial because it includes conduct by states, while some states argue that the criminalisation of terrorism should be limited to acts by non-state actors,[79] and because it assumes that there is a general crime of terrorism independent of the terrorist offences contained in suppression conventions. Although it is doubtful that customary international law today criminalises a general crime of terrorism as such,[80] the

[77] Draft Comprehensive Convention against International Terrorism, A/59/894, App. II, 12 August 2005, Art. 2. Disagreements over whether the definition of terrorism should be limited to terrorism by non-state actors, whether national liberation movements should be included and whether damage to property without causing any death or bodily injury can constitute terrorism have delayed the adoption of a treaty.

[78] *Interlocutory Decision on the Applicable Law, STL-II-0lI1 (16 February 2011)*, Special Tribunal for Lebanon, para. 85.

[79] See Note 77.

[80] For a critique of the tribunal's position that terrorism as such was a crime under customary law, see Ben Saul, 'Legislating from a Radical Hague: The United Nations Special Tribunal for Lebanon Invents an International Crime of Transnational Terrorism' (2011) 24 *Leiden Journal of International Law*, 677–700.

decision is useful here as it summarises the common elements of treaties against certain forms of terrorism and therefore facilitates the task to ascertain overlap between terrorist offences and ESCR violations. The transnational element requires that offences committed within a single state only fall within the scope of the definition of terrorism if the alleged offender and the victims have different nationalities, the alleged perpetrator is not found in the state in whose territory the offence was committed or more than one state has jurisdiction.[81] Where a transnational element is lacking, the alleged conduct does not fall under the definition of the offences that states must criminalise, but the cooperation clauses of the terrorism conventions continue to apply.[82]

We will first examine scenarios in which the offence is committed *within more than one state*, that is, where the transnational element of the definition of acts of terrorism is met because the conduct has a relationship with the territory of at least two states. In such cases, the demonstration of an overlap between the definition of terrorist offences under international law and violations of ESCR is contingent upon the extraterritorial applicability of human rights law in the same way as we saw it with the crime of aggression. Potential overlap between the terrorist offences and violations of the right to self-determination in the field of ESCR can therefore be demonstrated in the same way as above.

There is further overlap between terrorist offences and ESCR violations in situations of military occupation and other situations in which a foreign territory can be considered under the jurisdiction of State A to which the conduct is attributable.[83] Consider a hypothetical example in which terrorists destroy schools that offer education for girls in a border region of the neighbouring State B, where this border region is under the military control of State A. In such a scenario, the destruction of schools constitutes an offence under the International Convention for the Suppression of Terrorist Bombings.[84] If State A acknowledges and adopts the conduct in question as its own, it is internationally responsible for this

[81] International Convention for the Suppression of Terrorist Bombings, GA Res. 52/49, 15 December 1997 (entered into force 23 May 2001), Art. 3.

[82] See, for instance, ibid. or Convention for the Suppression of Unlawful Seizure of Aircraft, 860 UNTS 105 (1971), 16 December 1970 (entered into force 14 October 1971), Art. 3.

[83] Committee on Economic, Social and Cultural Rights, *General Comment 1 on Reporting by States Parties*, 24 February 1989, E/1989/22, para. 3. See also *Case Concerning Armed Activities on the Territory of the Congo (DRC* v. *Uganda), 19 December 2005*, ICJ, para. 216.

[84] Terrorist Bombing Convention, Art. 1(5).

conduct.[85] If it 'merely' encourages the conduct and fails to take measures against the terrorists operating in the border region under its control, the state is responsible for a failure to protect the right to education.[86] Even if the terrorists do not intend to kill or injure individuals, the conduct that harms the right to education is still covered under the Terrorist Bombing Convention, provided that the destruction is extensive and results, or is likely to result, in major economic loss.[87]

Second, there are also scenarios in which the offence is committed *within a single state*, but the transnational element required by the conventions suppressing terrorist acts is met because the alleged offender has a different nationality than the victims, or the offender has escaped from the country where the offence took place and is located in another state that is party to the relevant convention suppressing terrorist acts.[88] This could be the case, for instance, where a national of State A releases toxic chemicals, biological or radioactive agents or similar substances into food or water sources in State B. In such cases, the conduct can be covered by the Terrorism Bombing Convention,[89] or the Convention on Nuclear Terrorism if the substance is a nuclear or radioactive material.[90] The Terrorist Bombing Convention defines explosive or other lethal devices broadly: unlike most prohibitions of weapons under international humanitarian law (IHL), it is not necessary the devices be specifically *designed* as weapons.[91] Where the offence is committed within a single state, the applicability of human rights law is unproblematic. The release of substances covered by the instrument or the state's failure to protect the population from such a release can constitute a violation of ESCR,[92] and the conduct is also criminalised by anti-terrorism instruments. The broad definition of the items covered broadens the scope of the argument that ESCR violations can be addressed by conventions aiming at the suppression of terrorist offences.

85 ILC Articles on State Responsibility, Art. 11. Here, the state would fail to *respect* the right to education because the interference with access to education in the border region under its control is considered the state's own conduct.

86 ILC Articles on State Responsibility, Art. 4. Here, the state would fail to *protect* the right to education.

87 Terrorist Bombing Convention, Art. 2.

88 For instance, ibid., Art. 3; International Convention for the Suppression of Acts of Nuclear Terrorism, GA Res. 59/290, 13 April 2005 (entered into force 7 July 2007), Art. 3.

89 Terrorist Bombing Convention, Art. 1.

90 Nuclear Terrorism Convention, Art. 1(4).

91 Terrorist Bombing Convention, Art. 1(3).

92 Particularly, the right to food, health or water.

Another group of offences where such an argument is possible concerns treaties on certain weapons.

## 7.6 Unlawful use and emplacement of certain weapons

The unlawful use and emplacement of certain weapons can be an independent crime outside armed conflicts and is thus different from the war crimes analysed in Chapter 5.[93] State actors using and emplacing certain weapons are often simultaneously violating people's access to ESCR. For instance, the use of cluster munitions seriously inhibits access to agricultural land, water sources, schools or health facilities because unexploded bomblets contaminate wide areas and are difficult to locate and remove. The emplacement of cluster munitions most prominently affects the physical accessibility of food, water, education, health or cultural heritage and can constitute violations of ESCR.[94] If the cluster munitions are used by a state party to the Convention on Cluster Munitions, for instance, the same conduct in such a scenario both constitutes a violation of ESCR and is also covered by an international instrument with penal characteristics.[95]

Similarly, if the state allows persons to develop biological agents or toxins that have no justification for peaceful purposes, and such substances are deliberately released into food sources, the right to adequate food is violated.[96] Such conduct also falls within the scope of the Biological Weapons Convention, which requires states to criminalise such conduct by national legislation.[97] Analogous reasoning applies to the Chemical Weapons Convention when a government allows the release of toxic chemicals.[98]

[93] For the analysis of war crimes related to weapons, see Section 5.2.4.

[94] See, for instance, Committee on Economic, Social and Cultural Rights, *General Comment 15 on the Right to Water*, 20 January 2003, E/C.12/2002/11, para. 12.

[95] Convention on Cluster Munitions, Dublin, 30 May 2008 (entered into force 1 August 2010), Art. 9.

[96] Committee on Economic, Social and Cultural Rights, *General Comment 12 on the Right to Adequate Food*, 12 May 1999, E/C.12/1999/5, para. 19: the adoption of a policy to emplace cluster munitions would be 'manifestly incompatible with pre-existing legal obligations relating to the right to food'.

[97] Convention on the Prohibition of the Development, Production and Stockpiling of Bacteriological and Toxin Weapons and on Their Destruction, 10 April 1972 (entered into force 26 March 1975), Art. IV.

[98] Convention on the Prohibition of the Development, Production, Stockpiling and Use of Chemical Weapons and on Their Destruction, 3 September 1992 (entered into force 29 April 1997), Art. VII(1)a.

Laundering money and other proceeds of crime can also overlap with ESCR violations.

## 7.7 Laundering proceeds of crime

Various legal instruments attempt to fight the significant flows of money resulting from proceeds from the illegal drug trade, human trafficking, arms smuggling, waste dumping, illegal logging and other criminal activity. Proceeds of crime are any property derived from or obtained through the commission of an offence.[99] 'Laundering' is defined as hiding, disguising or otherwise legitimising proceeds of crime.[100]

States violate the duty to protect ESCR if they fail to properly regulate and monitor non-state actors engaged in laundering proceeds of crime. Let us consider just one scenario in which – provided the allegations by UN bodies, NGOs and the press are true – laundering proceeds of crimes overlaps with the state's failure to respect and protect ESCR. In this scenario, the laundering of proceeds not only gives rise to a violation of ESCR, but also falls within the scope of at least one international instrument criminalising such conduct:

Rainforest covered over 70 per cent of Cambodia's surface in 1970, but only 3 per cent of the territory in 2007.[101] As a state party to the main international human rights treaties, Cambodia has a duty to protect the livelihoods of the population, including the indigenous rural communities who depend on land and forest resources for their survival.[102] According to NGOs, rapid deforestation deprived the rural population of food, medicines and water resources.[103] In 2011, the World Bank Inspection Panel called on the government of Cambodia to stop housing rights violations after an inquiry showed that forced evictions in the

[99] UNTOC, Art. 2(e).

[100] David Luban et al., *International and Transnational Criminal Law* (Aspen, 2009), 597.

[101] Food and Agriculture Organization, *National Forest Inventory: Cambodia* (FAO, 2007), 3. See also Report of the Special Representative of the Secretary-General for Human Rights in Cambodia (Peter Leuprecht), E/CN.4/2005/116, 20 December 2004, paras. 42–57.

[102] See, for instance, ICESCR, Arts. 11, 12 and 15. The HRCttee interpreted that enjoyment of cultural life encompasses traditional livelihoods. See *Länsman et al.* v. *Finland, 22 November 1996, CCPR/C/52/D/511/1992*, HRCttee. Similarly, the IACommHR held that the right to health required that the state protect traditional livelihoods. *Yanomami Indians* v. *Brazil, 5 March 1985, IACommHR Report OEA/Ser.L/V/II.66*, IACommHR.

[103] Human Rights Watch, 'UPR Submission: Cambodia', (2009), Section C.

context of the Cambodia Land Management and Administration Project had taken place 'in violation of the Bank policy on Involuntary Resettlement'.[104] The UN Committee on Economic, Social and Cultural Rights (CESCR) has expressed concern that the rapid increase in economic land concessions resulted in the forced eviction of indigenous peoples from their lands and that the 'authorities of the State party are actively involved in land-grabbing', leading to large-scale forced evictions.[105] The CESCR linked these concerns with both the right to internal economic self-determination and the right to an adequate standard of living.[106] If these allegations are true, the rapid deforestation activities furthered, tolerated or directly implemented by government policies would seem to violate a range of ESCR.

Illegal logging (defined as harvesting timber in contravention of a country's laws) almost inevitably relies on laundering the proceeds of the crime. Those who engage in illegal logging are able and willing to continue the illegal activity only if they can legitimise their ill-gotten gains.[107] A 2007 report by a human rights and environmental group claimed that there was an officially sanctioned policy to illegally cut timber outside the boundaries of poorly demarcated plantations. The logs were allegedly moved inside the plantation boundaries, where they were presented as part of the officially authorised land conversion process or converted into plywood or pulp in order to disguise the origins of the timber.[108] According to these allegations, members of the armed forces oversaw this process.[109]

In this scenario, the laundering of proceeds of crime is an essential component of illegal logging. The logging in turn directly seems to constitute violations of various ESCR because the authorities, by their alleged involvement in or toleration of logging, failed to respect and protect people's access to food, water, housing and other rights.

What remains to be shown is that laundering proceeds is covered by at least one international instrument with penal characteristics. If

[104] World Bank, 'World Bank Board of Executive Directors Considers Inspection Panel Report on Cambodia Land Management and Administration Project', http://go.worldbank.org/MH5TANKPS0.

[105] Concluding Observations, Cambodia, E/CN.12/KHM/CO/1, 22 May 2009, para. 30.

[106] Ibid., paras. 15, 30.

[107] Luban et al., *International and Transnational Criminal Law*, 580.

[108] Witness, *Cambodia's Family Trees: Illegal Logging and the Stripping of Public Assets by Cambodia's Elite* (Witness, 2007), 35.

[109] Ibid.

government officials are intentionally involved in the conduct,[110] the alleged illegal logging may fall within the scope of two relevant (and *in casu* applicable) provisions: Art. 6 of UNTOC establishes that each state party must criminalise the laundering of proceeds of crime, including but not limited to the conversion or transfer of property for the purpose of concealing or disguising the illicit origin.[111] This provision therefore covers activities like the removal of illegally cut logs into demarcated plantation areas. The United Nations Convention against Corruption (UNCAC) contains a very similar provision obliging states to criminalise the laundering of proceeds of crime.[112] Regional conventions also contain penal characteristics concerning the laundering of criminal proceeds, although none of them applies in Asia.[113]

The above scenario illustrates that laundering of proceeds of crime cannot only give rise to several ESCR violations, but can, simultaneously, constitute one or several of the offences criminalised in international instruments of criminal law. Similarly, ESCR violations can sometimes overlap with corruption.

## 7.8 Corruption

Corruption not only fuels human rights abuses, but can itself constitute a violation of ESCR and is also the subject of international criminal law. In international law, corruption denotes the illegal abuse of entrusted power for private gain.[114] A range of instruments with penal characteristics address specific corrupt acts. The relevant legal instruments vary according to the forms of corrupt behaviour (including bribery, embezzlement, the trading of influence or the abuse of functions) as well as the type of actors they address (foreign or domestic public officials, the private sector, those who offer and those who accept bribes).[115] The purpose of

[110] Only intentional forms are covered. See UNTOC, Art. 6 and UN Convention against Corruption, GA Res. 58/4, 31 October 2003 (entered into force 14 December 2005), Art. 23(1). They only require states to criminalise the *intentional* laundering of proceeds of crime.

[111] UNTOC, Art. 6. [112] UNCAC, Art. 23.

[113] For an outline of relevant regional instruments, see Luban et al., *International and Transnational Criminal Law*, 584.

[114] On the legal definitions of corruption, see Julio Bacio Terracino, *The International Legal Framework against Corruption* (Intersentia, 2012), 18.

[115] For an overview of legal instruments, their commonalities and differences, see ibid., 48–71.

this section is to demonstrate that the same conduct can both constitute a form of corruption criminalised in one of the international criminal law instruments and give rise to a violation of ESCR.[116]

There are three ways that corruption constitutes a violation of ESCR and thus overlaps with the legal definition of corruption contained in international instruments with penal characteristics. They can be grouped according to the dimensions of state obligations in human rights law (the typology of respect, protect and fulfil).

First, corruption leads to *de facto* discrimination and substandard services for those who refuse or who cannot pay. Discrimination due to corrupt but unmonitored government officials in education, for instance, constitutes a violation of the duty to *respect* the right to education.[117] Simultaneously, the officials' conduct constitutes criminalised conduct defined in an international instrument of criminal law.

Second, corrupt officials may take bribes to neglect their duties related to the protection of ESCR. Consider a corrupt official tasked to control privately owned work sites to ensure that there is no child labour. If she accepts a bribe in exchange for controlling the facility, and if the government takes no steps to monitor the official's behaviour, her government fails to *protect* children's right to education as well as their right to be protected from performing any work that is harmful to their health and development.[118] Hence, tolerating corruption simultaneously violates the duty to protect children's right to be protected against child labour,

[116] This section is not interested in the full range of possible links between corruption and human rights violations. Corruption fuelling human rights abuse is not necessarily a violation of ESCR as such and thus is outside the interest of this section. Commentators have also argued that corruption can overlap with crimes against humanity. Ilias Bantekas, 'Corruption as an International Crime' (2006) 4 *Journal of International Criminal Justice*, 3, 466–84. Bantekas' argument is structurally different from the type of overlap analysed in this study. Bantekas examines the way corruption *results* in a lack of food or medicine, leading to forcible transfer or extermination. Here, the study is interested in how the penal characteristics of treaties against corruption overlap with violations of ESCR, which may in turn have been facilitated by corruption.

[117] ICESCR, Art. 2(2). UNESCO Convention against Discrimination in Education, 14 December 1960 (entered into force 22 May 1962), Art. 4; Committee on Economic, Social and Cultural Rights, *General Comment 13 on the Right to Education*, 8 December 1999, E/C.12/1999/10, para. 59. The failure to take measures that address *de facto* educational discrimination is a violation of the right to education.

[118] CRC, Art. 32. For a specific example, see International Trade Union Confederation, 'Report for the WTO General Council Review of Trade Policies of Pakistan' (WTO, 2008), 11.

including in privately owned establishments.[119] If intentional, the conduct falls under Art. 15 of UNCAC, which requires criminalisation of the acceptance of bribes by national public officials.[120] Failure to monitor and discipline officials tasked with supervising the implementation of legislation occurs in many sectors and can result in violations of almost any human right. Food quality and safety can be affected, and the right to water or health can be violated, if the state fails to protect the right to water and health by allowing companies to excessively abstract water or to dispose of toxic waste.[121]

Third, a government that tolerates corruption or that is involved in corrupt behaviour will often fail to *fulfil* ESCR.[122] The Committee on the Rights of the Child concluded that corruption in several countries seriously limits the resources available to implement children's socio-economic rights contained in the CRC.[123] The ACommHPR found that the right to education is violated if schools are closed for two years without explanation and if teachers are not paid because of widespread corruption.[124] By the same mechanism, a state tolerating corruption can also violate its duty to fulfil the right to social security.[125] Similarly,

[119] *International Commission of Jurists* v. *Portugal, Complaint No. 1/1998, 9 September 1999*, ECttSR, para. 42, finding that the allegations of corruption were not supported by evidence, but allowing for the conclusion that the obligation to verify that there is no child labour can be hampered by corruption.

[120] UNCAC, Art. 15.

[121] Report of the Special Rapporteur on the Adverse Effects of the Illicit Movement and Dumping of Toxic and Dangerous Products and Wastes on the Enjoyment of Human Rights (Okechukwu Ibeanu), A/HRC/7/21, 18 February 2008, para. 21, highlighting the role of corruption in the transboundary movement of hazardous materials.

[122] Corruption does not provide the state with an excuse that lower levels of resources are available. See also Committee on Economic, Social and Cultural Rights, *General Comment 3 on the Nature of States Parties Obligations*, 14 December 1990, E/1991/23, paras. 10–11.

[123] See, for instance, Concluding Observations, Tajikistan, CRC/C/TJK/CO/2, 5 February 2010, paras. 5, 17; Concluding Observations, Sri Lanka, CRC/C/LKA/CO/3-4, 19 October 2010, para. 17.

[124] *Free Legal Assistance Group and Others* v. *Zaire, Communications 25/89, 47/90, 56/91, 100/93, 1 October 2005*, ACommHPR (combination of a failure to respect and to fulfil rights). See also Paolo Mauro, 'Corruption and the Composition of Government Expenditure' (1998) 69 *Journal of Public Economics*, 2, 263–79: 264, finding a correlation between corruption and lower levels of investment in education.

[125] Julio Bacio Terracino, 'Hard Law Connections between Corruption and Human Rights', Paper presented at the Review Meeting: Corruption and Human Rights, Geneva, 2007, 30, explaining that 'embezzlement from a pension scheme will reduce the resources available for retired people and can result in payments that are not sufficient for living'.

cultural rights can be violated by corruption if the land resources used by a minority group to enjoy their culture are no longer available because a corrupt official bartered away land without consultation.[126]

In all these instances, ESCR are violated. Simultaneously, these violations overlap with conduct that is criminalised by an instrument of international criminal law – instruments that can thus potentially be invoked to curb at least some ESCR violations.

## 7.9 Destruction or theft of national treasures

Conventions prohibiting the illicit traffic in art and other forms of theft or destruction of national treasures also have the potential to address conduct that simultaneously amounts to an ESCR violation. The protection of natural treasures grew out of the regulation of armed conflict.[127] Over time, the concern for the protection of cultural property has extended to peacetime and to a wider range of national treasures and art.[128] The right to take part in cultural life can be affected by the destruction or the theft of national treasures, and this linkage deserves to be briefly analysed here.

The UNESCO Convention on the Means of Prohibiting and Preventing the Illicit Import, Export and Transfer of Ownership of Cultural Property expressly criminalises the unlawful import, export or transfer of ownership of cultural property.[129] The penal characteristics of the UNESCO Convention can overlap with violations of ESCR in the realm of the right of everyone to partake in cultural life. If public officials take part in the unlawful export of cultural property protected by the convention, such as 'objects of ethnological interest', and the state fails to monitor their conduct, the perpetrator's state likely violates the duty to protect cultural rights. The right to enjoy one's culture has been recognised to encompass physical access to

[126] Human Rights Committee, *General Comment 23 on the Rights of Minorities*, 8 April 1994, CCPR/C/21/Rev.1/Add.5, para. 7; *Ominayak and the Lubicon Lake Band* v. *Canada, 10 May 1990, CCPR/C/38/D/167/1984*, HRCttee, para. 33, concluding that the use of land is essential to the way of life and culture of minorities.

[127] See Section 5.2.2.3.

[128] Cherif Bassiouni, *International Criminal Law Conventions and Their Penal Provisions* (Transnational, 1997), 1019.

[129] Convention on the Means of Prohibiting and Preventing the Illicit Import, Export and Transfer of Ownership of Cultural Property, 14 November 1970 (entered into force 24 April 1972), Art. 3. The term 'shall be illicit' is equivalent to a duty to criminalise, confirmed by Arts. 6(b) and 8.

manifestations of culture,[130] thus including to cultural objects protected by the UNESCO Convention. Hence, if actors acting on behalf of a state allow the exportation of objects of ethnological interest, such as art objects unlawfully taken from indigenous peoples, such conduct simultaneously falls within the scope of the criminalised conduct of the international instrument as well as under the legal definition of a violation of ESCR.

## 7.10 Unlawful movements of hazardous waste and the use, import and export of persistent organic pollutants

International criminal law is also capable of addressing certain problems arising from hazardous waste and pollutants. Hazardous waste and persistent organic pollutants can have an adverse impact on the enjoyment of a range of human rights, particularly the right to health, the right to safe working conditions or the right to an adequate standard of living.[131] Unlawful transboundary movements of hazardous waste and, to a lesser extent, the use, import and export of persistent organic pollutants (POPs) are the subject of international instruments with penal characteristics. POPs are chemicals which remain intact in the environment for long periods and have adverse effects on human health. This section focuses on the overlap between the crime of transboundary waste movements and violations of ESCR, but the reasoning can be applied *mutatis mutandis* to the production and use of POPs, which is governed by the Stockholm Convention on Persistent Organic Pollutants, which establishes an explicit duty to prohibit the production and use of these substances.[132]

Given their severe impact on human rights, the international criminalisation of transboundary waste movement deserves more attention than it is currently given.[133] Unlawfully moving hazardous waste from

[130] Committee on Economic, Social and Cultural Rights, *General Comment 21 on the Right of Everyone to Take Part in Cultural Life*, 20 November 2009, E/C.12/GC/21, para. 49(d); Human Rights Committee, *General Comment 23 on the Rights of Minorities*, para. 7. For further references, see Chapter 5, Note 191.

[131] Stefano Sensi, 'The Adverse Effects of the Movement and Dumping of Toxic and Dangerous Products and Wastes on the Enjoyment of Human Rights', High-Level Expert Meeting, OHCHR, 2009.

[132] Stockholm Convention on Persistent Organic Pollutants, UNTS 2256, Stockholm, 22 May 2001 (entered into force 17 May 2004), Art. 3.

[133] The crime is not included in most textbooks on international criminal law, nor is it mentioned in Bassiouni's wide approach, despite the fact that the conventions would

one country to another not only constitutes a probable violation of the duty to respect or protect ESCR, but it can also fall within the scope of penal clauses of one or several of the treaties regulating the transnational movement of waste.

The subject of several court cases, the waste dumping in Côte d'Ivoire illustrates the possible overlap between violations of ESCR and conduct criminalised in international instruments. In July 2006, a ship chartered by Trafigura, a company operating from Geneva and Amsterdam, transported toxic waste from Dutch ports to Abidjan, where the waste was released by a local firm. The release of the chemicals resulted in 17 deaths and 30,000 injured.[134] A Dutch criminal court convicted the company itself and two employees for conduct occurring in The Netherlands.[135] In Côte d'Ivoire, a court found two non-Trafigura employees guilty of involvement in the dumping of the toxic waste.[136]

These court decisions do not, of course, prove the relationship between ESCR violations and the criminal provisions in the international instruments on the movement of hazardous waste. As previously explained, violations of ESCR require state responsibility, and that is something that criminal courts do not deal with, so the analysis of the courts must be complemented here. According to the domestic law of Côte d'Ivoire, the arrival of the ship must have been preceded by a permission to berth.[137] The officials who were informed about the arrival of the Trafigura ship apparently granted the company permission to clear the shipment in Abidjan.[138] No court has yet dealt with the allegations surrounding the possible involvement of Ivorian authorities.[139] But should it be accurate

meet his definitional criteria. Bassiouni, *International Criminal Law Conventions and Their Penal Provisions.*

134 The facts and the legal proceedings are summarised in FIDH et al., *L'Affaire du 'Probo Koala' ou la catastrophe du déversement des déchets toxiques en Côte d'Ivoire* (FIDH, 2011). See also Laura Pratt, 'Decreasing Dirty Dumping?' (2011) 35 *William and Mary Environmental Law and Policy Review*, 581–623: 581–5.

135 Probo Koala Case, *Uitspraak in Zaak Probo Koala (Broom II, Trafigura), 23 July 2010, Amsterdam District Court*, Netherlands. See also FIDH, 'L'affaire du Probo Koala relancée', www.fidh.org/L-affaire-du-PROBO-KOALA-relancee.

136 'Nigerian Gets 20 Years for Abidjan Toxic Waste Dumping', *Associated Press*, 23 October 2008.

137 Commission internationale d'enquête sur les déchets toxiques déversés dans le district d'Abidjan, *Rapport* (CIEDT, 2007), 85.

138 Ibid.

139 Rob White, 'Toxic Cities: Globalizing the Problem of Waste' (2008) 35 *Social Justice*, 3, 107–19: 111, referring to local press reports on the involvement of officials. See also FIDH et al., *L'Affaire du 'Probo Koala' ou la catastrophe du déversement des déchets toxiques en Côte d'Ivoire*, Section 1.3.2.

that Ivorian government officials were involved in this illegal conduct, the state of Côte d'Ivoire would have violated the duty to respect the right to health and other ESCR. Even without a direct and knowing involvement of state organs, Côte d'Ivoire would still be likely to have failed to protect ESCR, by insufficiently regulating and monitoring dangerous conduct affecting the right to health.[140]

Several instruments of international criminal law pertain to the issue. The most relevant instrument is the Basel Convention on the Control of Transboundary Movements of Hazardous Wastes and Their Disposal. The Basel Convention establishes rules aimed at regulating trade in waste, including by imposing strict liability on the corporate generator of such waste.[141] The instrument, however, only applies to 'waste', as opposed to 'products'.[142] This distinction is problematic in practice, and the legal distinction is 'irrelevant from the point of view of health and well-being'.[143] At the regional level, several relevant conventions have penal characteristics and are less limited in scope. The Convention on the Ban of Imports into Africa and the Control of Transboundary Movement and Management of Hazardous Wastes within Africa (Bamako Convention) addresses types of waste not covered in the Basel Convention.[144] In Europe, several conventions regulate liability for damage resulting in activities dangerous to the environment.[145]

Turning back to the Côte d'Ivoire case, we have established above that the waste dumping would be likely to constitute a violation of the right to health and other ESCR. The relevant provisions in the Basel and Bamako Conventions allow the conclusion that the unlawful movement

140 Committee on Economic, Social and Cultural Rights, *General Comment 14 on the Right to the Highest Attainable Standard of Health*, 11 August 2000, E/CN.12/2000/4, para. 51.

141 Basel Convention on the Control of Transboundary Movements of Hazardous Wastes and Their Disposal, UNTS 1673, 29 March 1989 (entered into force 5 May 1992).

142 Ibid., Art. 1.

143 Rob White, *Crimes against Nature* (Willan, 2008), 121.

144 Bamako Convention on the Ban of the Import into Africa and the Control of Transboundary Movement and Management of Hazardous Wastes within Africa, Bamako, 30 January 1991 (entered into force 22 April 1998). For instance, the Bamako Convention makes it harder than the Basel Convention to label exports as 'recycling'.

145 With penal characteristics: London Convention on the Prevention of Marine Pollution by Dumping of Wastes and Other Matter 1972 as amended by the 1996 Protocol Thereto, 13 November 1972 (the protocol entered into force 24 March 2006); Art. 10(2) of the Protocol establishes a duty to punish. The European Commission has the power to draft criminal laws on waste, because protecting the environment through a harmonisation of national criminal law is part of the objectives of the European Community. *Commission* v. *Council, C-176/03, on Council Framework Decision 2003/80 on the Protection of the Environment through Criminal Law, 13 September 2005 (Grand Chamber)*, European Court of Justice.

or disposal of waste not only constitutes a violation of ESCR but is also covered in international criminal law. The waste disposed in Abidjan squarely falls within the definitional scope of both conventions. First, the conduct is covered by Art. 4 of the Basel Convention, which requires state parties to criminalise the illegal transportation or disposal of hazardous wastes or other wastes.[146] Second, the conduct is covered by the Bamako Convention, which obliges state parties to establish a criminal offence over the import of all hazardous wastes, for any reasons, into Africa from non-contracting parties and which requires domestic criminalisation of all persons who have planned, carried out or assisted in illegal imports.[147] In such a scenario, the violations of ESCR fall within the ambit of the offences addressed in these two instruments of international criminal law.

## 7.11 Unlawful acts against internationally protected elements of the environment

Finally, there are treaties that suppress unlawful acts against internationally protected elements of the environment, and these treaties can simultaneously address certain ESCR violations. The protection of animal species by international conventions with penal characteristics dates back to the early twentieth century and started with the protection of fur seals, whales and the regulation of meshes of fishing nets.[148] Today, a wide range of acts against internationally protected elements of the environment are criminalised in a range of international conventions. They have potential, yet rarely acknowledged, links with ESCR violations.

Let us consider a scenario in which the same conduct constitutes a violation of certain ESCR and an offence under the Convention on International Trade in Endangered Species of Wild Fauna and Flora (CITES), the most widely ratified global instrument on trade in animals

[146] At least one of the substances dumped in Abidjan, sodium hydroxide, is inflammable and falls within several categories of the Basel Convention. Basel Convention, Art. I(1), covers inflammables; see Annex III. For the relevant criminalisation provisions, see Arts. 4(2)(g), 4(3), 4(4) and 4(7)(a).

[147] Inflammables are covered in the Bamako Convention, Annex I, at least by category Y35 and Annex II, category H8. For the relevant criminalisation provision, see Bamako Convention, Arts. 1 and 9(2).

[148] See Bassiouni, *International Criminal Law Conventions and Their Penal Provisions*, 1061–143.

and plants intended to prevent their extinction.[149] CITES heavily restricts the trade in extremely threatened species,[150] and requires export permits for other, less immediately threatened species.[151] States are obligated to penalise trade in violation of the treaty.[152] If government officials of a state party to CITES, for instance, participate in the export of endangered plants listed in Appendix I of the Convention, the conduct is not only covered by the suppression clause of CITES but may also constitute a violation of ESCR. Links between the successful protection of endangered species and the right to health were emphasised in an example of state practice when the South African government considered implementation measures for CITES.[153] A loss in biodiversity can result in the decline in animal and plant species containing therapeutic agents used in medicine,[154] including by indigenous groups, and may therefore hamper the right to health,[155] or the right to take part in cultural life of indigenous peoples.[156]

## 7.12 Conclusion

The definitions of international crimes examined in this chapter are scattered across a large number of sources. Their diversity in scope and context, their frequent requirement of transnationality and their reliance on the domestic criminal systems of each state suggest that these crimes are far from constituting a unified tool set for effectively addressing the

[149] Convention on International Trade in Endangered Species of Wild Fauna and Flora (CITES), 13 January 1976 (entered into force 1 July 1975).

[150] CITES, Arts. II and III and Appendix I. Species listed in Appendix I may only be traded if a scientific authority of the state has advised that such export will not be detrimental to the survival of that species.

[151] CITES, Arts. II and IV and Appendix II.

[152] CITES, Art. VIII(1)a.

[153] South African Human Rights Commission, 'Comments on National Environmental Management Biodiversity Act 2004: Draft CITES Regulations' (2009), 2.

[154] Belinda Hawkins, *Plants for Life: Medicinal Plant Conservation and Botanic Gardens* (Botanic Gardens Conservation International, 2008), 13, estimating that among the plants covered by CITES, about 240 are medical.

[155] Committee on Economic, Social and Cultural Rights, *General Comment 14 on the Right to the Highest Attainable Standard of Health*, para. 27, noting the relationship between the right to health, medicinal plants and indigenous peoples' traditional environment. See also *Yanomami Indians* v. *Brazil, 5 March 1985, IACommHR Report OEA/Ser.L/V/II.66*, IACommHR, para. 10(e), access to forests, the right to health and cultural life.

[156] Committee on Economic, Social and Cultural Rights, *General Comment 21 on the Right of Everyone to Take Part in Cultural Life*, para. 62. The CESCR notes that violations of the right to take part in cultural life can occur when states prevent access to cultural goods and services.

majority of ESCR violations. Nevertheless, the examined sources of definitions of international crimes do have the potential to address conduct that simultaneously gives rise to a violation of ESCR. Where overlap exists between violations of ESCR and the definition of one of the examined crimes, the violations of ESCR may thus also be addressed from the angle of international criminal law. Crucially, this implies that the cooperative mechanisms of the various instruments are pertinent to deal with certain ESCR violations. This is particularly valuable given that the international obligations contained in most treaties seen in this chapter include elaborate provisions of international cooperation that are often lacking in human rights law.

The potential to consider whether at least some ESCR abuses could be confronted by using the instruments of international criminal law – such as the ones studied in this chapter, but also those pertaining to crimes against humanity, war crimes and genocide – has been almost completely overlooked in the past. Chapter 8 thus undertakes to explore the legal corollaries of the findings made so far.

# 8

# Corollaries of qualifying ESCR violations as international crimes

Qualifying facts as international crimes carries a range of legal and other consequences. The legal corollaries vary for each category of crime and according to the different sources applicable to the situation.

Before we can consider the range of corollaries of the demonstration that ESCR violations can overlap with crimes relevant to international law, a cautionary note must be sounded. As we noted in Chapter 3, the international crimes analysed in this study are very diverse. Not all international crimes attract the same legal consequences. Although generalisations are difficult to draw, there are usually more legal consequences to classifying certain conduct as one of the international crimes that is directly criminalised at the international level than those that arise when an international treaty obliges states to suppress certain conduct in their domestic jurisdictions.

Table 8.1 provides an overview of legal corollaries of international crimes. In the following section (Section 8.1), we will consider how qualification of ESCR violations as an international crime influences whether the ICC has jurisdiction. Section 8.2 examines the jurisdiction (both criminal and civil) of national tribunals as well as state obligations that arise when international crimes have allegedly been committed. Sections 8.3, 8.4 and 8.5 address the corollaries of this study's findings for truth commissions and similar mechanisms, for non-state actors as well as for the UN Security Council.

## 8.1 Jurisdiction and reparation before the International Criminal Court

The qualification of ESCR violations as international crimes can imply that the ICC is competent and that it can potentially order reparations for victims.[1] The ICC can exercise jurisdiction over cases of alleged genocide, crimes against humanity, war crimes and – once amendments enter into force – the crime of aggression.[2] Where ESCR violations amount to one of these crimes (as defined in the Rome Statute) and where they can be traced to individual offenders, such abuses can be adjudicated before the ICC, if the court has jurisdiction over the situation and the alleged perpetrator, and if the case is admissible.

The rules establishing the jurisdiction and admissibility are obviously the same whether or not the facts of the case overlap with violations of ESCR. Reference is therefore made to the general literature on jurisdiction and admissibility.[3] Once a prosecution before the ICC is successful, the convicted individual can be sentenced to imprisonment, including life imprisonment. Whether or not the facts of a case involve ESCR abuses, the ICC (and other tribunals) must take care to respect the convicted individuals' right to not be subject to arbitrary penalty.[4]

If an accused is convicted, the court can also order that assets of the perpetrator be used for reparations: the court may order a fine or a forfeiture of proceeds, property and assets derived from the commission of the crime.[5] The Statute of the ICC is the first international criminal tribunal for which states have created a regime for reparations to victims. In the first case that reached a judgment, the trial chamber rendered a separate landmark decision on the principles and procedures that shall be applied to reparations for victims and emphasised the need for consulting the families and communities in setting up measures of restitution, compensation and rehabilitation. The chamber decided that the Trust Fund for Victims should implement the decision and award reparations.[6]

1 It is also possible that another international or hybrid tribunal is competent, depending on whether the case falls within the limited geographic, temporal and material jurisdiction of such an institution. The rules are specific to each tribunal and are not further examined in this study since they are dealt with elsewhere in the literature. For an overview of the jurisdictional regimes, see Ilias Bantekas, *International Criminal Law*, 4th edn (Hart, 2010).

2 Rome Statute of the International Criminal Court, 2187 UNTS 90, 17 July 1998 (entered into force 1 July 2002), Art. 5.

3 For example William Schabas, *Commentary on the Rome Statute* (Oxford University Press, 2010), 273–373.

4 Existing international criminal tribunals have handled sentences inconsistently in the case law, raising concerns of fairness. See Damien Scalia, *Du principe de légalité des peines en droit international pénal* (Bruylant, 2011).

5 Rome Statute, Art. 77.

6 *Prosecutor* v. *Lubanga Dyilo, Decision Establishing the Principles and Procedures to Be Applied to Reparations, 7 August 2012, Trial Chamber I, ICC-01/04-01/06*, ICC.

Table 8.1. *Legal corollaries of a finding that ESCR violations overlap with an international crime*

| | | Corollaries | | | | | | | | | |
|---|---|---|---|---|---|---|---|---|---|---|---|
| | | *ICC (subject matter jurisdiction, reparations)* | *National courts (permissive universal jurisdiction)* | *Duty of states to extradite or prosecute?* | *Duty of states to investigate and prosecute?* | *Duty of states to provide other remedies/ reparations?* | *Duty of states to avoid or remove obstacles (e.g., amnesties, limitations)?* | *Duty of states to cooperate?* | *Can truth commissions, national human rights institutions or vetting be used?* | *Liability of non-state actors?* | *Is the SC empowered to take measures under chapter VII, UN Charter?* |
| Crime | *Aggression* | yes | no | no | (no) – disputed | (probably not) | yes | yes, under Rome Statute | yes | no | yes, if threat to peace and security |
| | *Crimes against humanity (CAH)* | yes | yes | yes | not clearly established, but failure may amount to human rights violation | yes, under human rights law | yes | yes, under Rome Statute | yes | yes | yes, if threat to peace and security |
| | *Genocide* | yes | yes | yes | see above CAH | yes, under human rights law | yes | yes, under Rome Statute | yes | yes | yes, if threat to peace and security |
| | *Grave breaches* | yes | yes | yes | yes, particu-larly for grave breaches committed by the state's own nationals | yes, under human rights law and possi-bly IHL | yes | yes, under Rome Statute | yes | yes | yes, if threat to peace and security |

| | | | | | | | | | | | |
|---|---|---|---|---|---|---|---|---|---|---|---|
| | *Other war crimes* | yes | yes | no | see above CAH | yes, under human rights law and possibly IHL | yes | yes, under Rome Statute | yes | yes | yes, if threat to peace and security |
| | *Torture (UNCAT)* | no | yes | yes | see above CAH, explicit obligation to investigate | yes | no, if consistent with other obligations | yes | yes | yes | unlikely, but yes if threat to peace and security |
| | *Crimes such as laundering proceeds of crimes, unlawful movement of waste, etc.* | no | usually not, depends on terms of applicable instrument(s) | often yes, depends on terms of applicable instrument(s) | see above CAH | yes, under human rights law/specific obligations of applicable instruments | no, if consistent with other obligations | yes | yes | yes | yes, if threat to peace and security |
| | *Apartheid (Apartheid Convention)* | no, only if crime against humanity | yes | implicit in obligation to prosecute | yes | yes, under human rights law | yes | yes | yes | yes | yes, if threat to peace and security |
| | *Slavery and related practices* | no, only if crime against humanity | yes | often yes, depends on terms of applicable instrument(s) | often yes, depends on terms of applicable instrument(s) | yes, under human rights law/specific obligations of applicable instruments | no, if consistent with other obligations | yes | yes | yes | yes, if threat to peace and security |

This trust fund was set up by the Assembly of States Parties in 2002 and may use its funds for assistance 'for the benefits of victims' beyond individual reparation orders and before a conviction is made.[7]

As soon as overlap between ESCR violations and a crime under the ICC Statute is suspected, the avenues to rely on the jurisdiction and the corresponding remedial mechanisms of the ICC are potentially open to victims in the same way as they are for any alleged crimes under the Rome Statute.

Yet, even if the establishment of the ICC is a significant addition to the institutional landscape of international criminal law, it remains true that the international prosecution of international crimes is embryonic. Moreover, the principle of complementarity enshrined in the Rome Statute means that the ICC only steps in where national attempts to establish accountability are lacking or flawed. The authorities at the national level remain the primary enforcer of the prohibitions of international criminal law. We shall therefore consider the jurisdiction in national courts and the obligations of states to take action against international crimes.

## 8.2 Jurisdiction in national courts and state obligations to take action against international crimes

### *8.2.1 Jurisdiction*

National tribunals can assert jurisdiction over serious ESCR abuses that amount to international crimes. The following principles pertain to the establishment of jurisdiction in national courts and allow national tribunals to address certain international crimes overlapping with ESCR violations.[8]

#### 8.2.1.1 Territoriality, active personality, passive personality and the protective principle

The state on whose territory a crime has been perpetrated generally has jurisdiction over that crime. From a practical point of view, it is most

[7] ICC Rules of Procedure and Evidence, ICC-ASP/1/3 (Part.II-A), Rule 98(5). The fund has so far allocated general assistance to victims in Uganda and in the DRC. Trust Fund for Victims, www.trustfundforvictims.org.

[8] The most influential study systematically distinguishing such principles was Michael Akehurst, 'Jurisdiction' (1972) 46 *British Yearbook of International Law*, 145–257: 152, Section II.1 on criminal trials.

often the territorial state that is best placed to conduct the investigation and to prosecute the offence. Which state has *territorial jurisdiction* is frequently unproblematic to establish, particularly when all elements of the criminal conduct have taken place within the same jurisdiction.[9]

Domestic tribunals can also assert criminal jurisdiction over offences perpetrated by their nationals abroad. Many treaties on international crimes foresee the so-called *active personality* principle. The UN Convention against Torture (UNCAT) and UNTOC, for instance, oblige or permit states to establish jurisdiction over offences if the alleged offender is a national of that state.[10] A Dutch case based on the active nationality principle illustrates the relevance of this jurisdictional principle for the analysis of this study. The District Court of The Hague convicted Frans van Anraat, a Dutch businessman, of complicity in the war crime of inhumane treatment. By selling chemicals to Saddam Hussein's security forces, he knowingly enabled the regime to produce mustard gas for unlawful attacks against the Kurds in Iraq.[11] The mustard gas delivered to the Iraqi regime not only ruined the health of those who survived, but also enabled the regime to implement a 'strict economic blockade of the area permitting no foodstuffs, persons, cattle or machinery to reach the villages'.[12] The state of Iraq during the Anfal Campaign undoubtedly violated people's rights to food, health, housing or water of the Kurdish population living in the affected area. Van Anraat can thus be said to have been involved in conduct that can simultaneously be described as a gross violation of ESCR (attributable to the state of Iraq) and a war crime (giving rise to his personal criminal responsibility). Based on the active personality principle, the Dutch court was able to exercise jurisdiction over a war crime that overlapped with ESCR violations.

*Passive personality* is the exercise of jurisdiction based on the nationality of the victim, in situations where the crime takes place abroad. Many

[9] If a crime is not confined to the boundaries of one state and more than one state may want to exercise jurisdiction, states resort to international principles, considerations of comity or bilateral arrangements to decide which state should be given priority. For a useful outline, see Bantekas, *International Criminal Law*, 334.

[10] Convention against Torture and Other Cruel, Inhuman or Degrading Treatment or Punishment, GA Res. 39/46 (1984), 10 December 1984 (entered into force 26 June 1987), Art. 5(1)b (obligatory; UN Convention against Transnational Organized Crime, GA Res. 55/383, 15 November 2000 (entered into force 29 September 2003), Art. 15(2)b (permissive).

[11] *Prosecutor* v. *van Anraat, 23 December 2005, The Hague District Court, The Netherlands.*

[12] Ibid., para. 121.

multilateral treaties provide for permissive or mandatory jurisdiction based on the passive personality principle.[13] Article 5(1)c of UNCAT, for instance, authorises, but does not obligate, states to establish criminal jurisdiction if the victim is a national of the state asserting jurisdiction.[14] When an Israeli district court tried Eichmann for starvation, the court emphasised that there was a strong link between the victims of Eichmann's crimes and the state of Israel and that Israel could therefore exercise jurisdiction.[15]

The (controversial) *protective principle* purports that a state can criminalise conduct that occurs extraterritorially when such conduct affects its national interest. The Israeli district court in *Eichmann* also referred to the protection of its 'vital interests' as a ground for establishing jurisdiction over Eichmann.[16] The *Eichmann* case, however, most famously stands for what has become known as 'universal jurisdiction', the jurisdictional principle examined next.

#### 8.2.1.2 Universal jurisdiction

Universal jurisdiction refers to the exercise of jurisdiction over an alleged perpetrator of crimes that were not committed on the territory of the prosecuting state, nor by its nationals, nor with any other connection to the state.[17] 'The jurisdiction to try crimes under international law is universal',[18] said the Israeli district court when trying Eichmann. Because the starvation and the other crimes for which Eichmann was tried (war crimes and crimes against humanity) were grave offences against the law of nations, it was, according to the court, incumbent on the organs of every country 'to give effect to its criminal interdictions'.[19] This principle thus

[13] See for instance UNTOC, Art. 15(2) (permissive) or International Convention for the Suppression of Terrorist Bombings, GA Res. 52/49, 15 December 1997 (entered into force 23 May 2001), Art. 8 (mandatory establishment of jurisdiction).

[14] UNCAT, Art. 5(1)c. See, for instance, also UNTOC, Art. 15(2)a.

[15] *The Attorney-General of Israel* v. *Eichmann, 36 ILR 5 (1968), 24 July 1996, District Court of Jerusalem, Israel*, 38.

[16] Ibid., para. 35.

[17] ILC, Preliminary Report on the Obligation to Extradite or Prosecute (Zdzislaw Galicki), A/CN.4/571, 7 June 2006, para. 19.

[18] *The Attorney-General of Israel* v. *Eichmann, 36 ILR 5 (1968), 24 July 1996, District Court of Jerusalem, Israel*, 26. For the roots of the concept of universal jurisdiction: Emer de Vattel, *The Law of Nations* (Johnson, 1855), 54–5; Hugo Grotius, *On the Law of War and Peace, 1625* (Kessinger, 2004), Book 2, chapter 21.

[19] *The Attorney-General of Israel* v. *Eichmann, 36 ILR 5 (1968), 24 July 1996, District Court of Jerusalem, Israel*, 26.

enables national courts to exercise jurisdiction over ESCR-related abuses that overlap with international crimes.

Two forms of universal jurisdiction must be distinguished. First, permissive universal jurisdiction means that a state may, but is not required to, exercise jurisdiction over an alleged crime that has no link to the prosecuting state. Second, in some instances, international law not only permits universal jurisdiction, but imposes on states the obligation of 'extradite or prosecute' (*aut dedere aut judicare*). This second aspect will be discussed in Section 8.2.2.1.

State practice in the exercise of permissive universal jurisdiction is rare and inconsistent – sometimes the practice is inconsistent even within the same jurisdiction. Nevertheless, states, national courts and publicists widely agree that states may assert jurisdiction over the following crimes analysed in this study, even when there is no nexus with the prosecuting state and including where the factual background of the case relates to people's enjoyment of ESCR: war crimes,[20] crimes against humanity,[21] genocide,[22]

[20] Jean-Marie Henckaerts and Louise Doswald-Beck (eds.), *Customary IHL*, 2 vols., vol. 1 (Cambridge University Press, 2005), Rule 156. It should be noted that as with grave breaches, states are required to prosecute such war crimes if committed by their own nationals. *Prosecutor* v. *Đajić, 23 May 1997, in 92 American Journal of International Law 528, Supreme Court of Bavaria, Germany; Prosecutor v. Grabez, 18 April 1997, Tribunal militaire de division I, Switzerland*, finding that the tribunal has jurisdiction over war crimes committed in the former Yugoslavia.

[21] *The Attorney-General of Israel* v. *Eichmann, 36 ILR 5 (1968), 24 July 1996, District Court of Jerusalem, Israel; Fédération nationale des déportés et internés résistants et patriotes* v. *Barbie, 78 ILR 125 (1985), 20 December 1985, Cour de cassation, France, 130; In re Demjanjuk, 612 F. Supp. 544 (N.D. Ohio 1985), USA*, 556; Cherif Bassiouni, *Crimes against Humanity* (Kluwer, 1999), 240; *In re Pinochet, 8 November 1998, Tribunal of First Instance of Brussels (Investigating Magistrate), in American Journal of International Law, Vol. 93, 700–3, Belgium*, 703, 'as a matter of customary international law ... universal jurisdiction over crimes against humanity exists'. See also comments by governments: ILC, The Obligation to Extradite or Prosecute, A/CN.4/612, 6 March 2009, para. 19 (Belgium) and para. 36 (Canada). DeGuzman posits that although the concept of universal jurisdiction remains controversial, 'proponents of universal jurisdiction invariably include crimes against humanity within its scope'. Margaret DeGuzman, 'Crimes against Humanity', in *Research Handbook on International Criminal Law*, ed. Bartram Brown (Elgar, 2011), 62–83: 64.

[22] *In re Pinochet, in 93 American Journal of International Law 690 (1999), 4 November 1998, Spanish National Court, Criminal Division (Plenary Session), Spain; Guatemala Genocide Case, Resolución No. Stc 237/2005, 26 September 2005, Constitutional Court, Spain.* The Genocide Convention does not provide for compulsory universal jurisdiction, but a state fails to prevent genocide if it does not make genocide a crime in national law or fails to punish persons guilty of it. This is, for instance, the view adopted in the Restatement of the Law, Third, Foreign Relations Law of the United States, 1987.

apartheid,[23] torture,[24] certain terrorist offences[25] and slavery on the high seas.[26] Regional developments on the African continent suggest that, over time, states may accept to strengthen their national laws in order to rely on universal jurisdiction for a broader list of offences.[27] Moreover, civil society and legal experts have called for an expansion of universal jurisdiction to trafficking in human beings and 'certain other crimes that have major adverse economic, social or cultural consequences – such as acts of plunder and gross misappropriation of public resources, ... and serious environmental crimes'.[28]

While the scope of universal jurisdiction provisions in domestic law inevitably varies, most states provide for universal jurisdiction at least for genocide, war crimes and torture; many provide also for crimes against humanity. With continuing legislative efforts of states to implement the Rome Statute into domestic law, national legislation establishing jurisdiction over international crimes has become widespread.[29]

[23] International Convention on the Suppression and Punishment of the Crime of Apartheid, GA Res. 3068 (XXVIII), 30 November 1973 (entered into force 18 July 1976), Art. 4(b).

[24] *Regina* v. *Bartle (Ex Parte Pinochet No. 3); Regina* v. *Evans, 6 BHRC 24, 24 March 1999, House of Lords, United Kingdom; In re Munyeshyaka, 6 January 1998, Cour de cassation (Chambre criminelle), France; Prosecutor* v. *Nzapali, Trial Judgment, 7 April 2004, District Court of Rotterdam, The Netherlands.*

[25] Convention for the Suppression of Unlawful Seizure of Aircraft, 860 UNTS 105 (1971), 16 December 1970 (entered into force 14 October 1971), Art. 4; International Convention against the Taking of Hostages, GA Res. 34/146, 1035 UNTS 167, 18 December 1979 (entered into force 3 June 1983), Art. 5; Convention on the Safety of United Nations and Associated Personnel, GA Res. 49/49 (1994), 9 December 1994 (entered into force 15 January 1999), Art. 10.

[26] UN Convention on the Law of the Sea, GA Res. 48/263, 1833 UNTS 396, 10 December 1982 (entered into force 14 November 1994), Art. 99 (limited jurisdiction over slave transport on the high seas).

[27] African Union Model National Law on Universal Jurisdiction over International Crimes, Prepared at the Meeting of Government Experts and Ministers of Justice/Attorneys General on Legal Matters, 7–15 May 2012, Addis Ababa, Exp/Min/Legal/VI and Endorsed by the Assembly of the AU, 19th Ordinary Session, 15–16 July 2012, Assembly/AU/Dec.419(XIX). The model national law suggests that states should exercise universal jurisdiction over genocide, crimes against humanity, war crimes, piracy, trafficking in narcotics and terrorism as such (rather than only certain terrorist acts).

[28] Cairo-Arusha Principles on Universal Jurisdiction in Respect of Gross Human Rights Offences: An African Perspective, Adopted at Meetings Convened by Africa Legal Aid, 21 October 2002, Principle 4.

[29] Recent national legislation has been adopted in Albania, Argentina, Azerbaijan, Bosnia and Herzegovina, Burkina Faso, Cape Verde, Colombia, El Salvador, Estonia, Finland, Georgia, Kazakhstan, Kenya, Macedonia, Montenegro, Namibia, Peru, Portugal, Serbia, Switzerland and Uruguay. See Amnesty International, *Universal Jurisdiction: A Preliminary Survey of Legislation around the World* (Amnesty International, 2011).

Whenever a violation of ESCR is ascertained to be an international crime over which a state has universal jurisdiction, the specific domestic rules of this state have to be analysed in order to assess whether all requirements for the establishment of jurisdiction are met. Some jurisdictions require the physical presence of the alleged perpetrator on their territory.[30] Others only allow the exercise of universal jurisdiction if the defendant or the victim resides in their jurisdiction.[31] A third group of states grant the public prosecutor discretion in deciding whether to prosecute crimes with no other jurisdictional link.[32] A comparative study found that more than two-thirds of all states have laws that allow them to exercise universal jurisdiction over one or more crimes.[33] A database of the ICC contains such national legislation from most countries of the world.[34]

Despite existing legislation, few national tribunals have exercised universal jurisdiction, and existing universal jurisdiction cases for conduct that constitutes violations of ESCR are even rarer. Yet, it is notable that the 'founding case' of prosecutions based on universal jurisdiction, *Eichmann*, led to a conviction for starvation as a crime against humanity and as a war crime.[35] A more recent case that illustrates that certain ESCR violations can be part of universal jurisdiction prosecutions is the conviction of Mirsad Repak before the Norwegian Supreme Court. Among other charges, Repak, a former member of the Croatian Defence Forces, was found guilty of depriving victims of adequate access to food in a detention camp,[36] illustrating that universal jurisdiction is available to

[30] This, for instance, is the case in Switzerland and in the Netherlands: Code pénal suisse, 21 December 1937, Ro 54 781, Art. 264m; International Crimes Act of the Netherlands, Stb. 2003, 270, 19 June 2003, Art. 2(1a).

[31] Steven Ratner, 'Belgium's War Crimes Statute' (2003) 97 *American Journal of International Law*, 4, 888–97: after August 2003, universal jurisdiction is only possible if the defendant or victim is a citizen or resident of Belgium.

[32] For instance, Act to Introduce the Code of Crimes against International Law of 26 June 2002, Art. 3, Amendments to the Code of Criminal Procedure.

[33] *Amnesty International, Universal Jurisdiction: A Preliminary Survey of Legislation around the World*, 1. See also, ICRC, 'Analysis of the Punishments Applicable to International Crimes (War Crimes, Crimes against Humanity and Genocide) in Domestic Law and Practice', 2008) 90 *International Review of the Red Cross*, 870, 461–8.

[34] International Criminal Court, 'ICC Legal Tools Database', www.legal-tools.org/en/go-to-database.

[35] *The Attorney-General of Israel* v. *Eichmann, 36 ILR 277 (1968), 29 May 1962, Supreme Court, Israel*, 277–8.

[36] *Prosecutor* v. *Mirsad Repak, Hr-2011-00808-A, Case No. 2010/934, 13 April 2011, Supreme Court, Norway*, para. 82.

establish accountability over ESCR deprivations that overlap with international crimes.

### 8.2.2 *State obligations to take action against and to remedy international crimes*

For those ESCR violations that can be qualified as an international crime such as genocide, crimes against humanity or war crimes, states have a range of particular obligations under international law (i) to extradite or prosecute those alleged of crimes, (ii) to investigate and prosecute such crimes and provide remedies, (iii) to abstain from granting or to remove obstacles from prosecution, (iv) to cooperate with other states and (v) to deny refugee status to individuals if there are serious reasons for considering that they have committed such crimes. For other international crimes, states' obligations are specific to the terms of each suppression convention and generally include the obligation to cooperate with other states to bring alleged perpetrators to justice.

#### 8.2.2.1 The obligation to extradite or prosecute

Several international treaties oblige the state parties to either prosecute alleged perpetrators of certain crimes or extradite them. The so-called *aut dedere aut judicare* principle denotes the obligation of a state on whose territory a person suspected of a crime is located to either extradite that person or submit the case to its competent authorities for the purpose of prosecution whether or not the alleged conduct relates to ESCR violations or other abuses.

Clauses with an obligation to extradite or prosecute have been included in almost two dozen other widely ratified treaties,[37] showing that states have undisputed obligations to either prosecute or extradite alleged perpetrators of certain crimes. If ESCR violations overlap with such crimes, states must take care to comply with these obligations in order to deny safe haven to alleged perpetrators.

A related set of questions is whether in some cases states *must* prosecute individuals, and whether they must do so despite impediments such as amnesties or statutes of limitations, and what remedies states must grant to victims. The scope of obligations to investigate, prosecute and

[37] Amnesty International, *International Law Commission: The Obligation to Extradite or Prosecute* (Amnesty International, 2009), 29–30, identifying twenty treaties containing obligations to extradite or prosecute.

provide other remedies is the subject of debate in international law.[38] Nonetheless, there is enough support to conclude that states have particular obligations to address conduct amounting to international crimes committed by violating ESCR.

#### 8.2.2.2 Obligations to provide a remedy, to investigate and to prosecute

States have international obligations to investigate and prosecute allegations that, if true, amount to certain international crimes. Victims have a right to a remedy for grave human rights abuses, and judicial investigations and prosecutions often constitute such a remedy for abuses displaying overlap between ESCR violations and international crimes.

Sources for obligations to investigate and prosecute include IHL and human rights law, as well as the ICC Statute. The sources in IHL and human rights law are examined first, before turning to the obligations to prosecute under the Rome Statute.

Under IHL, states have the obligation to prosecute grave breaches committed by their own nationals.[39] The Geneva Conventions provide that each state party also has an obligation to 'take measures necessary for the suppression of all acts contrary to the provisions of the present Convention *other* than the grave breaches'.[40] There would also seem to be an implicit obligation to investigate all crimes for which a state has the obligation to extradite or prosecute alleged perpetrators, because without an investigation, states are unable to decide whether or not they must extradite or prosecute. The ICRC further posits that it identified sufficient state practice and *opinio juris* to conclude that this obligation extends to all war crimes committed by the state's nationals or on their territory, including in non-international armed conflict.[41]

Under human rights law, the failure to investigate and prosecute crimes can constitute a violation of the right to a remedy, and this conclusion is valid whether a state fails to investigate or prosecute crimes

[38] See, for instance, Diane Orentlicher, 'Settling Accounts Revisited' (2007) 1 *International Journal of Transitional Justice*, 1, 10–22; Michael Scharf, 'The Letter of the Law: The Scope of the International Legal Obligation to Prosecute Human Rights Crimes' (1996) 59 *Law and Contemporary Problems*, 4, 41–61: 44.

[39] This obligation is construed from the absolute obligation to extradite or prosecute those alleged of grave breaches, and the assumption that most states will prefer not to extradite their own nationals, and must, hence, prosecute them. For the definition of grave breaches, see Section 5.1.

[40] GVA Conventions, Arts. 49/50/129(3)/146 (emphasis added).

[41] Henckaerts and Doswald-Beck (eds.), *Customary IHL*, vol. 1, rule 158.

overlapping with ESCR violations or any other crimes.[42] Where the commission of a crime involves a violation of the right to life, case law of regional human rights courts affirms the duty of the state to investigate, including in cases in which life was under threat from non-state actors.[43] For states parties to the UN Genocide Convention, the state on whose territory genocide was committed bears a duty to prosecute alleged perpetrators.[44] Other states may do the same.[45] State parties to the Apartheid Convention undertook to prosecute apartheid, including in the absence of links to the prosecuting state.[46] The HRCttee concluded that the obligation of states to provide an effective remedy must include a criminal investigation in cases of abuses amounting to torture.[47] The obligation to investigate is explicit in UNCAT, which demands 'prompt and impartial investigations, wherever there is reasonable ground to believe that an act of torture has been committed'.[48] Regional human rights courts and commissions have also insisted on the obligations to investigate and prosecute serious abuses.[49] The Updated Set of Principles for the Protection and Promotion of Human Rights through Action to Combat Impunity refers to states' obligation to 'take appropriate measures in respect of the perpetrators, particularly in the area of criminal justice, by ensuring that those responsible for serious crimes under

[42] In *Pinochet*, Lord Hope and Lord Millet stated that the status of a norm of *jus cogens* – which would include all international crimes – implies an *erga omnes* obligation on all states to investigate and punish such conduct. *Regina* v. *Bartle (Ex Parte Pinochet No. 3); Regina* v. *Evans, 6 BHRC 24, 24 March 1999, House of Lords, United Kingdom*, Lord Hope, at 42, Lord Millet, at 66. The same was said of crimes against humanity. *Adolfo Scilingo, Sentencia por crímenes contra la humanidad, 19 April 2005, Audiencia nacional, Spain*: The *jus cogens* prohibition of crimes against humanity entails an *erga omnes* authorisation on all states to repress such crimes.

[43] For a typical case before the ECtHR, see *Ergi* v. *Turkey, Application No. 23818/94, 28 July 1998*, ECtHR, para. 82.

[44] Convention on the Prevention and Punishment of the Crime of Genocide, GA Res. 260 (III) A, 9 December 1948 (entered into force 12 January 1951), Art. VI.

[45] *Application of the Convention on the Prevention and Punishment of the Crime of Genocide (Bosnia and Herzegovina* v. *Serbia and Montenegro), 26 February 2007*, ICJ, para. 442.

[46] Apartheid Convention, Art. IV(b).

[47] The committee has held such in more than 50 views. For a recent example, see *Gapirjanova* v. *Uzbekistan, 11 May 2010, CCPR/C/98/D/1589/2007*, HRCttee, para. 8.3.

[48] UNCAT, Art. 12. The CAT Committee held that this obligation also applies to CIDT: *Abad* v. *Spain, 14 May 1998, CAT/C/20/D/59/1996*, CAT Committee, para. 8.2.

[49] *Velásquez* v. *Guatemala, Judgment (Merits) of 25 November 2000, Case No. 91/129, IACtHR Report (Ser. C) No. 70 (2000)*, IACtHR, para. 174. For allegations of torture and CIDT, the obligation to investigate is explicit. See Inter-American Convention to Prevent and Punish Torture, OAS Treaty Series, No. 67, 9 December 1985 (entered into force 28 February 1987), Art. 8.

international law are prosecuted, tried and duly punished'.[50] The obligation to provide effective remedies stemming from human rights law treaties also encompasses obligations to provide reparation, including, where appropriate, monetary compensation.[51] Given the evidence that ESCR violations can overlap with international crimes, it follows that states have particular duties to investigate, prosecute and remedy such abuses.

Other remedies, in addition to investigations and prosecutions, are often required to repair and overcome the legacy of past crimes. Developments over the last two decades illustrate the increasing prominence of remedial justice, not only for victims of international crimes, but also for victims of human rights violations and serious violations of IHL. In 2005, the GA adopted the UN Basic Principles and Guidelines on the Right to a Remedy and Reparation for Victims of Gross Violations of International Human Rights Law and Serious Violations of International Humanitarian Law.[52] While some aspects of these principles go beyond existing law, it is clear that the question of remedies and reparations for victims of international crimes is taken more and more seriously in international law and practice,[53] although remedies often fall short of victims' expectations and needs.[54] Those violations of ESCR that are deemed international crimes clearly fall within the scope of the UN Guiding Principles, which stipulate that states should 'make available all appropriate legal, diplomatic and consular means to ensure that victims can exercise their rights to remedy for gross violations of international human rights law or serious violations of international humanitarian law'.[55]

[50] Report of the Independent Expert to Update the Set of Principles to Combat Impunity (Diane Orentlicher), E/CN.4/2005/102/Add.1, 8 February 2005, Principle 19.

[51] Dinah Shelton, *Remedies*, 2nd edn (Oxford University Press, 2005), 14–22.

[52] Basic Principles and Guidelines on the Right to a Remedy and Reparation for Victims of Gross Violations of International Human Rights Law and Serious Violations of International Humanitarian Law, GA Res. 60/147, 16 December 2005.

[53] The Inter-American Court of Human Rights (IACtHR) has set a precedent on remedies for conflict-related ESCR problems: in the *Plan de Sánchez* case, the court recommended that Guatemala maintain and improve the sewage system and potable water supplies in the communities affected by the armed conflict. *Plan de Sánchez Massacre* v. *Guatemala, Reparations, Judgment of 19 November 2004, IACtHR Report (Ser. C) No. 116 (2004)*, IACtHR, para. 90.

[54] For systematic accounts of remedial justice, see Dinah Shelton, 'Principles and Guidelines on Reparations', in *Out of the Ashes: Reparation for Victims of Gross and Systematic Human Rights Violations*, ed. Marc Bossuyt, et al. (Intersentia, 2005), 11–34; Ilaria Bottigliero, *Redress for Victims of Crimes under International Law* (Nijhoff, 2004).

[55] Basic Principles and Guidelines on the Right to a Remedy and Reparation, Principle 12(d).

Where abuses have been widespread, out-of-court reparations programmes are often appropriate. Several states have established reparations programmes for survivors of international crimes. In the future, these programmes should be tailored in a way that does not automatically preclude access to reparations for survivors of ESCR abuses, at the very least those amounting to international crimes. It thus seems urgent to question which socio-economic abuses amount to international crimes whenever states set up a reparations programme as the *a priori* exclusion of ESCR will fall short of the requirements of the UN Guiding Principles. A number of countries emerging from a legacy of widespread abuse have designed reparations programmes that include at least some harm related to abuses in the realm of ESCR.[56]

In addition to IHL and human rights law, the Rome Statute also deals with obligations to provide remedies, to investigate and to prosecute. The preamble provides that 'the most serious crimes of concern to the international community as a whole must not go unpunished' and further recalls 'the duty of every State to exercise its criminal jurisdiction over those responsible for international crimes'.[57] By recalling obligations of *every* state, the drafters refer to duties incumbent upon states independent of the ICC Statute. This endorsement by states provides support of the above-stated view that states have certain duties to investigate and prosecute that pre-existed the adoption of the Rome Statute.[58] Since the preamble refers to those crimes for which there was or is an obligation to investigate and prosecute independent of the Rome Statute, such obligations must relate to violations which are recognised as international

[56] The literature on the experience on Guatemalan, Peruvian and Moroccan reparations programmes is particularly relevant. For an overview, see OHCHR, Transitional Justice and Economic, Social and Cultural Rights, HR/PUB/13/5, 2014, 40–4. The Commission for Historical Clarification in Guatemala recommended that victims of forced displacement receive reparations and that the reparations programme includes forced displacement on the list of abuses meriting reparation. Roger Duthie, 'Displacement' (2011) 5 *International Journal of Transitional Justice*, 241–61: 246. On Peru, see Lisa Laplante and Kimberly Theidon, 'Truth with Consequences' (2007) 29 *Human Rights Quarterly*, 228–50; Lisa Magarrell and Leonardo Filippini, *The Legacy of Truth* (ICTJ, 2006). For Morocco, see, for instance, Conseil consultatif des droits de l'homme and ICTJ, 'The Rabat Report: The Concept and Challenges of Collective Reparations' (2009). Generally, see Pablo de Greiff (ed.), *The Handbook of Reparations* (Oxford University Press, 2006).

[57] Rome Statute, Preamble, paras. 4, 6.

[58] This is also the view of Jann Kleffner, *Complementarity in the Rome Statute* (Oxford University Press, 2008), 243.

crimes in general international law.[59] The preamble thereby confirms the consensus of signatory states that there were such obligations even before the adoption of the Rome Statute. In addition, the preamble reinforces and emphasises that the object and purpose of the Statute is to address international crimes, hence including those ESCR violations that overlap with the international crimes over which the ICC has jurisdiction.

Does the text of the Rome Statute add further obligations in addition to the pre-existing obligations of states to exercise criminal jurisdiction over certain crimes? Belgian, French, South African and Swiss tribunals found that the ICC Statute and national implementing legislation imposed a duty on state parties to prosecute alleged perpetrators of ICC crimes,[60] including where this involves denying immunity *ratione materiae.*[61] Because the ICC will only be able to prosecute a small number of cases, obligations on state parties to investigate can be inferred clearly from the Rome Statute, while the same obligations are more equivocal for states that have not ratified the treaty. In any event, state parties to the ICC Statute must interpret the complementarity regime in light of the need for national systems to investigate and prosecute crimes under the jurisdiction of the court, including where the alleged conduct relates to people's enjoyment of ESCR.

If states shall bring to justice perpetrators of international crimes, the question arises whether states must also remove, or abstain from imposing, obstacles to legal accountability: must states abstain from granting amnesties or immunities to alleged perpetrators of abuses that give rise both to ESCR violations as well as to international crimes? Must they abstain from applying statutes of limitations? Other authors have dealt

[59] Based on the rule that a treaty cannot bind third parties. Vienna Convention on the Law of Treaties, 1155 UNTS 331, 23 May 1969 (entered into force 27 January 1980), Art. 34.

[60] *In re Sharon and Yaron, 26 June 2002, Cour d'appel de Bruxelles, Belgium; In re Gadaffi, 105 RGDIP 475–476, Judgment of 20 October 2000, Cour d'appel de Paris, France.* Both cited in *Kleffner, Complementarity in the Rome Statute*, 235; *Southern African Litigation Centre and Zimbabwe Exiles Forum* v. *National Director of Public Prosecutions et al., Case No. 77150/09, 8 May 2012, North Gauteng High Court, South Africa*, para. 33; *National Commissioner of the South African Police Service* v. *Southern African Human Rights Litigation Centre, Case No. 485/2012, 27 November 2013, Supreme Court of Appeal, South Africa.* As far as non-state parties are concerned, Lord Hutton in *Pinochet* relied upon the preamble of the ICC Statute and argued that there was a duty of *all* states to exercise jurisdiction over those alleged for international crimes. *Regina* v. *Bartle (Ex Parte Pinochet No. 3); Regina* v. *Evans, 6 BHRC 24, 24 March 1999, House of Lords, United Kingdom*, Lord Hutton.

[61] *A.* v. *Ministère public de la Confédération (Affaire Nezzar), Dossier BB.2011.140, 25 July 2012, Tribunal pénal fédéral, Switzerland*, 26.

with these questions in detail.[62] Here, amnesties, limitations and immunities can only be mentioned briefly in order to demonstrate that international law indeed restricts their use for cases of ESCR violations that overlap with international crimes.

#### 8.2.2.3 Obligations to remove or not to impose obstacles to the exercise of jurisdiction

**8.2.2.3.1 Amnesties** The use of blanket amnesties for international crimes is no longer accepted by the international community. The implementation of the Rome Statute in domestic law led a number of states to outlaw the granting of amnesties and other clemency measures for crimes under the jurisdiction of the ICC.[63] Where amnesties are granted domestically, alleged perpetrators may face prosecution before an international tribunal or in a foreign jurisdiction. Where they have jurisdiction, foreign authorities can validly prosecute alleged perpetrators of international crimes even if another state has granted them amnesties.[64]

For states parties to the Rome Statute, the granting of amnesties is further limited under Arts. 17 and 20(3), particularly if such an amnesty bars investigations.[65] The only place where room is left for states parties to the Rome Statute granting an amnesty or another clemency measure for ICC crimes is if such a measure is conferred after the individual is tried and convicted in independent and impartial proceedings which were not for the purpose of shielding the person concerned.[66]

Human rights courts and commissions have held that amnesties or pardons violate victims' right to an effective remedy.[67] Granting amnesties for international crimes that overlap with ESCR violations may therefore lead to a condemnation from a human rights court or supervisory body.

[62] Yasmin Naqvi, *Impediments to Exercising Jurisdiction over International Crimes* (Asser Press, 2010).

[63] For instance, Código penal de la República de Panamá, con las modificaciones introducidas por la Ley 14 De 2010, Art. 116; Ley N° 18.026, Cooperación con la Corte penal internacional, Diario oficial, 4 October 2006, Art. 8.

[64] *Prosecutor* v. *Kallon and Kamara, SCSL-2004-15-Ar72(E) and SCSL-2004-16-Ar72(E) (Challenge to Jurisdiction), 13 March 2004*, Special Court for Sierra Leone, para. 67.

[65] Kleffner, *Complementarity in the Rome Statute*, 264: such cases would often be admissible before the ICC.

[66] Ibid., 266, for further references.

[67] *Aguirre* v. *Peru (Barrios Altos Case), Judgment of 3 September 2001, IACtHR Report (Ser. C) No. 83 (2001)*, IACtHR. For a review of the case law of human rights bodies and many further references, see Anja Seibert-Fohr, *Prosecuting Serious Human Rights Violations* (Oxford University Press, 2009).

In short, states opting for amnesty clauses for those who have been involved in crimes overlapping with ESCR violations risk facing sizeable opposition, including by UN mediators, who will not acknowledge agreements containing broad or unconditional amnesties.[68] If international crimes have been committed by way of violating ESCR and if perpetrators have been given an amnesty, foreign or international tribunals may not have to respect it, and the state granting the amnesties may incur international responsibility for infringing victims' rights to a remedy.

**8.2.2.3.2 Limitations** For many international crimes, statutes of limitation do not apply. By virtue of the 1968 Convention on the Non-Applicability of Limitations, no prescription applies to war crimes and crimes against humanity.[69] States agreed that international crimes differed from ordinary domestic crimes and can therefore attract exceptional consequences, such as non-prescription.[70] Perpetrators of crimes against humanity or war crimes that overlap with ESCR violations can thus be brought to justice years after the facts.

**8.2.2.3.3 Immunities** The immunities that shield state representatives from criminal accountability are generally also not available for most international crimes, at least when trials are held before international tribunals.[71] There are still several caveats and uncertainties to this conclusion: The ICJ held that serving heads of state, prime ministers and foreign ministers remain immune before national courts, but not before international criminal tribunals.[72]

[68] See in particular Priscilla Hayner, *Negotiating Justice: Guidance for Mediators* (Centre for Humanitarian Dialogue, ICTJ, 2009). See also Belfast Guidelines on Amnesty and Accountability, Drafted by a Group of Experts Convened by the Transitional Justice Institute, University of Ulster, 2013, Guideline 4(b).

[69] Convention on the Non-Applicability of Statutory Limitations to War Crimes and Crimes against Humanity, GA Res. 2391, 26 November 1968 (entered into force 11 November 1970).

[70] Robert Miller, 'Convention on the Non-Applicability of Statutory Limitations' (1971) 65 *American Journal of International Law*, 3, 476–501: 484–5. The ICRC concluded that today, customary international law establishes that limitations do not apply to war crimes, independent of the ratification of the Convention on the Non-Applicability of Limitations. Henckaerts and Doswald-Beck, (eds.), *Customary IHL*, vol. 1, rule 160; *Fédération nationale des déportés et internés résistants et patriotes* v. *Barbie, 78 ILR 125 (1985), 20 December 1985, Cour de cassation, France; Carlos Prats, 2 December 2002, Supreme Court, Chile.*

[71] For the purposes of the Rome Statute, see Rome Statute, Art. 27. See also *Prosecutor* v. *Taylor, SCSL-2003-01-I, Decision on Immunity from Jurisdiction, 31 May 2004*, SCSL.

[72] *Arrest Warrant Case (DRC* v. *Belgium), 14 February 2002, ICJ*, para. 61.

To sum up, international law provides that states are not allowed to grant amnesties or immunities or to apply statutes of limitations to those involved in ESCR violations that amount to certain international crimes (such as genocide or crimes against humanity) in the same way as they could do in cases of ordinary crimes.

#### 8.2.2.4 Obligations to cooperate in criminal matters

International cooperation in criminal matters is a crucial aspect of the enforcement of international criminal law, both for prosecuting authorities, but also for the accused, who may seek to present exculpatory material located in another state.[73] Extradition, exchange of evidence and information or prisoner transfers are regulated in a cobweb of bilateral and multilateral arrangements.[74] Moreover, states parties to the Rome Statute have agreed on a complex set of rules of cooperation.[75] States are also obviously obliged to adhere to these cooperation rules in cases in which the factual background of a case relates to ESCR abuses, which further illustrates the need that states carefully assess whether specific ESCR abuses overlap with international crimes.

#### 8.2.2.5 The obligation to refuse refugee status

Another consequence of ESCR violations overlapping with certain international crimes is that refugee status is not available to perpetrators of such abuse. The 1951 Convention Relating to the Status of Refugees does not apply to any person if there are serious reasons for considering that he or she has committed a crime against peace, a war crime or a crime against humanity.[76] The Refugee Convention also does not apply to individuals if there are serious reasons for considering that they have 'been guilty of acts contrary to the purposes and principles of the United Nations',[77] or that they have 'committed a serious non-political crime'.[78]

[73] Bantekas, *International Criminal Law*, 355.

[74] For a database providing relevant legislation, see UN Office on Drugs and Crime, 'Legal Library', www.unodc.org/enl/searchIndex.do.

[75] Rod Rastan, 'Testing Co-Operation', 2008) 21 *Leiden Journal of International Law*, 2, 431–56. The GA has further adopted non-binding Principles of International Cooperation in the Detection, Arrest, Extradition and Punishment of Persons Guilty of War Crimes and Crimes against Humanity, GA Res. 3074 (XXVIII), 3 December 1973.

[76] Convention Relating to the Status of Refugees, GA Res. 429 (V), 189 UNTS 150, 28 July 1951 (entered into force 22 April 1954), Art. 1(F)a.

[77] Ibid., Art. 1(F)c.

[78] Ibid., Art. 1(F)b. For the interpretation of the term 'non-political crimes', see UNHCR, 'Statement on Article 1f of the 1951 Convention Issued in the Context of the Preliminary

Under certain limited circumstances, those suspected of aggression or offences covered by conventions for the suppression of terrorist acts, for instance, may fall under one of these exclusion provisions. 'Acts contrary to the purposes and principles of the United Nations' are understood to encompass 'serious and sustained violations of human rights' and thus also serious and sustained ESCR violations.[79]

Since the 1951 Convention Relating to the Status of Refugees is almost universally ratified, in practice the exclusion provisions of that convention imply that almost all states have an obligation to ascertain – prior to a refugee status decision – whether there are serious reasons for considering if the concerned person may have been involved in ESCR abuses that overlap with these categories of crimes. A case in point concerns an Iraqi physician who applied for asylum in the UK and confessed his role was to treat brutalised detainees so that they could face torture again. Based on allegations of crimes against humanity, the doctor was suspended from the British medical register for twelve months and was considered unworthy of asylum but allowed to stay on grounds of non-refoulement.[80]

Where serious reasons exist and provided that adequate procedural safeguards are in place, the authorities must deny refugee status to the concerned person. Given that these exclusion clauses entail serious consequences for the affected persons and are potentially open to misuse, care must, however, be taken that they are interpreted carefully and in light of the humanitarian object and purpose of the Refugee Convention.[81]

A number of states, including Belgium, Canada, Denmark, the Netherlands, Norway, Sweden, Switzerland and the United Kingdom, have established specialised units within their immigration, police or prosecution services for the investigation and prosecution of international crimes.[82] Such offices offer significant promise to overcome the legal,

Ruling References to the Court of Justice of the European Communities from the German Federal Administrative Court Regarding the Interpretation of Arts. 12(2)(b) and (c) of the Qualification Directive' (UNHCR, 2009), 12.

[79] UNHCR, 'Statement on Article 1f of the 1951 Convention Issued in the Context of the Preliminary Ruling References to the Court of Justice of the European Communities from the German Federal Administrative Court Regarding the Interpretation of Arts. 12(2)(b) and (c) of the Qualification Directive', 14, references omitted.

[80] 'Al-Byati: Iraqi Doctor Denies Tribunal Claims', *BBC News UK*, 26 February 2013.

[81] Jennifer Bond, 'Excluding Justice: The Dangerous Intersection between Refugee Claims, Criminal Law, and "Guilty" Asylum Seekers' (2012) 24 *International Journal of Refugee Law*, 1, 37–59.

[82] Redress and FIDH, 'Strategies for the Effective Investigation and Prosecution of Serious International Crimes: The Practice of Specialised War Crimes Units' (Redress, 2010). Switzerland recently established such a permanent unit within the Federal Prosecutor's

practical and political complexities of international crime cases, including for the systematic examination of immigration dossiers. As a corollary of the arguments presented in this study, the mandates of such units necessarily include that they examine whether the applicant was involved in ESCR violations overlapping with crimes over which the unit has competence. Civil society, meanwhile, is tasked to supply such units and immigration panels in general with relevant information about ESCR abuses overlapping with international crimes to deny safe haven to alleged perpetrators.

### *8.2.3 Legal consequences of a state failing to uphold these obligations*

Where a state fails to implement its obligations arising from the alleged commission of international crimes, the state's international responsibility is engaged.[83] Other states may have the right to take legal action against another state that fails to live up to these obligations,[84] as Belgium successfully did when Senegal failed to prosecute the former dictator of Chad, Hissène Habré, despite its ratification of UNCAT.[85]

Provided states have consented to the jurisdiction of the ICJ, other states can potentially bring a case for the failure to take action against those alleged of international crimes that overlap with ESCR violations.[86]

Office. See 'Réponse de l'autorité de surveillance du 20 février 2012 à l'interpellation 11.4168: Moyens mis à disposition pour la poursuite des criminels de guerre et création d'une unité spécialisée'.

[83] ILC Articles on State Responsibility, Art. 12.

[84] For an analysis of the *erga omnes* standing, see *Case Concerning Armed Activities on the Territory of the Congo (DRC* v. *Uganda), 19 December 2005*, ICJ, Separate Opinion of Judge Simma, paras. 32–41. As seen above, at least for international crimes, duties such as the prosecution or extradition of alleged perpetrators entail *erga omnes* obligations owed to the international community as a whole. *Barcelona Traction, Light and Power Company Limited (Belgium* v. *Spain), 2nd Phase, 5 February 1970*, ICJ, para. 34. See also *Fédération nationale des déportés et internés résistants et patriotes* v. *Barbie, 78 ILR 125 (1985), 20 December 1985, Cour de cassation, France*, summarising the earlier decision of the *cour d'appel*. The court found that the prosecution of crimes against humanity was an obligation owed to all members of the international community.

[85] The ICJ found that Senegal has failed to immediately make a preliminary inquiry relating to the crimes allegedly committed by Habré and to submit the case to its competent authorities for the purpose of prosecutions, if it does not extradite him. *Questions Relating to the Obligation to Prosecute or Extradite (Belgium* v. *Senegal), (Merits), 20 July 2012*, ICJ, para. 122.

[86] Statute of the International Court of Justice, 3 Bevans 1179, 26 June 1945 (entered into force 24 October 1945), Art. 36. Where states consent to the jurisdiction of the ICJ, legal disputes concerning 'the existence of any fact which, if established, would constitute a breach of an international obligation' can be referred to the ICJ.

In addition to the obligations of states discussed so far, states should also offer civil remedies for international crimes.

### *8.2.4 Civil jurisdiction in national courts*

#### 8.2.4.1 Overview

Obtaining civil remedies can be a crucial form of redress for victims, sometimes even in the absence of criminal proceedings against the alleged perpetrator(s). Victims of international crimes have successfully obtained civil damages in domestic courts in a number of jurisdictions. Where the crime occurred within one jurisdiction, the civil tribunals of that jurisdiction are often competent to hear civil damage claims for harm arising out of the commission of international crimes.[87] Rwandan courts, for instance, have awarded substantial civil damages in domestic courts against persons accused of genocide, and there is no reason to believe that other courts could not do the same in cases in which the international crime(s) overlap with ESCR violations.[88] Usually, states limit such jurisdiction to abuses committed within the territorial jurisdiction,[89] independent of whether or not international law would allow a wider establishment of civil jurisdiction for international crimes. Especially where governments were involved in the commission of abuses, victims often face insurmountable challenges to obtain civil redress within the jurisdiction of the state in which the abuses have occurred.

There are some exceptions of jurisdictions in which victims have successfully brought civil suits even if the abuses occurred abroad. In spring 2011, a French civil court ordered reparations to victims of war crimes in the Balkans, marking the first time in Europe that a civil court ordered reparations for war crimes in the absence of a criminal trial.[90] A year later, a court in the Netherlands awarded 1 million euros in compensation for torture in Libya in a civil trial based on universal jurisdiction. The plaintiff was a Palestinian medic illegally imprisoned in Libya

[87] For an outline of remedies in national law, see Shelton, *Remedies*, chapter 2.

[88] For instance: *Ministère public* v. *Higiro et al., Rmp 49932/S7, Rp 35/1/99, 14 March 2003, First Instance Tribunal of Butare, Rwanda*. The civil damage awards in this and other Rwandan cases are documented by Mark Drumbl, *Atrocity* (Cambridge University Press, 2007), 80–3.

[89] E.g. Ley federal para prevenir y sancionar la tortura (Mexico), 27 December 1991, Art. 1.

[90] *Radovan Karadžić et Biljana Plavsić, 14 March 2011, Tribunal de grande instance à Paris, France.*

for allegedly infecting children with HIV.[91] Canadian courts can moreover exercise jurisdiction over civil claims arising from extraterritorial conduct as long as there is a 'real and substantial connection' between the tort and the forum jurisdiction. In 2012, the Supreme Court of Canada indicated that Canadian courts can provide civil remedies for international crimes as long as the defendant is domiciled or resident in the jurisdiction, carries on business in the forum, and the tort was committed or a contract connected was made there.[92] These precedents show that the road to civil remedies for abuses committed extraterritorially is in principle open and should thus also be available for victims of international crimes that overlap with ESCR violations.

In addition, two pieces of American legislation allow for limited extraterritorial civil jurisdiction. Do they offer avenues for redressing some of the violations of ESCR that can be understood as international crimes?

#### 8.2.4.2 The United States Alien Torts Statute and Torture Victim Protection Act

In the United States, the Alien Torts Statute (ATS) of 1789, as well as the Torture Victim Protection Act (TVPA) of 1991 allow claimants to seek redress in US courts for certain abuses committed around the world.

The Torture Victim Protection Act allows US nationals to sue individuals for torture suffered abroad.[93] If torture was committed by way of violating the plaintiff's ESCR,[94] the victim may have a cause of action before US national tribunals. To date, cases under the Torture Victim Protection Act do not seem to have dealt with severe physical or mental pain or suffering inflicted by state actors who would simultaneously engage their state's responsibility for a violation of ESCR,[95] but courts are competent *ratione materiae* if such cases were brought.

[91] *Ashraf Ahmed El Hojouj, LJN: BV9748, 400882 / HA ZA 11-2252, 21 March 2012, Court of The Hague, Civil Division, The Netherlands*, pursuant with Art. 9 of the Dutch Code of Civil Procedure.

[92] *Club Resorts Ltd.* v. *Van Breda, 2012 SCC 17, 18 April 2012, Supreme Court, Canada.* Cited in Bruce Bromhall, 'Extraterritorial Civil Jurisdiction: Obstacles and Openings in Canada', www.ejiltalk.org/extraterritorial-civil-jurisdiction-obstacles-and-openings-in-canada.

[93] Torture Victim Protection Act of 1991, Pub. L. 102–256, 106 Stat. 73. Only individuals (but not other persons or entities) can be sued under the TVPA. See *Mohamad* v. *Palestinian Authority, 132 U.S. 1702, USA*, at 1708.

[94] See Section 7.2.

[95] Beth Stephens et al., *International Human Rights Litigation in U.S. Courts*, 2nd edn (Brill, 2008), 73–127.

A range of cases relevant to this study have been brought under the ATS. The ATS has been interpreted to allow US courts to hear extraterritorial civil claims of foreigners who allege that they have suffered a tort in violation of the laws of nations or a treaty of the United States.[96] The analysis of the extensive case law supports the view that violations of ESCR amounting to international crimes are actionable under the ATS before US courts as long as courts continue to recognise causes of action under the statute.

The US Supreme Court recently curtailed litigation under the ATS. In *Kiobel*, the Supreme Court of the United States decided that claims under the ATS can only succeed if they 'touch and concern' the territory of the United States.[97] There is no consensus about the precise meaning of *Kiobel* in general and its 'touch and concern' standard in particular. While the exact boundaries for extraterritorial liability after *Kiobel* will have to be litigated in the years to come, it would seem premature to conclude that the ATS is no longer relevant as a tool for civil remedies for serious ESCR violations. Although *Kiobel* implies additional jurisdictional and other hurdles, the qualification of what constitutes an actionable violation for the purpose of the ATS should not be affected. The following outlines how US courts have dealt with cases that touch upon ESCR-related abuses and/or international crimes.

To bring a claim under the ATS, the following requirements must be met. First, the plaintiff must be an *alien* (i.e., not a citizen of the United States). Second, the defendant must be an actor who committed an international tort and over whom US courts have personal jurisdiction, without defences such as immunity or the political question doctrine being available.[98] Third, the factual conduct alleged must constitute *a violation of the law of nations or a treaty of the United States*,[99] and the claims must 'touch and concern' the territory of the United States.[100] To assess these requirements, the US Supreme Court urged courts to exercise restraint in recognising claims.[101] Courts only allow claims if

96 Alien Torts Statute, 28 USC § 1391. Courts of the United States 'shall have original jurisdiction of any civil action by an alien for a tort only, committed in violation of the law of nations or a treaty of the United States'.

97 *Kiobel* v. *Royal Dutch Petroleum Co., 133 S.Ct. 1659, USA*, 1660.

98 The defences are statutes of limitations, *forum non conveniens*, act of state, political question, comity, prudention, case-specific deference, immunity and exhaustion.

99 Alien Torts Statute, 28 USC § 1391.

100 *Kiobel* v. *Royal Dutch Petroleum Co., 133 S.Ct. 1659, USA*, 1660.

101 *Sosa* v. *Alvarez-Machain, 542 US 692 (2004), USA*, at 729.

the alleged conduct violates a well-established norm of international law. The Supreme Court in *Sosa* held that the ATS should apply in cases of 'a handful of heinous actions – each of which violates definable, universal and obligatory norms'.[102]

US courts have recognised the following violations of contemporary international law as actionable under the ATS: genocide, crimes against humanity, war crimes, torture, summary executions, disappearance, arbitrary detention, slavery, instances of CIDT, non-consensual drug testing, arbitrary denationalisation and forms of forced labour.[103] If any of these abuses was committed in relation to ESCR violations and the general requirements of the ATS are satisfied, US courts can thus be expected to exercise jurisdiction over such claims under the ATS. To examine this conclusion, and because this study is concerned with the overlap between ESCR violations and crimes, the subsequent part analyses those ATS cases in which the alleged conduct related to ESCR violations. Note, however, that it is not necessary that violations of customary law must be of 'criminal gravity' to be actionable under the ATS.[104]

A considerable number of ATS cases involved abuses related to ESCR. The analysis here includes cases that have involved ESCR violations, including where this is not stated explicitly. For the purpose of analysing the possibilities of obtaining redress in US courts for ESCR violations *qua* international crimes, the existing cases on ESCR-related issues can be grouped into three categories.

The first group of cases involves applications that were dismissed either because the international law claims relied on apparently weak sources or because the conduct alleged was not covered by the norm invoked. In some of these cases, plaintiffs invoked international crimes. *Amlon Metals, Inc.* v. *FMC* involved an unsuccessful claim that toxic material posed a danger to human health and the environment. Plaintiffs relied on the Stockholm Declaration on the Human Environment, and

[102] Ibid., 732.

[103] For key cases on the determination which abuses are actionable, see *Doe I.* v. *Unocal, 395 F.3d 932 (9th Cir. 2002), USA*, at 946 (crimes 'to which the law of nations attributes individual liability'); *Kadić* v. *Karadžić, 70 F.3rd 232 (2nd Cir. 1995), USA, at 239; Kiobel* v. *Royal Dutch Petroleum, 621 F.3d 111 (2nd Cir. 2010), USA*, at 115 (crimes against humanity). Also: *Ken Wiwa et al.* v. *Royal Dutch Petroleum et al. 2002 US Dist. Lexis 3293, USA*, at 32 (crimes against humanity); *South African Apartheid Litigation, 617 F. Supp. 2d 228 (SDNY 2009), USA, at 253 (denationalisation); Abdullahi* v. *Pfizer, 562 F.3d 163 (2nd Cir. 2009), USA*, at 187 (non-consensual drug testing).

[104] *Flomo* v. *Firestone, 643 F.3d 1013 (7th Cir. 2011), USA*, at 21.

the court found that the almost exclusive reliance on an unbinding declaration was insufficient to plead a violation of international law.[105] Similarly, in *Beanal* v. *Freeport-McMoran*, plaintiffs relied on the non-binding Rio Declaration on Environment and Development as well as on an environmental law textbook.[106] The Appeals Court of the Fifth Circuit held that plaintiffs failed to show that Freeport's mining activities constituted abuses under well-established international law.[107] Plaintiffs further alleged that Freeport engaged in cultural genocide by destroying the habitat and religious symbols of the Amungme people of West Papua, thus forcing the Amungme to relocate.[108] Yet, the alleged facts did not demonstrate that the plaintiffs were victims of acts committed with the intent to destroy the Amungme.[109] The lack of support for the specific intent requirement of genocide led the court to dismiss the claim. The court did not exclude that the destruction of the tribe's cultural symbols and habitat, including the ensuing relocation of members of the tribe – allegations that are related to the Amungme's enjoyment of ESCR – *could* support a claim of genocide had the legal elements of the international definition of genocide been sufficiently pleaded. For very similar reasons, claims were dismissed in *Abagninin* v. *Amvac Chemical*. In this case, plaintiffs alleged genocide on the basis that the chemical corporation knowingly caused male sterility by the use of pesticides in Côte d'Ivoire and thus harmed plaintiffs' health. The case was dismissed because there were no indications that defendants intended to destroy a particular group.[110] In another case, plaintiffs alleged that the damage to health resulting from their exposure to Agent Orange manufactured by the defendants violated the law of nations. The court concluded that the prohibition of poison in IHL only covers poison specifically designed as a weapon.[111] The court held that there was no universally accepted norm that would have made the use of the defoliant during the Vietnam War a war crime.[112] The careful interpretation of the court of the IHL prohibition of poisonous weapons shows that the court would plausibly have accepted a war crimes claim related to harm to human health, had it been

[105] *Amlon Metals* v. *FMC Corp, 775 F. Supp. 668 (SDNY 1991), USA*, at 671.

[106] *Beanal* v. *Freeport-Mcmoran Inc., 197 F 3d 161 (5th Cir. 1999), USA*, at 167.

[107] Ibid. [108] Ibid., at 163. [109] Ibid., at 168.

[110] *Abagninin* v. *Amvac Chemical Corporation 545 F.3d 733 (9th Cir. 2008), USA*, at 740.

[111] *Vietnam Association for Victims of Agent Orange* v. *Dow Chemical 517 F.3d 104 (2dn Cir. 2008), USA*, at 119 20.

[112] Ibid.

convinced that the alleged conduct fell within the scope of a war crime.[113] More questionably, the 7th Circuit dismissed *Flomo* v. *Firestone* on the grounds that plaintiffs had not presented sufficient evidence that the worst forms of child labour were committed on rubber plantations in Liberia and thus found that no violation of customary international law was demonstrated.[114] In all of these cases, ESCR-related abuses were pleaded, but dismissed because the claims were not considered sufficiently strong.

In the second group of cases, established norms were well pleaded and covered the alleged conduct, but plaintiffs did not argue that the violation of the law of nations concerned an international crime. This category includes cases in which courts broadly stated that rights such as the rights to health or life were 'amorphous' under international law, but also cases in which plaintiffs succeeded in litigating abuses that implicitly dealt with plaintiffs' enjoyment of ESCR.

In *Flores* v. *Southern Peru Copper*, plaintiffs alleged that pollution from mines led to fatal illnesses, in violation of the rights to life and health.[115] The Second Circuit dismissed the case, holding that the rights to life and to health were too nebulous and indeterminate to constitute a cause of action under the ATS.[116] The ICESCR, but also the ICCPR, were described as 'boundless and indeterminate' because they leave discretion upon states on how to implement them.[117] This case illustrates the scepticism of US courts towards international human rights law in general and ESCR in particular.[118] *Flores* must, however, be distinguished from cases dealing with factual conduct amounting to an international crime that simultaneously violates plaintiffs' ESCR. It is notable for this analysis that plaintiffs did not argue that the company participated in the commission of an international crime, and the case therefore did not test the conclusion of this chapter that claims based on ESCR abuses that are pleaded *qua* international crimes should lead courts to conclude that the

[113] Ibid., at 119–20: the court dismissed the claim only 'inasmuch as Agent Orange was intended for defoliation and for destructing of crops only, its use did not violate the international norms relied upon here'.

[114] *Flomo* v. *Firestone, 643 F.3d 1013 (7th Cir. 2011), USA*, at 27.

[115] *Flores* v. *Southern Peru Copper Co., 414 F.3d 233 (2nd Cir. 2003), USA.*

[116] Ibid., at 254–6. [117] Ibid., at 255.

[118] If the court's reasoning was correct, courts would also have dismissed *Filartiga*, the first modern ATS case, since there is no reason to consider that the prohibition of torture is inherently more precise than aspects of other human rights norms. Further, state discretion in implementing international treaty obligations is a basic feature of international law and does not imply that a norm is devoid of obligatory character. *Filartiga* v. *Pena-Irala, 630 F.2d 878 (2d Cir. 1980), USA.*

cause is actionable.[119] Another ATS case in which ESCR-relevant abuses (but not international crimes) were alleged concerned a range of work-related abuses of impoverished Nepali labourers who were allegedly recruited under false pretences for labour abroad and who were captured and most of them killed by insurgents on the way to a US military base in Iraq. Shortly after *Kiobel*, the competent district court dismissed their ATS claims.[120]

Plaintiffs were more successful in *Abdullahi* v. *Pfizer*, where the court concluded that the prohibition of non-consensual medical experimentation is binding under customary international law, including without a nexus with international crimes.[121] The right to health was not mentioned in the complaint, but one could argue that plaintiffs suffered from a failure by Nigeria to protect their right to health.

The third category of ATS cases is the most interesting. In this group of cases, plaintiffs alleged international crimes, and the facts they describe in their complaints touch upon plaintiffs' enjoyment of ESCR. None of these cases reached a final decision on whether the invoked norm concerning an international crime overlapping with ESCR abuses meets the criteria of the ATS. Cases are either still ongoing, or they never reached a final decision because of a settlement or because of the availability of defences. Burmese plaintiffs, for instance, brought two cases against Unocal Corporation, alleging forced labour, the loss of homes and property, torture and crimes against humanity in Burma/Myanmar. These cases were settled and never reached a final decision that determined if the ESCR-related claims met the ATS requirements.[122] Involving a claim on home demolitions *qua* war

119 Similarly, two consolidated cases against Texaco, an oil corporation, alleged that the company dumped toxic water in the Amazon, damaging the environment and plaintiffs' health. The case was moved to Ecuador on a *forum non conveniens* motion. Plaintiffs did not plead that Texaco committed international crimes, and it thus remains open whether a *forum non conveniens* motion would have been granted if a claim on international crimes had been involved. *In re Aguinda, 303 F.3d 470 (2nd Cir. 2002), USA.*

120 Bonnie Barron, 'Legal Blow for Families of Slain Nepali Laborers', *Courthouse News Service*, 27 August 2013.

121 Pfizer was alleged to test an ineffective drug on Nigerian children suffering from meningitis. *Abdullahi* v. *Pfizer, 562 F.3d 163 (2nd Cir. 2009), USA*, at 187. In February 2011, the case was settled.

122 *Doe I.* v. *Unocal, 395 F.3d 932 (9th Cir. 2002), USA*. The original complaint claimed that forced labour and people's removal from their homes amounted to crimes against humanity. *Doe* v. *Unocal, Original Complaint, Filed 3 October 1996, (on file with the author), USA*, para. 120. The forced labour *qua* crimes against humanity claim was ultimately not pursued but the forced labour claim (independent of crimes against humanity) was allowed to proceed, and the case settled before the issue was resolved.

crimes, *Corrie* v. *Caterpillar* was dismissed on the basis of the political question defence.[123]

Three cases in this category came close to a decision on whether the argument of this study could succeed in an ATS claim: in the *Talisman* suit, a Canadian company was alleged to have aided and abetted abuses committed by the Sudanese military. The plaintiffs alleged forcible displacement as a crime against humanity, confiscation and destruction of property as war crimes and widespread and systematic forcible transfer of a civilian population as a crime against humanity and genocide. Ultimately, however, the Second Circuit dismissed the claims finding that plaintiffs supplied insufficient evidence that Talisman *purposely* supported abuses by the government.[124] The court extensively – but, in this author's view, incorrectly – dealt with the important choice of law issues, namely the source for the mental standard for aiding and abetting liability.[125] Because the court required a purpose standard and found that this standard had not been met, the court did not examine whether the claims of ESCR-related abuses as war crimes, crimes against humanity and genocide could have been sustained if the court had found the involvement of Talisman to be purposive.

The second case that came close to testing the conclusion that US courts exercise jurisdiction over ESCR abuses amounting to international crimes is the *Apartheid Litigation*. On behalf of massive classes of South African plaintiffs, multinational corporations were alleged of involvement in abuses of the apartheid regime.[126] The Southern District of New York

[123] *Corrie* v. *Caterpillar, Inc., 503 F.3d 974 (9th Cir. 2007), USA*, at 984. This case related to home demolitions in the Occupied Palestinian Territories. The court found that it would intrude upon the executive branch's foreign policy decisions because the US Congress appropriated the funds used by Israel to purchase the bulldozers involved in the alleged abuses. For the complaint that ESCR-related abuses amounted to war crimes, see *Corrie* v. *Caterpillar, First Amended Complaint, 2 May 2005, USA*.

[124] *Presbyterian Church of Sudan* v. *Talisman Energy and Republic of the Sudan, 453 F. Supp. 2d 633 (SDNY 2006), USA*, at 639. Upheld on appeal: *Presbyterian Church of Sudan* v. *Talisman Energy and Republic of the Sudan, 582 F.3d 244 (2nd Cir. 2009), USA*, at 247–8.

[125] To be held liable, it should be sufficient that actors act with knowledge, but not necessarily with purpose when they aid and abet human rights violations, as it is the case in international criminal law. See also *Doe* v. *Exxon, 2011 US App. Lexis 13934 (DC App., 8 July 2011), USA*, at 65.

[126] *South African Apartheid Litigation, 617 F. Supp. 2d 228 (SDNY 2009), USA*, p. 13. The US Judicial Panel on Multidistrict Litigation centralised pre-trial proceedings in the Southern District of New York. The original *Ntsebeza* v. *Daimler* complaint against 50 defendants failed to specifically link facts with allegations. In the second action, *Khulumani* v. *Barcleys National Bank*, plaintiffs claimed extrajudicial killing, sexual assault, torture, detention and cruel treatment. Plaintiffs filed two amended complaints.

accepted that apartheid as a crime against humanity could possibly be committed by forced removals and work discrimination (and therefore violations of ESCR).[127] As a consequence of *Kiobel*, the Court of Appeals for the Second Circuit returned the case to the lower court and recommended dismissing the case.[128] The lower court in December 2013 dismissed the claims against two of the defendants, Daimler and Rheinmetall, but allowed those against IBM and Ford to proceed.[129] In August 2014, however, the remaining claims were also dismissed based on *Kiobel*. The district court earlier agreed that the claim of apartheid as a crime against humanity, as defined in the Rome Statute, could proceed, including the claims that apartheid was committed by forced removals and labour discrimination.[130] Although the apartheid litigation was ultimately dismissed, it is notable that the claims related to international crimes, including those relating to abuses of ESCR, survived longest.

The third case in this category is particularly significant. Although the Court of Appeals for the Ninth Circuit also dismissed the case after *Kiobel*,[131] it had more or less successfully tested the conclusion drawn in this study that international crimes overlapping with ESCR violations can be claimed before US domestic courts: in *Sarei* v. *Rio Tinto*, residents of Papua New Guinea alleged that a mining group harmed their health by dumping toxic tailings into water sources.[132] Plaintiffs also accused Rio Tinto of complicity in crimes during the conflict in Bougainville, where the government blockaded the island, which resulted in severe shortages of medical services. The complaint claimed that crimes against humanity were committed, but the text for this count then confusingly referred to war crimes, genocide and torture.[133] The war crimes count did not articulate clearly whether plaintiffs considered the medical blockade a war crime, or whether their claim was limited to the alleged killings, rape and torture accompanying the blockade. The claims on violations of the right to life and health were confusing and contained in a separate

The *Ntsebeza* plaintiffs later claimed apartheid as a crime against humanity, torture, inhumane treatment and arbitrary denationalisation and extrajudicial killings. *Ntsebeza Complaint, 02 Mdl 1499, Docket No. 126 (SDNY Oct 27, 2008), USA. And Khulumani Complaint, 02 Mdl 1499, Docket No. 94 (SDNY Oct. 24, 2008), USA.*

127 *South African Apartheid Litigation, 617 F. Supp. 2d 228 (SDNY 2009), USA*, at 250–2.

128 *Balintulo* v. *Daimler, 2013 09-2778-Cv(L) (2nd Cir. 2013), USA.*

129 *South African Apartheid Litigation, Order 2 Md L 1499 (SAS) (SDNY 2013), USA.*

130 *South African Apartheid Litigation, 617 F. Supp. 2d 228 (SDNY 2009), USA*, at 250–2.

131 *Sarei* v. *Rio Tinto, No. 02-56256 (9th Cir. 2013), USA*

132 *Sarei* v. *Rio Tinto, Plc, 221 F.Supp.2d 1116 (C.D.Cal. 2002), USA*, at 1120.

133 *Sarei* v. *Rio Tinto Plc, Original Complaint (September 2000), USA.*

count.[134] In any event, the district court dismissed the claims on the violations of the rights to life and health, but allowed the claims on international crimes to proceed.[135] In late 2011, the Appeals Court of the Ninth Circuit issued an extended *en banc* decision in which it affirmed that the claims of genocide and war crimes were adequately alleged by the plaintiffs. Of interest in this study, the tribunal inferred that genocide against a protected group could have been committed based on allegations that Rio Tinto deliberately participated in the infliction of starvation by imposing a food and medical blockade on the island.[136] The court also accepted the war crimes claims: first, because the court affirmed that Rio Tinto induced the military action in Papua New Guinea 'to forcibly displace and destroy plaintiffs',[137] constituting murder as a war crime in NIAC, and, second, because in the court's view, the blockade constituted the 'war crime of intentional deprivation of essential supplies'.[138] As far as crimes against humanity were concerned, the court suggested that the food and medical blockade could constitute the crime against humanity of 'other inhumane acts'.[139] The court, however, summarily concluded that for purposes of an ATS claim, the statutes of international criminal tribunals would have to explicitly list medical and food blockades as an 'other inhumane act'.[140] This unconvincing conclusion apart,[141] the decision undoubtedly indicated that US legislation in principle allows US federal courts to deal with serious ESCR violations that overlap with international crimes, and this finding should remain unaffected even if the *Kiobel* decision by the US Supreme Court has added additional and challenging preliminary hurdles for ATS claims.

Two conclusions can be drawn from this analysis of ATS cases. First, plaintiffs must overcome numerous preliminary hurdles before courts will test the inference that certain ESCR violations can meet the ATS

[134] Ibid., para. 225: for instance, note 5 exclusively cites decisions of the IACommHR and the HRCttee for the argument that 'the ICESCR has found that environmental destruction and pollution . . . are cognizable violations of [customary] international law'.

[135] *Sarei* v. *Rio Tinto, Plc, 221 F.Supp.2d 1116 (C.D.Cal. 2002), USA, at 1156; Sarei* v. *Rio Tinto,650 F. Supp. 2d 1004 (9th Cir. 2009), USA*, at 1031.

[136] *Sarei* v. *Rio Tinto, 2011 US App. Lexis 21515 (9th Cir. Cal. 2011), USA*, at 57.

[137] Ibid., at 71. [138] Ibid., at 104.

[139] Ibid., at 77: 'A food and medical blockade may well be an "other inhumane act" constituting a crime against humanity.'

[140] Ibid., at 77.

[141] The conclusion is unconvincing because the medical blockade is simply one possible way of realising the *actus reus*. Other crimes, such as murder, also do not list all the specific ways in which they can be committed.

requirements because they overlap with international crimes. These preliminary hurdles have become even more complex after *Kiobel*. Second, the analysis supports the conclusion that plaintiffs can rely on claims of international crimes touching upon ESCR-related issues. If courts follow the guidance from the Supreme Court in *Sosa*, they will continue to allow claims of international crimes to proceed under the ATS, including when the facts of the case relate to ESCR. That said, it should be noted that plaintiffs do not have to characterise the pleaded violations as violations of ESCR. One of the hurdles of an ATS claim is that plaintiffs must show that the violation of the law of nations gives rise to a cause of action.[142] Yet, any claims based exclusively on human rights law related to ESCR will be confronted with the argument that the rights recognised in international instruments are not considered to create individual rights and/or are not self-executing for the purposes of domestic law.[143] It is unlikely that US courts would recognise a cause of action based upon international law norms solely derived from multilateral treaties such as the ICESCR, a treaty that is signed, but not ratified by the United States.[144] Nevertheless, where appropriate, the additional argument that ESCR-related abuses amount to international crimes holds promise. The requirement that a norm must both confer individual rights and be self-executing in order to be susceptible to judicial enforcement before a US court does not affect the finding that those ESCR violations that amount to international crimes are actionable. Since courts have recognised causes of action in those cases in which abuses amounted to international crimes, it is enough if plaintiffs show that the alleged facts constitute an international crime, and it is not necessary – and may not be advisable – that plaintiffs also qualify the same facts under human rights law.

In the next step, we will consider why the findings of this book are relevant for non-judicial or quasi-judicial processes employed at the national level in order to address a history of human rights abuses, namely truth commissions, national human rights institutions and vetting processes.

142 *Sosa* v. *Alvarez-Machain, 542 U.S. 692 (2004), USA*, 712.

143 Courts sometimes treat the question of whether a treaty grants individual rights together with the question of whether the treaty is self-executing. *Mora* v. *New York, 524 F.3d 183 (2d Cir. 2008), USA*, note 16, criticising that these two inquiries are, however, distinct.

144 United Nations, 'Treaty Collection, Status of Treaties', http://treaties.un.org/Pages/ParticipationStatus.aspx.

## 8.3 Legal corollaries for truth commissions, national human rights institutions and institutional vetting processes

Courts and tribunals are not the only actors dealing with international crimes. A growing number of countries establish non- or quasi-judicial mechanisms such as truth commissions or commissions of inquiry to provide an account of past abuses.[145] Truth commissions are bodies that investigate a pattern of past abuses that took place over a period of time. They are temporary and intended to conclude with a public report, and they are officially authorised or empowered by the state.[146] States can also set up programmes of lustration (vetting) and a range of institutional reforms tasked to address a legacy of abuses.[147] Many of these mechanisms have mandates that cover international crimes,[148] but very few of them have so far analysed violations of ESCR.[149] Because most scholars and practitioners have to date assumed that the elements of international crimes are confined to abuses related to a narrow set of civil and political liberties, as demonstrated in the introductory chapter, most mechanisms have not addressed ESCR violations.[150]

In particular, the mandates of truth commissions frequently cover crimes against humanity, war crimes or simply international crimes including, more recently, corruption. Truth commissioners must, therefore, interpret legal definitions of international crimes, and they may make recommendations on how to redress the abuses. If the argument of this book is accepted that international crimes overlap with ESCR violations,

145 Priscilla Hayner, *Unspeakable Truths*, 2nd edn (Routledge, 2011). 146 Ibid., 12.

147 See in particular the series of OHCHR Rule of Law Tools for Post-Conflict States (Geneva: OHCHR).

148 The mandates of truth commissions can be found in the following database, researched by the author of this study: United States Institute of Peace, 'Truth Commission Digital Collection', www.usip.org/publications/truth-commission-digital-collection.

149 Louise Arbour, 'Economic and Social Justice for Societies in Transition' (2007) 40 *New York University Journal of International Law and Politics*, 1, 1–28: 13. For an overview of the debate on the potential inclusion of socio-economic rights in transitional justice processes, see Evelyne Schmid and Aoife Nolan, 'Economic and Social Dimensions of Transitional Justice' (2014) 8 *International Journal of Transitional Justice* 3, 362–82.

150 Arbour, 'Economic and Social Justice for Societies in Transition', 14. For an overview of past truth commissions' experiences with considering issues which affect the enjoyment of ESCR, see OHCHR, Transitional Justice and Economic, Social and Cultural Rights, HR/PUB/13/5, 2014, 16–23. See also Evelyne Schmid, 'ESCR in Transitional Justice' (2009) 24 *PRAXIS - Fletcher Journal of Human Security*, 5–28; Lisa Laplante, 'On the Indivisibility of Rights' (2007) 10 *Yale Human Rights and Development Law Journal*, 141–77.

many, if not most, constitutive instruments of truth commissions task the relevant commissions to engage with at least some ESCR violations. This is significant, as it has been argued that the marginalisation of ESCR violations by truth commissions creates many missed opportunities. Louise Arbour posits that 'truth commissions lend themselves particularly well to the investigation and protection of ESCR'.[151] In his most recent report on the rule of law and transitional justice in conflict and post-conflict societies, the UN SG acknowledged that there 'is growing recognition that truth commissions should also address the economic, social and cultural rights dimensions of conflict to enhance long-term peace and security'.[152] A 2014 publication by OHCHR moreover emphasises that '[t]ruth commissions could be suitable platforms for considering ... violations of [ESCR], given their aim to uncover the truth about past events and their mandates to examine the causes, consequences and nature of gross human rights violations'.[153] Indeed, truth commissions can examine past abuses from a much broader perspective than criminal tribunals. Depending on their mandates, such commissions usually examine the antecedents, consequences and nature of crimes and/or human rights violations and they can make a broad range of recommendations on how best to repair the abuses and avoid their recurrence. The UN Special Rapporteur on the Promotion of Truth, Justice, Reparation and Guarantees of Non-Recurrence explains that the success of a truth commission hinges on its ability to recognise victims as rights holders, which in turn requires an official acknowledgement of atrocities.[154] Where a truth commission has reason to believe that ESCR violations in its jurisdiction have overlapped with international crimes, the findings made in this book provide the necessary guidance to identify the legal conclusions available to a truth commission. Rather than commanding the exclusion of ESCR abuses from the remit of truth commissions, international law bolsters the position that such commissions can legitimately deal with infringements of ESCR.

In addition, national human rights institutions can be vested to monitor abuses in their countries or they may be mandated to follow up on the implementation of recommendations of other mechanisms, such as truth

[151] Arbour, 'Economic and Social Justice for Societies in Transition', 14.

[152] Report of the SG on the Rule of Law and Transitional Justice in Conflict and Post-Conflict Societies, S/2011/634, 12 October 2011, para. 24.

[153] OHCHR, Transitional Justice and Economic, Social and Cultural Rights, HR/PUB/13/5, 2014, 17.

[154] Pablo de Greiff, Report of the Special Rapporteur on the Promotion of Truth, Justice, Reparation and Guarantees of Non-Recurrence, A/HRC/24/42, 28 August 2013, para. 24.

commissions or reparation programmes. These administrative bodies can play an important role in the qualification of facts as international crimes or in the discussions on how best to address a legacy of such crimes. The OHCHR recommended that national human rights institutions encourage, where appropriate, 'the prosecution of violations of ESCR'.[155] Similarly, commissions of inquiry can be established by national authorities or by international bodies, such as the UN Human Rights Council. They typically have a mandate to collect facts on specific incidents or situations, and they may sometimes also make legal qualifications to determine if international crimes have occurred and what should be done to address them.[156]

Vetting processes are another important tool in attempts to address legacies of an abusive past. These are administrative processes that exclude individuals associated with past abuse from serving in public offices outside or in combination with formal court proceedings. Where ESCR violations have characterised the experience of a large proportion of the surviving population and where due process is followed, it may be particularly appropriate to vet those credibly believed to have committed an international crime that overlapped with violations of socio-economic and cultural rights. OHCHR has prepared operational guidelines to support authorities and other actors in vetting initiatives.[157]

## 8.4 Liability of non-state actors

Another important implication of the findings of this study is that mechanisms applying international criminal law may address conduct by non-state actors. Whereas human rights law as traditionally understood binds states, prohibitions in international criminal law are also directed at non-state actors such as businesses and international organisations.[158] After World

[155] OHCHR, Guidance Note on National Human Rights Institutions and Transitional Justice, OHCHR, 27 September 2008, para. 31.

[156] On this issue, see Larissa van den Herik and Catherine Harwood, 'Sharing the Law' (2014) 2014/016-ICL Grotius Centre Working Paper.

[157] See OHCHR, Rule-of-Law Tools for Post-Conflict States: Vetting: An Operational Framework, OHCHR, 2006.

[158] For the argument that international criminal law is not solely addressed to crimes committed by individuals, see Andrew Clapham, 'Extending International Criminal Law' (2008) 6 *Journal of International Criminal Justice*, 5, 899–926. See also William Schabas, 'War Economies, Economic Actors and International Criminal Law', in *Profiting from Peace: Managing the Resource Dimensions of Civil War*, ed. Karen Ballentine and Heiko Nitzschke (Lynne Rienner, 2005), 425–46: 440, writing that corporations 'may find

War II, the international community made clear that corporations involved in the commission of international crimes can be punished,[159] and tribunals may hold non-state actors accountable for international crimes, including where these overlap with ESCR violations. Moreover, several conventions relevant to this study expressly criminalise conduct by corporations and other non-state actors: the Basel and Bamako Conventions on hazardous waste both impose liability on corporate actors.[160] UNCAC and the OECD Convention on Bribery require states to establish the liability of legal persons.[161] The Apartheid Convention provides that the crime of apartheid could be committed by 'organisations, institutions and individuals'.[162] Andrew Clapham and Bert Swart identify further multilateral instruments containing one or more provisions on corporate criminal liability.[163] Other conventions simply refer to 'persons', a term that can in principle apply to natural as well as legal persons.[164] In the course of legislative activity to incorporate ICC crimes in domestic law, a number of states have included legal entities other than physical persons in the list of potential perpetrators of international crimes.[165] If not

themselves – or their directors and managers – exposed to criminal prosecution as accomplices in international crimes. This is an area that deserves to be explored much further.' See also Section 3.2.2.1.

159 Although IG Farben was not prosecuted in a criminal trial in Nuremberg, the company faced the 'corporate death penalty' and was liquidated for its complicity in international crimes. Control Council Law No. 9, Seizure of Property Owned by IG Farbenindustrie and the Control Thereof, 30 November 1945, Preamble and Art. 1. Discussed in Tyler Giannini and Susan Farbstein, 'Corporate Accountability in Conflict Zones: How *Kiobel* Undermines the Nuremberg Legacy and Modern Human Rights' (2010) 52 *Harvard International Law Journal*, 119–35.

160 Basel Convention on the Control of Transboundary Movements of Hazardous Wastes and Their Disposal, UNTS 1673, 29 March 1989 (entered into force 5 May 1992), Arts. 2 (14) and 4; Bamako Convention on the Ban of the Import into Africa and the Control of Transboundary Movement and Management of Hazardous Wastes within Africa, Bamako, 30 January 1991 (entered into force 22 April 1998), Arts. 1(16) and 4.

161 UN Convention against Corruption, GA Res. 58/4, 31 October 2003 (entered into force 14 December 2005), Art. 26; OECD Convention on Combating Bribery of Foreign Public Officials in International Business Transactions, 21 November 1997 (entered into force 15 February 1999), Art. 2.

162 Apartheid Convention, Art. I(2).

163 Andrew Clapham, *Human Rights Obligations of Non-State Actors* (Oxford University Press, 2006), 247–52. And Bert Swart et al., 'Discussion: International Trends towards Establishing Some Form of Punishment for Corporations' (2008) 6 *Journal of International Criminal Justice*, 5, 947–79: 949.

164 See in this regard Note 112 in Chapter 3.

165 Report of the Special Representative of the SG on the Issue of Human Rights and Transnational Corporations and Other Business Enterprises (John Ruggie), A/HRC/4/35, 19 February 2007, paras. 22–5.

governed otherwise in an international treaty, international law leaves it to domestic legal systems to determine the precise standards of liability, and national courts can in many cases establish jurisdiction over non-state actors to hold them accountable for international crimes that overlap with ESCR violations in the same way they could do for other international crimes.

Moreover, the findings of this study are important for the UN Security Council as well as for the implementation of the concept of the responsibility to protect.

## 8.5 Security Council action and the responsibility to protect

Where ESCR violations overlap with international crimes, the UN system of collective security can possibly be employed. Without the consent of the concerned government, the UN Security Council can only authorise states to intervene in a situation if it acts under chapter VII of the UN Charter. Article 42 in chapter VII allows the SC to take any necessary means to maintain or restore international peace and security.[166] Before doing so, the SC must determine if the situation constitutes a threat to international peace and security in accordance with Art. 39 of the UN Charter.[167] Over the last two decades, the interpretation of Art. 39 has evolved to include situations such as massive population displacement, the hindrance of humanitarian aid or the commission of other crimes, including if committed within the territory of one state.[168] In 2005, states affirmed the responsibility to protect populations against genocide, war crimes, ethnic cleansing and crimes against humanity. This protection must entail the prevention of such crimes, including by encouraging and helping other states to build capacity to protect their populations from these crimes and to assist 'those which are under stress before crises and conflicts break out'.[169] The GA recalled that the SC should be prepared to take collective action 'should peaceful means be inadequate and national

[166] UN Charter, Art. 42. [167] UN Charter, Art. 39.

[168] For the earliest example: Somalia, S/RES/794, 3 December 1992, determining that the humanitarian situation in Somalia exacerbated by the blocking of relief assistance constitutes a threat to international peace and security. For a recent example: Libya, S/RES/1970, 27 February 2011, considering that the widespread and systematic attacks talking place in Libya may amount to crimes against humanity and deciding to act under chapter VII.

[169] World Summit Outcome, GA Res. 60/1, 24 October 2005, paras. 138–9.

authorities manifestly fail to protect their populations [from such crimes]'.[170]

The SC can establish economic or diplomatic sanctions or blockades or take any measures necessary to maintain or restore international peace and security.[171] If the SC determines that a situation represents a threat to international peace and security, it can also establish a tribunal or refer the situation to the ICC, opening the possibility for the ICC to open an investigation even where a state has not ratified the Rome Statute.[172] It is of interest for justice that the SC carefully takes into account the full spectrum of prohibited conduct in international criminal law, rather than exercising its powers only in respect of a small subset of abuses related to civil and political rights. Provided that certain ESCR violations are found to overlap with international crimes threatening international peace and security, the SC is vested with power to take a range of measures to address the situation, including by referring it to the ICC.

## 8.6 Conclusion

The actors of international criminal justice are multiple and so are the areas where the main findings of this study will have implications. As we saw in this chapter, some international crimes can be prosecuted before the ICC, and many national tribunals are competent to hear cases on alleged international crimes. For many international crimes, international law enables and sometimes requires their investigation and prosecution and the provision of remedies to victims independent of the state of national law. The granting of amnesties is restricted, and statutory limitations do not apply to most international crimes. With some caveats, immunity is not available to officials who are accused of international crimes. International refugee law prescribes that whoever is seriously believed to have committed certain international crimes may not be granted refugee status.[173] For other crimes, jurisdictional and other consequences are more limited and depend on the terms of a particular convention, but most instruments extend jurisdiction extraterritorially and apply the *aut dedere aut judicare* principle. Furthermore, and

170 Ibid. 171 UN Charter, Arts. 41 and 42.

172 Rome Statute, Arts. 13(b), 53. The SC has so far referred two situations to the ICC. See Sudan, S/RES/1593, 31 March 2005, Darfur; Libya, S/RES/1970, 27 February 2011, Libya.

173 Refugee Convention, Art. 1(F); Convention Relating to the Status of Stateless Persons, 360 UNTS 117, ECOSOC Res. 526 A (XVII), 28 September 1954 (entered into force 6 June 1960), Art. 1(2).

particularly relevant in attempts to address the legacies of widespread human rights abuses, it is crucial to emphasise that international criminal law is not the exclusive domain of courts. Other quasi-judicial or non-judicial mechanisms, such as truth commissions, international commissions of inquiry, reparations programmes or national human rights institutions, may have a mandate to determine whether crimes have occurred and how they should best be addressed. Moreover, non-state actors, such as businesses, can be liable for the commission of crimes, whereas human rights law, as traditionally understood, only binds states. Last but not least, the Security Council can take a range of measures to address crimes deemed to threaten international peace and security.

In light of the legal complexities in dealing with the legacy of international crimes, it seems warranted to emphasise the importance of preventing such crimes whether they overlap with economic, political, social, cultural or civil rights. The available institutional mechanisms have not always shone, and the political will to employ them has sometimes been lacking. Yet, the valuable efforts to monitor the human rights situation in zones of risk should take into account the overlap between international crimes and serious ESCR violations. Otherwise, monitors may miss signs of international crimes being committed and may fail to establish a complete picture of the situation. In armed conflicts, disclosing known and suspected violations is a legal obligation of all states and ensures respect for the Geneva Conventions.[174] Moreover, states have pledged to support the establishment of early-warning capabilities in order to prevent genocide, war crimes, ethnic cleansing and crimes against humanity.[175]

More broadly, the qualification of facts as an international crime implies wider social and political consequences going beyond the legal corollaries examined so far. International crimes are particularly stigmatised. Framing abuses as international crimes often results in increasing public attention. We must know, therefore, whether it is desirable to qualify ESCR violations as international crimes. The conclusions obtained in this enquiry give rise to a number of argued concerns and objections that shall be addressed in the concluding chapter.

[174] Geneva Conventions, Common Art. 1.

[175] World Summit Outcome, GA Res. 60/1, 24 October 2005, para. 138.

# 9

# Conclusions

Violations of economic, social and cultural rights continue to be a common occurrence, particularly in situations of armed conflict and massive human rights abuses. This study was designed to explore one particular set of legal questions that arise in attempts to address socio-economic and cultural abuses: the relationships between violations of ESCR and the substantive definitions of international crimes. The intention was to establish whether or not existing international law accommodates claims that existing processes of international criminal law can address ESCR violations. Our departing point was the observation that there is a tendency of lawyers, judges, scholars and practitioners to assume that such is not the case. Contrary to predominant views, the inquiry suggested that an international crime can sometimes simultaneously be understood as a violation of ESCR and vice versa. The preceding chapter surveyed the range of legal corollaries of the primary finding contained herein. This final chapter summarises the analysis underlying the study's overarching research question and reflects on the contribution of its findings.

## 9.1 The research, its objectives and main findings

This study provided a systematic account of the overlap between international crimes on the one hand, and violations of ESCR on the other. In the process, the legal relevance of claims was reviewed: should criminal lawyers be concerned with violations of rights such as the right to education, housing, work, food or health? Instead of tracing the contours of a possible expansion of international criminal law, the study set out to identify the circumstances under which ESCR abuses are already part of existing crimes. Its hypothesis was that current definitions of international crimes (leading to criminal responsibility) overlap with violations of ESCR (giving rise to state responsibility for internationally wrongful acts).

A nuanced analysis of the definitions of crimes showed that many types of abusive conduct depriving people of their rights to health, water, education, participation in cultural life, food or other ESCR are properly considered to be within the ambit of international criminal law. The analysis shows that focusing on civil and political rights in processes aimed to address serious abuses is both 'an arbitrary distinction for the victims of atrocities'[1] and legally unjustified.

The motivation for this study arose from the realisation that the majority of 'those who fall victim to adverse human agency are not injured by proximate violence but as a result of being compelled to live in subhuman conditions'.[2] Yet, the international community treats victims killed by soldiers firing into crowds differently than it treats those killed by hunger or by disease caused by government blockage of humanitarian aid.[3]

As described in the introductory chapter, the contemporary practice of mechanisms to address human rights abuses is limited by a tendency to focus on a narrow set of civil and political rights violations. In line with the findings of Leckie and Huggins, Miller, Roht-Arriaza and others, we observed how criminal proceedings, truth commissions and other mechanisms tend to portray violations of ESCR as a 'background' to what is perceived as more 'acute' violations of civil and political rights.[4] This study is based on the presumption that it is difficult to justify an ethics in which the differential treatment of human rights abuses and victims is apparent. The need for systematic analysis in this field has been recognised by scholars and practitioners. In Louise Arbour's words, by exposing violations of ESCR – including by considering how the scope of international criminal law relates to such abuses – attempts to address a legacy of an abusive past are 'poised to make the significant leap that would allow justice, in its full sense, to contribute as it should to societies in transition'.[5]

[1] Sigrun Skogly, 'Crimes against Humanity' (2001) 5 *International Journal of Human Rights*, 1, 58–80: 58.

[2] Elias Davidsson, 'Economic Oppression' (2005) 23 *Netherlands Quarterly of Human Rights*, 2, 173–212: 173.

[3] Ramesh Thakur, 'Macho Move Would Make Burma's Plight Even Worse', *Japan Times*, 2 June 2008.

[4] Scott Leckie and Christopher Huggins, *Conflict and Housing, Land, and Property Rights* (Cambridge University Press, 2011), 237; Zinaida Miller, 'Effects of Invisibility' (2008) 2 *International Journal of Transitional Justice*, 266–91: 266; Naomi Roht-Arriaza, 'Reparations and Economic and Social Rights', in *Justice and Economic Violence in Transition*, ed. Dustin Sharp (Springer, 2013), 109–38: 110.

[5] Louise Arbour, 'Economic and Social Justice for Societies in Transition' (2007) 40 *New York University Journal of International Law and Politics*, 1, 1–28: 2.

Nevertheless, treatment accorded to abuses of ESCR in international criminal law is still out of step with the contemporary legal understanding of ESCR in international human rights law. Though the significance of attempts to redress ESCR abuses in processes aimed to deal with past crimes is recognised, the literature displays uncertainty if the marginalisation of ESCR concerns can be remedied by a careful and principled interpretation of the definitions of existing international crimes, or whether an expansion of existing law is required. Against this background, it was particularly pressing to undertake a systematic analysis of the potential for existing international criminal law to accommodate claims related to ESCR abuses.

Chapter 2 began by tracing the intellectual roots of the tendency to assume that existing international criminal law prescribes an unavoidable focus on civil and political rights and leaves no or very little room for considerations of ESCR violations. Given that this legal impossibility argument is based on outdated perceptions of the legal nature of ESCR, a serious engagement with the underlying assumptions of the traditional view was timely and warranted.

Chapter 3 introduced the key legal concepts employed throughout the study: 'violations of ESCR' and 'international crimes'. Therein was presented the methodology that allowed us to ascertain if and how ESCR violations overlap with existing definitions of international crimes. The methodology required both that a criminal lawyer could correctly find the elements of an international crime, and that a human rights lawyer examining the same factual background could simultaneously and correctly identify a violation of ESCR under an existing human rights treaty.

Chapter 4 covered the overlap between the definitions of crimes against humanity and violations of ESCR. Because the law on crimes against humanity is to a great degree influenced by international human rights law, the point of convergence between crimes against humanity and ESCR violations is particularly significant. A range of crimes against humanity can be committed where perpetrators are involved in violations of ESCR. The definition of crimes against humanity requires that abuses were 'committed as part of a widespread or systematic attack directed against any civilian population'. We saw that in some circumstances, such an attack can itself be committed by violating ESCR. In other circumstances, ESCR violations can be the conduct fulfilling the elements of one of the underlying offences which will constitute crimes against humanity provided that they are committed in the context of a widespread or systematic attack directed against any civilian population.

The chapter considered numerous examples of cases World War II and abuses committed in Zimbabwe, Burma/Myanmar, North Korea and elsewhere, and identified particular ways in which ESCR violations can overlap with the crimes against humanity of deportation or forcible transfer of population, enslavement, sexual slavery, enforced prostitution, forced marriage, enforced sterilisation, persecution, apartheid, murder, extermination, torture and other inhumane acts.

Chapter 5 turned to the analysis of war crimes. We found that the legal definitions of war crimes against persons, war crimes against property, war crimes consisting in the use of prohibited methods of warfare as well as war crimes consisting in the use of prohibited means of warfare are all open to considerations of ESCR. The picture is complicated by the many distinctions in criminalisation between abuses committed during international armed conflict and conduct committed during non-international armed conflict, the status of the victim under IHL as well as whether the conduct is qualified according to the Rome Statute or another legal source. These difficulties, however, are not specific to whether or not the conduct deals with ESCR abuses. On the contrary, Chapter 5 revealed that the very first cases of international criminal justice already dealt with conduct that human rights lawyers today would qualify as violations of ESCR: we considered a number of first occurrences in international criminal law such as the trial of the first individual convicted according to the principles underpinning the IMT Charter, Arthur Greiser. We saw that the report of his trial details a brutal campaign exploiting the deprivation of people's access to ESCR by resettling them, evicting them from their homes, segregating them, shutting down cultural and educational institutions, depriving them of their right to work and health, confiscating entire libraries and destroying historical monuments.[6] Shortly after Greiser's trial, the first panel of NMT judges convicted Dr Karl Brandt and sixteen other defendants of atrocious interferences with victims' health.[7] In the first national trial known for the invocation of universal jurisdiction for international crimes, Adolf Eichmann was convicted for the deprivation of people's access to food.[8]

Chapter 6 argued that a principled interpretation of the definition of genocide implies that violations of ESCR can under certain circumstances overlap with genocide. The analysis considered how genocidal

[6] *Prosecutor* v. *Greiser, Case No. 74, XIII Law Reports of Trials of War Criminals 70, 7 July 1946, Supreme National Tribunal, Poland,* 73. See Section 5.2.

[7] See Section 5.2.1.4. [8] See Section 8.2.1.2.

intent to destroy a protected group can be inferred from violations of ESCR. While it is challenging to infer genocidal intent from the denial of food, water or other essential ESCR to a protected group, genocidal intent covers those ESCR violations that are intended to materially annihilate a protected group, including if the intention is to lead to the group's destruction over a significant time horizon. Importantly, we also saw that genocide can overlap with ESCR violations if one of the underlying acts is carried out by means of ESCR abuses and intent is inferred from other facts. Furthermore, we observed that the legal history of the crime of genocide indicates that considerations of people's enjoyment of ESCR have always been part and parcel of the law of genocide.

Chapter 7 complemented the analysis by studying the overlap of ESCR abuses with a range of other crimes. Crimes such as slavery and related practices, discrete instances of torture, corruption, the laundering of proceeds of crime or the unlawful movement of hazardous waste catch the headlines of international news less often, but they are all the subject of extensive international regulation and can overlap with ESCR violations. Where ESCR abuses overlap with crimes dealt with in numerous multilateral treaties, the human rights law framework can be complemented by the often-detailed provisions of suppression conventions in international criminal law. Governmental authorities can, and sometimes must, employ the specific provisions of a range of such treaties which states adopted to strengthen the effective repression and redress of criminalised conduct and hence ESCR violations.

Chapter 8 presented the legal corollaries of the finding that ESCR violations overlap with the existing definitions of international crimes. Rather than being a mere theoretical possibility, the main finding of this study bears a range of practical corollaries. Despite the contemporary hesitation to take into account ESCR violations in processes established to deal with an abusive past, prosecutors, lawyers, NGOs and judges at international and national tribunals can legitimately deal with those violations of ESCR that overlap with international crimes. International and national tribunals are competent to adjudicate claims based on conduct that can be understood as an international crime and that also relates to a simultaneous ESCR violation. Victims can claim the same remedies and reparations as for crimes touching upon their civil and political rights. States have a range of binding legal obligations to fight and remedy international crimes, and these obligations pertain to all violations of ESCR that amount to international crimes. Non-state actors can be liable for crimes overlapping with ESCR violations, and the UN

Security Council can take a range of measures to address such abuses. Of particular practical relevance is the consequence that mechanisms such as truth commissions, national human rights institutions or reparation programmes are competent to investigate and deal with ESCR violations amounting to international crimes given that the mandates of such mechanisms usually include international crimes.

## 9.2 Argued concerns and reflections on the contribution of the research findings

The main inference of this study is that there are no legal reasons to dismiss claims that conduct constitutes an international crime solely because the abuses relate to economic, social or cultural concerns. Not everyone, however, agrees that paying more attention to circumstances which human rights lawyers describe as violations of ESCR would be legally warranted and advisable in international criminal law. The main finding of this study – that the existing definitions of international crimes overlap with violations of ESCR – gives rise to a number of argued concerns and objections. The first of these concerns is the legal impossibility argument which we have already studied in detail in Chapter 2 and subsequently disproven throughout Chapters 3–7. The other concerns, which can be grouped under three headings, deserve to be addressed here.

### *9.2.1 Cherry-picking ESCR violations?*

A second concern that can potentially be raised is that the arguments made in this study might only hold true in extremely narrow circumstances. One might ask if the violations of ESCR studied in this book are selected in order to make a straightforward demonstration of overlap with international criminal law. Did the study simply concentrate on a very narrow understanding of ESCR while neglecting the majority of ESCR violations? Two enquiries are possible: first, whether all the ESCR violations dealt with in this study can also be understood as civil and political rights, and second, whether the ESCR violations in this study are limited to violations of states' duties to *respect* the rights by directly interfering with their enjoyment, rather than duties to protect and fulfil ESCR. For instance, it could be said that the crime against humanity of enforced sterilisations only overlaps with the right to health because the right to health, in this instance, could also be understood as (i) a civil and political rights violation (i.e., the right to bodily integrity) and (ii) a violation of the state's duty to respect rights (i.e., the duty to abstain from interference with bodily integrity). But then why would a 'detour' and a long argument on ESCR offer any advantages if all the rights studied can be understood as civil and political rights' infringements and negative rights?

Two responses must be made – one legal and the other one functional. The legal answer is two-pronged. First, not all violations of ESCR covered in this study can be understood as civil and political rights abuses. For example, deliberately attacking educational buildings can lead to the finding of a war crime that overlaps with an infringement of children's right to education.[9] If no person is injured in the attack, it will be difficult to argue that civil and political rights would simultaneously be affected – in which case the war crime overlaps with a violation of ESCR that cannot be understood as a violation of civil and political rights.

Second, not all the examined illustrations were concerned with the state's duty to respect ESCR. Examples touching upon the state's duty to protect, and sometimes the duty to fulfil, were also identified. Consider, for example, the overlap we examined in Chapter 5, between violations of the right to work in the former Yugoslavia and the war crime of forcible transfer. In that example, the ICTY found that discriminatory dismissals from employment were aimed at, and succeeded in, making it practically impossible for most Muslims and Croats to remain in municipalities controlled by Serb forces.[10] Not only is it impossible to frame the underlying human rights abuse as an infringement of civil and political rights, but the conduct also overlapped with the state's failure to protect against discriminatory dismissals. Similarly, we saw how violations of the right to housing or water can result from the state's failure to *protect* against abuses committed by non-state actors,[11] and can overlap both with war crimes and crimes against humanity.[12] Albeit in more limited circumstances, the dimension to fulfil ESCR was also relevant. For instance, when a state fails to fulfil the right to health based on discriminatory grounds or when a state fails to fulfil children's right to education, this violation of ESCR can overlap with the crime against humanity of persecution or with the crime of apartheid.[13]

9 See Section 5.2.2.3.

10 *Prosecutor* v. *Krajišnik, IT-00-39-T, 27 September 2006*, ICTY, para. 729. See Section 5.2.1.2.

11 *COHRE* v. *Sudan, Communication 296/05, 29 July 2010*, ACommHPR, para. 159 (housing) and paras. 209–12 (water).

12 For the analysis of how violations of the right to housing or water can overlap with war crimes and crimes against humanity, see, for instance, Section 4.3, 4.5, 5.2.1.1 or 5.2.4.

13 See Sections 4.5, 4.6 and 7.3.

In addition to the legal answer, a functional perspective suggests that the argument of this study is warranted even if those ESCR violations that most easily demonstrate overlap with international criminal definitions can often also be viewed as infringements of civil and political rights and/or violations of the duty to *respect* rights. As explained in the introductory chapter, there is a tendency to relegate certain crimes to the background as soon as they seem related primarily to people's enjoyment of ESCR. Imagine, for instance, a case of intentional killing by the deprivation of food. Although the underlying human rights violation can be understood as both a violation of the right to food and a violation of the right to life (which continues to be primarily understood as a civil and political right), such crimes tend to be more easily overlooked than intentional killings with firearms,[14] including in cases where the evidentiary challenges are not inherently more challenging than in cases of extrajudicial or summary executions. This neglect could be remedied if lawyers undertake a more conscious examination of ESCR-related abuses when identifying possible crimes and if the artificial perception of a separation of rights into two categories of human rights would be abandoned.

### 9.2.2 *Opening the floodgates?*

A third concern does not pertain to the legal analysis in this study, but raises doubts whether it would be an advisable policy to pay more attention to people's access to health, water, work or other ESCR when identifying international crimes. Some will ask whether paying more attention to ESCR would overstretch the capacities of international criminal law at best, and dilute the definitions of the various crimes at worst. A flood of claims might – according to this concern – follow and place an unmanageable burden upon the institutions and mechanisms that can be employed to fight international crimes, a worry well summarised by

[14] Sonja Starr has speculated as to why international criminal lawyers have tended to ignore abuses that cause suffering 'far out of proportion to the minimal headline ink expended on them'. Sonja Starr, 'Extraordinary Crimes at Ordinary Times' (2007) 101 *Northwestern University Law Review*, 3, 1257–314: 1257–8. Based on Hilary Charlesworth's description of international law as a 'discipline of crisis', Starr perceives an unjustified and unreflected reductionism in the focus of international criminal lawyers. By extension, her analysis of the 'crisis focus' of international criminal law could be expanded to the different treatment of abuses pertaining to people's enjoyment of ESCR on the one hand and civil and political rights abuses that are more easily associated with 'thundering and bloody history' on the other. Ibid., 1266. See also Hilary Charlesworth, 'A Discipline of Crisis' (2002) 65 *Modern Law Review*, 3, 377–92.

Rama Mani. While Mani advocates that we pay more attention to economic, social and cultural issues in attempts to redress past abuses, she cautions that tribunals, truth commissions and other 'existing transitional justice mechanisms are already overcharged, their responsibilities too heavy, public expectations too unrealistic and finances already too lean'.[15] In turn, if the institutional burden was to increase, this would, according to some, hamper the institutions, which will have to spend scarce resources on a wider array of criminal conduct. This concern is expressed by Mark Drumbl in relation to the ICC. Drumbl cautions that '[t]oo broad a swath of prosecutions for a variety of crimes may conflict with the ICC's focus on a small number of perpetrators of the most notorious offenses'.[16] Sigrun Skogly summarises the possible counter-argument to the application of the findings made in this study by voicing 'a concern that if we include too much in the concept of crimes against humanity [or other crimes], the concept may be watered down and lose its significant position in international law'.[17]

These concerns comprise a 'floodgates' argument – a concern based on the purported fear that too many claims could be justified on the basis of the analysis presented in this study. As other authors have noted, the problem with a floodgates argument is 'that it is clearly not a legal argument'.[18] As long as a correct interpretation based on principles of international law warrants the inclusion of considerations based on ESCR, international law is open to such claims and does not support the marginalisation of ESCR.

Although the floodgates concern is not a legal argument, it is nevertheless reasonable to consider the floodgates concern as a matter of policy. To ignore the concern is inapposite, given the frequency with which similar arguments are made by those who caution against giving

15 Rama Mani, 'Dilemmas' (2008) 2 *International Journal of Transitional Justice*, 3, 253–65: 255. See also Roger Duthie, 'Displacement' (2011) 5 *International Journal of Transitional Justice*, 241–61: 249–50: 'The sheer scale and complexity of the problem [of displacement] mean that transitional justice measures have a limited capacity to deal directly with the issue.'

16 Mark Drumbl, 'Accountability for Property and Environmental War Crimes' (ICTJ, November 2009), 23.

17 Skogly, 'Crimes against Humanity', 74.

18 Michelle Foster, *International Refugee Law and Socio-Economic Rights* (Cambridge University Press, 2007), 344, citing refugee law decisions rejecting the floodgates argument as 'no argument at all'. There was also significant opposition to a floodgates argument during the negotiation of the OP-ICESCR, with delegations rejecting the argument on the basis that it would 'seem to imply that some violations could be considered insignificant, which was unacceptable'. Fifth Report of the Open-Ended Working Group to Consider Options Regarding the Elaboration of an Optional Protocol to the International Covenant on Economic, Social and Cultural Rights, A/HRC/8/7, 6 May 2008, para. 59.

ESCR more attention. As long as the institutional capacity is not great enough to address all the international crimes that occur, policy considerations will remain relevant when lawyers identify what conduct to examine. It is thus warranted to give some notice to the floodgates concern, since, as Foster cautions, 'to ignore it may risk undermining the cogency of an otherwise valid [legal] argument'.[19]

Beyond the fact that it is no legal argument, there are three key answers to the floodgates appeal.

First, the floodgates argument assumes a significantly more expansive conclusion than what is justified by the analysis undertaken in this study.[20] Only few abuses of ESCR can be qualified as international crimes, and we saw that these crimes have formidable contextual thresholds and other legal elements that must be met. The analysis does not propose to change the definition of these crimes or to grant the status of victims to individuals who do not meet the required criteria. Hence, this study does not lend support to those who wish to apply the concept of international crimes to what Drumbl called conduct outside of 'the most notorious offenses'.[21] Rather, the analysis made evident that the marginalisation of claims based on conduct that primarily touches upon people's access and enjoyment of ESCR is an arbitrary distinction unwarranted by international law. As we saw, only a limited number of human rights violations fall within the category of international crimes, but the line is not to be drawn between ESCR violations and civil and political rights abuses.

[19] Foster, *International Refugee Law and Socio-Economic Rights*, 344.

[20] See also ibid., 345, for a similar structure in responding to a floodgates concern in relation to international refugee law.

[21] Drumbl cautions against prosecutions for crimes related to economic, social and environmental concerns because such an approach 'may conflict with the ICC's focus on a small number of perpetrators of the most notorious offenses'. However, prior to making this statement, Drumbl concluded that there are international 'crimes that are social, economic, cultural, or environmental in nature' and identified socio-economic crimes which are 'reasonably well articulated' in international criminal law. If these are international crimes, it is not clear why he would consider them less notorious offences than war crimes or crimes against humanity that do not relate to socio-economic wrongdoing. Drumbl, 'Accountability for Property and Environmental War Crimes', 5, 6. Drumbl seems to assume that 'what the public perceives as the more serious crimes of concern to humanity as a whole' will 'traditionally gravitate to massive and brutal violations of civil and political rights'. Ibid., 23. However, in another text, Drumbl contradicts this assumption when he explains how public pressure and insistence led the prosecutors of the Supreme National Tribunal in Poland to emphasise what can be conceptualised as infringements of cultural rights. Mark Drumbl, 'The Trial of Arthur Greiser in Poland', in *The Hidden Histories of War Crimes Trials*, ed. Kevin Heller and Gerry Simpson (Oxford University Press, 2013), 411–29: 419.

The second objection to the floodgates argument is that it misconstrues the main finding of this study. Nothing in this study has suggested that international and domestic criminal tribunals, national human rights institutions, truth commissions or other actors should accept all claims related to ESCR unconditionally and under all circumstances. What has been shown is that a correct and systematic interpretation of the definitions of international crimes indicates that ESCR violations are within the ambit of international criminal law. When Louise Arbour advocated for more attention to ESCR in post-conflict situations, she emphasised that she was 'not suggesting that courts and truth commissions should strive to investigate and provide remedies for violations of these rights under all circumstances and unconditionally'.[22] Similarly, this study has not advocated for an unconditional focus on ESCR abuses. Rather, the study demonstrated that there is no legal basis for the neglect of ESCR in international criminal justice.

Third, even where the argument of this study is used to encourage additional proceedings before criminal tribunals, fears of ensuing capacity constraints are not necessarily warranted. Whereas capacity concerns are real for international institutions – whether or not they pay attention to ESCR considerations – such is not necessarily the case for domestic tribunals. As we saw in Chapter 8, domestic tribunals are competent over a wide range of international crimes, including when the conduct has no or only minor links to the territory or nationality of the state exercising jurisdiction.[23] In many developed states, justice systems would seem capable of exercising jurisdiction over a greater number of cases, independent of whether or not the alleged conduct relates to abuses of ESCR. Provided there is political will, prosecutors and lawyers in many jurisdictions can rely on justice systems with the capacity to undertake additional investigations and prosecute those alleged of international crimes that overlap with ESCR violations.

### 9.2.3 *Decreasing or increasing the credibility of international justice?*

The last worry pertains to the credibility of international justice institutions. Will the credibility of mechanisms relying on international criminal law decrease or increase if their representatives pay more attention to

22 Arbour, 'Economic and Social Justice for Societies in Transition', 13.

23 See Section 8.2.

ESCR-related abuses? It would seem justified to believe that concern about the credibility of the international and national institutions dealing with crimes is not served by an unexplained bias towards certain rights and the marginalisation of others. If it is accepted that the philosophical justification of the international criminal order is based on the protection of human rights,[24] a focus on a very narrow set of human rights risks may undermine rather than bolster the legitimacy of international criminal law. Reflecting on the underlying conduct of persecution as a crime against humanity, the ICTY Appeals Chamber emphasised that '[t]he interest of justice would not be served by [providing an exhaustive list of rights that constitute fundamental rights], as the explicit inclusion of particular fundamental rights could be interpreted as the implicit exclusion of other rights'.[25]

At some point, difficult choices have to be made and explained by lawyers, NGOs, prosecutors, authorities or survivors about what abuses will be prioritised, who will be considered a victim and who might be entitled to redress. This is true independent of the inclusion of ESCR considerations in international criminal law approaches. Yet, the marginalisation of ESCR in attempts to address serious human rights abuses is usually not explained, but is often taken as a given or simply viewed as part of a wider problem of the limited capacity of tribunals, truth commissions, reparation programmes and other institutional mechanisms. But the institutions dealing with international crimes will not enhance their credibility if they fail to explain their focus. In this instance, the current approaches are 'creating two classes of victims – those who deserve assistance and those who do not; and two classes of crimes – those worthy of investigation and those that are not'.[26] Where institutional capacities are limited and where there may be good reasons to restrict the scope of a certain mechanism, such selectivity deserves to be explained and the deliberations made transparent, whether in relation to abuses affecting people's enjoyment of ESCR or their civil and political rights.[27] As argued in Chapter 2, selectivity in

[24] Otfried Höffe, *Democracy* (Springer, 2007), 264. Cited in Kai Ambos, 'Punishment without a Sovereign?' (2013) 33 *Oxford Journal of Legal Studies*, 2, 293–315: 17.

[25] *Prosecutor* v. *Krnojelac, IT-97-25-A, 17 September 2003*, ICTY, para. 185.

[26] Phuong Pham, 'Women & Justice in Conflict: Beyond Rape Victims', (29 October 2011), http://www.intlawgrrls.com/2011/10/women-justice-in-conflict-beyond-rape.html.

[27] It should be noted that certain civil and political rights also tend to attract less attention than others. The right to freedom of assembly, for instance, does not seem to have been an issue for international criminal lawyers after the post-World War II trials, even if violations thereof can overlap with crimes such as persecution.

international criminal law is a fact and one that is going to stay with us for the foreseeable future. Telford Taylor has vividly recounted how the Nuremberg prosecution staff wrestled with the decisions of who should be named as defendants in the indictment of the IMT.[28] The current capacity of institutions to deal with international criminal law today is equally constrained by limited resources and political realities, and there is no indication that states will remedy this situation in the near future. As Schabas writes, the selection of situations for prosecution 'may well be the greatest challenge to international justice'[29]:

> Because of its unavoidable political dimension, international justice (including its exercise at the national level) is by necessity not a comprehensive venture. Decisions must be made concerning those who are to be brought to justice. Inevitably, comparisons of the relative gravity and importance of atrocities perpetrated in different parts of the world must be made ... [T]hose who defend the system ... often attempt to show that the choices of targets for prosecution are based upon objective criteria, or at least insist that this is the intention. But it is a tortuous argument, because in fact highly subjective decisions are often at the origin of international prosecutions.[30]

If international law does not dictate an exclusion of considerations of ESCR in the realm of international crimes, this implies that international law cannot be blamed for the marginalisation of ESCR. Rather than being irrelevant when it comes to ESCR abuses, the scope of the existing definitions of international crimes is not fully explored. Instead of hastily concluding that international law does not allow us to deal with ESCR, we should spend more time reflecting on the way case selections are made and on what basis. It is possible, and not in contradiction with the findings of this study, that there are good reasons to advocate against a focus on ESCR abuses in addressing legacies of massive human rights abuse in a specific situation. The priority of abuses is a difficult question in any society and one that cannot be answered in the abstract. The population of one country may feel that it is most important to obtain the most complete historic record of patterns of past abuses, in which case it is likely that ESCR violations deserve to be addressed. But in another country, finding remains of a particular massacre might take priority, in which case it might be justifiable to focus exclusively on extrajudicial executions.[31]

[28] Telford Taylor, *The Anatomy of the Nuremberg Trials* (Bloomsbury, 1993), 79–115.
[29] William Schabas, *Unimaginable Atrocities* (Oxford University Press, 2012), 4.
[30] Ibid., 4–5.
[31] See also Evelyne Schmid, 'Truth Commissions', in *PeaceBrief* (USIP, 2012), 2.

To avoid sweeping conclusions about the priorities in a given situation, the OHCHR recommends the public at large be consulted before the mandate of, for example, a truth commission is designed or before decisions on how to craft recommendations on matters such as reparations or institutional reform are made.[32] When designing surveys for consultations, it is thus important to ensure that the survey does not in and of itself relegate ESCR violations to the fringes but employs a suitable methodology to ascertain opinions and expectations on the full range of past human rights abuses.[33]

In this context, it is also important not to pit justice for ESCR violations against development concerns. It is sometimes said that victims need development, not justice.[34] As the UN rapporteur on the promotion of truth, justice, reparation and guarantees of non-recurrence maintains,

> [g]overnments of some countries that emerge from conflict including systematic human rights violations are wont to say 'Victims do not call for justice; they want development'. This tendency is widespread . . . The diversity of Governments tempted by this position obviously does not make it correct.[35]
>
> Without denying the fact that scarcity makes choices inevitable, and that not all things come together all the time, priorities and sequences in discussions about development choices are set without sufficient attention to the interconnections between development on one hand, and rule of law, justice and rights, on the other hand.[36]

Quick assumptions on what the law is about must be avoided. Presenting selections of cases, strategies and emphases in international criminal law as objectively given is particularly problematic in periods when societies decide to address a legacy of massive abuse. During attempts to deal with an abusive past, the population can be expected to observe the official use of

[32] OHCHR, Rule-of-Law Tools for Post-Conflict States: National Consultations on Transitional Justice, OHCHR, 2009.

[33] Tafadzwa Pasipanodya, 'A Deeper Justice' (2008) 2 *International Journal of Transitional Justice*, 3, 378–97: 387–8. Pasipanodya criticises a population survey conducted in Nepal. This survey narrowly defined 'victims' as those who suffered disappearance, extrajudicial killings, torture or rape – leading to a skewed sample with an over-representation of some types of abuses and of male and economically privileged respondents.

[34] Lars Waldorf, 'Anticipating the Past' (2012) 21 *Social and Legal Studies*, 2, 171–86: 175. For a critique of Waldorf's use of rights language, see Evelyne Schmid and Aoife Nolan, 'Economic and Social Dimensions of Transitional Justice' (2014) 8 *International Journal of Transitional Justice*, 3, 362–82.

[35] Pablo de Greiff, Report of the Special Rapporteur on the Promotion of Truth, Justice, Reparation and Guarantees of Non-Recurrence, A/68/345, 23 August 2013, para. 11.

[36] Ibid., para. 6.

law very carefully and will (re)consider whether or not the state and its institutions are worthy of their trust and patience. The perceived legitimacy and usefulness of legal norms invoked will, amongst others factors, depend on whether or not the official references to law are seen to address what society considers the defining experiences of the abusive past. As de Greiff has put it: 'Transitional moments are periods of heightened normative sensitivity, where both institutions and individuals have strong incentives to articulate the principles, norms and values to which they commit themselves.'[37] Given that ESCR violations overlapping with international crimes entail a 'defeat of normative expectations fundamental to our sense of agency in the world',[38] just as this is the case for other crimes, attempts to address the legacies of past human rights violations are most promising if they are conceptualised as 'measures that serve to signal the significance of the status of persons as rights bearers'.[39] Conversely, where ESCR abuses overlapping with international crimes marked victims' experiences, the absence of any efforts to integrate ESCR violations into mainstream strategies to deal with an abusive past will signal that these abuses are less worthy of condemnation than crimes overlapping with civil and political rights violations.

In line with Rawls' *Theory of Justice*, we can expect that the use of law to address abuses of ESCR can catalyse trust and constitute the 'grounds upon which persons can rely on one another and rightly object when their expectations are not fulfilled'.[40] Setting ESCR aside implicitly informs societies that depriving people of food, health care or education is 'not to be prosecuted or amnestied'.[41] The risk of such an approach, as alluded to in the introductory chapters, is that the marginalisation of ESCR considerations will lead to perceptions that international law, or law as such, is irrelevant and cannot contribute to or address issues of socio-economic deprivation and cultural rights abuses. With this in mind, sensitivity to ESCR abuses and a conscious and transparent engagement with the question to what extent ESCR violations should be addressed do not decrease the credibility of institutions dealing with international crimes, but, on the contrary, help to strengthen their relevance.

[37] Pablo de Greiff (ed.), *The Handbook of Reparations* (Oxford University Press, 2006), 465.

[38] de Greiff, Report of the Special Rapporteur on the Promotion of Truth, Justice, Reparation and Guarantees of Non-Recurrence, A/68/345, 23 August 2013, paras. 16, 38.

[39] Ibid. [40] John Rawls, *A Theory of Justice*, original edn (Belknap, 1971), 235.

[41] Miller, 'Effects of Invisibility', 268.

That said, even the most careful treatment of ESCR in international criminal law will not solve all problems associated with the legacies of socio-economic and cultural abuses.

## 9.3 The limits of the main finding

The converse argument to the floodgates concern described above may also be advanced, namely that reliance on international criminal law does not provide sufficient avenues to address abuses of ESCR.[42] This leads us to consider the obstacles to the reach and contribution of the finding made in this study.

There is a risk of overemphasising the use of international criminal law to remedy violations of ESCR (or any other human rights violations). First of all, there are important general limitations of international criminal law that deserve to be taken into account. Even where it is legally appropriate to rely on international criminal law, reliance on this body of law will rarely be sufficient to redress past abuses. Moreover, while legal analysis based on appropriate principles of treaty interpretation has shown that definitions of international crimes overlap with violations of ESCR, insurmountable obstacles prevent the application of international criminal law in many situations that deserve to be addressed. Regardless of how open the actors applying international criminal law are towards considering abuses of ESCR, the proper application and interpretation of international criminal law will result in the exclusion of many arguably deserving claims.[43] Four formidable obstacles limit the reach of the findings made in this study.

### *9.3.1 General limitations of international criminal law*

First, as Theodor Meron has succinctly expressed it, '[i]nternational criminal law, of course, is just one element in the life of the society. Addressed in isolation, it will not eliminate abuses'.[44] Meron's fundamental note of caution emphasises that criminal tribunals are limited in their ability to address societal ills. Prosecutions in criminal tribunals have potentially serious drawbacks. In particular, the job of a criminal

[42] Similarly, Foster, *International Refugee Law and Socio-Economic Rights*, 348.

[43] Foster raises a similar point in relation to ESCR abuses and refugee law. Ibid., 349.

[44] Theodor Meron, 'Criminalization of Internal Atrocities' (1995) 89 *American Journal of International Law*, 554–77: 556.

tribunal is first and foremost to decide upon the guilt or innocence of specific individuals – a task that entails a necessarily limited focus on the accused and the need to apply particular standards of evidence. Criminal proceedings are not particularly well placed to provide a holistic understanding of what happened. Moreover, trials for international crimes are costly, lengthy and often frustrating for survivors, and there is no solid evidence of their alleged deterrent effect.[45] Unrealistic expectations about the potential of international criminal law thus have to be avoided, and the question whether courtrooms are the proper place to grapple with past human rights violations should always be raised – whether the crimes overlap with ESCR violations or not.

### *9.3.2 Demanding elements of crimes and evidentiary challenges*

Second, and stressed repeatedly throughout the study, ESCR abuses must meet specific legal criteria before they overlap with international crimes. It is often challenging to demonstrate that all the elements of a crime are present, in particular where contextual threshold criteria must be met (such as the existence of an armed conflict, or a widespread or systematic attack directed against a civilian population). It is often difficult to gather the necessary evidence to prove both the objective and the subjective elements of a crime.

Demanding elements of crimes and related evidentiary challenges arise whether or not the alleged criminal conduct touches upon civil and political rights, ESCR or a combination of both. Linking abuses to specific perpetrators is easier in some cases than in others, but the dividing line is again not between civil and political rights and ESCR violations. On the one hand, cases of traditional looting of personal property, the burning of civilians' homes in armed conflicts or the starvation of detainees are among the most straightforward examples demonstrating that dealing with abuses of ESCR is not inherently more complex than the prosecution of abuses touching upon people's civil and political rights.[46] On the

[45] On the limitations of international criminal law in general, see Drumbl, 'Accountability for Property and Environmental War Crimes', 22–3. On deterrence, see Kate Cronin-Furman, 'Managing Expectations: International Criminal Trials and the Prospects for Deterrence of Mass Atrocity' (2013) 7 *International Journal of Transitional Justice*, 3, 434–54.

[46] This goes back to the idea outlined in Chapter 2 that not all violations of ESCR are necessarily 'structural'. Nor are all civil and political rights infringements always 'discrete' abuses. See Section 2.2.1.3.

other hand, the evidentiary challenges are particularly challenging for conduct which is compartmentalised into a large number of individual abuses that collectively demonstrate the existence of an international crime. Such constellations can arise in cases of alleged crimes committed by way of violating ESCR but they are not unique to abuses in the realm of ESCR. Consider, for example, the crime of forcible transfer as a crime against humanity. The attack itself must be widespread or systematic (not the perpetrator's underlying act of forcible transfer), but it is in practice usually necessary to consider a large number of involuntary evictions. To prove the *mens rea* elements of the crime, the prosecutor will need to consider how the individual instances of forced evictions are interrelated. While we need to acknowledge such evidentiary difficulties, the same challenges arise if the underlying abuses primarily touch upon victims' civil and political rights, such as when prosecutors attempt to link a perpetrator's role in massive infringements of freedom to arbitrary deprivation of liberty with the *mens rea* elements for the crime of persecution. Throughout this study, numerous examples of court cases have been listed in which such evidentiary problems could be overcome in cases that related to infringements of ESCR.[47]

In addition, something does not cease to be a crime merely because it is difficult to prove and to eradicate. After all, evidentiary challenges are inherent to any proceedings of international criminal law and not intrinsically negative, considering the requirements of due process and the need to avoid miscarriages of justice.

These challenges are much less acute outside criminal tribunals. Other mechanisms applying international criminal law do not necessarily have to relate the criminal conduct to specific perpetrators, and we saw that the findings of this study also pertain to quasi- or non-judicial mechanisms. A truth commission or an international commission of inquiry, for instance, can legitimately find that an international crime has occurred, without identifying individual perpetrators, and hence without the need to examine the mental state of specific individuals. At the same time, it remains accurate that the demonstration of the elements of international crimes is a complex endeavour that excludes many harmful abuses.

[47] To mention just one example, the case of *Krajišnik* (see Section 5.2.1.2) is illustrative (displacement of civilians by way of inflicting severe living conditions touching upon people's access to ESCR).

### 9.3.3 *Abuses by non-state actors*

The third limitation of this study is that it has not addressed the full range of abuses committed by non-state actors. Given that this study has dealt with violations of ESCR, the law of international responsibility of states for internationally wrongful acts prescribed that it was necessary to establish the role the state played in the abuses. As explained in Chapter 3, the traditional understanding of human rights violations requires that the state failed to comply with an international obligation by conduct that is attributable to that state. The most common way attribution to a state can be established is if a state actor is directly involved in the abuses or when the state fails to regulate the behaviour of non-state actors, that is, when the state fails to protect ESCR. Multiple examples in this study demonstrate that a violation of ESCR can be found if the state has violated its duty to protect where non-state actors interfere with people's enjoyment of ESCR. Yet, non-state actors can, of course, also harm people's socio-economic and cultural well-being independent of the behaviour of a state.[48] This study has only considered violations of ESCR as they are traditionally understood in relation to the law of state responsibility for internationally wrongful acts. The numerous other ways people's socio-economic and cultural interests can be affected have not been the subject of this study.

### 9.3.4 *Incomplete criminalisation*

The fourth reason why many deserving claims are excluded from the reach of the argument presented in this study is that international criminalisation is incomplete and depends on contextual elements that states introduce for political rather than legal reasons.[49] The elements of crimes imply that conduct can be a crime under certain circumstances, but not in others. For instance, some abuses are only criminalised if

[48] If such is the case, the lack of attribution implies that we cannot consider the conduct a violation of ESCR, at least as traditionally understood. This does, of course, not exclude a finding of an international crime. Where the non-state actor is a collective entity (such as an armed group or a corporation), it is uncertain, but at least possible to envisage that international criminal law may impose liability on actors other than individuals. See the last paragraphs of Section 3.2.2.1.

[49] On this point, see, for instance, Bruce Broomhall, *International Justice and the International Criminal Court: Between Sovereignty and the Rule of Law* (Oxford University Press, 2004), 39. Broomhall aptly concludes that '[b]ecause the judgment of states, individually and collectively, is subject to diverse extra-legal influences, the process of international criminalization will always be less orderly than its conceptual foundation'.

committed in international conflicts but not in civil wars. These complex distinctions are referable 'to no moral reason or legal necessity'.[50] The degree of international criminalisation depends on states' willingness to hold officials and other actors accountable for abuses. Ratner concludes that '[t]he portrait of international criminal law is one of a legal environment resembling more a patchwork than a coherent, let alone, complete system'.[51] Ratner famously called the result the 'schizophrenias of international criminal law'.[52] By schizophrenias, the author refers to the schisms in international criminal law, which distinguishes '(1) between criminality for atrocities in wartime and those in peacetime; (2) a distinction among wartime atrocities between the criminality of those committed in interstate conflicts and those in civil wars; and (3) a distinction among peacetime atrocities among the criminality of seemingly equally egregious acts (for example, torture versus murder)'.[53]

In relation to abuses discussed in this study, an individual treated inhumanely because he or she is deprived of food or water, for instance, can often be recognised as a victim of a crime if the conduct takes place in the context of an armed conflict.[54] If the same conduct takes place in peacetime, the individual could only be a victim of an international crime if the perpetrator acts within the context of a crime against humanity or genocide. To add just one illustration, it will often be possible to qualify attacks against buildings dedicated to education as a war crime, but if educational buildings are harmed in peacetime, the same conduct will rarely constitute an international crime. These distinctions in criminalisation are difficult to justify ethically.[55] The effects for the concerned individual's enjoyment of ESCR are the same, independent of the context in which the abuses were committed. Yet, the distinctions in criminalisation cannot be overcome by the analysis made in this study. They are inherent to any approaches based on existing international

[50] Steven Ratner, 'Schizophrenias' (1998) 33 *Texas International Law Journal*, 2, 237–56: 249–50.

[51] Ibid., 250. [52] Ibid., 237.

[53] Ibid., 238. Unconnected instances of torture in peacetime are considered an international crime, whereas murder is not. See Chapter 7, Note 29.

[54] In particular, the status of the victim is decisive: he or she must be a 'protected person' for the purpose of IHL. For the circumstances where this is the case, see Section 5.2.1.4.

[55] In relation to the distinctions in criminalisation between atrocities committed in NIAC as opposed to IAC, see also Meron, 'Criminalization of Internal Atrocities', 561. Meron writes that '[t]here is no moral justification, and no truly persuasive legal reason, for treating perpetrators of atrocities in internal conflicts more leniently than those engaged in international wars'.

criminal law. This leads us to the question of whether international criminal law should be revised.

## 9.4 Whether international criminal law should be revised

We saw in the introduction that the literature displays uncertainty about whether overlap between ESCR violations and international crimes could exist without an expansion of existing law. Sigrun Skogly advocated for 'an inclusion [of ESCR-related abuses] into the crimes against humanity concept, such as deliberate starvation or forced evictions',[56] in addition to the crimes listed in the various instruments. In 1994, UN Special Rapporteur Guissé exemplified the belief that international criminal law could only be used to address ESCR abuses once its ambit would be expanded: '[v]iolations of economic, social and cultural rights could be *declared* international crimes',[57] he suggested.

This study makes evident that an expansion is not required to consider that ESCR violations can properly fall within the ambit of international crimes. In fact, we saw that violations of treaties protecting ESCR are already part of the definitions of many existing crimes. Whether international criminal law should be revised for other reasons – such as to criminalise additional ESCR-related abuses – is a multifaceted and complex question that is beyond the scope of this study. In a perfect world, states would agree to revise international criminal law in a way that eradicates the schisms mentioned in the previous section. However ideal, such a need for revision is unrelated to the fact that ESCR violations are already included in many of the definitions of existing crimes.

## 9.5 Further research

Independent of the question of revision of international criminal law, this study also excludes a range of other issues and different potential avenues that may be required to address the legacy of past ESCR violations and that warrant further research and consideration. First, the analysis in this study has not considered the consequences of international crimes on individuals' enjoyment of ESCR. In conjunction with pre-existing

[56] Skogly, 'Crimes against Humanity', 58–60.

[57] Final Report of the Special Rapporteur on the Question of the Impunity of Perpetrators of Human Rights Violations: Economic, Social and Cultural Rights (El Hadji Guissé), E/CN.4/Sub.2/1997/8, 27 June 1997, para. 142 (emphasis added). The verb 'declare' seems to imply that Guissé refers to *de lege ferenda*.

inequalities, many crimes, whether or not they relate to ESCR, can have a plethora of *consequences* for victims' and their families' access to ESCR. In cases of enforced disappearances or rape, for instance, the enjoyment of ESCR of the victims and the family members who are left behind is often severely affected, in particular when they are female.[58] Families may not be able to access essential social security benefits in the absence of a death certificate,[59] or the surviving partner may not be able to inherit land or to remarry, which may in turn exacerbate poverty and marginalisation. Many other international crimes have serious consequences on ESCR. Corruption is well known for draining resources away from government spending on education or health care. Moreover, a UN task force mentioned how governments reacted to terrorist offences by taking measures that impact on ESCR, for instance, because farmers suspected of terrorism are detained at the high seasons for agriculture, making it difficult for their families to harvest the crops.[60] Such consequences of crimes upon the enjoyment of ESCR were not the subject of this study, but they would seem to encompass a range of legal and policy issues that need to be considered in the future.

Second, further research is also needed to *complement approaches* focused on criminal law. Given the limitations of international criminal law outlined above, criminal law approaches to economic, social and cultural issues in the aftermath of a legacy of human rights abuses should

[58] Gendered differences in entitlements are of importance in determining what impact abuses have on people's livelihoods. See, for instance, David Bloomfield et al. (eds.), *Reconciliation after Violent Conflict* (IDEA, 2003), 56. See also Larissa van den Herik's analysis of references to socio-economic consequences of other crimes in existing international crimes cases, for example, instances in which '[t]he ICC Prosecutor has included, on occasion, references to these consequences [infections with HIV/AIDS as a consequence of rape] without necessarily making them part of the core charges'. Larissa van den Herik, 'ESCR – International Criminal Law's Blind Spot?', in *Economic, Social, and Cultural Rights: Contemporary Issues and Challenges*, ed. Eibe Riedel, et al., *Economic, Social, and Cultural Rights* (Oxford University Press, 2014), 343–66: 359. Care must also be taken not to downplay ESCR violations as mere aggravating circumstances where they themselves overlap with a crime.

[59] In Algeria, for instance, reparations were only awarded with the presentation of a death certificate, which many were reluctant to obtain without knowing the fate of the disappeared. Victims argued that the government was trying to bribe them to stop asking for information. Evelyne Schmid, 'Socio-Economic and Cultural Rights and Wrongs after Armed Conflicts' (2013) 31 *Netherlands Quarterly of Human Rights*, 3, 241–71: 263.

[60] UN Counter-Terrorism Implementation Task Force Working Group Protecting Human Rights While Countering Terrorism, Expert Seminar on the Impact of Terrorism and Counter-Terrorism Measures on the Enjoyment of ESCR, Summary of Discussions, 5–7 November 2008, para. 27.

be combined with the other reforms that may be simultaneously ongoing in the same country. As the Secretary-General of the UN has suggested, issues surrounding disputes related to housing, land, property, natural resource extraction and the realisation of economic and social rights generally 'are critical to peace and security in multiple settings',[61] and '[t]he United Nations must promote dialogue on the realization of economic and social rights, and provide concrete results through transitional justice mechanisms, legal reform, capacity-building, and land and identity registration efforts, among other initiatives'.[62] Similarly, Arbour advocated that where ESCR abuses have occurred in situations of armed conflict or massive human rights violations, efforts to take into account international law on ESCR should start even before a peace agreement or a blueprint agreement for dealing with the past is forged and be much more broadly focused than on criminal sanctions, for instance, by reconsidering the place accorded to ESCR in the domestic legal system.[63]

Third, *cultural rights* should be given further attention. Cultural rights remain marginalised even within the literature on ESCR, and further research should explore whether cultural rights are or should be dealt with differently to economic or social rights in the context of attempts to address a legacy of past human rights violations.

Fourth and most importantly, further consideration deserves to be given to how ESCR violations can be monitored more effectively as a *preventive tool*. In his 'Agenda for Peace', former UN Secretary-General Boutros Boutros-Ghali called upon states to strengthen the international prevention of conflicts and massive human rights abuses.[64] States endorsed this idea of protecting populations from international crimes in the 2005 summit outcome document.[65] As is well known at least since Lemkin's work on genocide and since the UN's efforts to prevent

[61] Report of the SG on the Rule of Law and Transitional Justice in Conflict and Post-Conflict Societies, S/2011/634, 12 October 2011, para. 51.

[62] Ibid., para. 52.

[63] Arbour, 'Economic and Social Justice for Societies in Transition', 21. See also Evelyne Schmid, 'Thickening the Rule of Law in Transition', in *International Law in Domestic Courts: Rule of Law Reform in Post-Conflict States*, ed. Edda Kristjansdottir, André Nollkaemper and Cedric Ryngaert, *Rule of Law Reform in Post-Conflict States* (Intersentia, 2012), 59–81.

[64] An Agenda for Peace: Preventive Diplomacy, Peacemaking and Peace-Keeping, A/47/277, 17 June 1992.

[65] World Summit Outcome, GA Res. 60/1, 24 October 2005, para. 138.

genocide, atrocities often start by abuses in the realm of ESCR.[66] To complement the analysis made in this study, further research should systematically explore whether, and how, early responses to violations of ESCR can enhance the prevention of widespread abuses.

## 9.6 Final remarks

The main finding of this book holds promise despite the obstacles limiting its reach. While narrow in many respects, existing international law allows us to take into account many more abuses of ESCR than what has traditionally been recognised. The fact that international criminal law is insufficient to provide an adequate response to the full range of problems involved in dealing with legacies of human rights abuses does not mean that this body of law is irrelevant or useless. As Ratner has concluded, despite the shortcomings in the law, 'the current definitions [of international crimes] have the advantage of covering the vast majority of atrocities that governments and non-governmental entities have wreaked upon their populations'.[67] A principled approach based on the traditional rules of legal treaty interpretation has suggested that the existing definitions of international crimes clearly accommodate claims based on contemporary legal understandings of socio-economic and cultural abuses.

While certainly not constituting an ideal scheme for dealing with all violations of ESCR, the qualification of human rights abuses as international crimes also serves an important symbolic purpose that goes beyond the legal corollaries of characterising ESCR violations as international offences, which were identified in Chapter 8. As already discussed in Chapter 2, expressionist theories of international criminal law convincingly point out that the description of an abuse as an international offence serves as an expression of international concern about the seriousness of the condemned conduct. Paraphrasing Feinberg, Sloane

[66] Raphael Lemkin, *Axis Rule* (Carnegie Endowment for International Peace, 1944), 80, expressing the view that genocide has two phases, starting with the 'destruction of the national pattern of the oppressed group', meaning the destruction of the cultural rights of the group; Office of the UN Special Adviser on the Prevention of Genocide, 'Analysis Framework', www.un.org/en/preventgenocide/adviser/pdf/osapg_analysis_framework.pdf. See also CERD Committee, Decision on Follow-Up to the Declaration on the Prevention of Genocide: Indicators of Patterns of Systematic and Massive Racial Discrimination, CERD/C/67/1, 14 October 2005, paras. 3, 14, 15; or Report of the UN High Commissioner for Human Rights on the Question of the Realization in All Countries of Economic, Social and Cultural Rights, A/HRC/20/4, 10 April 2012, para. 56.

[67] Steven Ratner et al., *Accountability*, 3rd edn (Oxford University Press, 2009), 81.

points out that 'by punishing the perpetrators of serious international crimes . . ., the international community attempts authoritatively to disavow that conduct, to indicate symbolically its refusal to acquiesce in the crimes'.[68] Similarly, Mark Drumbl eloquently describes how international criminal law has the potential to enhance 'expressive value in asserting the importance of law, the stigmatization of the offender who transgresses that law, and the authenticity of the historical narrative that ensues'.[69] Based on international relations scholarship, Dixon and Tenove argue that international criminal law provides 'strategic openings for diplomatic, legal and civil society actors to convert their authority into forms recognizable in their own and adjacent fields' and is 'able to mobilize authority in ways that make it more powerful at a global level' than other approaches employed to address legacies of a violent past.[70] Qualifying abuses in the realm of ESCR as international crimes is thus no mere technical matter, but reminds one that the law does not tolerate perpetrators' involvement in serious threats to ESCR.

Over time, application of the approach presented in this study will serve towards a more nuanced and less agitated approach to considerations of ESCR in international law. It will become evident that there are abuses in the realm of ESCR that can be addressed in the context of international criminal law just like international criminal lawyers address other criminal conduct. Paying more attention to ESCR when identifying international crimes will expose abusive policies on ESCR, lead to investigations, secure remedies and debunk myths that socio-economic deprivation is a result of natural misfortune. What Scott Leckie wrote about violations of housing, land and property rights that overlap with war crimes and crimes against humanity pertains more generally to ESCR violations:

> For too long these particular actions – forced displacement, the wanton destruction of property, land theft/grabbing, unlawful expropriation of land, ethnic cleansing, deprivation of basic services crucial for life such as water and electricity, and so many others – have been treated as

[68] Robert Sloane, 'The Expressive Capacity of International Punishment' (2007) 43 *Stanford Journal of International Law*, 1, 39–94: 71. Citing Joel Feinberg, *Doing & Deserving* (Princeton University Press, 1970), 101–5.

[69] Mark Drumbl, *Atrocity* (Cambridge University Press, 2007), 175; see generally 3–6.

[70] Peter Dixon and Chris Tenove, 'International Criminal Justice as a Transnational Field: Rules, Authority and Victims' (2013) 7 *International Journal of Transitional Justice*, 3, 393–412: 393, 405.

> unfortunate side effects of conflict, political transition or processes of economic development, rather than as the crimes these acts so clearly constitute.[71]

Where widespread ESCR abuses have ruined institutional trust and legitimacy, authorities can more easily re-establish such trust and legitimacy if they are willing to investigate and prosecute those crimes that most closely relate to survivors' experiences of the past abuses. The potential of exploring the full range of international law on ESCR is promising. For the first time, a systematic analysis of the existing international crimes demonstrates that the responsibility does not belong solely to the territorial state and its government or to the international human rights machinery, but that 'the sharp edge of the sword which establishes individual responsibility'[72] can be employed to address abuses of ESCR. This sharp edge of the sword warrants to be given thought to for a very simple reason: international crimes that overlap with ESCR violations deserve to be taken seriously for much the same reasons that other international crimes are.

[71] Displacement Solutions, *Housing, Land and Property Rights and International Criminal Justice* (Displacement Solutions, 2012), foreword by Scott Leckie.

[72] Robert Woetzel, 'International Criminal Law and Human Rights' (1968) 62 *Proceedings of the American Society of International Law at Its Annual Meeting*, 117–23: 117.

# SELECT BIBLIOGRAPHY


Abtahi, Hirad and Philippa Webb, *The Genocide Convention: The Travaux Préparatoires* (Nijhoff, 2008).

Acquaviva, Guido, 'Forced Displacement and International Crimes', *Legal and Protection Policy Research Series* (UNHCR, 2011).

Ainley, Kirsten, 'Individual Agency and Responsibility for Atrocity', in *Confronting Evil in International Relations: Ethical Responses to Problems of Moral Agency*, edited by Renée Jeffery (Palgrave, 2008), 37–60.

Akehurst, Michael, 'Jurisdiction in International Law' (1972) 46 *British Yearbook of International Law*, 145–257.

Akhavan, Payam, *Reducing Genocide to Law: Definition, Meaning, and the Ultimate Crime* (Cambridge University Press, 2012).

Alston, Philip, 'Establishing a Right to Petition under the Covenant on Economic Social and Cultural Rights', in *Collected Courses of the Academy of European Law. The Protection of Human Rights in Europe* (European University Institute, 1993), 115–53.

'US Ratification of the Covenant on Economic, Social and Cultural Rights: The Need for an Entirely New Strategy' (1990) 84 *American Journal of International Law*, 2, 365–93.

Alston, Philip and Gerard Quinn, 'The Nature and Scope of States Parties' Obligations under the International Covenant on Economic, Social and Cultural Rights' (1987) 9 *Human Rights Quarterly*, 156–299.

Ambos, Kai, *Der allgemeine Teil des Völkerstrafrechts: Ansätze einer Dogmatisierung* (Duncker & Humblot, 2002).

'Punishment without a Sovereign? The Ius Puniendi Issue of International Criminal Law: A First Contribution Towards a Consistent Theory of International Criminal Law' (2013) 33 *Oxford Journal of Legal Studies*, 2, 293–315.

'What Does Intent to Destroy in Genocide Mean?' (2009) 91 *International Review of the Red Cross*, 876, 833–58.

Ambos, Kai and Steffen Wirth, 'The Current Law of Crimes against Humanity: An Analysis of UNTAET Regulation 15/2000' (2002) 13 *Criminal Law Forum*, 1, 1–90.

Amnesty International, *International Law Commission: The Obligation to Extradite or Prosecute* (Amnesty International, 2009).

*Left Behind: The Impact of Zimbabwe's Mass Forced Evictions on the Right to Education* (Amnesty International, 2011).

*The State of the World's Human Rights 2010* (Amnesty International, 2010).

*Universal Jurisdiction: A Preliminary Survey of Legislation around the World* (Amnesty International, 2011).

Andreu-Guzman, Federico, 'Criminal Justice and Forced Displacement: International and National Perspectives', in *Transitional Justice and Displacement*, edited by Roger Duthie (Social Science Research Council, 2012), 233–53.

Annas, George and Michael Grodin (eds.), *The Nazi Doctors and the Nuremberg Code: Human Rights in Human Experimentation* (Oxford University Press, 1992).

Arambulo, Kitty, *Strengthening the Supervision of the International Covenant on Economic, Social and Cultural Rights* (Intersentia, 1999).

Arbour, Louise, 'Economic and Social Justice for Societies in Transition' (2007) 40 *New York University Journal of International Law and Politics*, 1, 1–28.

Askin, Kelly, 'Prosecuting Wartime Rape and Other Gender-Related Crimes under International Law: Extraordinary Advances, Enduring Obstacles' (2003) 21 *Berkeley Journal of International Law*, 2, 288–349.

Bacio Terracino, Julio, *The International Legal Framework against Corruption: States' Obligations to Prevent and Repress Corruption* (Intersentia, 2012).

Bantekas, Ilias, 'Corruption as an International Crime and Crime against Humanity: An Outline of Supplementary Criminal Justice Policies' (2006) 4 *Journal of International Criminal Justice*, 3, 466–84.

*International Criminal Law*. 4th edn (Hart, 2010).

Bassiouni, Cherif, *Crimes against Humanity in International Criminal Law* (Kluwer, 1999).

'Enslavement as an International Crime' (1991) 23 *Journal of International Law and Politics*, 2, 445–517.

*International Criminal Law* 3 vols. Vol. 1 (Transnational, 1986).

*International Criminal Law Conventions and Their Penal Provisions* (Transnational, 1997).

*The Legislative History of the International Criminal Court, International and Comparative Criminal Law Series* (Transnational, 2005).

Benvenisti, Eyal, 'Water Conflicts During the Occupation of Iraq' (2003) 97 *American Journal of International Law*, 4, 860–72.

Boas, Gideon, James Bischoff and Natalie Reid, *Elements of Crimes under International Law* (Cambridge University Press, 2008).

Boister, Neil, 'Transnational Criminal Law?' (2003) 14 *European Journal of International Law*, 5, 953–76.

Boister, Neil and Robert Cryer, *Documents on the Tokyo International Military Tribunal: Charter, Indictment and Judgments* (Oxford University Press, 2008).

*The Tokyo International Military Tribunal* (Oxford University Press, 2008).

Bossuyt, Marc, 'La distinction juridique entre les droits civil et politiques et les droits économiques, sociaux et culturels' (1981) 7 *Revue des droits de l'homme*, 783–820.

Boulesbaa, Ahcene, *The U.N. Convention on Torture and the Prospects for Enforcement* (Nijhoff, 1999).

Buckingham, Donald, 'A Recipe for Change: Towards an Integrated Approach to Food under International Law' (1994) 6 *Pace International Review*, 285–321.

Butler, David, 'Enforced Starvation: Exploring Individual Criminal Responsibility for State-Induced Famines' (2007) 3 *Human Rights Law Commentary*, http://www.nottingham.ac.uk/hrlc/publications/humanrightslawcommentary.aspx.

Cahill-Ripley, Amanda, 'Foregrounding Economic and Social Rights in Transitional Justice: Realising Justice for Violations of Economic, Social and Cultural Rights' (2014) 32 *Netherlands Quarterly of Human Rights*, 2, 183–213.

Carranza, Ruben, 'Plunder and Pain: Should Transitional Justice Engage with Corruption and Economic Crimes?' (2008) 2 *International Journal of Transitional Justice*, 3, 310–30.

Cassese, Antonio, 'Can the Notion of Inhuman and Degrading Treatment Be Applied to Socio-Economic Conditions?' (1991) 2 *European Journal of International Law* 1, 141–5.

*International Criminal Law*. 2nd edn (Oxford University Press, 2008).

'The Policy Element in Genocide: When Is It Required by International Rules?', in *The Genocide Convention Sixty Years after Its Adoption*, edited by Christoph Safferling and Eckart-Alexander Conze (Asser, 2010), 133–40.

Chapman, Audrey, 'A "Violations Approach" for Monitoring the International Covenant on Economic, Social and Cultural Rights' (1996) 18 *Human Rights Quarterly*, 1, 23–66.

Charlesworth, Hilary, 'International Law: A Discipline of Crisis' (2002) 65 *The Modern Law Review*, 3, 377–92.

Clapham, Andrew, 'Extending International Criminal Law Beyond the Individual to Corporations and Armed Opposition Groups' (2008) 6 *Journal of International Criminal Justice*, 5, 899–926.

*Human Rights Obligations of Non-State Actors* (Oxford University Press, 2006).

Combacau, Jean, 'Le droit international: bric-a-brac ou système?' (1986) 31 *Annuaire de philosophie du droit*, 85–105.

Comisión para el Esclarecimiento Histórico, 'Guatemala: memoria del silencio' (Asociación Americana para el Avance de las Ciencia, 2000).

Commission for Reception, Truth and Reconciliation in Timor-Leste, *Chega! Final Report* (CAVR, 2005).

Coomans, Fons and Fried van Hoof (eds.), *The Right to Complain About Economic, Social and Cultural Rights* (SIM, 1995).

Coomans, Fons and Rolf Künnemann, *Cases and Concepts on Extraterritorial Obligations in the Area of Economic, Social and Cultural Rights* (Intersentia, 2012).

Craven, Matthew, 'The Domestic Application of the International Covenant on Economic, Social and Cultural Rights' (1993) 40 *Netherlands International Law Review*, 3, 367–404.

*The International Covenant on Economic, Social, and Cultural Rights: A Perspective on Its Development* (Clarendon Press, 1995).

Cryer, Robert, 'General Principles of Liability', in *The Permanent International Criminal Court: Legal and Policy Issues*, edited by Dominic McGoldrick, Peter Rowe and Eric Donnelly (Hart, 2004), 233–62.

'The Interplay of Human Rights and Humanitarian Law: The Approach of the ICTY' (2009) 14 *Journal of Conflict and Security Law*, 3, 511–27.

*Prosecuting International Crimes: Selectivity and the International Criminal Law Regime* (Cambridge University Press, 2005).

Dankwa, Victor, Cees Flinterman and Scott Leckie, 'Commentary to the Maastricht Guidelines on Violations of Economic, Social and Cultural Rights' (1998) 20 *Human Rights Quarterly*, 3, 705–30.

Darcy, Shane, 'Prosecuting the War Crime of Collective Punishment' (2010) 8 *Journal of International Criminal Justice*, 1, 29–51.

Davidsson, Elias, 'Economic Oppression as an International Wrong or as Crime against Humanity' (2005) 23 *Netherlands Quarterly of Human Rights*, 2, 173–212.

DeFalco, Randle, 'Accounting for Famine at the Extraordinary Chambers in the Courts of Cambodia: The Crimes against Humanity of Extermination, Inhumane Acts and Persecution' (2011) 5 *International Journal of Transitional Justice*, 1, 142–58.

de Greiff, Pablo (ed.), *The Handbook of Reparations* (Oxford University Press, 2006).

DeGuzman, Margaret, 'Choosing to Prosecute: Expressive Selection at the International Criminal Court' (2012) 33 *Michigan Journal of International Law*, 2, 265–320.

'Crimes against Humanity', *in Research Handbook on International Criminal Law*, edited by Bartram Brown (Elgar, 2011), 62–83.

'The Road from Rome: The Developing Law of Crimes against Humanity' (2000) 22 *Human Rights Quarterly*, 2, 335–403.

De Preux, Jean, Frédéric Siordet, Claude Pilloud, Henri Coursier, Oscar Uhler, René-Jean Wilhelm and Jean-Pierre Schoenholzer, *The Geneva Conventions of 12 August 1949: Commentary, Third Geneva Convention* (ICRC, 1960).

De Waal, Alex, *Famine Crimes: Politics, and the Disaster Relief Industry in Africa* (International African Institute, 1997).

Dennis, Michael and David Stewart, 'Justiciability of Economic, Social, and Cultural Rights: Should There Be an International Complaints Mechanism to Adjudicate the Rights to Food, Water, Housing, and Health?' (2004) 98 *American Journal of International Law*, 3, 462–515.

Dinstein, Yoram, 'Case Analysis: Crimes against Humanity after Tadic' (2000) 13 *Leiden Journal of International Law*, 2, 373–93.

*The Conduct of Hostilities under the Law of International Armed Conflict* (Cambridge University Press, 2004).

'Siege Warfare and the Starvation of Civilians', in *Humanitarian Law of Armed Conflict: Essays in Honour of F. Kalshoven*, edited by Astrid Delissen and Gerard Tanja (Nijhoff, 1991), 145–52.

Dinstein, Yoram and Mala Tabory (eds.), *War Crimes in International Law* (Nijhoff, 1996).

Displacement Solutions, *Housing, Land and Property Rights and International Criminal Justice: Holding HLP Rights Violators Accountable* (Displacement Solutions, 2012).

Dolan, Chris, *Social Torture: The Case of Northern Uganda* (Berghahn Books, 2009).

Dörmann, Knut, Louise Doswald-Beck and Robert Kolb, *Elements of War Crimes under the Rome Statute of the International Criminal Court: Sources and Commentary* (Cambridge University Press, 2003).

Doswald-Beck, Louise and Sylvain Vité, 'International Humanitarian Law and Human Rights Law' (1993) 33 *International Review of the Red Cross*, 293, 95–105.

Drumbl, Mark, 'Accountability for Property and Environmental War Crimes: Prosecution, Litigation, and Development' (ICTJ, November 2009).

*Atrocity, Punishment, and International Law* (Cambridge University Press, 2007).

'"Germans Are the Lords and Poles Are the Servants": The Trial of Arthur Greiser in Poland, 1946', in *The Hidden Histories of War Crimes Trials*, edited by Kevin Heller and Gerry Simpson (Oxford University Press, 2013), 411–29.

Dungel, Joakim, 'Humanitarian Assistance in Internal Armed Conflicts: Respecting Sovereignty, Neutrality and Legitimacy: Practical Proposals to Practical Problems' (2004) *Journal of Humanitarian Assistance*, http://sites.tufts.edu/jha/archives/838.

Duthie, Roger, 'Transitional Justice and Displacement' (2011) 5 *International Journal of Transitional Justice*, 241–61.

Duttweiler, Michael, 'Liability for Omission in International Criminal Law' (2006) 6 *International Criminal Law Review*, 1, 1–61.

Eide, Asbjørn, Catarina Krause and Allan Rosas (eds.), *Economic, Social, and Cultural Rights: A Textbook* (Nijhoff, 1995).

Epstein, Catherine, *Model Nazi: Arthur Greiser and the Occupation of Western Poland* (Oxford University Press, 2010).

Farmer, Paul, *Pathologies of Power: Health, Human Rights, and the New War on the Poor* (University of California Press, 2003).

Fein, Helen, 'Genocide by Attrition 1939–1993: The Warsaw Ghetto, Cambodia, and Sudan: Links between Human Rights, Health, and Mass Death' (1997) 2 *Health and Human Rights*, 2, 10–45.

Feinberg, Joel, *Doing & Deserving: Essays in the Theory of Responsibility* (Princeton University Press, 1970).

'The Expressive Function of Punishment' (1965) 49 *The Monist*, 3, 397–423.

Fischer-Lescano, Andreas and Gunther Teubner, 'Regime-Collisions: The Vain Search for Legal Unity in the Fragmentation of Global Law' (2004) 25 *Michigan Journal of International Law*, 4, 999–1046.

Foster, Michelle, *International Refugee Law and Socio-Economic Rights: Refuge from Deprivation* (Cambridge University Press, 2007).

Francioni, Francesco and Martin Scheinin (eds.), *Cultural Human Rights* (Nijhoff, 2008).

Gasser, Hans-Peter, 'The Changing Relationship between International Criminal Law, Human Rights Law and Humanitarian Law', in *The Legal Regime of the International Criminal Court: Essays in Honour of Professor Igor Blishchenko*, edited by José Doria, Hans-Peter Gasser, M. Cherif Bassiouni and I. P. Blishchenko (Nijhoff, 2009), 1111–9.

Giacca, Gilles, *Economic, Social, and Cultural Rights in Armed Conflict* (Oxford University Press, 2014).

Gilligan, James, *Violence: Reflections on a National Epidemic* (Vintage Books, 1997).

Golay, Christophe, *Droit à l'alimentation et l'accès à la justice* (Bruylant, 2011).

Gready, Paul, 'Telling Truth? The Methodological Challenges of Truth Commissions', in *Methods of Human Rights Research*, edited by Fons Coomans, Fred Grünfeld and Menno T. Kamminga (Intersentia, 2009), 159–85.

Hannum, Hurst, 'International Law and Cambodian Genocide: The Sounds of Silence' (1989) 11 *Human Rights Quarterly*, 1, 82–138.

Hart, Herbert and Tony Honoré, *Causation in the Law*. 2nd edn (Clarendon, 1985).

Harvard Law School Human Rights Clinic, *Crimes in Burma* (Harvard Law School, 2009).

Hausler, Kristin, Nicole Urban and Robert McCorquodale, *Protecting Education in Armed Conflict: An International Law Handbook* (British Institute of International and Comparative Law, Education Above All, 2012).

Hayner, Priscilla, *Unspeakable Truths: Transitional Justice and the Challenge of Truth Commissions*. 2nd edn (Routledge, 2011).

Heintze, Hans-Joachim and Andrej Zwitter, *International Law and Humanitarian Assistance* (Springer, 2011).

Heller, Kevin, *The Nuremberg Military Tribunals and the Origins of International Criminal Law* (Oxford University Press, 2011).

Henckaerts, Jean-Marie and Louise Doswald-Beck (eds.), *Customary International Humanitarian Law* 2 vols., Vol. 1 (Cambridge University Press, 2005).
(eds.), *Customary International Humanitarian Law* 2 vols., Vol. 2 (Cambridge University Press, 2005).
Higgins, Rosalyn, *Problems and Process: International Law and How We Use It* (Clarendon, 1994).
Höffe, Otfried, *Democracy in an Age of Globalisation* (Springer, 2007).
Hughes, Katherine, 'Operations "Drive out the Trash": The Case for Imposing Targeted United Nations Sanctions against Zimbabwean Officials' (2007) 76 *Fordham Law Review*, 1, 323–86.
ICRC, 'Analysis of the Punishments Applicable to International Crimes (War Crimes, Crimes against Humanity and Genocide) in Domestic Law and Practice' (2008) 90 *International Review of the Red Cross*, 870, 461–8.
'Health Care in Danger: Making the Case' (ICRC, 2011).
ICRC and Tristan Ferraro, *Occupation and Other Forms of Administration of Foreign Territory: Report of Expert Meetings* (ICRC, 2012).
Irish Centre for Human Rights, *Crimes against Humanity in Western Burma: The Situation of the Rohingyas* (University of Ireland, 2010).
Jackson, Robert, *Report of Robert H. Jackson, United States Representative to the International Conference on Military Trials, London, 1945* (U.S. Government Printing Office, 1949).
Jacobs, Steven, 'Raphael Lemkin and the Holodomor: Was It Genocide?', in *Holodomor: Reflections on the Great Famine of 1932–1933 in Soviet Ukraine*, edited by Lubomyr Luciuk and Lisa Grekul (Kashtan, 2008), 159–70.
Jacques, Mélanie, *Armed Conflict and Displacement: The Protection of Refugees and Displaced Persons under International Humanitarian Law* (Cambridge University Press, 2012).
Jasanoff, Sheila, 'What Judges Should Know About the Sociology of Science' (1992) 32 *Jurimetrics*, 3, 345–59.
Jasudowicz, Tadeusz, 'The Legal Character of Social Rights from the Perspective of International Law as a Whole', in *Social Rights as Human Rights: A European Challenge*, edited by Krzysztof Drzewicki, Catarina Krause and Allan Rosas (Åbo Akademi University, 1994), 34–9.
Kälin, Walter and Jörg Künzli, *The Law of International Human Rights Protection* (Oxford University Press, 2009).
Kiernan, Ben, *The Pol Pot Regime: Race, Power, and Genocide in Cambodia under the Khmer Rouge* (Yale University Press, 1996).
Kleffner, Jann, *Complementarity in the Rome Statute and National Criminal Jurisdictions* (Oxford University Press, 2008).
Kofele-Kale, Ndiva, *The International Law of Responsibility for Economic Crimes* (Ashgate, 2006).

Kress, Claus, 'The Crime of Genocide under International Law' (2006) 6 *International Criminal Law Review*, 4, 461–502.

'The Darfur Report and Genocidal Intent' (2005) 3 *Journal of International Criminal Justice*, 3, 562–78.

Langford, Malcolm (ed.), *Social Rights Jurisprudence: Emerging Trends in International and Comparative Law* (Cambridge University Press, 2008).

Langford, Malcolm, Martin Scheinin, Wouter Vandenhole and Willem van Genugten, *Global Justice, State Duties: The Extra-Territorial Scope of Economic, Social and Cultural Rights in International Law* (Cambridge University Press, 2012).

Laplante, Lisa, 'On the Indivisibility of Rights: Truth Commissions, Reparations, and the Right to Development' (2007) 10 *Yale Human Rights & Development Law Journal*, 141–77.

'Transitional Justice and Peace Building: Diagnosing and Addressing the Socioeconomic Roots of Violence through a Human Rights Framework' (2008) 2 *International Journal of Transitional Justice*, 3, 331–55.

Laplante, Lisa and Kimberly Theidon, 'Truth with Consequences: Justice and Reparations in Post-Truth Commission Peru' (2007) 29 *Human Rights Quarterly*, 228–50.

Latour, Bruno and Steve Woolgar, *Laboratory Life: The Construction of Scientific Facts* (Princeton University Press, 1986).

Leary, Virginia, 'Justiciability and Beyond, Complaint Procedures and the Right to Health' (1995) *Review – International Commission of Jurists*, 55, 105–22.

Leckie, Scott, 'Another Step Towards Indivisibility: Identifying the Key Features of Violations of Economic, Social and Cultural Rights' (1998) 20 *Human Rights Quarterly*, 1, 81–124.

'The UN Committee on Economic, Social and Cultural Rights and the Right to Adequate Housing: Towards an Appropriate Approach' (1989) 11 *Human Rights Quarterly*, 522–60.

*When Push Comes to Shove: Forced Evictions and Human Rights* (Habitat International Coalition, 1995).

Leckie, Scott and Christopher Huggins, *Conflict and Housing, Land, and Property Rights: A Handbook on Issues, Frameworks, and Solutions* (Cambridge University Press, 2011).

Lemkin, Raphael, *Axis Rule in Occupied Europe* (Carnegie Endowment for International Peace, 1944).

'Genocide as a Crime under International Law' (1947) 41 *The American Journal of International Law*, 1, 145–51.

*Les actes constituant un danger général considerés comme delits de droit des gens* (Pedone, 1933).

'Soviet Genocide in the Ukraine (Untitled Speech to the Ukrainian American Congress Committee, 1953)', in *Holodomor: Reflections on the Great Famine of 1932–1933 in Soviet Ukraine*, edited by Lubomyr Luciuk and Lisa Grekul (Kashtan, 2008), 235–44.

Liebenberg, Sandra, 'South Africa: Adjudicating Socio-Economic Rights under a Transformative Constitution', in *Social Rights Jurisprudence: Emerging Trends in International and Comparative Law*, edited by Malcolm Langford (Cambridge University Press, 2009), 75–101.

Luban, David, 'A Theory of Crimes against Humanity' (2004) 29 *Yale Journal of International Law*, 1, 85–167.

Luban, David, Julie O'Sullivan and David Stewart, *International and Transnational Criminal Law* (Aspen, 2009).

Magarrell, Lisa and Leonardo Filippini, *The Legacy of Truth: Criminal Justice in the Peruvian Transition* (ICTJ, 2006).

Mamdani, Mahmood, 'Amnesty or Impunity? A Preliminary Critique of the Report of the TRC of South Africa' (2002) 32 *Diacritics*, 3–4, 33–59.

Mani, Rama, 'Dilemmas of Expanding Transitional Justice, or Forging the Nexus between Transitional Justice and Development' (2008) 2 *International Journal of Transitional Justice*, 3, 253–65.

Marcus, David, 'Famine Crimes in International Law' (2003) 97 *American Journal of International Law*, 2, 245–81.

McCarthy, Thomas and World Organisation Against Torture, *Attacking the Root Causes of Torture: Poverty, Inequality and Violence* (OMCT, 2006).

McClean, David, *Transnational Organized Crime: A Commentary on the UN Convention and Its Protocols* (Oxford University Press, 2007).

McCrudden, Christopher, 'Human Dignity and Judicial Interpretation of Human Rights' (2008) 19 *European Journal of International Law*, 4, 655–724.

McEvoy, Kieran, 'Beyond Legalism: Towards a Thicker Understanding of Transitional Justice' (2007) 34 *Journal of Law and Society*, 4, 411–40.

Mehring, Sigrid, 'The Rights and Duties of Physicians in Armed Conflict' (2010) 103 *Militair Rechtelijk Tijdschrift*, 205–21.

Meron, Theodor, 'Deportation of Civilians as a War Crime under Customary Law', in *Broadening the Frontiers of Human Rights*, edited by Donna Gomien and Asbjørn Eide (Scandinavian University Press, 1993), 201–18.

'Human Rights in Time of Peace and in Time of Armed Strife', in *Contemporary Issues in International Law*, edited by Thomas Buergenthal (Engel, 1984), 1–21.

'International Criminalization of Internal Atrocities' (1995) 89 *American Journal of International Law*, 554–77.

'On a Hierarchy of International Human Rights' (1986) 80 *American Journal of International Law*, 1, 1–23.

Mettraux, Guénaël, 'Crimes against Humanity in the Jurisprudence of the International Criminal Tribunals for the Former Yugoslavia and for Rwanda' (2002) 43 *Harvard International Law Journal*, 237–316.

*International Crimes and the ad hoc Tribunals* (Oxford University Press, 2005).

Miller, Zinaida, 'Effects of Invisibility: In Search of the "Economic" in Transitional Justice' (2008) 2 *International Journal of Transitional Justice*, 266–91.

Mottershaw, Elizabeth, 'Economic, Social and Cultural Rights in Armed Conflict' (2008) 12 *The International Journal of Human Rights*, 3, 449–70.

Mourey, Alain, 'Famine and War' (1991) 31 *International Review of the Red Cross*, 285, 549–57.

Müller, Amrei, 'Limitations to and Derogations from Economic, Social and Cultural Rights' (2009) 9 *Human Rights Law Review*, 4, 557–601.

*The Relationship between Economic, Social and Cultural Rights and International Humanitarian Law: An Analysis of Health-Related Issues in Non-International Armed Conflicts* (Nijhoff, 2013).

Muvingi, Ismael, 'Sitting on Powder Kegs: Socioeconomic Rights in Transitional Societies' (2009) 3 *International Journal of Transitional Justice*, 2, 163.

Nolan, Aoife, 'Addressing Economic and Social Rights Violations by Non-State Actors through the Role of the State: A Comparison of Regional Approaches to the "Obligation to Protect"' (2009) 9 *Human Rights Law Review*, 2, 225–55.

'"Aggravated Violations", Roma Housing Rights and Forced Expulsions in Italy: Recent Developments under the European Social Charter Collective Complaints System' (2011) 11 *Human Rights Law Review*, 2, 343–61.

O'Keefe, Roger, 'Protection of Cultural Property', in *The Handbook of International Humanitarian Law*, edited by Dieter Fleck (Oxford University Press, 2008), 433–74.

Obokata, Tom, *Transnational Organised Crime in International Law* (Hart, 2010).

Ocheje, Paul, 'Refocusing International Law on the Quest for Accountability in Africa: The Case against the "Other" Impunity' (2002) 15 *Leiden Journal of International Law*, 4, 749–79.

Office of the High Commissioner for Human Rights, *Rule-of-Law Tools for Post-Conflict States: Reparations Programmes* (United Nations, 2008).

Oosterveld, Valerie, 'Sexual Slavery and the International Criminal Court' (2004) 25 *Michigan Journal of International Law*, 3, 605–51.

Oré Aguilar, Gaby and Felipe Gómez Isa (eds.), *Rethinking Transitions: Equality and Social Justice in Societies Emerging from Conflict* (Intersentia, 2011).

Orentlicher, Diane, 'Settling Accounts Revisited: Reconciling Global Norms with Local Agency' (2007) 1 *International Journal of Transitional Justice*, 1, 10–22.

Pasipanodya, Tafadzwa, 'A Deeper Justice: Economic and Social Justice as Transitional Justice in Nepal' (2008) 2 *International Journal of Transitional Justice*, 3, 378–97.

Paust, Jordan, 'The Human Rights to Food, Medicine and Medical Supplies, and Freedom from Arbitrary and Inhumane Detention and Controls in Sri Lanka' (1998) 31 *Vanderbilt Journal of Transnational Law*, 3, 617–40.

Pham, Phuong, Patrick Vinck, Marieke Wierda, Eric Stover and Adrian Di Giovanni, *Forgotten Voices: A Population-Based Survey of Attitudes About*

*Peace and Justice in Northern Uganda* (ICTJ, Berkeley Human Rights Center, 2005).

Physicians for Human Rights, 'Experiments in Torture: Evidence of Human Subject Research and Experimentation in the "Enhanced" Interrogation Program' (Physicians for Human Rights, 2010).

'Stateless and Starving: Persecuted Rohingya Flee Burma and Starve in Bangladesh' (Physicians for Human Rights, 2010).

Platzky, Laurine and Cherryl Walker, *The Surplus People: Forced Removals in South Africa* (Ravan, 1985).

Pocar, Fausto, 'Persecution as a Crime under International Law' (2008) 2 *Journal of National Security Law & Policy*, 365, 355–65.

Präg, Werner and Wolfgang Jacobmeyer (eds.), *Das Diensttagebuch des deutschen Generalgouverneurs in Polen 1939–1945* (Deutsche Verlagsanstalt, 1975).

Rassam, Yasmine, 'International Law and Contemporary Forms of Slavery: An Economic and Social Rights-Based Approach' (2004) 23 *Penn State International Law Review*, 3, 809–55.

Rastan, Rod, 'Testing Co-Operation: The International Criminal Court and National Authorities' (2008) 21 *Leiden Journal of International Law*, 2, 431–56.

Ratner, Steven, 'Belgium's War Crimes Statute: A Postmortem' (2003) 97 *American Journal of International Law*, 4, 888–97.

'The Schizophrenias of International Criminal Law' (1998) 33 *Texas International Law Journal*, 2, 237–56.

Ratner, Steven, Jason Abrams and James Bischoff, *Accountability for Human Rights Atrocities in International Law*. 3rd edn (Oxford University Press, 2009).

Rawls, John, *A Theory of Justice*. Original edn (Belknap, 1971).

Robbins, Peter and Kevin Bales, 'No One Shall Be Held in Slavery or Servitude: A Critical Analysis of International Slavery Agreements and Concepts of Slavery' (2001) 2 *Human Rights Review*, 2, 18–45.

Robinson, Darryl, 'The Identity Crisis of International Criminal Law' (2008) 21 *Leiden Journal of International Law*, 4, 925–63.

Robinson, Nehemiah, *The Genocide Convention* (Institute of Jewish Affairs, 1960).

Roht-Arriaza, Naomi, 'Editorial Note to the Special Issue on the Role of International Criminal Justice in Transitional Justice' (2013) 7 *International Journal of Transitional Justice*, 3, 383–92.

'Reparations and Economic and Social Rights after Violent Conflict', in *Justice and Economic Violence in Transition*, edited by Dustin Sharp (Springer, 2013), 109–38.

Röling, Bernard and Antonio Cassese, *The Tokyo Trial and Beyond: Reflections of a Peacemonger* (Polity Press, 1993).

Rottensteiner, Christa, 'The Denial of Humanitarian Assistance as a Crime under International Law' (1999) 81 *International Review of the Red Cross*, 555–82.

Ryngaert, Cedric, 'State Responsibility, Necessity and Human Rights' (2011) 41 *Netherlands Yearbook of International Law*, 79–98.

Sadat Wexler, Leila, 'International Criminal Law Comes of Age: Reviewing Jordan Paust, Cherif Bassiouni, Sharon Williams, Michael Scharf, Jimmy Gurule and Bruce Zagaris (eds.), International Criminal Law: Cases and Materials' (1997) 8 *Criminal Law Forum*, 3, 461–505.

Sandoz, Yves, Christophe Swinarski and Bruno Zimmermann, *Commentary on the Additional Protocols of 8 June 1977* (Nijhoff, 1987).

Sautenet, Vincent, 'Crimes against Humanity and the Principles of Legality: What Could the Potential Offender Expect?' (2000) 7 *Murdoch Electronic Journal of Law*, 1, 1–6.

Schabas, William, *Genocide in International Law: The Crime of Crimes*. 1st edn (Cambridge University Press, 2000).

*Genocide in International Law: The Crime of Crimes*. 2nd edn (Cambridge University Press, 2009).

*The International Criminal Court: A Commentary on the Rome Statute* (Oxford University Press, 2010).

*Unimaginable Atrocities: Justice, Politics, and Rights at the War Crimes Tribunals* (Oxford University Press, 2012).

'War Economies, Economic Actors and International Criminal Law', in *Profiting from Peace: Managing the Resource Dimensions of Civil War*, edited by Karen Ballentine and Heiko Nitzschke (Lynne Rienner, 2005), 425–46.

Scheinert, Josh, 'Refusal to Save Lives: A Perspective from International Criminal Law' (2013) 13 *International Criminal Law Review*, 3, 627–63.

Schmid, Evelyne, 'Liberia's Truth Commission Report: Economic, Social and Cultural Rights in Transitional Justice' (2009) 24 *PRAXIS – The Fletcher Journal of Human Security*, 5–28.

'Socio-Economic and Cultural Rights and Wrongs after Armed Conflicts: Using the State Reporting Procedure before the UN CESCR More Effectively' (2013) 31 *Netherlands Quarterly of Human Rights*, 3, 241–71.

'Thickening the Rule of Law in Transition: The Constitutional Entrenchment of Economic and Social Rights in South Africa', in *International Law in Domestic Courts: Rule of Law Reform in Post-Conflict States*, edited by Edda Kristjansdottir, André Nollkaemper and Cedric Ryngaert (Intersentia, 2012), 59–81.

'War Crimes Related to Violations of Economic, Social and Cultural Rights' (2011) 71 *Heidelberg Journal of International Law*, 3, 523–41.

Schmid, Evelyne and Aoife Nolan, 'Economic and Social Dimensions of Transitional Justice: Doing Harm through Terminological Misunderstandings?' (2014) 8 *International Journal of Transitional Justice*, 3, 362–82.

Seibert-Fohr, Anja, *Prosecuting Serious Human Rights Violations* (Oxford University Press, 2009).

Sepúlveda, Magdalena, *The Nature of the Obligations under the International Covenant on Economic, Social, and Cultural Rights* (Intersentia, 2003).

Shahabuddeen, Mohamed, 'Does the Principle of Legality Stand in the Way of Progressive Development of Law?' (2004) 2 *Journal of International Criminal Justice*, 4, 1007–17.

Sharp, Dustin, 'Addressing Economic Violence in Times of Transition' (2012) 35 *Fordham International Law Journal*, 780–814.

(ed.), *Justice and Economic Violence in Transition* (Springer, 2013).

Shelton, Dinah, *Remedies in International Human Rights Law*. 2nd edn (Oxford University Press, 2005).

'The United Nations Principles and Guidelines on Reparations: Context and Contents', in *Out of the Ashes: Reparation for Victims of Gross and Systematic Human Rights Violations*, edited by Marc Bossuyt, Paul Lemmens, Koen De Feyter and Stephan Parmentier (Intersentia, 2005), 11–34.

Shue, Henry, 'The Interdependence of Duties', in *The Right to Food*, edited by Philip Alston and Katarina Tomasevski (Nijhoff, 1984), 83–95.

'Rights in the Light of Duties', in *Human Rights and US Foreign Policy*, edited by Peter Brown and Douglas MacLean (Lexington Books, 1979), 65–81.

Sieghart, Paul, *The Lawful Rights of Mankind* (Oxford University Press, 1985).

Simma, Bruno and Dirk Pulkowski, 'Of Planets and the Universe: Self-Contained Regimes in International Law' (2006) 17 *European Journal of International Law*, 3, 483–529.

Skogly, Sigrun, 'Crimes against Humanity – Revisited: Is There a Role for Economic and Social Rights?' (2001) 5 *The International Journal of Human Rights*, 1, 58–80.

Sloane, Robert, 'The Expressive Capacity of International Punishment: The Limits of the National Law Analogy and the Potential of International Criminal Law' (2007) 43 *Stanford Journal of International Law*, 1, 39–94.

Sluiter, Göran, '"Chapeau Elements" of Crimes against Humanity in the Jurisprudence of the UN ad hoc Tribunals', in *Forging a Convention for Crimes against Humanity*, edited by Leila Sadat (Cambridge University Press, 2011), 102–41.

Sørensen, Max, 'Autonomous Legal Orders: Some Considerations Relating to a Systems Analysis of International Organisations in the World Legal Order' (1983) 32 *The International and Comparative Law Quarterly*, 3, 559–76.

Stamatopoulou, Elsa, *Cultural Rights in International Law: Article 27 of the Universal Declaration of Human Rights and Beyond* (Nijhoff, 2007).

Starr, Sonja, 'Extraordinary Crimes at Ordinary Times: International Justice Beyond Crisis Situations' (2007) 101 *Northwestern University Law Review*, 3, 1257–314.

Stavropoulou, Maria, 'Displacement and Human Rights: Reflections on UN Practice' (1998) 20 *Human Rights Quarterly*, 3, 515–54.

Stewart, James, *Corporate War Crimes: Prosecuting the Pillage of Natural Resources* (Open Society Institute, 2010).

Symonides, Janusz, 'Cultural Rights: A Neglected Category of Human Rights' (1998) 50 *International Social Science Journal*, 4, 559–72.

Taylor, Telford, *The Anatomy of the Nuremberg Trials* (Bloomsbury, 1993).

Tignino, Mara, *L'eau et la guerre: éléments pour un régime juridique* (Bruylant, 2011).

'The Right to Water and Sanitation in Post-Conflict Peacebuilding' (2011) 36 *Water International*, 2, 241–9.

Tournaye, Cécile, 'Genocidal Intent before the ICTY' (2003) 52 *International and Comparative Law Quarterly*, 2, 447–62.

Triffterer, Otto (ed.), *Commentary on the Rome Statute of the International Criminal Court* (Beck, 2008).

Uhler, Oscar, Henri Coursier, Frédéric Siordet, Claude Pilloud, Roger Boppe, René-Jean Wilhelm and Jean-Pierre Schoenholzer, *The Geneva Conventions of 12 August 1949: Commentary, Fourth Geneva Convention* (ICRC, 1958).

UNESCO, *Education under Attack* (UNESCO, 2007).

Valticos, Nicolas, *International Labour Law* (Kluwer, 1979).

Van den Herik, Larissa, 'Economic, Social and Cultural Rights – International Criminal Law's Blind Spot?', in *Economic, Social, and Cultural Rights: Contemporary Issues and Challenges*, edited by Eibe Riedel, Christophe Golay, Claire Mahon and Gilles Giacca (Oxford University Press, 2014), 343–66.

'The Meaning of the Word Destroy and Its Implications for the Wider Understanding of the Concept of Genocide', in *The Genocide Convention: The Legacy of 60 Years*, edited by Harmen van der Wilt, Jeroen Vervliet, Göran Sluiter and Cate Houwink ten (Nijhoff, 2012), 51–8.

Van den Herik, Larissa and Daniëlla Dam-De Jong, 'Revitalizing the Antique War Crime of Pillage: The Potential and Pitfalls of Using International Criminal Law to Address Illegal Resource Exploitation During Armed Conflict' (2011) 22 *Criminal Law Forum*, 3, 237–73.

Van den Herik, Larissa and Catherine Harwood, 'Sharing the Law: The Appeal of International Criminal Law for International Commissions of Inquiry' (2014) 2014/016-ICL *Grotius Centre Working Paper*.

Van Hoof, Godfried, 'The Legal Nature of Economic, Social and Cultural Rights: A Rebuttal of Some Traditional Views', in *Right to Food*, edited by Philip Alston and Katarina Tomasevski (Nijhoff, 1984), 97–110.

Vité, Sylvain, 'The Interrelation of the Law of Occupation and Economic, Social and Cultural Rights' (2008) 90 *International Review of the Red Cross*, 871, 629–52.

Waldorf, Lars, 'Anticipating the Past: Transitional Justice and Socio-Economic Wrongs' (2012) 21 *Social & Legal Studies*, 2, 171–86.

Weber, Max, *From Max Weber: Essays in Sociology*, Translated by Hans Heinrich Gerth and Charles Wright Mills (Routledge, 1991).
Weindling, Paul, *Nazi Medicine and the Nuremberg Trials: From Medical War Crimes to Informed Consent* (Palgrave, 2004).
White, Rob, *Crimes against Nature: Environmental Criminology and Ecological Justice* (Willan, 2008).
'Toxic Cities: Globalizing the Problem of Waste' (2008) 35 *Social Justice*, 3, 107–19.
Willms, Jan, 'Without Order, Anything Goes? The Prohibition of Forced Displacement in Non-International Armed Conflict' (2009) 91 *International Review of the Red Cross*, 875, 547–65.
Woetzel, Robert, 'International Criminal Law and Human Rights: The Sharp Edge of the Sword' (1968) 62 *Proceedings of the American Society of International Law at Its Annual Meeting*, 117–23.
World Health Organization, *Health Implications of Apartheid in South Africa* (WHO, 1975).
Zemmali, Ameur, 'The Protection of Water in Times of Armed Conflict' (1995) *International Review of the Red Cross*, 308, 550–64.

# INDEX

# CAMBRIDGE STUDIES IN INTERNATIONAL AND COMPARATIVE LAW

*Books in the series*

*Taking Economic, Social and Cultural Rights Seriously in International Criminal Law* Evelyne Schmid

*Climate Change Litigation: Regulatory Pathways to Cleaner Energy?* Jacqueline Peel and Hari Osofsky

*Mestizo International Law: A Global Intellectual History 1842–1933* Arnulf Becker Lorca

*Sugar and the Making of International Trade Law* Michael Fakhri

*Strategically Created Treaty Conflicts and the Politics of International Law* Surabhi Ranganathan

*Investment Treaty Arbitration as Public International Law: Procedural Aspects and Implications* Eric De Brabandere

*The New Entrants Problem in International Fisheries Law* Andrew Serdy

*Substantive Protection under Investment Treaties: A Legal and Economic Analysis* Jonathan Bonnitcha

*Popular Governance of Post-Conflict Reconstruction: The Role of International Law* Matthew Saul

*Evolution of International Environmental Regimes: The Case of Climate Change* Simone Schiele

*Judges, Law and War: The Judicial Development of International Humanitarian Law* Shane Darcy

*Religious Offence and Human Rights: The Implications of Defamation of Religions* Lorenz Langer

*Forum Shopping in International Adjudication: The Role of Preliminary Objections* Luiz Eduardo Ribeiro Salles

*International Law and the Arctic* Michael Byers

*Cooperation in the Law of Transboundary Water Resources* Christina Leb

*Underwater Cultural Heritage and International Law* Sarah Dromgoole

*State Responsibility: The General Part* James Crawford

*The Origins of International Investment Law* Kate Miles

*The Crime of Aggression under the Rome Statute of the International Criminal Court* Carrie McDougall

*Crimes against Peace and International Law* Kirsten Sellars

*The Non-Legal in International Law* Fleur Johns

*Armed Conflict and Displacement: The Protection of Refugees and Displaced Persons under International Humanitarian Law* Mélanie Jacques

*Foreign Investment and the Environment in International Law* Jorge Viñuales

*The Human Rights Treaty Obligations of Peacekeepers* Kjetil Larsen

*Cyberwarfare and the Laws of War* Heather Harrison Dinniss

*The Right to Reparation in International Law for Victims of Armed Conflict* Christine Evans

*Global Public Interest in International Investment Law* Andreas Kulick

*State Immunity in International Law* Xiaodong Yang

*Reparations and Victim Support in the International Criminal Court* Conor McCarthy

*Reducing Genocide to Law: Definition, Meaning, and the Ultimate Crime* Payam Akhavan

*Decolonizing International Law: Development, Economic Growth and the Politics of Universality* Sundhya Pahuja

*Complicity and the Law of State Responsibility* Helmut Philipp Aust

*State Control over Private Military and Security Companies in Armed Conflict* Hannah Tonkin

*'Fair and Equitable Treatment' in International Investment Law* Roland Kläger

*The UN and Human Rights: Who Guards the Guardians?* Guglielmo Verdirame

*Sovereign Defaults before International Courts and Tribunals* Michael Waibel

*Making the Law of the Sea: A Study in the Development of International Law* James Harrison

*Science and the Precautionary Principle in International Courts and Tribunals: Expert Evidence, Burden of Proof and Finality* Caroline E. Foster

*Transition from Illegal Regimes in International Law* Yaël Ronen

*Access to Asylum: International Refugee Law and the Globalisation of Migration Control* Thomas Gammeltoft-Hansen

*Trading Fish, Saving Fish: The Interaction between Regimes in International Law* Margaret Young

*The Individual in the International Legal System: Continuity and Change in International Law* Kate Parlett

*The Participation of States in International Organisations: The Role of Human Rights and Democracy* Alison Duxbury

*'Armed Attack' and Article 51 of the UN Charter: Evolutions in Customary Law and Practice* Tom Ruys

*Science and Risk Regulation in International Law* Jacqueline Peel

*Theatre of the Rule of Law: Transnational Legal Intervention in Theory and Practice* Stephen Humphreys

*The Public International Law Theory of Hans Kelsen: Believing in Universal Law* Jochen von Bernstorff

*Vicarious Liability in Tort: A Comparative Perspective* Paula Giliker

*Legal Personality in International Law* Roland Portmann

*Legitimacy and Legality in International Law: An Interactional Account* Jutta Brunnée and Stephen J. Toope

*The Concept of Non-International Armed Conflict in International Humanitarian Law* Anthony Cullen

*The Challenge of Child Labour in International Law* Franziska Humbert

*Shipping Interdiction and the Law of the Sea* Douglas Guilfoyle

*International Courts and Environmental Protection* Tim Stephens

*Legal Principles in WTO Disputes* Andrew D. Mitchell

*War Crimes in Internal Armed Conflicts* Eve La Haye

*Humanitarian Occupation* Gregory H. Fox

*The International Law of Environmental Impact Assessment: Process, Substance and Integration* Neil Craik

*The Law and Practice of International Territorial Administration: Versailles to Iraq and Beyond* Carsten Stahn

*Cultural Products and the World Trade Organization* Tania Voon

*United Nations Sanctions and the Rule of Law* Jeremy Farrall

*National Law in WTO Law: Effectiveness and Good Governance in the World Trading System* Sharif Bhuiyan

*The Threat of Force in International Law* Nikolas Stürchler

*Indigenous Rights and United Nations Standards* Alexandra Xanthaki

*International Refugee Law and Socio-Economic Rights* Michelle Foster

*The Protection of Cultural Property in Armed Conflict* Roger O'Keefe

*Interpretation and Revision of International Boundary Decisions* Kaiyan Homi Kaikobad

*Multinationals and Corporate Social Responsibility: Limitations and Opportunities in International Law* Jennifer A. Zerk

*Judiciaries within Europe: A Comparative Review* John Bell

*Law in Times of Crisis: Emergency Powers in Theory and Practice* Oren Gross and Fionnuala Ní Aoláin

*Vessel-Source Marine Pollution: The Law and Politics of International Regulation* Alan Tan

*Enforcing Obligations* Erga Omnes *in International Law* Christian J. Tams

*Non-Governmental Organisations in International Law* Anna-Karin Lindblom

*Democracy, Minorities and International Law* Steven Wheatley
*Prosecuting International Crimes: Selectivity and the International Law Regime* Robert Cryer
*Compensation for Personal Injury in English, German and Italian Law: A Comparative Outline* Basil Markesinis, Michael Coester, Guido Alpa, Augustus Ullstein
*Dispute Settlement in the UN Convention on the Law of the Sea* Natalie Klein
*The International Protection of Internally Displaced Persons* Catherine Phuong
*Imperialism, Sovereignty and the Making of International Law* Antony Anghie
*Necessity, Proportionality and the Use of Force by States* Judith Gardam
*International Legal Argument in the Permanent Court of International Justice: The Rise of the International Judiciary* Ole Spiermann
*Great Powers and Outlaw States: Unequal Sovereigns in the International Legal Order* Gerry Simpson
*Local Remedies in International Law* C. F. Amerasinghe
*Reading Humanitarian Intervention: Human Rights and the Use of Force in International Law* Anne Orford
*Conflict of Norms in Public International Law: How WTO Law Relates to Other Rules of International Law* Joost Pauwelyn
*Transboundary Damage in International Law* Hanqin Xue
*European Criminal Procedures* Edited by Mireille Delmas-Marty and John Spencer
*The Accountability of Armed Opposition Groups in International Law* Liesbeth Zegveld
*Sharing Transboundary Resources: International Law and Optimal Resource Use* Eyal Benvenisti
*International Human Rights and Humanitarian Law* René Provost
*Remedies against International Organisations* Karel Wellens
*Diversity and Self-Determination in International Law* Karen Knop
*The Law of Internal Armed Conflict* Lindsay Moir
*International Commercial Arbitration and African States: Practice, Participation and Institutional Development* Amazu A. Asouzu
*The Enforceability of Promises in European Contract Law* James Gordley
*International Law in Antiquity* David J. Bederman
*Money Laundering: A New International Law Enforcement Model* Guy Stessens
*Good Faith in European Contract Law* Reinhard Zimmermann and Simon Whittaker

*On Civil Procedure* J. A. Jolowicz
*Trusts: A Comparative Study* Maurizio Lupoi
*The Right to Property in Commonwealth Constitutions* Tom Allen
*International Organizations before National Courts* August Reinisch
*The Changing International Law of High Seas Fisheries* Francisco Orrego Vicuña
*Trade and the Environment: A Comparative Study of EC and US Law* Damien Geradin
*Unjust Enrichment: A Study of Private Law and Public Values* Hanoch Dagan
*Religious Liberty and International Law in Europe* Malcolm D. Evans
*Ethics and Authority in International Law* Alfred P. Rubin
*Sovereignty over Natural Resources: Balancing Rights and Duties* Nico Schrijver
*The Polar Regions and the Development of International Law* Donald R. Rothwell
*Fragmentation and the International Relations of Micro-States: Self-Determination and Statehood* Jorri Duursma
*Principles of the Institutional Law of International Organizations* C. F. Amerasinghe

Lightning Source UK Ltd.
Milton Keynes UK
UKOW06n2144130515

251476UK00003B/40/P

9 781107 063969